AZ GREAT BRITAIN
NORTHERN IRELAND
Handy Road Atlas

A-Z Az AtoZ
registered trade marks of
Geographers' A-Z Map Company Ltd

www./az.co.uk

EDITION 24 2016
Copyright © Geographers' A-Z Map Company Ltd.
Telephone: 01732 781000 (Enquiries & Trade Sales)
          01732 783422 (Retail Sales)
Contains Ordnance Survey data © Crown copyright and database right 2015

Northern Ireland: This is Based upon Crown Copyright and is reproduced with
the permission of Land & Property Services under delegated authority from the
Controller of Her Majesty's Stationery Office, © Crown copyright and database
right 2015 PMLPA No 100508. The inclusion of parts or all of the Republic of
Ireland is by permission of the Government of Ireland who retain copyright in
the data used. © Ordnance Survey Ireland and Government of Ireland.

Land & Property Services
Paper Map Licensed Partner
ORDNANCE SURVEY
OF NORTHERN IRELAND

This is a registered Trade Mark of
Department of Finance and Personnel.

Motorway
Autoroute
Autobahn
≡M1≡

Motorway Under Construction
Autoroute en construction
Autobahn im Bau

Motorway Proposed
Autoroute prévue
Geplante Autobahn

Motorway Junctions with Numbers
Autoroute échangeur numéroté
Beschränkter Fahrtrichtungswechsel
4 ≡ 5

Unlimited Interchange ④	**Limited Interchange** ⑤
Echangeur complet	Echangeur partiel
Autobahnanschlußstelle mit Nummer	Unbeschränkter Fahrtrichtungswechsel

Motorway Service Area
with access from one carriageway only
Aire de services d'autoroute   Rastplatz oder Raststätte
accessible d'un seul côté   Einbahn
Ⓢ

Major Road Service Areas with 24 hour facilities
Aire de services sur route prioritaire ouverte 24h sur 24
Raststätte durchgehend geöffnet

Primary Route ≡Ⓢ≡	**Class A Road**
Route à grande circulation	Route de type A
Hauptverkehrsstraße	A- Straße ≡Ⓢ≡

Truckstop (selection of)
Sélection d'aire pour poids lourds
Auswahl von Fernfahrerrastplatz
≡Ⓣ≡

Major Road Junctions
Jonctions grands routiers
Hauptverkehrsstrasse Kreuzungen

Other Autre Andere

Primary Route
Route à grande circulation
Hauptverkehrsstraße
A40

Primary Route Junction with Number
Echangeur numéroté
Hauptverkehrsstraßenkreuzung mit Nummer
④

Primary Route Destination
Route prioritaire, direction
Hauptverkehrsstraße Richtung
DOVER

Dual Carriageways (A & B roads)
Route à double chaussées séparées (route A & B)
Zweispurige Schnellstraße (A- und B- Straßen)

Class A Road
Route de type A
A- Straße
A129

Class B Road
Route de type B
B- Straße
B177

Narrow Major Road (passing places)
Route prioritaire étroite (possibilité de dépassement)
Schmale Hauptverkehrsstaße (mit Überholmöglichkeit)

Major Roads Under Construction
Route prioritaire en construction
Hauptverkehrsstaße im Bau

Major Roads Proposed
Route prioritaire prévue
Geplante Hauptverkehrsstaße

Gradient 1:7 (14%) **& steeper**
(Descent in direction of arrow)
Pente égale ou supérieure à 14% (dans le sens de la descente)
14% Steigung und steiler (in Pfeilrichtung)
»

Toll
Barrière de péage
Gebührenpflichtig
Toll

Dart Charge
www.gov.uk/pay-dartford-crossing-charge
Ⓒ

Park & Ride
Parking avec Service Navette
Parken und Reisen
P+R

Mileage between markers
Distence en miles entre les flèches
Strecke zwischen Markierungen in Meilen
8

Airport
Aéroport
Flughafen
✈

Railway and Station
Voie ferrée et gare
Eisenbahnlinie und Bahnhof

Level Crossing and Tunnel
Passage à niveau et tunnel
Bahnübergang und Tunnel

River or Canal
Rivière ou canal
Fluß oder Kanal

County or Unitary Authority Boundary
Limite de comté ou de division administrative
Grafschafts- oder Verwaltungsbezirksgrenze

National Boundary
Frontière nationale
Landesgrenze
+ — +

Built-up Area
Agglomération
Geschloßene Ortschaft

Town, Village or Hamlet
Ville, Village ou hameau
Stadt, Dorf oder Weiler
○

Wooded Area
Zone boisée
Waldgebiet

Spot Height in Feet
Altitude (en pieds)
Höhe in Fuß
· 813

Height Above Sea Level   1,400'-2000' 427m-610m
Altitude par rapport au niveau de la mer 2000'+   610m+
Höhe über Meeresspiegel

National Grid Reference (kilometres)
Coordonnées géographiques nationales (Kilomètres)
Nationale geographische Koordinaten (Kilometer)
¹00

Page Continuation
Suite à la page indiquée
Seitenfortsetzung
24

Scale to Map Pages 1:316,800 = 5 miles to 1 inch / 3.1 km to 1 cm

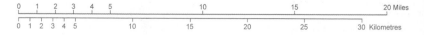

0	1	2	3	4	5		10		15		20 Miles

| 0 | 1 | 2 | 3 | 4 | 5 | | 10 | 15 | 20 | 25 | 30 Kilometres |

Airfield
Terrain d'aviation
Flugplatz

Heliport
Héliport
Hubschrauberlandeplatz

Abbey, Church, Friary, Priory
Abbaye, église, monastère, prieuré
Abtei, Kirche, Mönchskloster, Kloster

Animal Collection
Ménagerie
Tiersammlung

Aquarium
Aquarium
Aquarium

Arboretum, Botanical Garden
Jardin Botanique
Botanischer Garten

Aviary, Bird Garden
Volière
Voliere

Battle Site and Date
Champ de bataille et date
Schlachtfeld und Datum
1066

Blue Flag Beach
Plage Pavillon Bleu
Blaue Flagge Strand

Bridge
Pont
Brücke

Castle (open to public)
Château (ouvert au public)
Schloß / Burg (für die Öffentlichkeit zugänglich)

Castle with Garden (open to public)
Château avec parc (ouvert au public)
Schloß mit Garten (für die Öffentlichkeit zugänglich)

Cathedral
Cathédrale
Kathedrale

Cidermaker
Cidrerie (fabrication)
Apfelwein Hersteller

Country Park
Parc régional
Landschaftspark

Distillery
Distillerie
Brennerei

Farm Park, Open Farm
Park Animalier
Bauernhof Park

Ferry (vehicular, sea)
        (vehicular, river)
        (foot only)
Bac (véhicules, mer)
    (véhicules, rivière)
    (piétons)
Fähre (auto, meer)
      (auto, fluß)
      (nur für Personen)

Fortress, Hill Fort
Château Fort
Festung

Garden (open to public)
Jardin (ouvert au public)
Garten (für die Öffentlichkeit zugänglich)

Golf Course
Terrain de golf
Golfplatz

Historic Building (open to public)
Monument historique (ouvert au public)
Historisches Gebäude (für die Öffentlichkeit zugänglich)

Historic Building with Garden (open to public)
Monument historique avec jardin (ouvert au public)
Historisches Gebäude mit Garten (für die Öffentlichkeit zugänglich)

Horse Racecourse
Hippodrome
Pferderennbahn

Industrial Monument
Monument Industrielle
Industriedenkmal

Leisure Park, Leisure Pool
Parc d'Attraction, Loisirs Piscine
Freizeitpark, Freizeit pool

Lighthouse
Phare
Leuchtturm

Mine, Cave
Mine, Grotte
Bergwerk, Höhle

Monument
Monument
Denkmal

Motor Racing Circuit
Circuit Automobile
Automobilrennbahn

Museum, Art Gallery
Musée
Museum, Galerie

National Park
Parc national
Nationalpark

National Trust Property
National Trust Property
National Trust- Eigentum

Nature Reserve or Bird Sanctuary
Réserve naturelle botanique ou ornithologique
Natur- oder Vogelschutzgebiet

Nature Trail or Forest Walk
Chemin forestier, piste verte
Naturpfad oder Waldweg

Place of Interest   *Craft Centre* •
Site, curiosité
Sehenswürdigkeit

Prehistoric Monument
Monument Préhistorique
Prähistorische Denkmal

Railway, Steam or Narrow Gauge
Chemin de fer, à vapeur ou à voie étroite
Eisenbahn, Dampf- oder Schmalspurbahn

Roman Remains
Vestiges Romains
Römischen Ruinen

Theme Park
Centre de loisirs
Vergnügungspark

Tourist Information Centre (All year)
Office de Tourisme   (ouvert toute l'année)
Touristeninformationen   (ganzjährig geöffnet)
                            (Summer season only)
                            (été seulement)
                            (nur im Sommer geöffnet)

Viewpoint   (360 degrees)   (180 degrees)
Vue panoramique   (360 degrés)   (180 degrés)
Aussichtspunkt   (360 Grade)   (180 Grade)

Vineyard
Vignoble
Weinberg

Visitor Information Centre
Centre d'information touristique
Besucherzentrum

Wildlife Park
Réserve de faune
Wildpark

Windmill
Moulin à vent
Windmühle

Zoo or Safari Park
Parc ou réserve zoologique
Zoo oder Safari-Park

Please note: symbols have been enlarged for clarity

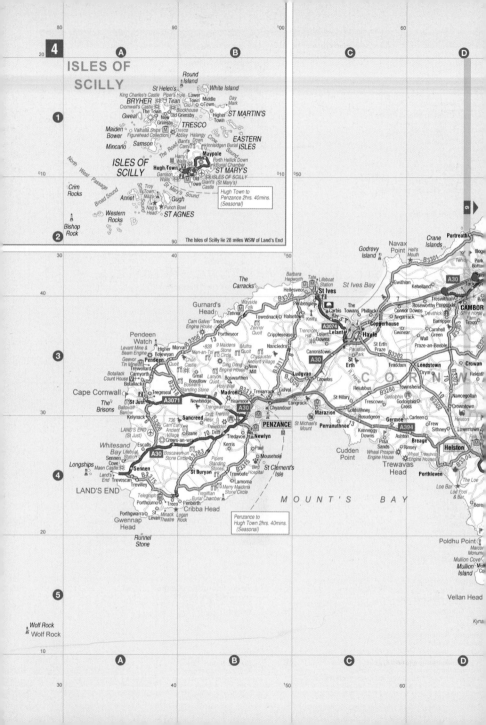

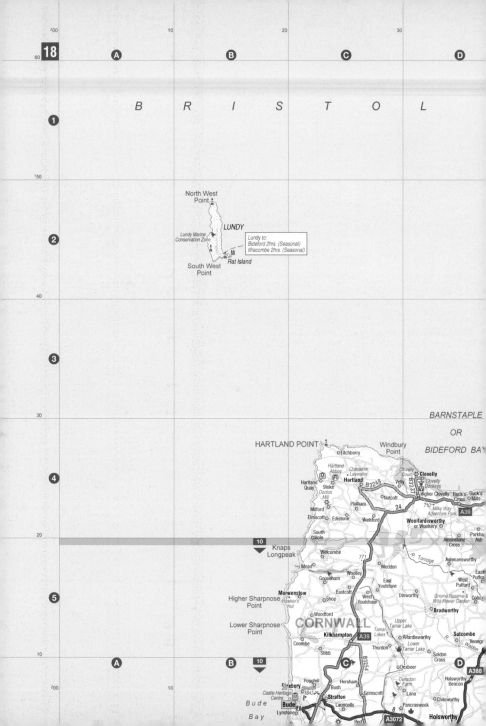

200 · 10 · 20 · 30

Ⓐ   Ⓑ   Ⓒ   Ⓓ

60

B R I S T O L

⓵

150

North West
Point

⓶

*Lundy Marine
Conservation Zone*   *LUNDY*

Lundy to:
Bideford 2hrs. (Seasonal)
Ilfracombe 2hrs. (Seasonal)

Rat Island

South West
Point

40

⓷

30

BARNSTAPLE

OR

BIDEFORD BAY

HARTLAND POINT   Windbury
Point

⓸

Titchberry   Clovelly
Court   **Clovelly**
Hartland
Abbey   Chalcstow
Lavender   Clovelly
Donkeys
Hartland   **Hartland**   B3248   Velly   Higher Clovelly   Buck's Buck's
Quay   Stoke   Natcott   Cross Mills
Docton
Mill   710 Milky Way
Milford   Philham   24   Adventure Park   A39
Elmscott   Edistone   Welsford   **Woolfardisworthy**
               or Woolsery   Parkha
South   Ash
Hole   Alminstone
Cross

20

▽ 10   Knaps
Longpeak   Welcombe   R. Torridge   Ashmansworthy

Mead   771   Meddon   East
Woolley   Putford
Gooseh_am   West   West
Youlstone   Putford

⓹

Higher Sharpnose   **Morwenstow**   Eastcott   West   Dimworthy   Gnome Reserve &
Point   Hawker's Hut   Shop   Youlstone   Wild Flower Garden
       Woodford   **Bradworthy**
Lower Sharpnose   **CORNWALL**   Upper
Point   Tamar Lake   Alfardisworthy   **Sutcombe**
       Kilkhampton   A39   Tamar   Lower   Venny
           Lakes   Thurdon   Tamar Lake   Weldon
Coombe   Soldon
       Stibb   Cross

10

Ⓐ   Ⓑ   ▽ 10   Ⓒ   B3254   Ⓓ   A388

                   Dexbeer   Dunsdon
                       Farm   Holsworthy
Poughill   Hersham   Beacon
Flexbury   Bush   Lana   Chilsworthy
Castle Heritage   1643   Grimscott   Pancrasweek
Centre   **Stratton**
Bude   Launcells   8   **Holsworthy**
Lynstone

Bude
Bay   A3072

200 · 10

N O R T H

1

S E A

2

90

80

3

South Channel
Turner
Contemporary
Lifeboat
Station
Walpole
Bay Hotel
Foreness Point

Westgate
on Sea
Westbrook
MARGATE
Cliftonville
Palaces
Kingsgate

Quex House
Westwood
B2051

Minnis Bay
Spitfire &
Hurricane
**NORTH
FORELAND**

Herne Bay
Reculver
Reculver Towers
Regulbium
Roman Fort
Birchington
ISLE OF THANET
St
Peter's

HERNE BAY
Hillborough
A28
Acol
Lydden
A255
BROADSTAIRS
Dickens House

WHITSTABLE
Swalecliffe
Beltinge
A299
St Nicholas
at Wade
B2050
Manston
Tower
B2052

Tankerton
Greenhill
Sarre
A256
A254
RAMSGATE

Seasalter
A2990
Hunters
Forstal
Broomfield
Maypole
A28
Monkton
Minster
A299
Maritime

Whitstable Bay
Chestfield
West
End
Herne
Boyden
Gate
A253
Abbey
Cliffsend

Shell
Ness
A299
Herne
Common
Chislet
East Stourmouth
Richborough Port
Pegwell
Bay

Graveney
Radfall
Hoath
West
Stourmouth
Plucks
Gutter
Westmarsh
River
Richborough
Sandwich
Bay

Leysdown-on-Sea
A291
Wildwood
Calcott
Broad Oak
Upstreet
Grove
Paramour
Street
Cooper
Street
Great Stonar

Yorkletts
Denstroude
Honey Hill
Druidstone
Park
Hersden
Preston
Elmstone
Ware
Amphitheatre
A257
Sandwich

Goodnestone
Dargate
Tyler
Hill
Stodmarsh
Hoaden
Nash
Sandown
Castle

Preston
Mount
Blean
Rough
Common
Fordwich
Westbere
Wickhambreaux
Ickham
Wingham
11
Staple
Woodnesborough
Worth

Boughton
under
Blean
A290
A2050
Harbledown
CANTERBURY
Littlebourne
A257
Bramling
Marshborough
Eastry
A258
Sholden

South Street
Dunkirk
Thannington
Without
Bekesbourne
Barnsole
Ham
Finglesham
DEAL

Old Wives
Lees
A28
Chartham
Hatch
Patrixbourne
Goodnestone
Chillenden
Heronden
Betteshanger
Walmer

Chilham
Shalmsford
Street
Bridge
Nackington
Adisham
Knowlton
Northbourne
Great Mongeham
Ringwould

A252
Mountain
Street
Street
End
Lower
Hardres
Pett
Bottom
Nonington
Elvington
A256
Kingsdown

Godmersham
Petham
Bishopsbourne
Kingston
Tilmanstone
Martin Mill

A28
Sole
Street
Upper
Hardres Court
Barham
29
Woolage Village
Barfrestone
Eythorne
Martin

Boughton
Aluph
Billing
E
Crundale
B2068
F
Denton
Woolage
Green
East Kent
Railway
G
Shepherdswell
or Sibertswold
West
Langdon
A258
St Margaret's

Wye
Waltham
Stelling
Minnis
A260
Wootton
Lydden
Whitfield
Guston

❶

90

❷

80

C A R D I G A N   B A Y

(B A E   C E R E D I G I O N)

❸

70

❹

60

Aberaeron

Ffos-y-ffin   A48

New Quay   ⓘ
(Ceinewydd)   Marine Wildlife Centre

Maen-y-groes   Gilfachreda

Cwmtudu   Llwyncelyn

Cross   Llanarth
Inn   Oakford   (Derwen Gam)
New Quay   Geneva
Honey Farm   Pen-cae

Ynys-Lochtyn   Nantemis   Caerwedros

Blaen   Llwyndafydd   A486   Synod Inn
Celyn   (Post-Mawr)

❺   Llangranog   Mydroilye

Morfa   Pontgarreg   A487

Penbryn   Brynhoffnant

Cardigan   Sarnau   A487   Talgarreg
Island

Rainforest   Pentregat   Plwmp   B43
Centre   Aberporth

250   Cardigan Island   Parcllyn   Tresaith   Capel   Bwlch-y-fadfa
Coastal Farm Park   Cynon

Allt-y-goedo   44   Tan-y-groes   B4334
Felinwynt

Pwllygranant   Y Ferwig   mannerch   B4350

Cippyn   Tremain   Blaenporth   Felin   Brithdir   Rhydlewis   Ffostrasol   40   Pont-Sian
10   Penparc   Wnda   B4571   B4459

St   Cardigan   20   Bettws   Hawen   Penrhiw-   A475
Dogmaels   (Aberteifi)   Noyadd   Ifan   Curlew Weavers   pal   Rhydowen
(Llandudoch)   A487   Trefawr   Woollen Mill   Maes
Moylgrove   Abbey   Castle   Pantgwyn   B4570   Beulah   Troedyraur   Llyn   Tre-groes
(Trewyddel)   Watermill   Llangoedmor   Ponthirwaun   Brongest   Coed-y-   A475

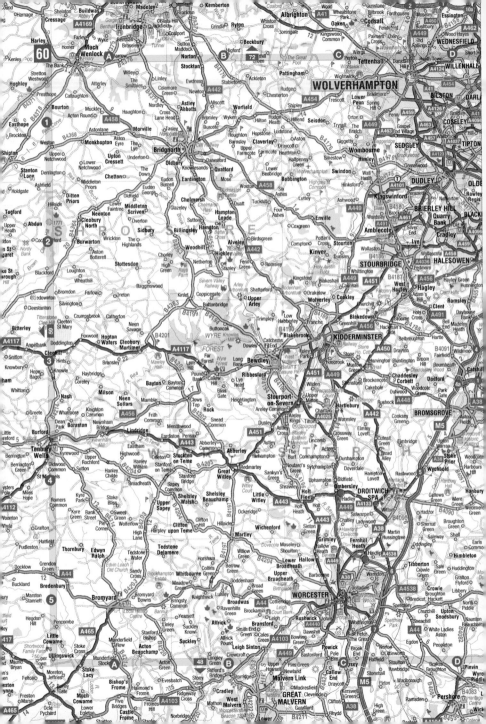

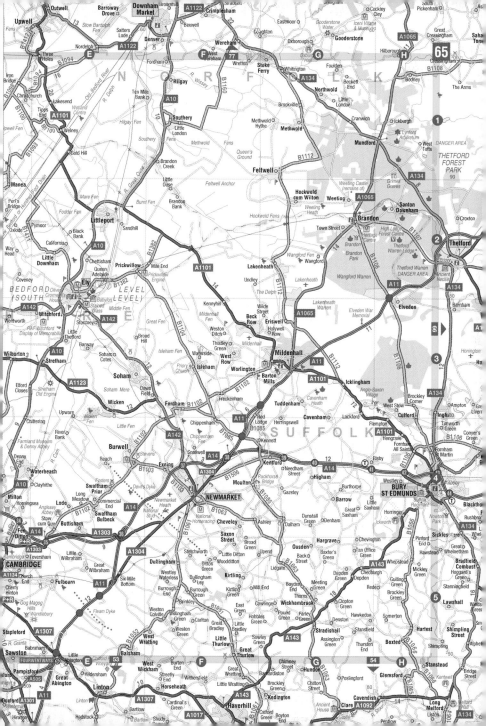

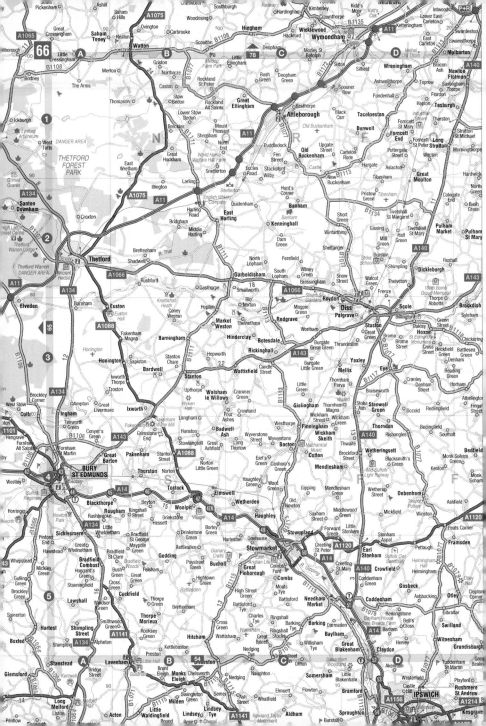

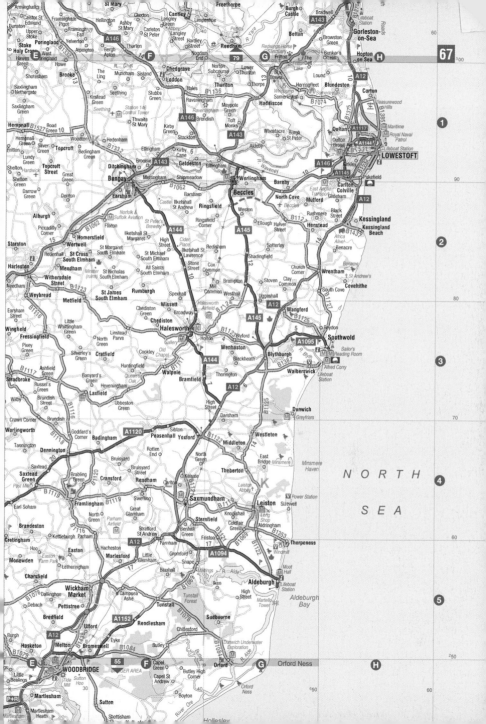

1

30

N O R T H

S E A

2

20

Brotton
Skinningrove   *Boulby Cliffs*
Carlin How   Loftus   Boulby   *Lifeboat Station*   *Captain Cook &*
How   *Cleveland*   Cowbar   *Staithes Heritage*
Ironstone Mining
North   Kilton   A174   Staithes
Ironstone   Thorpe   Easington   Dalehouse   Port
Stanghow   *Liverton Mines*   Hinderwell   Mulgrave   *Runswick Bay*
Moorsholm   Liverton   Roxby   Borrowby   Runswick
Moorsholm   *Newton*   Kettleness
Mulgrave   Goldsborough   **3**
Moorsholm   A171   Scaling   Scaling   14   A174   Lythe   Sandsend
Moor   *Scaling Dam*   *Reservoir*   West   East   East Row   *Dracula*   10
21   Mickleby   Barnby   Barnby   Raithwaite   *Experience*   **WHITBY**
Roxby High Moor   Ugthorpe   Dunsley   *Castleton*   *Abbey*   *Captain Cook*
Danby Low Moor   *Lealholm*   *Hutton*   Newholm   Ruswarp   *Memorial*   *Saltwick*
Danby   *Danby Moor*   Mulgrave   Briggswath   Golden   *Bay*
Danby   *Beacon*   Stonegate   Aislaby   Grove   Long   High
Botton   *981*   Houlsyke   Hutton   Sleights   Stainsacre   Lease   Hawsker
Ainthorpe   Leaholm   Egton   Sleights   Ugglebarnby   Low   *Ness Point or*
Danby   *Victorian*   Egton   Grosmont   Sneaton   Hawsker   *North Cheek*
Botton   *Science*   Bridge   A169   Sneatonthorpe   Row   *Robin*   **4**
Botton   Glaisdale   Key   *Lease*   Esk Valley   Fylingthorpe   Hood's Bay
Glaisdale   Green   *Rigg*   Green End   *Robin Hood's Bay*   *Old Coastguard Station*
Rigg   *The*   *Falling Foss*   *& Fylingdales*   *Boggle Hole*
NORTH YORK MOORS   Beck   *Hermitage*   *(Waterfall)*   *Old Peak or*
Loose Howe   Hole   *Mallyan*   *Thomason Foss*   *Coastal Centre*   *South Cheek*
Spout   Goathland   *Waterfall*   *Peak Alum Works*   **500**
NATIONAL PARK   *Pike Hill Moor*   *Fylingdales Moor*   Ravenscar
YORK   *Nelly Ayre Foss*   *Lilla Cross*   20
MOORS   *Waterfall*   *959*   *Burn*   Staindondale
Low   *Wheeldale Moor*   *Wheeldale*   *Howe Rigg*   Crowdon   *Staindondale Shire Horse Farm*
Thorgill   *Bell End*   *Roman Road*   *Goathland*   *Harwood Dale*   Cloughton
Rosedale   *North Yorkshire Moors Railway*   *Moor*   *Forest*   Newlands
Abbey   *Newton Dale Spring*   *Sattergate*   *Harwood Dale*
Rosedale   *Mauley*   *Malo*   **LANGDALE**   Burniston
Chimney Ironworks   Toll   *Cross*   Cross   *Blakey*   **FOREST**   A165   **5**
River Severn   *Skelton*   *Topping*   Scalby
Spaunton   Stape   *Hole of*   *Bickley*   Broxa   Silpho   Mills   *Sea Life*
Moor   Hartoft   *Horcum*   Bridestones   *Toll*   Suffield   A171   *North Bay Railway*
Ryedale   End   A169   *Langdale*   Hackness   Scalby   Thro   101   *by*   *Rotunda*
Folk   Lastingham   Levisham   Everley   *Art Gallery*
Hutton-   Spaunton   Newton-on-   Lockton   *Wykeham*   Barrowcliff   **SCARBOROUGH**
le-Hole   100   Rawcliffe   Low   **Dalby**   **Forest**   *Forest*   Falsgrave
Appleton-   Cropton   Cawthorne   Dalby   *Dalby Forest Drive*   *North*   East   A170
le-Moors   *Brewery*   *Moor*   Ayton
kbymoorside   Cropton   *North Yorkshire Moors Railway*   *Wykeham Woods*   P+R   P+R
Sinnington   Wrelton   Aislaby   *Hutton*   Sawdon   A170   *Cayton*
Kirkby   Keldholme   Middleton   Newbridge
Mills   A170

POINT OF AYRE

Rue Point

Shellag Point

Jurby Head

Ramsey
Bay

Orrisdale Head

Maughold
Head
Port Mooar

Gob y Deigan

Port Cornaa

Bulgham Bay

St Patrick's Isle

Peel

Contrary Head

Patrick

Laxey Bay

Clay Head

Dalby Point

Port Groudle

Onchan Head

Niarbyl Bay

DOUGLAS

Stroin Vuigh

Douglas Head

Fleshwick
Bay

Little Ness

Santon Head

Bradda Head

Port Erin

Dreswick
Point

SPANISH HEAD

Calf of Man

Douglas to:
Belfast 2hrs.45mins.
(Fast Ferry, Seasonal)
Birkenhead 4hrs. 15mins.
(Seasonal)
Heysham 3hrs. 30mins.
Dublin 2hrs. 45mins.
(Fast Ferry, Seasonal)
Liverpool 2hrs. 30mins.
(Fast Ferry, Seasonal)

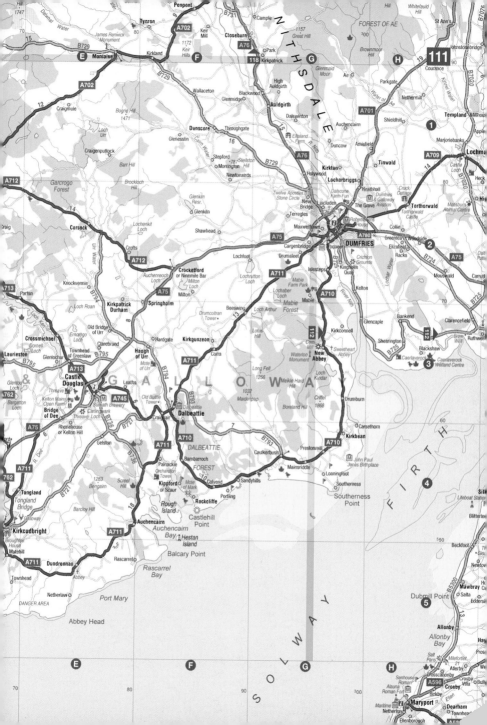

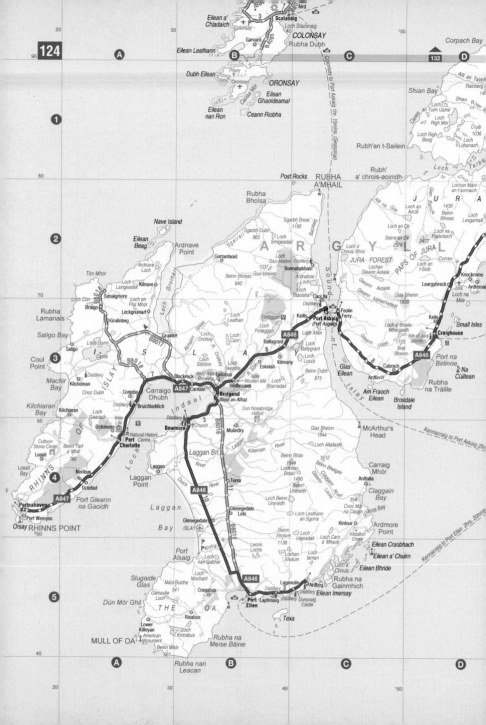

NORTH SEA

NORTHUMBERLAND

BERWICK-UPON-TWEED

Tweedmouth

Spittal

HOLY ISLAND

Fast Castle Head

ST ABB'S HEAD

A B C D

'00 10 20 30

Oban to
Lochboisdale 5hrs. 20mins.
(Seasonal)

Oban to
Castlebay 5hrs.

Cairns of Coll

Eag na
Maoile

Rubha Mòr

Eilean Mòr

Rubh'a' Bhinnein

Bousd

COLL

Cornaigmore
Sorisdale
Loch
Fada

Clad Bay

Grishipoll

Rubha Hogh

Clabhach

Bagh Feisdlum

Hogh Bay

340
Ben Nogh

Loch Clad

Arinagour

Loch nan
Cinneachan

Stables

Loch
Anlaimh

Acha

Totronald

Eilean
Ornsay

Tiree to
Barra 2hrs. 45mins.
(Seasonal)

Feall
Bay

Coll

Uig

Port na
h-Eathar

Calgary Point

Gunna

Caolas Bàn

Crossapol
Bay

Soa

Port
a' Mhurain

Gunna Sound

Rubha Dubh

Friesland
Bay

Breachacha

Oban to Tiree 3hrs. 20mins. (Seasonal)

Coll to Tiree 55mins.

Vaul
Bay

Miodar

Caman

Treshnis

Balephetrish
Bay

Vaul

Salum

Sràid
Ruadh

Cornaigmore

Balephetrish

Loch
Riaghain

Gott

Caolas

Rubha Dubh

Ruaig

Kirkapol

Cairn na
Burgh Beg

Balevullin

Kennovay

TIREE
(Port Adhair Thiriodh)

Gott Bay

Kilmoluaig

Cornaigbeg

Hough

An
Iodhlann

Kilkenneth

Moss

Loch an
Eilein

Scarinish

Fladda

Sandaig

Baugh

Rubha Tràigh
an Duin

Middleton

Crossapol

Heanish

Isles

Port Mor

Barrapol

Heylipol

Hynish
Bay

TIREE

Lunga

Port
Bharrapool

Island Lile

Loch a'
Phuill

Balephuil

Balemartine

Mannal

Bac Mor or
Dutchman's Cap

Treshnish

Balephuil
Bay

West
Hynish

Hynish

Bac Beag

Port Snoig

Skerryvore
Lighthouse

Staffa
Fingal's
Cave

INNER

Hough
Skerries

HEBRIDES

I N N E R

70

60

50

40

30

Réidh
Eilean

Eilean
Annraidh

Rubha
nan Cea

Macleans
Cross

Abbey &
Nunnery

Kintra
Creich

IONA

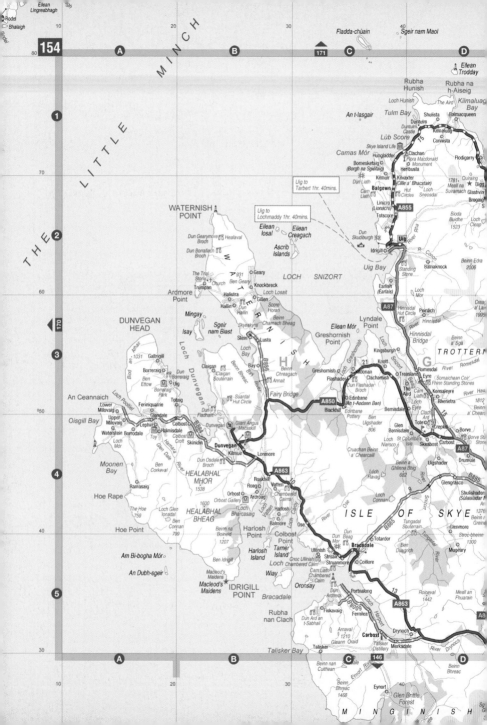

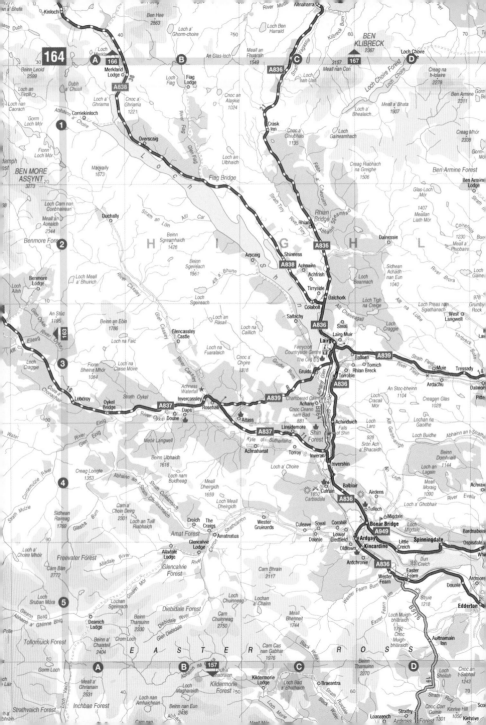

STRATHY POINT

Whiten Head or An Ceann Geal

Eilean Hoan

Eilean Clüimhrig

Rispond

Loch Eriboll

tnancon

Hope

Eriboll

Loch Hope

Cashel Dhu

ocach

BEN HOPE
3040

Meallan Liath
1902

Loch na Seilg

Alltnacaillich

Dun Dornaigil

Strathmore River

Loch Meadie

ruisgach
odge

Loch Coire na Saidhe Duibhe

Allt Coire na Saidhe Duibhe

Meadie Burn

Ben Hutig
1338

Achininver
Lubinvullin
West Strathan
Strathan
Achinahuagh

Port Vasgo
Midfield

Talmine

Skinnet
Midtown
Loch a' Mhuilinn

Coldbackie
Rhitongue

Achuvoldrach

Ribigill

Tongue
Braetongue

Caisteal Bharraigh

Blandy
Dalchan

Loch Cormaic

Rabbit Islands

Port Raineach
Clasheddy
Strathan Skerray
Skerray

Eilean nan Ron

Neave or Coombe Island

Tongue Bay

Caol Raineach

Achtoty
Modsarie
Torrisdale

Borgie

Achina

Farr

Farr Point

Farr Bay

Torrisdale Bay

Bay of Swordly

Swordly
Clerkhill

Bettyhill

Invernaver

Leckfurin

Coille na Borgie Chambered Tomb

Kirtomy Point

Ardmore Point

Armadale Bay

Armadale

Kirtomy
Crask

Clachan

Loch Gaineimh

Loch Meadle

Loch Buidhe Beag

Loch Buidhe Mor

STRATHY POINT

Totegan
Aultivullin

Port Allt a' Mhuilinn

Brawl
Aultiphurst

Lednagullin

Strathy
Bali

Strathy Bay

River Strathy

Strathy Forest

Bowside Lodge

Beinn nam Bo
751

Loch Meala

Loch Mor na Caorach

Loch nan Clach

Rhitongue

Loch Maovaly

Loch na Mhuilinn

Loch Fhionnaich

Kinloch Lodge

Loch Hakel

Kinloch River

Loch an Dherue

Loch Haluim

Loch Coulside

A836

Cnoc Craggie 1043

Loch Craggie

Beinn Bhreac 1018

Beinn Stumanadh 1728

Loch nam Breac

Ben Loyal 2509

Loch Loyal

Loch Loyal Lodge 1828

Cnoc nan Cuilean

Loch nan Ealachan

Loch Eileanach

Loch Bad na Gallaig

Borgie Forest

Lochan nan Carn

Loch nan Ealachan

Na Caol Lochan

Loch Slephon

Skelpick

Archargary

Carnachy

Rhifail

Rough Haugh

Skail

Skall Chambered Cairn

Syre

Rhifail Loch

Rosal Clearance Village

Naval Forest

Rimsdale

Loch Meleag

Dunviden Lochs

Beinn Rifa-gil 963

Loch Strathy

Loch Mor 1133

Cnoc nan Tri-chlach

Loch Badanloch

Badanloch Lodge

B871

Loch Druim a' Chliabhain

Ben Griam Mor 1902

Ben Griam Beg 1938

Garvault

Badanloch Forest

Loch nan Clàr

Loch Rimsdale

Loch Truderscaig

Loch an Alltan Fhearna

Loch na Gaineimh

Loch Achnamoine

River Helmsdale

Achento

Loch Ruath

B871

Kinb

Pole Hill 965

Grumbeg Settlement

Grummore

Mudale

River Mudale

Aultnaharra

B873

Loch Naver

Kilbreck Burn

BEN KLIBRECK 3367

Meall nan Con 3157

Loch Choire Lodge

Loch Choire Forest

Creag na h-Iolaire 2278

An Liath Mheall Mhòr 1423

Ben Armine 2311

Gorm-Loch Beag

Borrobol Forest

Strathy Forest

168

STRATHY POINT

An Glas-loch

Meall an Fhuarain 1549

Meall a' Bhata 1907

Loch a' Bhealaich

Loch nan Uan

Cnc50h Alaskie 1024

Loch Fiag

Fiag Lodge

E   F   G   H

164   165

Abhainn na

Altanduin

Cnoc na

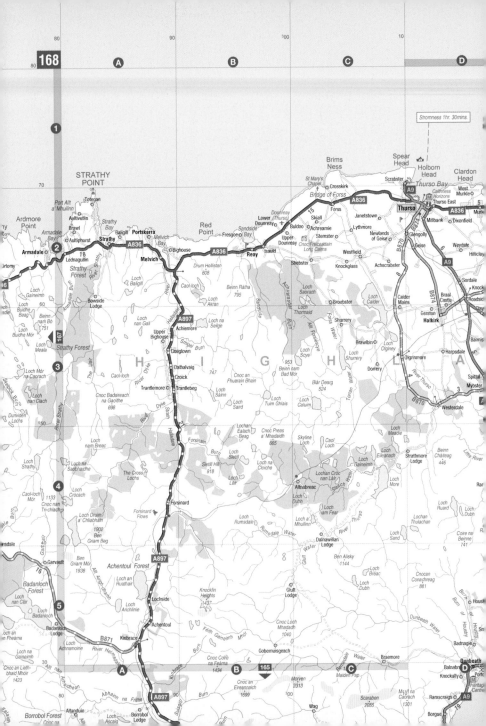

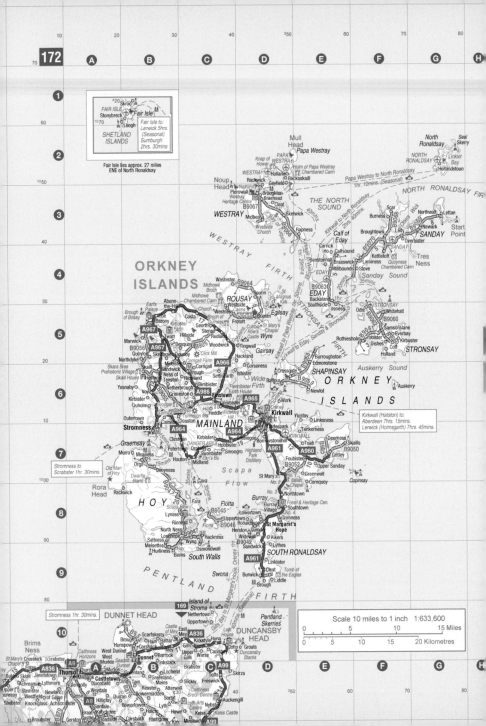

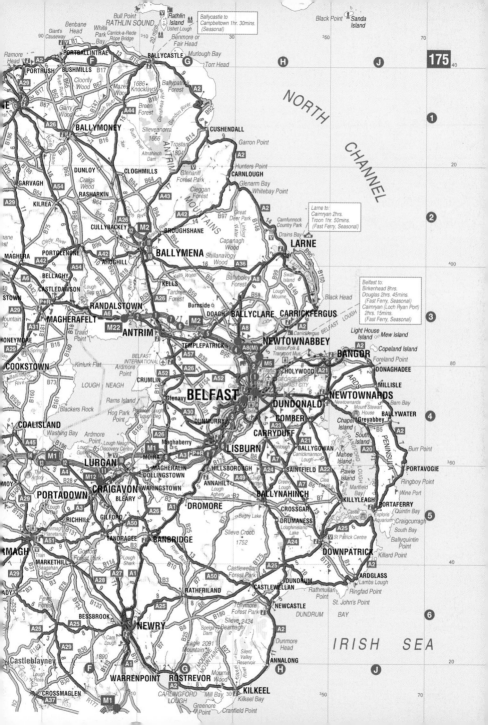

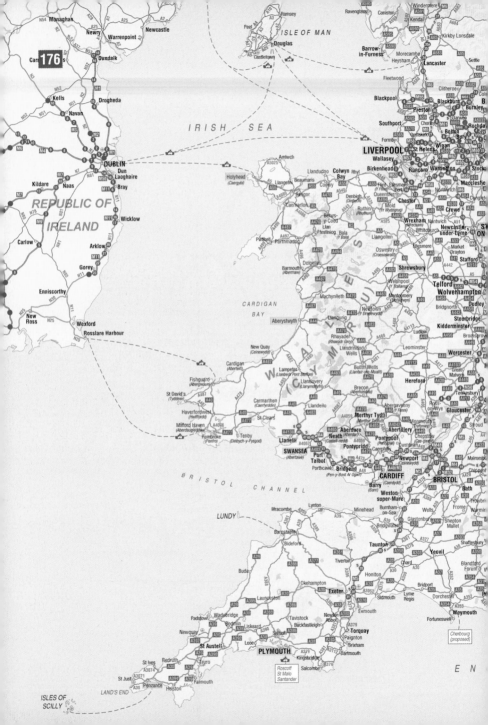

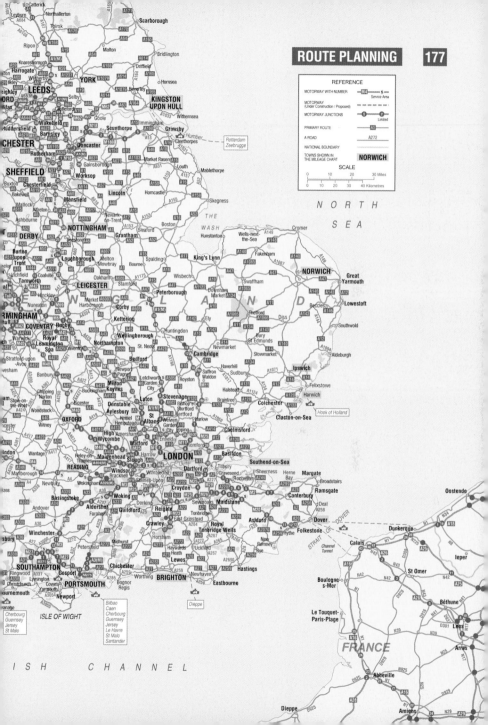

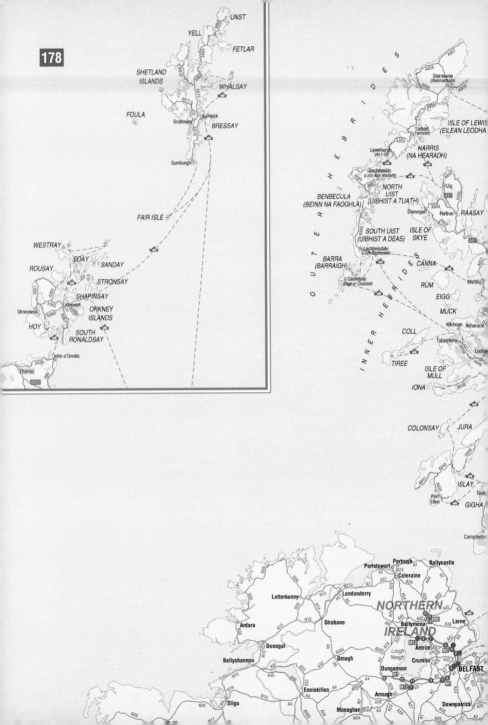

UNST
YELL
FETLAR
SHETLAND ISLANDS
WHALSAY
FOULA
Scalloway
Lerwick
BRESSAY
Sumburgh

FAIR ISLE

WESTRAY
EDAY
ROUSAY
SANDAY
STRONSAY
SHAPINSAY
Kirkwall
ORKNEY ISLANDS
Stromness
HOY
SOUTH RONALDSAY
John o'Groats
Thurso

ISLE OF LEWIS (EILEAN LEODHA
Stornoway (Steòrnabhagh)
Tarbert (Tairbeart)
HARRIS (NA HEARADH)
Leverburgh (An t-Ob)
Lochmaddy (Loch nam Madadh)
Uig
NORTH UIST (UIBHIST A TUATH)
BENBECULA (BEINN NA FAOGHLA)
Dunvegan
Portree
RAASAY
SOUTH UIST (UIBHIST A DEAS)
ISLE OF SKYE
Lochboisdale (Loch Baghasdail)
BARRA (BARRAIGH)
CANNA
Castlebay (Bàgh a' Chaisteil)
RÙM
EIGG
MUCK
Kilchoan
Acharacle
COLL
Tobermory
TIREE
ISLE OF MULL
IONA

COLONSAY
JURA

ISLAY
Port Ellen
Tayic
GIGHA

Campbeltow

OUTER HEBRIDES
INNER HEBRIDES

NORTHERN IRELAND
Portstewart
Portrush
Ballycastle
Coleraine
Letterkenny
Londonderry
Ballymena
Larne
Ardara
Strabane
Antrim
Crumlin
Donegal
Omagh
Lough Neagh
BELFAST
Ballyshannon
Dungannon
Enniskillen
Armagh
Downpatrick
Sligo
Monaghan

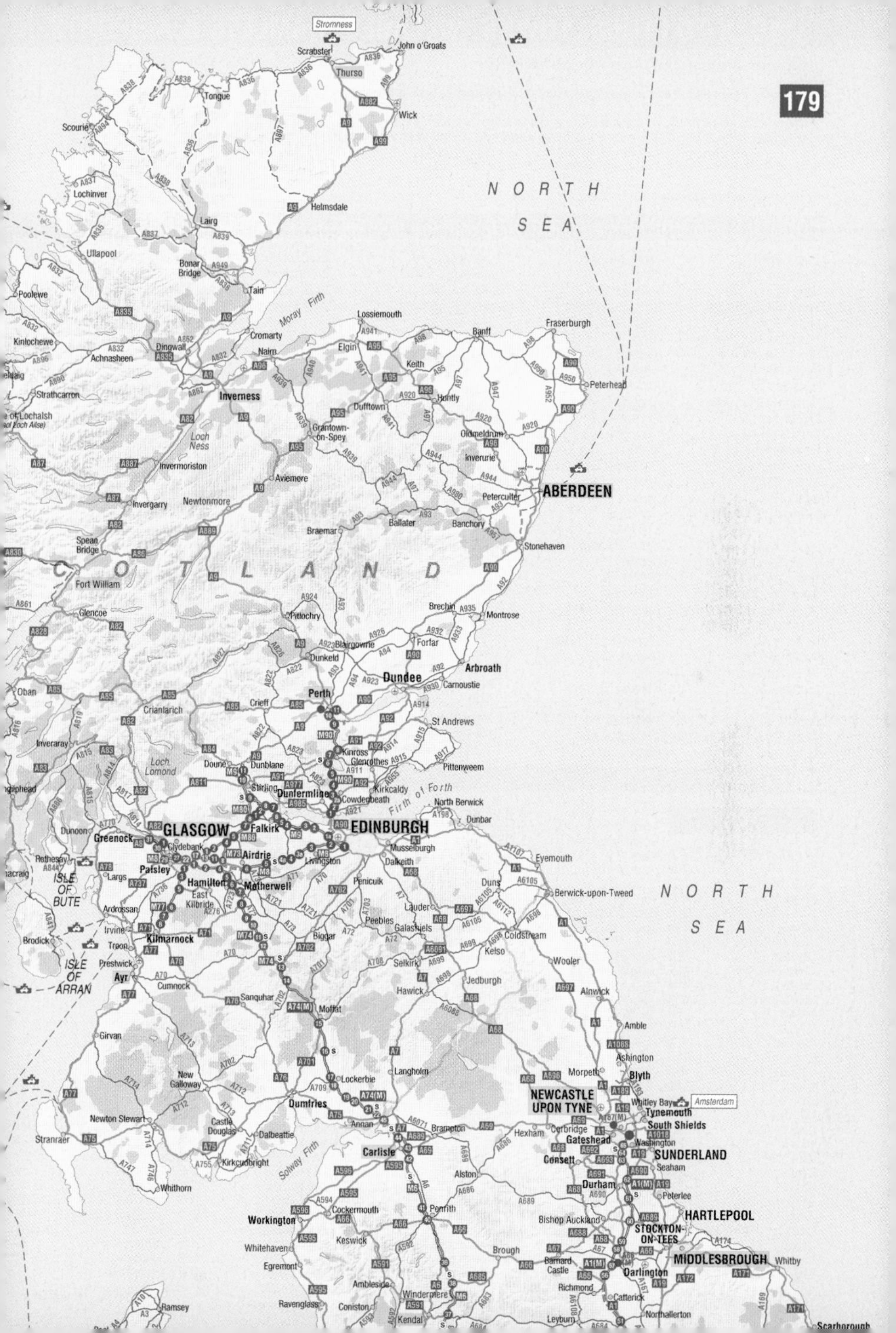

NORTH SEA
SCOTLAND
Stromness
Scrabster
John o'Groats
Thurso
Tongue
Wick
Scourie
Lochinver
Helmsdale
Lairg
Ullapool
Bonar Bridge
Tain
Poolewe
Moray Firth
Lossiemouth
Fraserburgh
Kinlochewe
Achnasheen
Dingwall
Cromarty
Nairn
Elgin
Banff
Keith
Peterhead
Strathcarron
Inverness
Huntly
Dufftown
Grantown-on-Spey
Loch Ness
Oldmeldrum
Inverurie
Invermoriston
Aviemore
Peterculter
ABERDEEN
Invergarry
Newtonmore
Braemar
Ballater
Banchory
Stonehaven
Spean Bridge
Fort William
Glencoe
Pitlochry
Brechin
Montrose
Blairgowrie
Forfar
Arbroath
Dunkeld
Dundee
Carnoustie
Oban
Perth
Crianlarich
Crieff
St Andrews
Inveraray
Kinross
Glenrothes
Pittenweem
Loch Lomond
Doune
Dunblane
Stirling
Dunfermline
Kirkcaldy
Cowdenbeath
Firth of Forth
North Berwick
Dunbar
Dunoon
GLASGOW
Falkirk
EDINBURGH
Greenock
Clydebank
Musselburgh
Airdrie
Livingston
Dalkeith
Eyemouth
Rothesay
ISLE OF BUTE
Largs
Paisley
Hamilton
Motherwell
Penicuik
Duns
Berwick-upon-Tweed
East Kilbride
Ardrossan
Lauder
Irvine
Peebles
Galashiels
Coldstream
Brodick
Troon
Kilmarnock
Biggar
Kelso
ISLE OF ARRAN
Prestwick
Selkirk
Wooler
Ayr
Cumnock
Sanquhar
Hawick
Jedburgh
Alnwick
Moffat
Amble
Girvan
Ashington
Langholm
Morpeth
Blyth
New Galloway
Lockerbie
NEWCASTLE UPON TYNE
Whitley Bay
Amsterdam
Tynemouth
South Shields
Dumfries
Newton Stewart
Castle Douglas
Dalbeattie
Annan
Brampton
Hexham
Corbridge
Gateshead
Washington
Stranraer
Carlisle
SUNDERLAND
Consett
Seaham
Kirkcudbright
Solway Firth
Alston
Durham
Whithorn
Peterlee
Cockermouth
Penrith
Workington
Bishop Auckland
HARTLEPOOL
STOCKTON-ON-TEES
Whitehaven
Keswick
Brough
MIDDLESBROUGH
Whitby
Egremont
Barnard Castle
Darlington
Ambleside
Richmond
Catterick
Ramsey
Ravenglass
Coniston
Windermere
Northallerton
Kendal
Leyburn
Scarborough

(1) A strict alphabetical order is used e.g. An Dùnan follows Andreas but precedes Andwell.

(2) The map reference given refers to the actual map square in which the town spot or built-up area is located and not to the place name.

(3) Where two or more places of the same name occur in the same County or Unitary Authority, the nearest large town is also given;
e.g. Achiemore. High . . . .2D **166** (nr. Durness) indicates that Achiemore is located in square 2D on page **166** and is situated near Durness in the Unitary Authority of Highland.

(4) Only one reference is given although due to page overlaps the place may appear on more than one page.

(5) Major towns and destinations are shown in bold, i.e. **Aberdeen**. *Aber* 3G **153**

COUNTIES and UNITARY AUTHORITIES with the abbreviations used in this index

Aberdeen : *Aber*
Aberdeenshire : *Abers*
Angus : *Ang*
Antrim & Newtownabbey : *Ant*
Argyll & Bute : *Arg*
Armagh, Banbridge & Craigavon : *Arm*
Bath & N E Somerset : *Bath*
Bedford : *Bed*
Belfast : *Bel*
Blackburn with Darwen : *Bkbn*
Blackpool : *Bkpl*
Blaenau Gwent : *Blae*
Bournemouth : *Bour*
Bracknell Forest : *Brac*
Bridgend : *B'end*
Brighton & Hove : *Brig*
Bristol : *Bris*
Buckinghamshire : *Buck*
Caerphilly : *Cphy*
Cambridgeshire : *Cambs*
Cardiff : *Card*
Carmarthenshire : *Carm*
Causeway Coast & Glens : *Caus*
Central Bedfordshire : *C Beds*
Ceredigion : *Cdgn*
Cheshire East : *Ches E*
Cheshire West & Chester : *Ches W*
Clackmannanshire : *Clac*
Conwy : *Cnwy*
Cornwall : *Corn*
Cumbria : *Cumb*
Darlington : *Darl*

Denbighshire : *Den*
Derby : *Derb*
Derbyshire : *Derbs*
Derry & Strabane : *Derr*
Devon : *Devn*
Dorset : *Dors*
Dumfries & Galloway : *Dum*
Dundee : *D'dee*
Durham : *Dur*
East Ayrshire : *E Ayr*
East Dunbartonshire : *E Dun*
East Lothian : *E Lot*
East Renfrewshire : *E Ren*
East Riding of Yorkshire : *E Yor*
East Sussex : *E Sus*
Edinburgh : *Edin*
Essex : *Essx*
Falkirk : *Falk*
Fermanagh & Omagh : *Ferm*
Fife : *Fife*
Flintshire : *Flin*
Glasgow : *Glas*
Gloucestershire : *Glos*
Greater London : *G Lon*
Greater Manchester : *G Man*
Gwynedd : *Gwyn*
Halton : *Hal*
Hampshire : *Hants*
Hartlepool : *Hart*
Herefordshire : *Here*
Hertfordshire : *Herts*
Highland : *High*

Inverclyde : *Inv*
Isle of Anglesey : *IOA*
Isle of Man : *IOM*
Isle of Wight : *IOW*
Isles of Scilly : *IOS*
Kent : *Kent*
Kingston upon Hull : *Hull*
Lancashire : *Lanc*
Leicester : *Leic*
Leicestershire : *Leics*
Lincolnshire : *Linc*
Lisburn & Castlereagh : *Lis*
Luton : *Lutn*
Medway : *Medw*
Merseyside : *Mers*
Merthyr Tydfil : *Mer T*
Mid & East Ant : *ME Ant*
Middlesbrough : *Midd*
Midlothian : *Midl*
Mid Ulster : *M Ulst*
Milton Keynes : *Mil*
Monmouthshire : *Mon*
Moray : *Mor*
Neath Port Talbot : *Neat*
Newport : *Newp*
Newry, Mourne & Down : *New M*
Norfolk : *Norf*
Northamptonshire : *Nptn*
North Ayrshire : *N Ayr*
North Down & Ards : *N Dwn*
North East Lincolnshire : *NE Lin*

North Lanarkshire : *N Lan*
North Lincolnshire : *N Lin*
North Somerset : *N Som*
Northumberland : *Nmbd*
North Yorkshire : *N Yor*
Nottingham : *Nott*
Nottinghamshire : *Notts*
Orkney : *Orkn*
Oxfordshire : *Oxon*
Pembrokeshire : *Pemb*
Perth & Kinross : *Per*
Peterborough : *Pet*
Plymouth : *Plym*
Poole : *Pool*
Portsmouth : *Port*
Powys : *Powy*
Reading : *Read*
Redcar & Cleveland : *Red C*
Renfrewshire : *Ren*
Rhondda Cynon Taff : *Rhon*
Rutland : *Rut*
Scottish Borders : *Bord*
Shetland : *Shet*
Shropshire : *Shrp*
Slough : *Slo*
Somerset : *Som*
Southampton : *Sotn*
South Ayrshire : *S Ayr*
Southend-on-Sea : *S'end*
South Gloucestershire : *S Glo*
South Lanarkshire : *S Lan*

South Yorkshire : *S Yor*
Staffordshire : *Staf*
Stirling : *Stir*
Stockton-on-Tees : *Stoc T*
Stoke-on-Trent : *Stoke*
Suffolk : *Suff*
Surrey : *Surr*
Swansea : *Swan*
Swindon : *Swin*
Telford & Wrekin : *Telf*
Thurrock : *Thur*
Torbay : *Torb*
Torfaen : *Torf*
Tyne & Wear : *Tyne*
Vale of Glamorgan, The : *V Glam*
Warrington : *Warr*
Warwickshire : *Warw*
West Berkshire : *W Ber*
West Dunbartonshire : *W Dun*
Western Isles : *W Isl*
West Lothian : *W Lot*
West Midlands : *W Mid*
West Sussex : *W Sus*
West Yorkshire : *W Yor*
Wiltshire : *Wilts*
Windsor & Maidenhead : *Wind*
Wokingham : *Wok*
Worcestershire : *Worc*
Wrexham : *Wrex*
York : *York*

INDEX

A

Alresford. Essx ... 3D 54
Alrewas. Staf ... 4F 73
Alsager. Ches E ... 5B 84
Alsagers Bank. Staf ... 1C 72
Alsop en le Dale. Derbs ... 5F 85
Alston. Cumb ... 5A 114
Alston. Devn ... 2G 13
Alstone. Glos ... 2E 49
Alstone. Som ... 2G 21
Alstonefield. Staf ... 5F 85
Alston Sutton. Som ... 1H 21
Alswear. Devn ... 4H 19
Altandhu. High ... 2D 163
Altanduin. High ... 1F 165
Altarnun. Corn ... 4C 10
Altass. High ... 3B 164
Alterwall. High ... 2E 169
Altgaltraig. Arg ... 2B 126
Altham. Lanc ... 1F 91
Althorne. Essx ... 1D 40
Althorpe. N Lin ... 4B 94
Altnabreac. High ... 4C 168
Altnacealgach. High ... 2G 163
Altnafeadh. High ... 3G 141
Altnaharra. High ... 5F 167
Altofts. W Yor ... 2D 93
Alton. Derbs ... 4A 86
Alton. Hants ... 3F 25
Alton. Staf ... 1E 73
Alton Barnes. Wilts ... 5G 35
Altonhill. E Ayr ... 1D 116
Alton Pancras. Dors ... 2C 14
Alton Priors. Wilts ... 5G 35
Altrincham. G Man ... 2B 84
Altrua. High ... 4E 149
Alva. Clac ... 4A 136
Alvanley. Ches W ... 3G 83
Alvaston. Derb ... 2A 74
Alvechurch. Worc ... 3E 61
Alvecote. Warw ... 5G 73
Alvediston. Wilts ... 4E 23
Alveley. Shrp ... 2B 60
Alverdiscott. Devn ... 4F 19
Alverstoke. Hants ... 3D 16
Alverstone. IOW ... 4D 16
Alverthorpe. W Yor ... 2D 92
Alverton. Notts ... 1E 75
Alves. Mor ... 2F 159
Alvescot. Oxon ... 5A 50
Alveston. S Glo ... 3B 34
Alveston. Warw ... 5G 61
Alvie. High ... 3C 150
Alvingham. Linc ... 1C 88
Alvington. Glos ... 5B 48
Alwalton. Cambs ... 1A 64
Alweston. Dors ... 1B 14
Alwington. Devn ... 4E 19
Alwinton. Nmbd ... 4D 120
Alwoodley. W Yor ... 5E 99
Alyth. Per ... 4B 144
Amatnatua. High ... 4B 164
Am Baile. W Isl ... 7C 170
Ambaston. Derbs ... 2B 74
Ambergate. Derbs ... 5H 85
Amber Hill. Linc ... 1B 76
Amberley. Glos ... 5D 48
Amberley. W Sus ... 4B 26
Amble. Nmbd ... 4G 121
Amblecote. W Mid ... 2C 60
Ambler Thorn. W Yor ... 2A 92
Ambleside. Cumb ... 4E 103
Ambleston. Pemb ... 2E 43
Ambrosden. Oxon ... 4E 50
Amcotts. N Lin ... 3B 94
Amersham. Buck ... 1A 38
Amerton. Staf ... 3D 73
Amesbury. Wilts ... 2G 23
Amisfield. Dum ... 1B 112
Amlwch. IOA ... 1D 80
Amlwch Port. IOA ... 1D 80
Ammanford. Carm ... 4G 45
Amotherby. N Yor ... 2B 100
Ampfield. Hants ... 4B 24
Ampleforth. N Yor ... 2H 99
Ampleforth College. N Yor ... 2H 99

Ampney Crucis. Glos ... 5F 49
Ampney St Mary. Glos ... 5F 49
Ampney St Peter. Glos ... 5F 49
Amport. Hants ... 2A 24
Ampthill. C Beds ... 2A 52
Ampton. Suff ... 3A 66
Amroth. Pemb ... 4F 43
Amulree. Per ... 5G 143
Amwell. Herts ... 4B 52
Anaheilt. High ... 2C 140
An Aird. High ... 3D 147
An Camus Darach. High ... 4E 147
Ancaster. Linc ... 1G 75
Anchor. Shrp ... 2D 58
Anchorsholme. Lanc ... 5C 96
Anchor Street. Norf ... 3F 79
An Cnoc. W Isl ... 4G 171
An Cnoc Ard. W Isl ... 1H 171
An Coroghon. High ... 3A 146
Ancroft. Nmbd ... 5G 131
Ancrum. Bord ... 2A 120
Ancton. W Sus ... 5A 26
Anderby. Linc ... 3E 89
Anderby Creek. Linc ... 3E 89
Anderson. Dors ... 3D 15
Anderton. Ches W ... 3A 84
Andertons Mill. Lanc ... 3D 90
Andover. Hants ... 2B 24
Andover Down. Hants ... 2B 24
Andoversford. Glos ... 4F 49
Andreas. IOM ... 2D 108
An Dùnan. High ... 1D 147
Andwell. Hants ... 1E 25
Anelog. Gwyn ... 3A 68
Anfield. Mers ... 1F 83
Angarrack. Corn ... 3C 4
Angelbank. Shrp ... 3H 59
Angersleigh. Som ... 1E 13
Angerton. Cumb ... 4D 112
Angle. Pemb ... 4C 42
An Gleann Ur. W Isl ... 4G 171
Angmering. W Sus ... 5B 26
Angmering-on-Sea. W Sus ... 5B 26
Angram. N Yor ... 5B 104
Angram. N Yor ... 5H 99
Anick. Nmbd ... 3C 114
Ankerbold. Derbs ... 4A 86
Ankerville. High ... 1C 158
Anlaby. E Yor ... 2D 94
Anlaby Park. Hull ... 2D 94
An Leth Meadhanach. W Isl ... 7C 170
Anmer. Norf ... 3G 77
Anmore. Hants ... 1E 17
Annahilt. Lis ... 5G 175
Annalong. New M ... 6H 175
Annan. Dum ... 3D 112
Annaside. Cumb ... 1A 96
Annat. Arg ... 1H 133
Annat. High ... 3A 156
Annathill. N Lan ... 2A 128
Anna Valley. Hants ... 2B 24
Annbank. S Ayr ... 2D 116
Annesley. Notts ... 5C 86
Annesley Woodhouse. Notts ... 5C 86
Annfield Plain. Dur ... 4E 115
Annscroft. Shrp ... 5G 71
An Sailean. High ... 2A 140
Ansdell. Lanc ... 2B 90
Ansford. Som ... 3B 22
Ansley. Warw ... 1G 61
Anslow. Staf ... 3G 73
Anslow Gate. Staf ... 3F 73
Ansteadbrook. Surr ... 2A 26
Anstey. Herts ... 2E 53
Anstey. Leics ... 5C 74
Anston. S Lan ... 5D 128
Anstruther Easter. Fife ... 3H 137
Anstruther Wester. Fife ... 3H 137
Ansty. Warw ... 2A 62
Ansty. W Sus ... 3D 27
Ansty. Wilts ... 4E 23
An Taobh Tuath. W Isl ... 9B 171
An t-Aodann Ban. High ... 3C 154

An t Ath Leathann. High ... 1E 147
An Teanga. High ... 3E 147
Anthill Common. Hants ... 1E 17
Anthorn. Cumb ... 4C 112
Antingham. Norf ... 2E 79
An t-Ob. W Isl ... 9C 171
Anton's Gowt. Linc ... 1B 76
Antony. Corn ... 3A 8
An t-Ord. High ... 2E 147
Antrim. Ant ... 3G 175
Antrobus. Ches W ... 3A 84
Anvil Corner. Devn ... 2D 10
Anwick. Linc ... 5A 88
Anwoth. Dum ... 4C 110
Apethorpe. Nptn ... 1H 63
Apeton. Staf ... 4C 72
Apley. Linc ... 3A 88
Apperknowle. Derbs ... 3A 86
Apperley. Glos ... 3D 48
Apperley Dene. Nmbd ... 4D 114
Appersett. N Yor ... 5B 104
Appin. Arg ... 4D 140
Appleby. N Lin ... 3C 94
Appleby-in-Westmorland.
  Cumb ... 2H 103
Appleby Magna. Leics ... 5H 73
Appleby Parva. Leics ... 5H 73
Applecross. High ... 4G 155
Appledore. Devn ... 1D 12
  (nr. Bideford)
Appledore. Devn ... 2D 12
  (nr. Tiverton)
Appledore. Kent ... 3D 28
Appledore Heath. Kent ... 2D 28
Appleford. Oxon ... 2D 36
Applegarthtown. Dum ... 1C 112
Applemore. Hants ... 2B 16
Appleshaw. Hants ... 2B 24
Applethwaite. Cumb ... 2D 102
Appleton. Hal ... 2H 83
Appleton. Oxon ... 5C 50
Appleton-le-Moors. N Yor ... 1B 100
Appleton-le-Street. N Yor ... 2B 100
Appleton Roebuck. N Yor ... 5H 99
Appleton Thorn. Warr ... 2A 84
Appleton Wiske. N Yor ... 4A 106
Appletree. Nptn ... 1C 50
Appletreehall. Bord ... 3H 119
Appletreewick. N Yor ... 3C 98
Appley. Som ... 4D 20
Appley Bridge. Lanc ... 3D 90
Apse Heath. IOW ... 4D 16
Apsley End. C Beds ... 2B 52
Apuldram. W Sus ... 2G 17
Arabella. High ... 1C 158
Arasaig. High ... 5E 147
Arbeadie. Abers ... 4D 152
Arberth. Pemb ... 3F 43
Arbirlot. Ang ... 4F 145
Arborfield. Wok ... 5F 37
Arborfield Cross. Wok ... 5F 37
Arborfield Garrison. Wok ... 5F 37
Arbourthorne. S Yor ... 2A 86
Arbuthnott. Abers ... 1H 145
Arcan. High ... 3H 157
Archargary. High ... 3H 157
Archdeacon Newton. Darl ... 3F 105
Archiestown. Mor ... 4G 159
Arclid. Ches E ... 4B 84
Arclid Green. Ches E ... 4B 84
Ardachu. High ... 3D 164
Ardalanish. Arg ... 2A 132
Ardaneaskan. High ... 5H 155
Ardarroch. High ... 5H 155
Ardbeg. Arg ... 1C 126
  (nr. Dunoon)
Ardbeg. Arg ... 5C 124
  (on Islay)
Ardbeg. Arg ... 3B 126
  (on Isle of Bute)
Ardcharnich. High ... 5F 163
Ardchiavaig. Arg ... 2A 132
Ardchonnell. Arg ... 2G 133
Ardchrishnish. Arg ... 1B 132

Ardchronie. High ... 5D 164
Ardchullarie. Stir ... 2E 135
Ardchyle. Stir ... 1E 135
Ard-dhubh. High ... 4G 155
Arddleen. Powy ... 4E 71
Ardeley. Herts ... 3D 52
Ardelve. High ... 1A 148
Arden. Arg ... 1E 127
Ardendrain. High ... 5H 157
Arden Hall. N Yor ... 5C 106
Ardens Grafton. Warw ... 5F 61
Ardentinny. Arg ... 1C 126
Ardeonaig. Stir ... 5D 142
Ardersier. High ... 3B 158
Ardery. High ... 2B 140
Ardessie. High ... 5E 163
Ardfern. Arg ... 3F 133
Ardfernal. Arg ... 2D 124
Ardfin. Arg ... 3C 124
Ardgartan. Arg ... 3B 134
Ardgay. High ... 4D 164
Ardglass. New M ... 6J 175
Ardgour. High ... 2E 141
Ardheslaig. High ... 3G 155
Ardindrean. High ... 5F 163
Ardingly. W Sus ... 3E 27
Ardington. Oxon ... 3C 36
Ardlamont House. Arg ... 3A 126
Ardleigh. Essx ... 3D 54
Ardler. Per ... 4B 144
Ardley. Oxon ... 3D 50
Ardlui. Arg ... 2C 134
Ardlussa. Arg ... 1E 125
Ardmair. High ... 4F 163
Ardmay. Arg ... 3B 134
Ardminish. Arg ... 5E 125
Ardmolich. High ... 1B 140
Ardmore. High ... 3C 166
  (nr. Kinlochbervie)
Ardmore. High ... 5E 164
  (nr. Tain)
Ardnacross. Arg ... 4G 139
Ardnadam. Arg ... 1C 126
Ardnagrask. High ... 4H 157
Ardnamurach. High ... 4G 147
Ardnarff. High ... 5A 156
Ardnastang. High ... 2C 140
Ardoch. High ... 5H 143
Ardochy House. High ... 3E 148
Ardoyne. Abers ... 1D 152
Ardpeaton. Arg ... 1D 126
Ardrishaig. Arg ... 1G 125
Ardroag. High ... 4B 154
Ardross. High ... 1A 158
Ardrossan. N Ayr ... 5D 126
Ardshealach. High ... 2A 140
Ardsley. S Yor ... 4D 93
Ardslignish. High ... 2G 139
Ardtalla. Arg ... 4C 124
Ardtalnaig. Per ... 5E 142
Ardtoe. High ... 1A 140
Arduaine. Arg ... 2E 133
Ardullie. High ... 2H 157
Ardvasar. High ... 3E 147
Ardvorlich. Per ... 1F 135
Ardwell. Dum ... 5G 109
Ardwell. Mor ... 5A 160
Arean. High ... 1A 140
Areley Common. Worc ... 3C 60
Areley Kings. Worc ... 3C 60
Arford. Hants ... 3G 25
Argoed. Cphy ... 2E 33
Argoed Mill. Powy ... 4B 58
Argos Hill. E Sus ... 3G 27
Aridhglas. Arg ... 2B 132
Arinacrinachd. High ... 3G 155
Arinagour. Arg ... 3D 138
Arisaig. High ... 5E 147
Ariundle. High ... 2C 140
Arivegaig. High ... 2A 140
Arkendale. N Yor ... 3F 99
Arkesden. Essx ... 2E 53
Arkholme. Lanc ... 2E 97
Arkle Town. N Yor ... 4D 104
Arkley. G Lon ... 1D 38

Arksey. S Yor ... 4F 93
Arkwright Town. Derbs ... 3B 86
Arlecdon. Cumb ... 3B 102
Arlescote. Warw ... 1B 50
Arlesey. C Beds ... 2B 52
Arleston. Telf ... 4A 72
Arley. Ches E ... 2A 84
Arlingham. Glos ... 4C 48
Arlington. Devn ... 2G 19
Arlington. E Sus ... 5G 27
Arlington. Glos ... 5G 49
Arlington Beccott. Devn ... 2G 19
Armadail. High ... 3E 147
Armadale. High ... 3E 147
  (nr. Isleornsay)
Armadale. High ... 2H 167
  (nr. Strathy)
Armadale. W Lot ... 3C 128
Armagh. Arm ... 5E 175
Armathwaite. Cumb ... 5G 113
Arminghall. Norf ... 5E 79
Armitage. Staf ... 4E 73
Armitage Bridge. W Yor ... 3B 92
Armley. W Yor ... 1C 92
Armscote. Warw ... 1H 49
Arms, The. Norf ... 1A 66
Armston. Nptn ... 2H 63
Armthorpe. S Yor ... 4G 93
Arncliffe. N Yor ... 2B 98
Arncliffe Cote. N Yor ... 2B 98
Arncroach. Fife ... 3H 137
Arne. Dors ... 4E 15
Arnesby. Leics ... 1D 62
Arnicle. Arg ... 2B 122
Arnisdale. High ... 2G 147
Arnish. High ... 4E 155
Arniston. Midl ... 3G 129
Arnol. W Isl ... 3F 171
Arnold. E Yor ... 5F 101
Arnold. Notts ... 1C 74
Arnprior. Stir ... 4F 135
Arnside. Cumb ... 2D 96
Aros Mains. Arg ... 4G 139
Arpafeelie. High ... 3A 158
Arrad Foot. Cumb ... 1C 96
Arram. E Yor ... 5E 101
Arras. E Yor ... 5D 100
Arrathorne. N Yor ... 5E 105
Arreton. IOW ... 4D 16
Arrington. Cambs ... 5C 64
Arrochar. Arg ... 3B 134
Arrow. Warw ... 5E 61
Arscaig. High ... 2C 164
Artafallie. High ... 4A 158
Arthington. W Yor ... 5E 99
Arthingworth. Nptn ... 2E 63
Arthog. Gwyn ... 4F 69
Arthrath. Abers ... 5G 161
Arthurstone. Per ... 4B 144
Artington. Surr ... 1A 26
Arundel. W Sus ... 5B 26
Asby. Cumb ... 2B 102
Ascog. Arg ... 3C 126
Ascot. Wind ... 4A 38
Ascott-under-Wychwood. Oxon ... 4B 50
Asenby. N Yor ... 2F 99
Asfordby. Leics ... 4E 74
Asfordby Hill. Leics ... 4E 74
Asgarby. Linc ... 4C 88
  (nr. Horncastle)
Asgarby. Linc ... 1A 76
  (nr. Sleaford)
Ash. Devn ... 4E 9
Ash. Dors ... 1D 14
Ash. Kent ... 5G 41
  (nr. Sandwich)
Ash. Kent ... 4H 39
  (nr. Swanley)
Ash. Som ... 4H 21
Ash. Surr ... 1G 25
Ashampstead. W Ber ... 4D 36
Ashbocking. Suff ... 5D 66
Ashbourne. Derbs ... 1F 73
Ashbrittle. Som ... 4D 20
Ashbrook. Shrp ... 1G 59

Barnhead—Belper

Barnhead. Ang 3F 145
Barnhill. D'dee 5D 145
Barnhill. Mor 3F 159
Barnhill. Per 1D 136
Barnhills. Dum 2E 109
Barningham. Dur 3D 105
Barningham. Suff 3B 66
Barnoldby le Beck. NE Lin 4F 95
Barnoldswick. Lanc 5A 98
Barns Green. W Sus 3C 26
Barnsley. Glos 5F 49
Barnsley. Shrp 1B 60
Barnsley. S Yor 4D 92
Barnstaple. Devn 3F 19
Barnston. Essx 4G 53
Barnston. Mers 2E 83
Barnstone. Notts 2E 75
Barnt Green. Worc 3E 61
Barnton. Ches W 3A 84
Barnwell. Cambs 5D 64
Barnwell. Nptn 2H 63
Barnwood. Glos 4D 48
Barons Cross. Here 5G 59
Barony, The. Orkn 5B 172
Barr. Dum 4G 117
Barr. S Ayr 5B 116
Barra Airport. W Isl 8B 170
Barrachan. Dum 5A 110
Barraglom. W Isl 4D 171
Barrahormid. Arg 1F 125
Barrapol. Arg 4A 138
Barrasford. Nmbd 2C 114
Barravullin. Arg 3F 133
Barregarrow. IOM 3C 108
Barrhead. E Ren 4G 127
Barrhill. S Ayr 1H 109
Barri. V Glam 5E 32
Barrington. Cambs 1D 53
Barrington. Som 1G 13
Barripper. Corn 3D 4
Barrmill. N Ayr 4E 127
Barrock. High 1E 169
Barrow. Lanc 1F 91
Barrow. Rut 4F 75
Barrow. Shrp 5A 72
Barrow. Som 3C 22
Barrow. Suff 4G 65
Barroway Drove. Norf 5E 77
Barrow Bridge. G Man 3E 91
Barrowburn. Nmbd 3C 120
Barrowby. Linc 2F 75
Barrowcliff. N Yor 1E 101
Barrow Common. N Som 5A 34
Barrowden. Rut 5G 75
Barrowford. Lanc 1G 91
Barrow Gurney. N Som 5A 34
Barrow Haven. N Lin 2D 94
Barrow Hill. Derbs 3B 86
Barrow-in-Furness. Cumb 3B 96
Barrow Nook. Lanc 4C 90
Barrows Green. Cumb 1E 97
Barrow's Green. Hal 2H 83
Barrow Street. Wilts 3D 22
Barrow upon Humber. N Lin 2D 94
Barrow upon Soar. Leics 4C 74
Barrow upon Trent. Derbs 3A 74
Barry. Ang 5E 145
Barry. V Glam 5E 32
Barry Island. V Glam 5E 32
Barsby. Leics 4D 74
Barsham. Suff 2F 67
Barston. W Mid 3G 61
Bartestree. Here 1A 48
Barthol Chapel. Abers 5F 161
Bartholomew Green. Essx 3H 53
Barthomley. Ches E 5B 84
Bartley. Hants 1B 16
Bartley Green. W Mid 2E 61
Bartlow. Cambs 1F 53
Barton. Cambs 5D 64
Barton. Ches W 5G 83
Barton. Cumb 2F 103
Barton. Glos 3G 49
Barton. IOW 4D 16
Barton. Lanc 4B 90 (nr. Ormskirk)
Barton. Lanc 1D 90 (nr. Preston)
Barton. N Som 1G 21
Barton. N Yor 4F 105
Barton. Oxon 5D 50
Barton. Torb 2F 9
Barton. Warw 5F 61
Barton Bendish. Norf 5G 77
Barton Gate. Staf 4F 73
Barton Green. Staf 4F 73
Barton Hartsthorn. Buck 2E 51
Barton Hill. N Yor 3B 100
Barton in Fabis. Notts 2C 74
Barton in the Beans. Leics 5A 74
Barton-le-Clay. C Beds 2A 52
Barton-le-Street. N Yor 2B 100
Barton-le-Willows. N Yor 3B 100
Barton Mills. Suff 3G 65
Barton on Sea. Hants 3H 15
Barton-on-the-Heath. Warw 2A 50
Barton St David. Som 3A 22
Barton Seagrave. Nptn 3F 63
Barton Stacey. Hants 2C 24
Barton Town. Devn 2G 19
Barton Turf. Norf 3F 79
Barton-under-Needwood. Staf 4F 73
Barton-upon-Humber. N Lin 2D 94
Barton Waterside. N Lin 2D 94
Barugh Green. S Yor 4D 92
Barway. Cambs 3E 65
Barwell. Leics 1B 62
Barwick. Herts 4D 53
Barwick. Som 1A 14
Barwick in Elmet. W Yor 1D 93
Baschurch. Shrp 3G 71
Bascote. Warw 4B 62
Basford Green. Staf 5D 85
Bashall Eaves. Lanc 5F 97
Bashall Town. Lanc 5G 97
Bashley. Hants 3H 15
Basildon. Essx 2B 40
Basingstoke. Hants 1E 25
Baslow. Derbs 3G 85
Bason Bridge. Som 2G 21
Bassaleg. Newp 3F 33
Bassendean. Bord 5C 130
Bassenthwaite. Cumb 1D 102
Bassett. Sotn 1C 16
Bassingbourn. Cambs 1D 52
Bassingfield. Notts 2D 74
Bassingham. Linc 4G 87
Bassingthorpe. Linc 3G 75
Bassus Green. Herts 3D 52
Basta. Shet 2G 173
Baston. Linc 4A 76
Bastonford. Worc 5C 60
Bastwick. Norf 4G 79
Batchley. Worc 4E 61
Batchworth. Herts 1B 38
Batcombe. Dors 2B 14
Batcombe. Som 3B 22
Bate Heath. Ches E 3A 84
Bath. Bath 5C 34
Bathampton. Bath 5C 34
Bathealton. Som 4D 20
Batheaston. Bath 5C 34
Bathford. Bath 5C 34
Bathgate. W Lot 3C 128
Bathley. Notts 5E 87
Bathpool. Corn 5C 10
Bathpool. Som 4F 21
Bathville. W Lot 3C 128
Bathway. Som 1A 22
Batley. W Yor 2C 92
Batsford. Glos 2G 49
Batson. Devn 5D 8
Battersby. N Yor 4C 106
Battersea. G Lon 3D 39
Battisborough Cross. Devn 4C 8
Battisford. Suff 5C 66
Battisford Tye. Suff 5C 66
Battle. E Sus 4B 28
Battle. Powy 2D 46
Battleborough. Som 1G 21
Battledown. Glos 3E 49
Battlefield. Shrp 4H 71
Battlesbridge. Essx 1B 40
Battlesden. C Beds 3H 51
Battlesea Green. Suff 3E 66
Battleton. Som 4C 20
Battram. Leics 5B 74
Battramsley. Hants 3B 16
Batt's Corner. Surr 2G 25
Bauds of Cullen. Mor 2B 160
Baugh. Arg 4B 138
Baughton. Worc 1D 49
Baughurst. Hants 5D 36
Baulking. Oxon 2B 36
Baumber. Linc 3B 88
Baunton. Glos 5F 49
Baverstock. Wilts 3F 23
Bawburgh. Norf 5D 78
Bawdeswell. Norf 3C 78
Bawdrip. Som 3G 21
Bawdsey. Suff 1G 55
Bawdsey Manor. Suff 2G 55
Bawsey. Norf 4F 77
Bawtry. S Yor 1D 86
Baxenden. Lanc 2F 91
Baxterley. Warw 1G 61
Baxter's Green. Suff 5G 65
Bay. High 3B 154
Baybridge. Hants 4D 24
Baybridge. Nmbd 4C 114
Baycliff. Cumb 2B 96
Baydon. Wilts 4A 36
Bayford. Herts 5D 52
Bayford. Som 4C 22
Bayles. Cumb 5A 114
Baylham. Suff 5D 66
Baynard's Green. Oxon 3D 50
Bayston Hill. Shrp 5G 71
Baythorn End. Essx 1H 53
Baythorpe. Linc 1B 76
Bayton. Worc 3A 60
Bayton Common. Worc 3B 60
Bayworth. Oxon 5D 50
Beach. S Glo 4C 34
Beachampton. Buck 2F 51
Beachamwell. Norf 5G 77
Beachley. Glos 2A 34
Beacon. Devn 2E 13
Beacon End. Essx 3C 54
Beacon Hill. Surr 3G 25
Beacon's Bottom. Buck 2F 37
Beaconsfield. Buck 1A 38
Beacrabhaic. W Isl 8D 171
Beadlam. N Yor 1A 100
Beadnell. Nmbd 2G 121
Beaford. Devn 1F 11
Beal. Nmbd 5G 131
Beal. N Yor 2F 93
Bealsmill. Corn 5D 10
Beam Hill. Staf 3G 73
Beamhurst. Staf 2E 73
Beaminster. Dors 2H 13
Beamish. Dur 4F 115
Beamond End. Buck 1A 38
Beamsley. N Yor 4C 98
Bean. Kent 3G 39
Beanacre. Wilts 5E 35
Beanley. Nmbd 3E 121
Beaquoy. Orkn 5C 172
Beardwood. Bkbn 2E 91
Beare Green. Surr 1C 26
Bearley. Warw 4F 61
Bearpark. Dur 5F 115
Bearsbridge. Nmbd 4A 114
Bearsden. E Dun 2G 127
Bearsted. Kent 5B 40
Bearstone. Shrp 2B 72
Bearwood. Pool 3F 15
Bearwood. W Mid 2E 61
Beattock. Dum 4C 118
Beauchamp Roding. Essx 4F 53
Beauchief. S Yor 2H 85
Beaufort. Blae 4E 47
Beaulieu. Hants 2B 16
Beauly. High 4H 157
Beaumaris. IOA 3F 81
Beaumont. Cumb 4E 113
Beaumont. Essx 3E 55
Beaumont Hill. Darl 3F 105
Beaumont Leys. Leic 5C 74
Beausale. Warw 3G 61
Beauvale. Notts 1B 74
Beauworth. Hants 4D 24
Beaworthy. Devn 3E 11
Beazley End. Essx 3H 53
Bebington. Mers 2F 83
Bebside. Nmbd 1F 115
Beccles. Suff 2G 67
Becconsall. Lanc 2C 90
Beckbury. Shrp 5B 72
Beckenham. G Lon 4E 39
Beckermet. Cumb 4B 102
Beckett End. Norf 1G 65
Beckfoot. Cumb 1A 96 (nr. Broughton in Furness)
Beck Foot. Cumb 5H 103 (nr. Kendal)
Beckfoot. Cumb 4C 102 (nr. Seascale)
Beckfoot. Cumb 5B 112 (nr. Silloth)
Beckford. Worc 2E 49
Beckhampton. Wilts 5F 35
Beck Hole. N Yor 4F 107
Beckingham. Linc 5F 87
Beckingham. Notts 1E 87
Beckington. Som 1D 22
Beckley. E Sus 3C 28
Beckley. Hants 3H 15
Beckley. Oxon 4D 50
Beck Row. Suff 3F 65
Beck Side. Cumb 1C 96 (nr. Cartmel)
Beckside. Cumb 1F 97 (nr. Sedbergh)
Beck Side. Cumb 1B 96 (nr. Ulverston)
Beckton. G Lon 2F 39
Beckwithshaw. N Yor 4E 99
Becontree. G Lon 2F 39
Bedale. N Yor 1E 99
Bedburn. Dur 1E 105
Bedchester. Dors 1D 14
Beddau. Rhon 3D 32
Beddgelert. Gwyn 1E 69
Beddingham. E Sus 5F 27
Beddington. G Lon 4E 39
Bedfield. Suff 4E 66
Bedford. Bed 1A 52
Bedford. G Man 1A 84
Bedham. W Sus 3B 26
Bedhampton. Hants 2F 17
Bedingfield. Suff 4D 66
Bedingham Green. Norf 1E 67
Bedlam. N Yor 3E 99
Bedlar's Green. Essx 3F 53
Bedlington. Nmbd 1F 115
Bedlinog. Mer T 5D 46
Bedminster. Bris 4A 34
Bedmond. Herts 5A 52
Bednall. Staf 4D 72
Bedrule. Bord 3A 120
Bedstone. Shrp 3F 59
Bedwas. Cphy 3E 33
Bedwellty. Cphy 5E 47
Bedworth. Warw 2A 62
Beeby. Leics 5D 74
Beech. Hants 3E 25
Beech. Staf 2C 72
Beechcliffe. W Yor 5C 98
Beech Hill. W Ber 5E 37
Beechingstoke. Wilts 1F 23
Beedon. W Ber 4C 36
Beeford. E Yor 4F 101
Beeley. Derbs 4G 85
Beelsby. NE Lin 4F 95
Beenham. W Ber 5D 36
Beeny. Corn 3B 10
Beer. Devn 4F 13
Beer. Som 3H 21
Beercrocombe. Som 4G 21
Beer Hackett. Dors 1B 14
Beesands. Devn 4E 9
Beesby. Linc 2D 88
Beeson. Devn 4E 9
Beeston. C Beds 1B 52
Beeston. Ches W 5H 83
Beeston. Norf 4B 78
Beeston. Notts 2C 74
Beeston. W Yor 1C 92
Beeston Regis. Norf 1D 78
Beeswing. Dum 3F 111
Beetham. Cumb 2D 97
Beetham. Som 1F 13
Beetley. Norf 4B 78
Beffcote. Staf 4C 72
Began. Card 3F 33
Begbroke. Oxon 4C 50
Begdale. Cambs 5D 76
Begelly. Pemb 4F 43
Beggar Hill. Essx 5G 53
Beggar's Bush. Powy 4E 59
Beggearn Huish. Som 3D 20
Beguildy. Powy 3D 58
Beighton. Norf 5F 79
Beighton. S Yor 2B 86
Beighton Hill. Derbs 5G 85
Beinn Casgro. W Isl 5G 171
Beith. N Ayr 4E 127
Bekesbourne. Kent 5F 41
Belaugh. Norf 4E 79
Belbroughton. Worc 3D 60
Belchalwell. Dors 2C 14
Belchalwell Street. Dors 2C 14
Belchamp Otten. Essx 1B 54
Belchamp St Paul. Essx 1A 54
Belchamp Walter. Essx 1B 54
Belchford. Linc 3B 88
Belfast. Bel 4H 175
Belfast International Airport. Ant 3G 175
Belfatton. Abers 3H 161
Belford. Nmbd 1F 121
Belgrano. Cnwy 3B 82
Belhaven. E Lot 2C 130
Belhelvie. Abers 2G 153
Belhinnie. Abers 1B 152
Bellabeg. Abers 2A 152
Belladrum. High 4H 157
Bellaghy. M Ulst 3F 175
Bellamore. S Ayr 1H 109
Bellanoch. Arg 4F 133
Bell Busk. N Yor 4B 98
Belleau. Linc 3D 88
Belleheiglash. Mor 5F 159
Bell End. Worc 3D 60
Bellerby. N Yor 5E 105
Bellerby Camp. N Yor 5D 105
Bellever. Devn 5G 11
Belle Vue. Cumb 1C 102
Belle Vue. Shrp 4G 71
Bellfield. S Lan 1H 117
Belliehill. Ang 2E 145
Bellingdon. Buck 5H 51
Bellingham. Nmbd 1B 114
Bellmount. Norf 3E 77
Bellochantuy. Arg 2A 122
Bellsbank. E Ayr 4D 117
Bell's Cross. Suff 5D 66
Bellshill. N Lan 4A 128
Bellshill. Nmbd 1F 121
Bellside. N Lan 4B 128
Bellspool. Bord 1D 118
Bellsquarry. W Lot 3D 128
Bells Yew Green. E Sus 2H 27
Belmaduthy. High 3A 158
Belmesthorpe. Rut 4H 75
Belmont. Bkbn 3E 91
Belmont. Shet 1G 173
Belmont. S Ayr 2C 116
Belnacraig. Abers 2A 152
Belnie. Linc 2B 76
Belowda. Corn 2D 6
Belper. Derbs 1A 74

Birchall. *Staf* 5D 85
Bircham Newton. *Norf* 2G 77
Bircham Tofts. *Norf* 2G 77
Birchanger. *Essx* 3F 53
Birchburn. *N Ayr* 3D 122
Birch Cross. *Staf* 2F 73
Bircher. *Here* 4G 59
Birch Green. *Essx* 4C 54
Birchgrove. *Card* 3E 33
Birchgrove. *Swan* 3G 31
Birch Heath. *Ches W* 4H 83
Birch Hill. *Ches W* 3H 83
Birchill. *Devn* 2G 13
Birchington. *Kent* 4G 41
Birchley Heath. *Warw* 1G 61
Birchmoor. *Warw* 5G 73
Birchmoor Green. *C Beds* 2H 51
Birchover. *Derbs* 4G 85
Birch Vale. *Derbs* 2E 85
Birchview. *Mor* 5F 159
Birchwood. *Linc* 4G 87
Birchwood. *Som* 1F 13
Birchwood. *Warr* 1A 84
Bircotes. *Notts* 1D 86
Birdbrook. *Essx* 1H 53
Birdham. *W Sus* 2G 17
Birdholme. *Derbs* 4A 86
Birdingbury. *Warw* 4B 62
Birdlip. *Glos* 4E 49
Birds Edge. *W Yor* 4C 92
Birdsgreen. *Shrp* 2B 60
Birdsmoorgate. *Dors* 2G 13
Birdston. *E Dun* 2H 127
Birdwell. *S Yor* 4D 92
Birdwood. *Glos* 4C 48
Birgham. *Bord* 1B 120
Birichen. *High* 4E 165
Birkby. *Cumb* 1B 102
Birkby. *N Yor* 4A 106
Birkdale. *Mers* 3B 90
Birkenhead. *Mers* 2F 83
Birkenhills. *Abers* 4E 161
Birkenshaw. *N Lan* 3H 127
Birkenshaw. *W Yor* 2C 92
Birkhall. *Abers* 4H 151
Birkholme. *Linc* 3G 75
Birkin. *N Yor* 2F 93
Birley. *Here* 5G 59
Birling. *Kent* 4A 40
Birling. *Nmbd* 4G 121
Birling Gap. *E Sus* 5G 27
Birlingham. *Worc* 1E 49
Birmingham. *W Mid* 2E 61
Birmingham Airport. *W Mid* ...2F 61
Birnam. *Per* 4H 143
Birse. *Abers* 4C 152
Birsemore. *Abers* 4C 152
Birstall. *Leics* 5C 74
Birstall. *W Yor* 2C 92
Birstall Smithies. *W Yor* 2C 92
Birstwith. *N Yor* 4E 99
Birthorpe. *Linc* 2A 76
Birtle. *Lanc* 3G 91
Birtley. *Here* 4F 59
Birtley. *Nmbd* 2B 114
Birtley. *Tyne* 4F 115
Birtley. *Worc* 4A 60
Birts Street. *Worc* 2C 48
Bisbrooke. *Rut* 1F 63
Bisham. *Wind* 3G 37
Bishampton. *Worc* 5D 61
Bish Mill. *Devn* 4H 19
Bishop Auckland. *Dur* 2F 105
Bishopbridge. *Linc* 1H 87
Bishopbriggs. *E Dun* 2H 127
Bishop Burton. *E Yor* 1C 94
Bishop Middleham. *Dur* 1A 106
Bishopmill. *Mor* 2G 159
Bishop Monkton. *N Yor* 3F 99
Bishop Norton. *Linc* 1G 87
Bishopsbourne. *Kent* 5F 41

Bishops Cannings. Wilts 5F 35
Bishop's Castle. Shrp 2F 59
Bishop's Caundle. Dors 1B 14
Bishop's Cleeve. Glos 3E 49
Bishop's Down. Dors 1B 14
Bishop's Frome. Here 1B 48
Bishop's Green. Essx 4G 53
Bishop's Green. Hants 5D 36
Bishop's Hull. Som 4F 21
Bishop's Itchington. Warw 5A 62
Bishops Lydeard. Som 4E 21
Bishop's Norton. Glos 3D 48
Bishop's Nympton. Devn 4A 20
Bishop's Offley. Staf 3B 72
Bishop's Stortford. Herts 3E 53
Bishop's Sutton. Hants 3E 24
Bishop's Tachbrook.
   Warw 4H 61
Bishop's Tawton. Devn 3F 19
Bishopsteignton. Devn 5C 12
Bishopstoke. Hants 1C 16
Bishopston. Swan 4E 31
Bishopstone. Buck 4G 51
Bishopstone. E Sus 5F 27
Bishopstone. Here 1H 47
Bishopstone. Swin 3H 35
Bishopstone. Wilts 4F 23
Bishopstrow. Wilts 2D 23
Bishop Sutton. Bath 1A 22
Bishop's Waltham. Hants 1D 16
Bishopswood. Som 1F 13
Bishops Wood. Staf 5C 72
Bishopsworth. Bris 5A 34
Bishop Thornton. N Yor 3E 99
Bishopthorpe. York 5H 99
Bishopton. Darl 2A 106
Bishopton. Dum 5B 110
Bishopton. N Yor 2E 99
Bishopton. Warw 5F 61
Bishop Wilton. E Yor 4B 100
Bishton. Newp 3G 33
Bishton. Staf 3E 73
Bisley. Glos 5E 49
Bisley. Surr 5A 38
Bispham. Bkpl 5C 96
Bispham Green. Lanc 3C 90
Bissoe. Corn 4B 6
Bisterne. Hants 2G 15
Bisterne Close. Hants 2H 15
Bitchfield. Linc 3G 75
Bittadon. Devn 2F 19
Bittaford. Devn 3C 8
Bittering. Norf 4B 78
Bitterley. Shrp 3H 59
Bitterne. Sotn 1C 16
Bitteswell. Leics 2C 62
Bitton. S Glo 5B 34
Bix. Oxon 3F 37
Bixter. Shet 6E 173
Blaby. Leics 1C 62
Blackawton. Devn 3E 9
Black Bank. Cambs 2E 65
Black Barn. Linc 3D 76
Blackborough. Devn 2D 12
Blackborough. Norf 4F 77
Blackborough End. Norf 4F 77
Black Bourton. Oxon 5A 50
Blackboys. E Sus 3G 27
Blackbrook. Derbs 1H 73
Blackbrook. Mers 1H 83
Blackbrook. Staf 2B 72
Blackbrook. Surr 1C 26
Blackburn. Abers 2F 153
Blackburn. Bkbn 2E 91
Blackburn. W Lot 3C 128
Black Callerton. Tyne 3E 115
Black Carr. Norf 1C 66
Black Clauchrie. S Ayr 1H 109
Black Corries. High 3G 141
Black Crofts. Arg 5D 140
Black Cross. Corn 2D 6
Blackden Heath. Ches E 3B 84
Blackditch. Oxon 5C 50
Blackdog. Abers 2G 153

Black Dog. Devn 2B 12
Blackdown. Dors 2G 13
Blackdyke. Cumb 4C 112
Blacker Hill. S Yor 4D 92
Blackfen. G Lon 3F 39
Blackfield. Hants 2C 16
Blackford. Cumb 3E 113
Blackford. Per 3A 136
Blackford. Shrp 2H 59
Blackford. Som 2H 21
   (nr. Burnham-on-Sea)
Blackford. Som 2H 21
   (nr. Wincanton)
Blackfordby. Leics 4H 73
Blackgang. IOW 5C 16
Blackhall. Edin 2F 129
Blackhall. Ren 3F 127
Blackhall Colliery. Dur 1B 106
Blackhall Mill. Tyne 4E 115
Blackhall Rocks. Dur 1B 106
Blackham. E Sus 2F 27
Blackheath. Essx 3D 54
Blackheath. G Lon 3E 39
Blackheath. Suff 3G 67
Blackheath. Surr 1B 26
Blackheath. W Mid 2D 61
Black Heddon. Nmbd 2D 115
Blackhill. Abers 4H 161
Blackhill. High 3C 154
Blackhills. Abers 2G 161
Blackhills. High 3D 158
Blackjack. Linc 2B 76
Blackland. Wilts 5F 35
Black Lane. G Man 4F 91
Blackleach. Lanc 1C 90
Blackley. G Man 4G 91
Blackley. W Yor 3B 92
Blacklunans. Per 2A 144
Blackmill. B'end 3C 32
Blackmoor. G Man 4E 91
Blackmoor. Hants 3F 25
Blackmoor Gate. Devn 2G 19
Blackmore. Essx 5G 53
Blackmore End. Essx 2H 53
Blackmore End. Herts 4B 52
Black Mount. Arg 4G 141
Blackness. Falk 2D 128
Blacknest. Hants 2F 25
Blackney. Dors 3H 13
Blacknoll. Dors 4D 14
Black Notley. Essx 3A 54
Blacko. Lanc 5A 98
Black Pill. Swan 3F 31
Blackpool. Bkpl 1B 90
Blackpool. Devn 4E 9
Blackpool Corner. Devn 3G 13
Blackpool Gate. Cumb 2G 113
Blackridge. W Lot 3B 128
Blackrock. Arg 3B 124
Blackrock. Mon 4F 47
Blackrod. G Man 3E 90
Blackshaw. Dum 3B 112
Blackshaw Head. W Yor 2H 91
Blackshaw Moor. Staf 5E 85
Blacksmith's Green. Suff 4D 66
Blacksnape. Bkbn 2F 91
Blackstone. W Sus 4D 26
Black Street. Suff 2H 67
Black Tar. Pemb 4D 43
Blackthorn. Oxon 4E 50
Blackthorpe. Suff 4B 66
Blacktoft. E Yor 2B 94
Blacktop. Aber 3F 153
Black Torrington. Devn 2E 11
Blacktown. Newp 3F 33
Blackwall Tunnel. G Lon 2E 39
Blackwater. Corn 4B 6
Blackwater. Hants 1G 25
Blackwater. IOW 4D 16
Blackwater. Som 1F 13
Blackwaterfoot. N Ayr 3C 122
Blackwell. Darl 3F 105
Blackwell. Derbs 5B 86
   (nr. Alfreton)

Blackwell. Derbs 3F 85
   (nr. Buxton)
Blackwell. Som 4D 20
Blackwell. Warw 1H 49
Blackwell. Worc 3D 61
Blackwood. Cphy 2E 33
Blackwood. Dum 1G 111
Blackwood. S Lan 5A 128
Blackwood Hill. Staf 5D 84
Blacon. Ches W 4F 83
Bladnoch. Dum 4B 110
Bladon. Oxon 4C 50
Blaenannerch. Cdgn 1C 44
Blaenau Dolwyddelan. Cnwy 5F 81
Blaenau Ffestiniog. Gwyn 1G 69
Blaenavon. Torf 5F 47
Blaenawey. Mon 4F 47
Blaen Celyn. Cdgn 5C 56
Blaen Clydach. Rhon 2C 32
Blaencwm. Rhon 2C 32
Blaendulais. Neat 5B 46
Blaenffos. Pemb 1F 43
Blaengarw. B'end 2C 32
Blaen-geuffordd. Cdgn 2F 57
Blaengwrach. Neat 5B 46
Blaengwynfi. Neat 2B 32
Blaenllechau. Rhon 2D 32
Blaenpennal. Cdgn 4F 57
Blaenplwyf. Cdgn 3E 57
Blaenporth. Cdgn 1C 44
Blaenrhondda. Rhon 2C 32
Blaenwaun. Carm 2G 43
Blaen-y-coed. Carm 2H 43
Blagdon. N Som 1A 22
Blagdon. Torb 2E 9
Blagdon Hill. Som 1F 13
Blagill. Cumb 5A 114
Blaguegate. Lanc 4C 90
Blaich. High 1E 141
Blain. High 2A 140
Blaina. Blae 5F 47
Blair Atholl. Per 2F 143
Blair Drummond. Stir 4G 135
Blairgowrie. Per 4A 144
Blairhall. Fife 1D 128
Blairingone. Per 4B 136
Blairlogie. Stir 4H 135
Blairmore. Abers 5B 160
Blairmore. Arg 1C 126
Blairmore. High 3B 166
Blairquhanan. W Dun 1F 127
Blaisdon. Glos 4C 48
Blakebrook. Worc 3C 60
Blakedown. Worc 3C 60
Blakemere. Here 1G 47
Blakeney. Glos 5B 48
Blakeney. Norf 1C 78
Blakenhall. Ches E 1B 72
Blakeshall. Worc 2C 60
Blakesley. Nptn 5D 62
Blanchland. Nmbd 4C 114
Blandford Camp. Dors 2E 15
Blandford Forum. Dors 2D 15
Blandford St Mary. Dors 2D 15
Bland Hill. N Yor 4E 98
Blandy. High 2G 167
Blanefield. Stir 2G 127
Blankney. Linc 4H 87
Blantyre. S Lan 4H 127
Blarmachfoldach. High 2E 141
Blarnalearoch. High 4F 163
Blashford. Hants 2G 15
Blaston. Leics 1F 63
Blatchbridge. Som 2C 22
Blathaisbhal. W Isl 1D 170
Blatherwycke. Nptn 1G 63
Blawith. Cumb 1B 96
Blaxhall. Suff 5F 67
Blaxton. S Yor 4G 93
Blaydon. Tyne 3E 115
Bleadney. Som 2H 21
Bleadon. Som 1G 21
Blean. Kent 4F 41
Bleary. Arm 5F 175

Bleasby. Linc 2A 88
Bleasby. Notts 1E 74
Bleasby Moor. Linc 2A 88
Blebocraigs. Fife 2G 137
Bleddfa. Powy 4E 58
Bledington. Glos 3H 49
Bledlow. Buck 5F 51
Bledlow Ridge. Buck 2F 37
Blencarn. Cumb 1H 103
Blencogo. Cumb 5C 112
Blendworth. Hants 1F 17
Blennerhasset. Cumb 5C 112
Bletchingdon. Oxon 4D 50
Bletchingley. Surr 5E 39
Bletchley. Mil 2G 51
Bletchley. Shrp 2A 72
Bletherston. Pemb 2E 43
Bletsoe. Bed 5H 63
Blewbury. Oxon 3D 36
Blickling. Norf 3D 78
Blidworth. Notts 5C 86
Blindburn. Nmbd 3C 120
Blindcrake. Cumb 1C 102
Blindley Heath. Surr 1E 27
Blindmoor. Som 1F 13
Blisland. Corn 5B 10
Blissford. Hants 1G 15
Bliss Gate. Worc 3B 60
Blists Hill. Telf 5A 72
Blisworth. Nptn 5E 63
Blithbury. Staf 3E 73
Blitterlees. Cumb 4C 112
Blockley. Glos 2G 49
Blofield. Norf 5F 79
Blofield Heath. Norf 4F 79
Blo' Norton. Norf 3C 66
Bloomfield. Bord 2H 119
Blore. Staf 1F 73
Blount's Green. Staf 2E 73
Bloxham. Oxon 2C 50
Bloxholm. Linc 5H 87
Bloxwich. W Mid 5D 73
Bloxworth. Dors 3D 15
Blubberhouses. N Yor 4D 98
Blue Anchor. Som 2D 20
Blue Anchor. Swan 3E 31
Blue Bell Hill. Kent 4B 40
Blue Row. Essx 4D 54
Bluetown. Kent 5D 40
Blundeston. Suff 1H 67
Blunham. C Beds 5A 64
Blunsdon St Andrew. Swin 3G 35
Bluntington. Worc 3C 60
Bluntisham. Cambs 3C 64
Blunts. Corn 2H 7
Blurton. Stoke 1C 72
Blyborough. Linc 1G 87
Blyford. Suff 3G 67
Blymhill. Staf 4C 72
Blymhill Lawns. Staf 4C 72
Blyth. Nmbd 1G 115
Blyth. Notts 2D 86
Blyth Bank. Bord 5E 129
Blyth Bridge. Bord 5E 129
Blythburgh. Suff 3G 67
Blythe Bridge. Staf 1D 72
Blythe Marsh. Staf 1D 72
Blythe, The. Staf 3E 73
Blyton. Linc 1F 87
Boarhills. Fife 2H 137
Boars Hill. Oxon 2E 16
Boarshead. E Sus 2G 27
Boar's Head. G Man 4D 90
Boars Hill. Oxon 5C 50
Boarstall. Buck 4E 51
Boasley Cross. Devn 3F 11
Boath. High 1H 157
Boat of Garten. High 2D 150
Bobbing. Kent 4C 40
Bobbington. Staf 1C 60
Bobbingworth. Essx 5F 53
Bocaddon. Corn 3F 7
Bocking. Essx 3A 54
Bocking Churchstreet. Essx 3A 54

Boddam. Abers 4H 161
Boddam. Shet 10E 173
Boddington. Glos 3D 49
Bodedern. IOA 2C 80
Bodelwyddan. Den 3C 82
Bodenham. Here 5H 59
Bodenham. Wilts 4G 23
Bodewryd. IOA 1C 80
Bodfari. Den 3C 82
Bodffordd. IOA 3D 80
Bodham. Norf 1D 78
Bodiam. E Sus 3B 28
Bodicote. Oxon 2C 50
Bodieve. Corn 1D 6
Bodinnick. Corn 3F 7
Bodle Street Green. E Sus 4A 28
Bodmin. Corn 2E 7
Bodnant. Cnwy 3H 81
Bodney. Norf 1H 65
Bodorgan. IOA 4C 80
Bodrane. Corn 2G 7
Bodsham. Kent 1F 29
Boduan. Gwyn 2C 68
Bodymoor Heath. Warw 1F 61
Bogallan. High 3A 158
Bogbrae Croft. Abers 5H 161
Bogend. S Ayr 1C 116
Boghall. Midl 3F 129
Boghall. W Lot 3C 128
Boghead. S Lan 5A 128
Bogindollo. Ang 3D 144
Bogmoor. Mor 2A 160
Bognebrae. Abers 4C 160
Bognor Regis. W Sus 3H 17
Bograxie. Abers 2E 152
Bogside. N Lan 4B 128
Bog, The. Shrp 1F 59
Bogton. Abers 3D 160
Bogue. Dum 1D 110
Bohenie. High 5E 149
Bohortha. Corn 5C 6
Boirseam. W Isl 9C 171
Bokiddick. Corn 2E 7
Bolam. Dur 2E 105
Bolam. Nmbd 1D 115
Bolberry. Devn 5C 8
Bold Heath. Mers 2H 83
Boldon. Tyne 3G 115
Boldon Colliery. Tyne 3G 115
Boldre. Hants 3B 16
Boldron. Dur 3D 104
Bole. Notts 2E 87
Bolehall. Staf 5G 73
Bolehill. Derbs 5G 85
Bolenowe. Corn 5A 6
Boleside. Bord 1G 119
Bolham. Devn 1C 12
Bolham Water. Devn 1E 13
Bolingey. Corn 3B 6
Bolney. W Sus 3D 26
Bolnhurst. Bed 5H 63
Bolshan. Ang 3F 145
Bolsover. Derbs 3B 86
Bolsterstone. S Yor 1G 85
Bolstone. Here 2A 48
Boltachan. Per 3F 143
Boltby. N Yor 1G 99
Bolton. Cumb 2H 103
Bolton. E Lot 2B 130
Bolton. E Yor 4B 100
Bolton. G Man 4F 91
Bolton. Nmbd 3F 121
Bolton Abbey. N Yor 4C 98
Bolton-by-Bowland. Lanc 5G 97
Boltonfellend. Cumb 3F 113
Boltongate. Cumb 5D 112
Bolton Green. Lanc 3D 90
Bolton-le-Sands. Lanc 3D 97
Bolton Low Houses. Cumb 5D 112
Bolton New Houses. Cumb 5D 112
Bolton-on-Swale. N Yor 5F 105
Bolton Percy. N Yor 5H 99
Bolton Town End. Lanc 3D 97
Bolton upon Dearne. S Yor 4E 93

Bolton Wood Lane—Brafferton

Bolton Wood Lane. *Cumb* 5D 112
Bolventor. *Corn* 5B 10
Bomarsund. *Nmbd* 1F 115
Bomere Heath. *Shrp* 4G 71
Bonar Bridge. *High* 4D 164
Bonawe. *Arg* 5E 141
Bonby. *N Lin* 3D 94
Boncath. *Pemb* 1G 43
Bonchester Bridge. *Bord* 3H 119
Bonchurch. *IOW* 5D 16
Bond End. *Staf* 4F 73
Bondleigh. *Devn* 2G 11
Bonds. *Lanc* 5D 97
Bonehill. *Devn* 5H 11
Bonehill. *Staf* 5F 73
Bo'ness. *Falk* 1C 128
Boney Hay. *Staf* 4E 73
Bonham. *Wilts* 3C 22
Bonhill. *W Dun* 2E 127
Boningale. *Shrp* 5C 72
Bonjedward. *Bord* 2A 120
Bonkle. *N Lan* 4B 128
Bonnington. *Ang* 5E 145
Bonnington. *Edin* 3E 129
Bonnington. *Kent* 2E 29
Bonnybank. *Fife* 3F 137
Bonnybridge. *Falk* 1B 128
Bonnykelly. *Abers* 3F 161
Bonnyrigg. *Midl* 3G 129
Bonnyton. *Ang* 5C 144
Bonnytown. *Fife* 2H 137
Bonsall. *Derbs* 5G 85
Bont. *Mon* 4G 47
Bontddu. *Gwyn* 4F 69
Bont Dolgadfan. *Powy* 5A 70
Bontgoch. *Cdgn* 2F 57
Bonthorpe. *Linc* 3D 89
Bontnewydd. *Cdgn* 4F 57
Bont-newydd. *Cnwy* 3C 82
Bontnewydd. *Gwyn* 4D 81 (nr. Caernarfon)
Bont Newydd. *Gwyn* 1G 69 (nr. Llan Ffestiniog)
Bontuchel. *Den* 5C 82
Bonvilston. *V Glam* 4D 32
Bon-y-maen. *Swan* 3F 31
Booker. *Buck* 2G 37
Booley. *Shrp* 3H 71
Boorley Green. *Hants* 1D 16
Boosbeck. *Red C* 3D 106
Boot. *Cumb* 4C 102
Booth. *W Yor* 2A 92
Boothby Graffoe. *Linc* 5G 87
Boothby Pagnell. *Linc* 2G 75
Booth Green. *Ches E* 2D 84
Booth of Toft. *Shet* 4F 173
Boothstown. *G Man* 4F 91
Boothville. *Nptn* 4E 63
Booth Wood. *W Yor* 3A 92
Bootle. *Cumb* 1A 96
Bootle. *Mers* 1F 83
Booton. *Norf* 3D 78
Booze. *N Yor* 4D 104
Boquhan. *Stir* 1G 127
Boraston. *Shrp* 3A 60
Borden. *Kent* 4C 40
Borden. *W Sus* 4G 25
Bordlands. *Bord* 5E 129
Bordley. *N Yor* 3B 98
Bordon. *Hants* 3F 25
Boreham. *Essx* 5A 54
Boreham. *Wilts* 2D 23
Boreham Street. *E Sus* 4A 28
Borehamwood. *Herts* 1C 38
Boreland. *Dum* 5D 118
Boreston. *Devn* 3D 8
Borestone Brae. *Stir* 4G 135
Boreton. *Shrp* 5H 71
Borgh. *W Isl* 8B 170 (on Barra)
Borgh. *W Isl* 3C 170 (on Benbecula)
Borgh. *W Isl* 1E 170 (on Berneray)
Borgh. *W Isl* 2G 171 (on Isle of Lewis)
Borghasdal. *W Isl* 9C 171
Borghastan. *W Isl* 3D 171
Borgh na Sgiotaig. *High* 1C 154
Borgie. *High* 3G 167
Borgue. *Dum* 5D 110
Borgue. *High* 1H 165
Borley. *Essx* 1B 54
Borley Green. *Essx* 1B 54
Borley Green. *Suff* 4B 66
Borlum. *High* 1H 149
Bornais. *W Isl* 6C 170
Bornesketaig. *High* 1C 154
Boroughbridge. *N Yor* 3F 99
Borough Green. *Kent* 5H 39
Borras Head. *Wrex* 5F 83
Borreraig. *High* 3A 154
Borrobol Lodge. *High* 1F 165
Borrodale. *High* 4A 154
Borrowash. *Derbs* 2B 74
Borrowby. *N Yor* 1G 99 (nr. Northallerton)
Borrowby. *N Yor* 3E 107 (nr. Whitby)
Borrowston. *High* 4F 169
Borrowstonehill. *Orkn* 7D 172
Borrowstoun. *Falk* 1C 128
Borstal. *Medw* 4B 40
Borth. *Cdgn* 2F 57
Borthwick. *Midl* 4G 129
Borth-y-Gest. *Gwyn* 2E 69
Borve. *High* 4D 154
Borwick. *Lanc* 2E 97
Bosbury. *Here* 1B 48
Boscastle. *Corn* 3A 10
Boscombe. *Bour* 3G 15
Boscombe. *Wilts* 3H 23
Boscoppa. *Corn* 3E 7
Bosham. *W Sus* 2G 17
Bosherston. *Pemb* 5D 42
Bosley. *Ches E* 4D 84
Bossall. *N Yor* 3B 100
Bossiney. *Corn* 4A 10
Bossingham. *Kent* 1F 29
Bossington. *Som* 2B 20
Bostadh. *W Isl* 3D 171
Bostock Green. *Ches W* 4A 84
Boston. *Linc* 1C 76
Boston Spa. *W Yor* 5G 99
Boswarthen. *Corn* 3B 4
Boswinger. *Corn* 4D 6
Botallack. *Corn* 3A 4
Botany Bay. *G Lon* 1D 39
Botcheston. *Leics* 5B 74
Botesdale. *Suff* 3C 66
Bothal. *Nmbd* 1F 115
Bothampstead. *W Ber* 4D 36
Bothamsall. *Notts* 3D 86
Bothel. *Cumb* 1C 102
Bothenhampton. *Dors* 3H 13
Bothwell. *S Lan* 4A 128
Botley. *Buck* 5H 51
Botley. *Hants* 1D 16
Botley. *Oxon* 5C 50
Botloe's Green. *Glos* 3C 48
Botolph Claydon. *Buck* 3F 51
Botolphs. *W Sus* 5C 26
Bottacks. *High* 2G 157
Bottesford. *Leics* 2F 75
Bottesford. *N Lin* 4B 94
Bottisham. *Cambs* 4E 65
Bottlesford. *Wilts* 1G 23
Bottomcraig. *Fife* 1F 137
Bottom o' th' Moor. *G Man* 3E 91
Botton. *N Yor* 4D 107
Botton Head. *Lanc* 3F 97
Bottreaux Mill. *Devn* 4B 20
Botus Fleming. *Corn* 2A 8
Botwnnog. *Gwyn* 2B 68
Bough Beech. *Kent* 1F 27
Boughrood. *Powy* 2E 47
Boughspring. *Glos* 2A 34
Boughton. *Norf* 5F 77
Boughton. *Nptn* 4E 63
Boughton. *Notts* 4D 86
Boughton Aluph. *Kent* 1E 29
Boughton Green. *Kent* 5B 40
Boughton Lees. *Kent* 1E 28
Boughton Malherbe. *Kent* 1C 28
Boughton Monchelsea. *Kent* 5B 40
Boughton under Blean. *Kent* 5E 41
Boulby. *Red C* 3E 107
Bouldnor. *IOW* 4B 16
Bouldon. *Shrp* 2H 59
Boulmer. *Nmbd* 3G 121
Boulston. *Pemb* 3D 42
Boultham. *Linc* 4G 87
Boulton. *Derb* 2A 74
Boundary. *Staf* 1D 73
Bounds. *Here* 2B 48
Bourn. *Cambs* 5C 64
Bournbrook. *W Mid* 2E 61
Bourne. *Linc* 3H 75
Bourne End. *Bed* 4H 63
Bourne End. *Buck* 3G 37
Bourne End. *C Beds* 1H 51
Bourne End. *Herts* 5A 52
Bournemouth. *Bour* 3F 15
Bournemouth Airport. *Dors* 3G 15
Bournes Green. *Glos* 5E 49
Bournes Green. *S'end* 2D 40
Bourne, The. *Surr* 2G 25
Bournheath. *Worc* 3D 60
Bournmoor. *Dur* 4G 115
Bournville. *W Mid* 2E 61
Bourton. *Dors* 3C 22
Bourton. *N Som* 5G 33
Bourton. *Oxon* 3H 35
Bourton. *Shrp* 1H 59
Bourton. *Wilts* 5F 35
Bourton on Dunsmore. *Warw* 3B 62
Bourton-on-the-Hill. *Glos* 2G 49
Bourton-on-the-Water. *Glos* 3G 49
Bousd. *Arg* 2D 138
Bousta. *Shet* 6D 173
Boustead Hill. *Cumb* 4D 112
Bouth. *Cumb* 1C 96
Bouthwaite. *N Yor* 2D 98
Boveney. *Buck* 3A 38
Boveridge. *Dors* 1F 15
Boverton. *V Glam* 5C 32
Bovey Tracey. *Devn* 5B 12
Bovingdon. *Herts* 5A 52
Bovingdon Green. *Buck* 3G 37
Bovinger. *Essx* 5F 53
Bovington Camp. *Dors* 4D 14
Bow. *Devn* 2H 11
Bowbank. *Dur* 2C 104
Bow Brickhill. *Mil* 2H 51
Bowbridge. *Glos* 5D 48
Bowburn. *Dur* 1A 106
Bowcombe. *IOW* 4C 16
Bowd. *Devn* 4E 12
Bowden. *Devn* 4E 9
Bowden. *Bord* 1H 119
Bowden Hill. *Wilts* 5E 35
Bowdens. *Som* 4H 21
Bowderdale. *Cumb* 4H 103
Bowdon. *G Man* 2B 84
Bower. *Nmbd* 1A 114
Bowerchalke. *Wilts* 4F 23
Bowerhill. *Wilts* 5E 35
Bower Hinton. *Som* 1H 13
Bowermadden. *High* 2E 169
Bowers. *Staf* 2C 72
Bowers Gifford. *Essx* 2B 40
Bowershall. *Fife* 4C 136
Bowertower. *High* 2E 169
Bowes. *Dur* 3C 104
Bowgreave. *Lanc* 5D 97
Bowhousebog. *N Lan* 4B 128
Bowithick. *Corn* 4B 10
Bowland Bridge. *Cumb* 1D 96
Bowlees. *Dur* 2C 104
Bowley. *Here* 5H 59
Bowlhead Green. *Surr* 2A 26
Bowling. *W Dun* 2F 127
Bowling. *W Yor* 1B 92
Bowling Bank. *Wrex* 1F 71
Bowling Green. *Worc* 5C 60
Bowlish. *Som* 2B 22
Bowmanstead. *Cumb* 5E 102
Bowmore. *Arg* 4B 124
Bowness-on-Solway. *Cumb* 3D 112
Bowness-on-Windermere. *Cumb* 5F 103
Bow of Fife. *Fife* 2F 137
Bowriefauld. *Ang* 4E 145
Bowscale. *Cumb* 1E 103
Bowsden. *Nmbd* 5F 131
Bowside Lodge. *High* 2A 168
Bowston. *Cumb* 5F 103
Bow Street. *Cdgn* 2F 57
Bowthorpe. *Norf* 5D 78
Box. *Glos* 5D 48
Box. *Wilts* 5D 34
Boxbush. *Glos* 3B 48
Box End. *Bed* 1A 52
Boxford. *Suff* 1C 54
Boxford. *W Ber* 4C 36
Boxgrove. *W Sus* 5A 26
Box Hill. *Wilts* 5D 34
Boxley. *Kent* 5B 40
Boxmoor. *Herts* 5A 52
Box's Shop. *Corn* 2C 10
Boxted. *Essx* 2C 54
Boxted. *Suff* 5H 65
Boxted Cross. *Essx* 2D 54
Boxworth. *Cambs* 4C 64
Boxworth End. *Cambs* 4C 64
Boyden End. *Suff* 5G 65
Boyden Gate. *Kent* 4G 41
Boylestone. *Derbs* 2F 73
Boylestonfield. *Derbs* 2F 73
Boyndie. *Abers* 2D 160
Boynton. *E Yor* 3F 101
Boys Hill. *Dors* 1B 14
Boythorpe. *Derbs* 4A 86
Boyton. *Corn* 3D 10
Boyton. *Suff* 1G 55
Boyton. *Wilts* 3E 23
Boyton Cross. *Essx* 5G 53
Boyton End. *Essx* 2G 53
Boyton End. *Suff* 1H 53
Bozeat. *Nptn* 5G 63
Braaid. *IOM* 4C 108
Braal Castle. *High* 3D 168
Brabling Green. *Suff* 4E 67
Brabourne. *Kent* 1F 29
Brabourne Lees. *Kent* 1E 29
Brabster. *High* 2F 169
Bracadale. *High* 5C 154
Bracara. *High* 4F 147
Braceborough. *Linc* 4H 75
Bracebridge. *Linc* 4G 87
Bracebridge Heath. *Linc* 4G 87
Braceby. *Linc* 2H 75
Bracewell. *Lanc* 5A 98
Brackenber. *Cumb* 3A 104
Brackenfield. *Derbs* 5A 86
Brackenlands. *Cumb* 5D 112
Brackenthwaite. *Cumb* 5D 112
Brackenthwaite. *N Yor* 4E 99
Brackla. *B'end* 4C 32
Brackla. *High* 3C 158
Bracklesham. *W Sus* 3G 17
Brackletter. *High* 5D 148
Brackley. *Nptn* 2D 50
Brackley Hatch. *Nptn* 1E 51
Brackloch. *High* 1F 163
Bracknell. *Brac* 5G 37
Braco. *Per* 3H 135
Bracobrae. *Mor* 3C 160
Bracon. *N Lin* 4A 94
Bracon Ash. *Norf* 1D 66
Bradbourne. *Derbs* 5G 85
Bradbury. *Dur* 2A 106
Bradda. *IOM* 4A 108
Bradden. *Nptn* 1E 51
Bradenham. *Buck* 2G 37
Bradenham. *Norf* 5B 78
Bradenstoke. *Wilts* 4F 35
Bradfield. *Essx* 2E 55
Bradfield. *Norf* 2E 79
Bradfield. *W Ber* 4E 36
Bradfield Combust. *Suff* 5A 66
Bradfield Green. *Ches E* 5A 84
Bradfield Heath. *Essx* 3E 55
Bradfield St Clare. *Suff* 5B 66
Bradfield St George. *Suff* 4B 66
Bradford. *Derbs* 4G 85
Bradford. *Devn* 2E 11
Bradford. *Nmbd* 1F 121
Bradford. *W Yor* 1B 92
Bradford Abbas. *Dors* 1A 14
Bradford Barton. *Devn* 1B 12
Bradford Leigh. *Wilts* 5D 34
Bradford-on-Avon. *Wilts* 5D 34
Bradford-on-Tone. *Som* 4E 21
Bradford Peverell. *Dors* 3B 14
Bradiford. *Devn* 3F 19
Brading. *IOW* 4E 16
Bradley. *Ches W* 3H 83
Bradley. *Derbs* 1G 73
Bradley. *Glos* 2C 34
Bradley. *Hants* 2E 25
Bradley. *NE Lin* 4F 95
Bradley. *N Yor* 1C 98
Bradley. *Staf* 4C 72
Bradley. *W Mid* 1D 60
Bradley. *W Yor* 2B 92
Bradley. *Wrex* 5F 83
Bradley Cross. *Som* 1H 21
Bradley Green. *Ches W* 1H 71
Bradley Green. *Som* 3F 21
Bradley Green. *Warw* 5G 73
Bradley Green. *Worc* 4D 61
Bradley in the Moors. *Staf* 1E 73
Bradley Mount. *Ches E* 3D 84
Bradley Stoke. *S Glo* 3B 34
Bradlow. *Here* 2C 48
Bradmore. *Notts* 2C 74
Bradmore. *W Mid* 1C 60
Bradninch. *Devn* 2D 12
Bradnop. *Staf* 5E 85
Bradpole. *Dors* 3H 13
Bradshaw. *G Man* 3F 91
Bradstone. *Devn* 4D 11
Bradwall Green. *Ches E* 4B 84
Bradway. *S Yor* 2H 85
Bradwell. *Derbs* 2F 85
Bradwell. *Essx* 3B 54
Bradwell. *Mil* 2G 51
Bradwell. *Norf* 5H 79
Bradwell-on-Sea. *Essx* 5D 54
Bradwell Waterside. *Essx* 5C 54
Bradworthy. *Devn* 1D 10
Brae. *High* 5C 162
Brae. *Shet* 5E 173
Braeantra. *High* 1H 157
Braefield. *High* 5G 157
Braefindon. *High* 3A 158
Braegrum. *Per* 1C 136
Braehead. *Ang* 3F 145
Braehead. *Dum* 4B 110
Braehead. *Mor* 4G 159
Braehead. *Orkn* 3D 172
Braehead. *S Lan* 1H 117 (nr. Coalburn)
Braehead. *S Lan* 4C 128 (nr. Forth)
Braehoulland. *Shet* 4D 173
Braemar. *Abers* 4F 151
Braemore. *High* 5C 168 (nr. Dunbeath)
Braemore. *High* 1D 156 (nr. Ullapool)
Brae of Achnahaird. *High* 2E 163
Brae Roy Lodge. *High* 4F 149
Braeside. *Abers* 5G 161
Braeside. *Inv* 2D 126
Braes of Coul. *Ang* 3B 144
Braeswick. *Orkn* 4F 172
Braetongue. *High* 3F 167
Braeval. *Stir* 3E 135
Braevallich. *Arg* 3G 133
Braewick. *Shet* 6E 173
Brafferton. *Darl* 2F 105
Brafferton. *N Yor* 2G 99

Brafield-on-the-Green—Broadholme

Brafield-on-the-Green. *Nptn* 5F **63**
Bragar. *W Isl* 3E **171**
Bragbury End. *Herts* 3C **52**
Bragleenbeg. *Arg* 1G **133**
Braichmelyn. *Gwyn* 4F **81**
Braides. *Lanc* 4D **96**
Braidwood. *S Lan* 5B **128**
Braigo. *Arg* 3A **124**
Brailsford. *Derbs* 1G **73**
Braintree. *Essx* 3A **54**
Braiseworth. *Suff* 3D **66**
Braishfield. *Hants* 4B **24**
Braithwaite. *Cumb* 2D **102**
Braithwaite. *S Yor* 3G **93**
Braithwaite. *W Yor* 5C **98**
Braithwell. *S Yor* 1C **86**
Brakefield Green. *Norf* 5C **78**
Bramber. *W Sus* 4C **26**
Brambledown. *Kent* 3D **40**
Brambridge. *Hants* 4C **24**
Bramcote. *Notts* 2C **74**
Bramcote. *Warw* 2B **62**
Bramdean. *Hants* 4E **24**
Bramerton. *Norf* 5E **79**
Bramfield. *Herts* 4C **52**
Bramfield. *Suff* 3F **67**
Bramford. *Suff* 1E **54**
Bramhall. *G Man* 2C **84**
Bramham. *W Yor* 5G **99**
Bramhope. *W Yor* 5E **99**
Bramley. *Hants* 1E **25**
Bramley. *S Yor* 1B **86**
Bramley. *Surr* 1B **26**
Bramley. *W Yor* 1C **92**
Bramley Green. *Hants* 1E **25**
Bramley Head. *N Yor* 4D **98**
Bramley Vale. *Derbs* 4B **86**
Bramling. *Kent* 5G **41**
Brampford Speke. *Devn* 3C **12**
Brampton. *Cambs* 3B **64**
Brampton. *Cumb* 2H **103**
(nr. Appleby-in-Westmorland)
Brampton. *Cumb* 3G **113**
(nr. Carlisle)
Brampton. *Linc* 3F **87**
Brampton. *Norf* 3E **78**
Brampton. *S Yor* 4E **93**
Brampton. *Suff* 2G **67**
Brampton Abbotts. *Here* 3B **48**
Brampton Ash. *Nptn* 2E **63**
Brampton Bryan. *Here* 3F **59**
Brampton en le Morthen. *S Yor* 2B **86**
Bramshall. *Staf* 2E **73**
Bramshaw. *Hants* 1A **16**
Bramshill. *Hants* 5F **37**
Bramshott. *Hants* 3G **25**
Branault. *High* 2G **139**
Brancaster. *Norf* 1G **77**
Brancaster Staithe. *Norf* 1G **77**
Brancepeth. *Dur* 1F **105**
Branch End. *Nmbd* 3D **114**
Branchill. *Mor* 3E **159**
Brand End. *Linc* 1C **76**
Branderburgh. *Mor* 1G **159**
Brandesburton. *E Yor* 5F **101**
Brandeston. *Suff* 4E **67**
Brand Green. *Glos* 3C **48**
Brandhill. *Shrp* 3G **59**
Brandis Corner. *Devn* 2E **11**
Brandish Street. *Som* 2C **20**
Brandiston. *Norf* 3D **78**
Brandon. *Dur* 1F **105**
Brandon. *Linc* 1G **75**
Brandon. *Nmbd* 3E **121**
Brandon. *Suff* 2G **65**
Brandon. *Warw* 3B **62**
Brandon Bank. *Cambs* 2F **65**
Brandon Creek. *Norf* 1F **65**
Brandon Parva. *Norf* 5C **78**
Brandsby. *N Yor* 2H **99**
Brandy Wharf. *Linc* 1H **87**
Brane. *Corn* 4B **4**
Bran End. *Essx* 3G **53**
Branksome. *Pool* 3F **15**
Bransbury. *Hants* 2C **24**
Bransby. *Linc* 3F **87**
Branscombe. *Devn* 4E **13**
Bransford. *Worc* 5B **60**
Bransgore. *Hants* 3G **15**
Bransholme. *Hull* 1E **94**
Bransley. *Shrp* 3A **60**
Branston. *Leics* 3F **75**
Branston. *Linc* 4H **87**
Branston. *Staf* 3G **73**
Branston Booths. *Linc* 4H **87**
Branstone. *IOW* 4D **16**
Bransty. *Cumb* 3A **102**
Brant Broughton. *Linc* 5G **87**
Brantham. *Suff* 2E **54**
Branthwaite. *Cumb* 1D **102**
(nr. Caldbeck)
Branthwaite. *Cumb* 2B **102**
(nr. Workington)
Brantingham. *E Yor* 2C **94**
Branton. *Nmbd* 3E **121**
Branton. *S Yor* 4G **93**
Branton Green. *N Yor* 3G **99**
Branxholme. *Bord* 3G **119**
Branxton. *Nmbd* 1C **120**
Brassington. *Derbs* 5G **85**
Brasted. *Kent* 5F **39**
Brasted Chart. *Kent* 5F **39**
Bratch, The. *Staf* 1C **60**
Brathens. *Abers* 4D **152**
Bratoft. *Linc* 4D **88**
Brattleby. *Linc* 2G **87**
Bratton. *Som* 2C **20**
Bratton. *Telf* 4A **72**
Bratton. *Wilts* 1E **23**
Bratton Clovelly. *Devn* 3E **11**
Bratton Fleming. *Devn* 3G **19**
Bratton Seymour. *Som* 4B **22**
Braughing. *Herts* 3D **53**
Braulen Lodge. *High* 5E **157**
Braunston. *Nptn* 4C **62**
Braunstone Town. *Leics* 5C **74**
Braunston-in-Rutland. *Rut* 5F **75**
Braunton. *Devn* 3E **19**
Brawby. *N Yor* 2B **100**
Brawl. *High* 2A **168**
Brawlbin. *High* 3C **168**
Bray. *Wind* 3A **38**
Braybrooke. *Nptn* 2E **63**
Brayford. *Devn* 3G **19**
Bray Shop. *Corn* 5D **10**
Braystones. *Cumb* 4B **102**
Brayton. *N Yor* 1G **93**
Bray Wick. *Wind* 4G **37**
Brazacott. *Corn* 3C **10**
Brea. *Corn* 4A **6**
Breach. *W Sus* 2F **17**
Breachwood Green. *Herts* 3B **52**
Breacleit. *W Isl* 4D **171**
Breaden Heath. *Shrp* 2G **71**
Breadsall. *Derbs* 1A **74**
Breadstone. *Glos* 5C **48**
Breage. *Corn* 4D **4**
Breakachy. *High* 4G **157**
Breakish. *High* 1E **147**
Bream. *Glos* 5B **48**
Breamore. *Hants* 1G **15**
Bream's Meend. *Glos* 5B **48**
Brean. *Som* 1F **21**
Breanais. *W Isl* 5B **171**
Brearton. *N Yor* 3F **99**
Breascleit. *W Isl* 4E **171**
Breaston. *Derbs* 2B **74**
Brecais Àrd. *High* 1E **147**
Brecais Iosal. *High* 1E **147**
Brechfa. *Carm* 2F **45**
Brechin. *Ang* 3F **145**
Breckles. *Norf* 1B **66**
Brecon. *Powy* 3D **46**
Brecon Beacons. *Powy* 3C **46**
Bredbury. *G Man* 1D **84**
Brede. *E Sus* 4C **28**
Bredenbury. *Here* 5A **60**
Bredfield. *Suff* 5E **67**
Bredgar. *Kent* 4C **40**
Bredhurst. *Kent* 4B **40**
Bredicot. *Worc* 5D **60**
Bredon. *Worc* 2E **49**
Bredon's Norton. *Worc* 2E **49**
Bredwardine. *Here* 1G **47**
Breedon on the Hill. *Leics* 3B **74**
Breibhig. *W Isl* 9B **170**
(on Barra)
Breibhig. *W Isl* 4G **171**
(on Isle of Lewis)
Breich. *W Lot* 3C **128**
Breightmet. *G Man* 4F **91**
Breighton. *E Yor* 1H **93**
Breinton. *Here* 2H **47**
Breinton Common. *Here* 2H **47**
Breiwick. *Shet* 7F **173**
Brelston Green. *Here* 3A **48**
Bremhill. *Wilts* 4E **35**
Brenachie. *High* 1B **158**
Brenchley. *Kent* 1A **28**
Brendon. *Devn* 2A **20**
Brent Cross. *G Lon* 2D **38**
Brent Eleigh. *Suff* 1C **54**
Brentford. *G Lon* 3C **38**
Brentingby. *Leics* 4E **75**
Brent Knoll. *Som* 1G **21**
Brent Pelham. *Herts* 2E **53**
Brentwood. *Essx* 1G **39**
Brenzett. *Kent* 3E **28**
Brereton. *Staf* 4E **73**
Brereton Cross. *Staf* 4E **73**
Brereton Green. *Ches E* 4B **84**
Brereton Heath. *Ches E* 4C **84**
Bressingham. *Norf* 2C **66**
Bretby. *Derbs* 3G **73**
Bretford. *Warw* 3B **62**
Bretforton. *Worc* 1F **49**
Bretherdale Head. *Cumb* 4G **103**
Bretherton. *Lanc* 2C **90**
Brettabister. *Shet* 6F **173**
Brettenham. *Norf* 2B **66**
Brettenham. *Suff* 5B **66**
Bretton. *Flin* 4F **83**
Bretton. *Pet* 5A **76**
Brewlands Bridge. *Ang* 2A **144**
Brewood. *Staf* 5C **72**
Briantspuddle. *Dors* 3D **14**
Bricket Wood. *Herts* 5B **52**
Bricklehampton. *Worc* 1E **49**
Bride. *IOM* 1D **108**
Bridekirk. *Cumb* 1C **102**
Bridell. *Pemb* 1B **44**
Bridestowe. *Devn* 4F **11**
Brideswell. *Abers* 5C **160**
Bridford. *Devn* 4B **12**
Bridge. *Corn* 4A **6**
Bridge. *Kent* 5F **41**
Bridge. *Som* 2G **13**
Bridge End. *Bed* 5H **63**
Bridge End. *Cumb* 5D **102**
(nr. Broughton in Furness)
Bridge End. *Cumb* 5E **113**
(nr. Dalston)
Bridge End. *Linc* 2A **76**
Bridge End. *Shet* 8E **173**
Bridgefoot. *Ang* 5C **144**
Bridgefoot. *Cumb* 2B **102**
Bridge Green. *Essx* 2E **53**
Bridgehampton. *Som* 4A **22**
Bridge Hewick. *N Yor* 2F **99**
Bridgehill. *Dur* 4D **115**
Bridgemary. *Hants* 2D **16**
Bridgemere. *Ches E* 1B **72**
Bridgemont. *Derbs* 2E **85**
Bridgend. *Abers* 5C **160**
(nr. Huntly)
Bridgend. *Abers* 5H **161**
(nr. Peterhead)
Bridgend. *Ang* 2E **145**
(nr. Brechin)
Bridgend. *Ang* 4C **144**
(nr. Kirriemuir)
Bridgend. *Arg* 4F **133**
(nr. Lochgilphead)
Bridgend. *Arg* 3B **124**
(on Islay)
Bridgend. *B'end* 3C **32**
Bridgend. *Cumb* 3E **103**
Bridgend. *Devn* 4B **8**
Bridgend. *Fife* 2F **137**
Bridgend. *High* 3F **157**
Bridgend. *Mor* 5A **160**
Bridgend. *Per* 1D **136**
Bridgend. *W Lot* 2D **128**
Bridgend of Lintrathen. *Ang* 3B **144**
Bridgeness. *Falk* 1D **128**
Bridge of Alford. *Abers* 2C **152**
Bridge of Allan. *Stir* 4G **135**
Bridge of Avon. *Mor* 5F **159**
Bridge of Awe. *Arg* 1H **133**
Bridge of Balgie. *Per* 4C **142**
Bridge of Brown. *High* 1F **151**
Bridge of Cally. *Per* 3A **144**
Bridge of Canny. *Abers* 4D **152**
Bridge of Dee. *Dum* 3E **111**
Bridge of Don. *Aber* 2G **153**
Bridge of Dun. *Ang* 3F **145**
Bridge of Dye. *Abers* 5D **152**
Bridge of Earn. *Per* 2D **136**
Bridge of Ericht. *Per* 3C **142**
Bridge of Feugh. *Abers* 4E **152**
Bridge of Gairn. *Abers* 4A **152**
Bridge of Gaur. *Per* 3C **142**
Bridge of Muchalls. *Abers* 4F **153**
Bridge of Oich. *High* 3F **149**
Bridge of Orchy. *Arg* 5H **141**
Bridge of Walls. *Shet* 6D **173**
Bridge of Weir. *Ren* 3E **127**
Bridge Reeve. *Devn* 1G **11**
Bridgerule. *Devn* 2C **10**
Bridge Sollers. *Here* 1H **47**
Bridge Street. *Suff* 1B **54**
Bridgetown. *Devn* 2E **9**
Bridgetown. *Som* 3C **20**
Bridge Town. *Warw* 5G **61**
Bridge Trafford. *Ches W* 3G **83**
Bridgeyate. *S Glo* 4B **34**
Bridgham. *Norf* 2B **66**
Bridgnorth. *Shrp* 1B **60**
Bridgtown. *Staf* 5D **73**
Bridgwater. *Som* 3G **21**
Bridlington. *E Yor* 3F **101**
Bridport. *Dors* 3H **13**
Bridstow. *Here* 3A **48**
Brierfield. *Lanc* 1G **91**
Brierley. *Glos* 4B **48**
Brierley. *Here* 5G **59**
Brierley. *S Yor* 3E **93**
Brierley Hill. *W Mid* 2D **60**
Brierton. *Hart* 1B **106**
Briestfield. *W Yor* 3C **92**
Brigg. *N Lin* 4D **94**
Briggate. *Norf* 3F **79**
Briggswath. *N Yor* 4F **107**
Brigham. *Cumb* 1B **102**
Brigham. *E Yor* 4E **101**
Brighouse. *W Yor* 2B **92**
Brighstone. *IOW* 4C **16**
Brightgate. *Derbs* 5G **85**
Brighthampton. *Oxon* 5B **50**
Brightholmlee. *S Yor* 1G **85**
Brightley. *Devn* 3G **11**
Brightling. *E Sus* 3A **28**
Brightlingsea. *Essx* 4D **54**
Brighton. *Brig* 5E **27**
Brighton. *Corn* 3D **6**
Brighton Hill. *Hants* 2E **24**
Brightons. *Falk* 2C **128**
Brightwalton. *W Ber* 4C **36**
Brightwalton Green. *W Ber* 4C **36**
Brightwell. *Suff* 1F **55**
Brightwell Baldwin. *Oxon* 2E **37**
Brightwell-cum-Sotwell. *Oxon* 2D **36**
Brigmerston. *Wilts* 2G **23**
Brignall. *Dur* 3D **104**
Brig o' Turk. *Stir* 3E **135**
Brigsley. *NE Lin* 4F **95**
Brigsteer. *Cumb* 1D **97**
Brigstock. *Nptn* 2G **63**
Brill. *Buck* 4E **51**
Brill. *Corn* 4E **5**
Brilley. *Here* 1F **47**
Brimaston. *Pemb* 2D **42**
Brimfield. *Here* 4H **59**
Brimington. *Derbs* 3B **86**
Brimley. *Devn* 5B **12**
Brimpsfield. *Glos* 4E **49**
Brimpton. *W Ber* 5D **36**
Brims. *Orkn* 9B **172**
Brimscombe. *Glos* 5D **48**
Brimstage. *Mers* 2F **83**
Brincliffe. *S Yor* 2H **85**
Brind. *E Yor* 1H **93**
Brindister. *Shet* 6D **173**
(nr. West Burrafirth)
Brindister. *Shet* 8F **173**
(nr. West Lerwick)
Brindle. *Lanc* 2D **90**
Brindley. *Ches E* 5H **83**
Brindley Ford. *Stoke* 5C **84**
Brineton. *Staf* 4C **72**
Bringhurst. *Leics* 1F **63**
Bringsty Common. *Here* 5A **60**
Brington. *Cambs* 3H **63**
Brinian. *Orkn* 5D **172**
Briningham. *Norf* 2C **78**
Brinkhill. *Linc* 3C **88**
Brinkley. *Cambs* 5F **65**
Brinklow. *Warw* 3B **62**
Brinkworth. *Wilts* 3F **35**
Brinscall. *Lanc* 2E **91**
Brinscombe. *Som* 1H **21**
Brinsley. *Notts* 1B **74**
Brinsworth. *S Yor* 2B **86**
Brinton. *Norf* 2C **78**
Brisco. *Cumb* 4F **113**
Brisley. *Norf* 3B **78**
Brislington. *Bris* 4B **34**
Brissenden Green. *Kent* 2D **28**
Bristol. *Bris* 4A **34**
Bristol Airport. *N Som* 5A **34**
Briston. *Norf* 2C **78**
Britannia. *Lanc* 2G **91**
Britford. *Wilts* 4G **23**
Brithdir. *Cphy* 5E **47**
Brithdir. *Cdgn* 1D **44**
Brithdir. *Gwyn* 4G **69**
Briton Ferry. *Neat* 3G **31**
Britwell Salome. *Oxon* 2E **37**
Brixham. *Torb* 3F **9**
Brixton. *Devn* 3B **8**
Brixton. *G Lon* 3E **39**
Brixton Deverill. *Wilts* 3D **22**
Brixworth. *Nptn* 3E **63**
Brize Norton. *Oxon* 5B **50**
Broad Alley. *Worc* 4C **60**
Broad Blunsdon. *Swin* 2G **35**
Broadbottom. *G Man* 1D **85**
Broadbridge. *W Sus* 2G **17**
Broadbridge Heath. *W Sus* 2C **26**
Broad Campden. *Glos* 2G **49**
Broad Chalke. *Wilts* 4F **23**
Broadclyst. *Devn* 3C **12**
Broadfield. *Inv* 2E **127**
Broadfield. *Pemb* 4F **43**
Broadfield. *W Sus* 2D **26**
Broadford. *High* 1E **147**
Broadford Bridge. *W Sus* 3B **26**
Broadgate. *Cumb* 1A **96**
Broad Green. *Cambs* 5F **65**
Broad Green. *C Beds* 1H **51**
Broad Green. *Worc* 3D **61**
(nr. Bromsgrove)
Broad Green. *Worc* 5B **60**
(nr. Worcester)
Broadhaven. *High* 3F **169**
Broad Haven. *Pemb* 3C **42**
Broadheath. *G Man* 2B **84**
Broad Heath. *Staf* 3C **72**
Broadheath. *Worc* 4A **60**
Broadhembury. *Devn* 2E **12**
Broadhempston. *Devn* 2E **9**
Broad Hill. *Cambs* 3E **65**
Broad Hinton. *Wilts* 4G **35**
Broadholm. *Derbs* 1A **74**
Broadholme. *Linc* 3F **87**

Buckland Dinham. Som 1C 22
Buckland Filleigh. Devn ...2E 11
Buckland in the Moor. Devn ...5H 11
Buckland Monachorum. Devn ...2A 8
Buckland Newton. Dors ...2B 14
Buckland Ripers. Dors ...4B 14
Buckland St Mary. Som ...1F 13
Buckland-tout-Saints. Devn ...4D 8
Bucklebury. W Ber ...4D 36
Bucklegate. Linc ...2C 76
Buckleigh. Devn ...4E 19
Buckler's Hard. Hants ...3C 16
Bucklesham. Suff ...1F 55
Buckley. Flin ...4E 83
Buckley Green. Warw ...4F 61
Buckley Hill. Mers ...1F 83
Bucklow Hill. Ches E ...2B 84
Buckminster. Leics ...3F 75
Bucknall. Linc ...4A 88
Bucknall. Stoke ...1D 72
Bucknell. Oxon ...3D 50
Bucknell. Shrp ...3F 59
Buckpool. Mor ...2B 160
Bucksburn. Aber ...3F 153
Buck's Cross. Devn ...4D 18
Bucks Green. W Sus ...2B 26
Buckshaw Village. Lanc ...2D 90
Bucks Hill. Herts ...5A 52
Bucks Horn Oak. Hants ...2G 25
Buck's Mills. Devn ...4D 18
Buckton. E Yor ...2F 101
Buckton. Here ...3F 59
Buckton. Nmbd ...1E 121
Buckton Vale. G Man ...4H 91
Buckworth. Cambs ...3A 64
Budby. Notts ...4D 86
Bude. Corn ...2C 10
Budge's Shop. Corn ...3H 7
Budlake. Devn ...2C 12
Budle. Nmbd ...1F 121
Budleigh Salterton. Devn ...4D 12
Budock Water. Corn ...5B 6
Buerton. Ches E ...1A 72
Buffler's Holt. Buck ...2E 51
Bugbrooke. Nptn ...5D 62
Buglawton. Ches E ...4C 84
Bugle. Corn ...3E 6
Bugthorpe. E Yor ...4B 100
Buildwas. Shrp ...5A 72
Builth Road. Powy ...5C 58
Builth Wells. Powy ...5C 58
Bulbourne. Buck ...4H 51
Bulby. Linc ...3H 75
Bulcote. Notts ...1D 74
Buldoo. High ...2B 168
Bulford. Wilts ...2G 23
Bulford Camp. Wilts ...2G 23
Bulkeley. Ches E ...5H 83
Bulkington. Warw ...2A 62
Bulkington. Wilts ...1E 23
Bulkworthy. Devn ...1D 11
Bullamoor. N Yor ...5A 106
Bull Bay. IOA ...1D 80
Bullbridge. Derbs ...5A 86
Bullgill. Cumb ...1B 102
Bull Hill. Hants ...3B 16
Bullinghope. Here ...2A 48
Bull's Green. Herts ...4C 52
Bullwood. Arg ...2C 126
Bulmer. Essx ...1B 54
Bulmer. N Yor ...3A 100
Bulmer Tye. Essx ...2B 54
Bulphan. Thur ...2H 39
Bulverhythe. E Sus ...5B 28
Bulwark. Abers ...4G 161
Bulwell. Nott ...1C 74
Bulwick. Nptn ...1G 63
Bumble's Green. Essx ...5E 53
Bun Abhainn Eadarra. W Isl ...7D 171
Bunacaimb. High ...5E 147
Bun a' Mhuilinn. W Isl ...7C 170
Bunarkaig. High ...5D 148
Bunbury. Ches E ...5H 83
Bunchrew. High ...4A 158
Bundalloch. High ...1A 148

Buness. Shet ...1H 173
Bunessan. Arg ...1A 132
Bungay. Suff ...2F 67
Bunkegivie. High ...2H 149
Bunker's Hill. Cambs ...5D 76
Bunkers Hill. Linc ...5B 88
Bunkers Hill. Suff ...5H 79
Bunloit. High ...1H 149
Bunnahabhain. Arg ...2C 124
Bunny. Notts ...3C 74
Buntait. High ...5G 157
Buntingford. Herts ...3D 52
Buntings Green. Essx ...2B 54
Bunwell. Norf ...1D 66
Burbage. Derbs ...3E 85
Burbage. Leics ...1B 62
Burbage. Wilts ...5H 35
Burcher. Here ...4F 59
Burcombe. Wilts ...3F 23
Burcot. Oxon ...2D 36
Burcot. Worc ...3D 61
Burcote. Shrp ...1B 60
Burcott. Buck ...3G 51
Burcott. Som ...2A 22
Burdale. N Yor ...3C 100
Burdrop. Oxon ...2B 50
Bures. Suff ...2C 54
Burford. Oxon ...4A 50
Burford. Shrp ...4H 59
Burg. Arg ...4E 139
Burgate Great Green. Suff ...3C 66
Burgate Little Green. Suff ...3C 66
Burgess Hill. W Sus ...4E 27
Burgh. Suff ...5E 67
Burgh by Sands. Cumb ...4E 113
Burgh Castle. Norf ...5G 79
Burghclere. Hants ...5C 36
Burghead. Mor ...2F 159
Burghfield. W Ber ...5E 37
Burghfield Common. W Ber ...5E 37
Burghfield Hill. W Ber ...5E 37
Burgh Heath. Surr ...5D 38
Burghill. Here ...1H 47
Burgh le Marsh. Linc ...4E 89
Burgh Muir. Abers ...2E 153
Burgh next Aylsham. Norf ...3E 78
Burgh on Bain. Linc ...2B 88
Burgh St Margaret. Norf ...4G 79
Burgh St Peter. Norf ...1G 67
Burghwallis. S Yor ...3F 93
Burham. Kent ...4B 40
Buriton. Hants ...4F 25
Burland. Ches E ...5A 84
Burland. Shet ...8E 173
Burlawn. Corn ...2D 6
Burleigh. Brac ...4G 37
Burleigh. Glos ...5D 48
Burlescombe. Devn ...1D 12
Burleston. Dors ...3C 14
Burlestone. Devn ...4E 9
Burley. Hants ...2H 15
Burley. Rut ...4F 75
Burley. W Yor ...1C 92
Burleydam. Ches E ...1A 72
Burley Gate. Here ...1A 48
Burley in Wharfedale. W Yor ...5D 98
Burley Street. Hants ...2H 15
Burley Woodhead. W Yor ...5D 98
Burlingjobb. Powy ...5E 59
Burlington. Shrp ...4B 72
Burlton. Shrp ...3G 71
Burmantofts. W Yor ...1D 92
Burmarsh. Kent ...2F 29
Burmington. Warw ...2A 50
Burn. N Yor ...2F 93
Burnage. G Man ...1C 84
Burnaston. Derbs ...2G 73
Burnbanks. Cumb ...3G 103
Burnby. E Yor ...5C 100
Burncross. S Yor ...1H 85

Burneside. Cumb ...5G 103
Burness. Orkn ...3F 172
Burneston. N Yor ...1F 99
Burnett. Bath ...5B 34
Burnfoot. E Ayr ...4D 116
Burnfoot. Per ...3B 136
Burnfoot. Bord ...3H 119
(nr. Hawick)
Burnfoot. Bord ...3G 119
(nr. Roberton)
Burngreave. S Yor ...2A 86
Burnham. Buck ...2A 38
Burnham. Linc ...3D 94
Burnham Deepdale. Norf ...1H 77
Burnham Green. Herts ...4C 52
Burnham Market. Norf ...1H 77
Burnham Norton. Norf ...1H 77
Burnham-on-Crouch. Essx ...1D 40
Burnham-on-Sea. Som ...2G 21
Burnham Overy Staithe. Norf ...1H 77
Burnham Overy Town. Norf ...1H 77
Burnham Thorpe. Norf ...1A 78
Burnhaven. Abers ...4H 161
Burnhead. Dum ...5A 118
Burnhervie. Abers ...2E 153
Burnhill Green. Staf ...5B 72
Burnhope. Dur ...5E 115
Burnhouse. N Ayr ...4E 127
Burniston. N Yor ...5H 107
Burnlee. W Yor ...4B 92
Burnley. Lanc ...1G 91
Burnmouth. Bord ...3F 131
Burn Naze. Lanc ...5C 96
Burn of Cambus. Stir ...3G 135
Burnopfield. Dur ...4E 115
Burnsall. N Yor ...3C 98
Burnside. Ang ...3E 145
Burnside. Ant ...3G 175
Burnside. E Ayr ...3E 117
Burnside. Per ...3D 136
Burnside. Shet ...4D 173
Burnside. S Lan ...4H 127
Burnside. W Lot ...2D 129
(nr. Broxburn)
Burnside. W Lot ...2D 128
(nr. Winchburgh)
Burntcommon. Surr ...5B 38
Burnthouse. Derbs ...2G 73
Burnt Heath. Essx ...3D 54
Burnt Hill. W Ber ...4D 36
Burnt Houses. Dur ...2E 105
Burntisland. Fife ...1F 129
Burnt Oak. G Lon ...1D 38
Burntstalk. Norf ...2G 77
Burntwood. Staf ...5E 73
Burntwood Green. Staf ...5E 73
Burnt Yates. N Yor ...3E 99
Burnwynd. Edin ...3E 129
Burpham. Surr ...5B 38
Burpham. W Sus ...5B 26
Burradon. Nmbd ...4D 121
Burradon. Tyne ...2F 115
Burrafirth. Shet ...1H 173
Burraigarth. Shet ...1G 173
Burras. Corn ...5A 6
Burraton. Corn ...3A 8
Burravoe. Shet ...3E 173
(nr. North Roe)
Burravoe. Shet ...5E 173
(on Mainland)
Burravoe. Shet ...4G 173
(on Yell)
Burray Village. Orkn ...8D 172
Burrells. Cumb ...3H 103
Burrelton. Per ...5A 144
Burridge. Devn ...3F 19
Burridge. Hants ...1D 16
Burrill. N Yor ...1E 99
Burringham. N Lin ...4B 94
Burrington. Devn ...1G 11
Burrington. Here ...3G 59
Burrington. N Som ...1H 21
Burrough End. Cambs ...5F 65

Burrough Green. Cambs ...5F 65
Burrough on the Hill. Leics ...4E 75
Burroughston. Orkn ...5E 172
Burrow. Devn ...4D 12
Burrow. Som ...2C 20
Burrowbridge. Som ...4G 21
Burrowhill. Surr ...4A 38
Burry. Swan ...3D 30
Burry Green. Swan ...3D 30
Burry Port. Carm ...5E 45
Burscough. Lanc ...3C 90
Burscough Bridge. Lanc ...3C 90
Bursea. E Yor ...1B 94
Burshill. E Yor ...5E 101
Bursledon. Hants ...2C 16
Burslem. Stoke ...1C 72
Burstall. Suff ...1D 54
Burstock. Dors ...2H 13
Burston. Devn ...2H 11
Burston. Norf ...2D 66
Burston. Staf ...2D 72
Burstow. Surr ...1E 27
Burstwick. E Yor ...2F 95
Burtersett. N Yor ...1A 98
Burtholme. Cumb ...3G 113
Burthorpe. Suff ...4G 65
Burthwaite. Cumb ...5F 113
Burtle. Som ...2H 21
Burtoft. Linc ...2B 76
Burton. Ches W ...4H 83
(nr. Kelsall)
Burton. Ches W ...3F 83
(nr. Neston)
Burton. Dors ...3G 15
(nr. Christchurch)
Burton. Dors ...3B 14
(nr. Dorchester)
Burton. Nmbd ...1F 121
Burton. Pemb ...4D 43
Burton. Som ...2E 21
Burton. Wilts ...4D 34
(nr. Chippenham)
Burton. Wilts ...3D 22
(nr. Warminster)
Burton. Wrex ...5F 83
Burton Agnes. E Yor ...3F 101
Burton Bradstock. Dors ...4H 13
Burton-by-Lincoln. Linc ...3G 87
Burton Coggles. Linc ...3G 75
Burton Constable. E Yor ...1E 95
Burton Corner. Linc ...1C 76
Burton End. Cambs ...1G 53
Burton End. Essx ...3F 53
Burton Fleming. E Yor ...2E 101
Burton Green. W Mid ...3G 61
Burton Green. Wrex ...5F 83
Burton Hastings. Warw ...2B 62
Burton-in-Kendal. Cumb ...2E 97
Burton in Lonsdale. N Yor ...2F 97
Burton Joyce. Notts ...1D 74
Burton Latimer. Nptn ...3G 63
Burton Lazars. Leics ...4E 75
Burton Leonard. N Yor ...3F 99
Burton on the Wolds. Leics ...3C 74
Burton Overy. Leics ...1D 62
Burton Pedwardine. Linc ...1A 76
Burton Pidsea. E Yor ...1F 95
Burton Salmon. N Yor ...2E 93
Burton's Green. Essx ...3B 54
Burton Stather. N Lin ...3B 94
Burton upon Stather. N Lin ...3B 94
Burton upon Trent. Staf ...3G 73
Burton Wolds. Leics ...3D 74
Burtonwood. Warr ...1H 83
Burwardsley. Ches W ...5H 83
Burwarton. Shrp ...2A 60
Burwash. E Sus ...3A 28
Burwash Common. E Sus ...3H 27
Burwash Weald. E Sus ...3A 28
Burwell. Cambs ...4E 65
Burwell. Linc ...3C 88
Burwen. IOA ...1D 80
Burwick. Orkn ...9D 172
Bury. Cambs ...2B 64
Bury. G Man ...3G 91

Bury. Som ...4C 20
Bury. W Sus ...4B 26
Burybank. Staf ...2C 72
Bury End. Worc ...2F 49
Bury Green. Herts ...3E 53
Bury St Edmunds. Suff ...4H 65
Burythorpe. N Yor ...3B 100
Busbridge. Surr ...1A 26
Busby. Per ...1C 136
Busby. S Lan ...4G 127
Buscot. Oxon ...2H 35
Bush. Corn ...2C 10
Bush Bank. Here ...5G 59
Bushbury. W Mid ...5D 72
Bushby. Leics ...5D 74
Bushey. Dors ...4E 15
Bushey. Herts ...1C 38
Bushey Heath. Herts ...1C 38
Bush Green. Norf ...1C 66
(nr. Attleborough)
Bush Green. Norf ...2E 66
(nr. Harleston)
Bush Green. Suff ...5B 66
Bushley. Worc ...2D 48
Bushley Green. Worc ...2D 48
Bushmead. Bed ...4A 64
Bushmills. Caus ...1F 175
Bushmoor. Shrp ...2G 59
Bushton. Wilts ...4F 35
Bushy Common. Norf ...4B 78
Busk. Cumb ...5H 113
Buslingthorpe. Linc ...2H 87
Bussage. Glos ...5D 49
Bussex. Som ...3G 21
Busta. Shet ...5E 173
Butcher's Cross. E Sus ...3G 27
Butcombe. Som ...5A 34
Bute Town. Cphy ...5E 46
Butleigh. Som ...3A 22
Butleigh Wootton. Som ...3A 22
Butlers Marston. Warw ...1B 50
Butley. Suff ...5F 67
Butley High Corner. Suff ...1G 55
Bullocks Heath. Hants ...2C 16
Butterburn. Cumb ...2H 113
Buttercrambe. N Yor ...4B 100
Butterknowle. Dur ...2E 105
Butterleigh. Devn ...2C 12
Buttermere. Cumb ...3C 102
Buttermere. Wilts ...5B 36
Buttershaw. W Yor ...2B 92
Butterstone. Per ...4H 143
Butterton. Staf ...5E 85
(nr. Leek)
Butterton. Staf ...1C 72
(nr. Stoke-on-Trent)
Butterwick. Dur ...2A 106
Butterwick. Linc ...1C 76
Butterwick. N Yor ...2B 100
(nr. Malton)
Butterwick. N Yor ...2D 101
(nr. Weaverthorpe)
Butteryhaugh. Nmbd ...5A 120
Butt Green. Ches E ...5A 84
Buttington. Powy ...5E 71
Buttonbridge. Shrp ...3B 60
Buttonoak. Shrp ...3B 60
Buttsash. Hants ...2C 16
Butt's Green. Essx ...5A 54
Butt Yeats. Lanc ...3E 97
Buxhall. Suff ...5C 66
Buxted. E Sus ...3F 27
Buxton. Derbs ...3E 85
Buxton. Norf ...3E 78
Buxworth. Derbs ...2E 85
Bwcle. Flin ...4E 83
Bwlch. Powy ...3E 47
Bwlchderwin. Gwyn ...1D 68
Bwlchgwyn. Wrex ...5E 83
Bwlch-Llan. Cdgn ...5E 57
Bwlchnewydd. Carm ...3D 44
Bwlchtocyn. Gwyn ...3C 68
Bwlch-y-cibau. Powy ...4D 70
Bwlchyddar. Powy ...3D 70
Bwlch-y-fadfa. Cdgn ...1E 45

Bwlch-y-ffridd. Powy ...1C 58
Bwlch y Garreg. Powy ...1C 58
Bwlch-y-groes. Pemb ...1G 43
Bwlch-y-sarnau. Powy ...3C 58
Bybrook. Kent ...1E 28
Byermoor. Tyne ...4E 115
Byers Garth. Dur ...5G 115
Byers Green. Dur ...1F 105
Byfield. Nptn ...5C 62
Byfleet. Surr ...4B 38
Byford. Here ...1G 47
Bygrave. Herts ...2C 52
Byker. Tyne ...3F 115
Byland Abbey. N Yor ...2H 99
Bylchau. Cnwy ...4B 82
Byley. Ches W ...4B 84
Bynea. Carm ...3E 31
Byram. N Yor ...2E 93
Byrness. Nmbd ...4B 120
Bystock. Devn ...4D 12
Bythorn. Cambs ...3H 63
Byton. Here ...4F 59
Bywell. Nmbd ...3D 114
Byworth. W Sus ...3A 26

C

Cabharstadh. W Isl ...6F 171
Cabourne. Linc ...4E 95
Cabrach. Arg ...3C 124
Cabrach. Mor ...1A 152
Cabus. Lanc ...5D 97
Cadbury. Devn ...2C 12
Cadder. E Dun ...2H 127
Caddington. C Beds ...4A 52
Caddonfoot. Bord ...1G 119
Cadeby. Leics ...5B 74
Cadeby. S Yor ...4F 93
Cadeleigh. Devn ...2C 12
Cade Street. E Sus ...3H 27
Cadgwith. Corn ...5E 5
Cadham. Fife ...3E 137
Cadishead. G Man ...1B 84
Cadle. Swan ...3F 31
Cadley. Lanc ...1D 90
Cadley. Wilts ...1H 23
(nr. Ludgershall)
Cadley. Wilts ...5H 35
(nr. Marlborough)
Cadmore End. Buck ...2F 37
Cadnam. Hants ...1A 16
Cadney. N Lin ...4D 94
Cadole. Flin ...4E 82
Cadoxton-Juxta-Neath. Neat ...2A 32
Cadwell. Herts ...2B 52
Cadwst. Den ...2C 70
Caeathro. Gwyn ...4E 81
Caehopkin. Powy ...4B 46
Caenby. Linc ...2H 87
Caerau. B'end ...2C 32
Caerau. Card ...4E 33
Cae'r-bont. Powy ...4B 46
Cae'r-bryn. Carm ...4F 45
Caerdeon. Gwyn ...4F 69
Caerdydd. Card ...4E 33
Caerfarchell. Pemb ...2B 42
Caerffili. Cphy ...3E 33
Caerfyrddin. Carm ...4E 45
Caergeiliog. IOA ...3C 80
Caergwrle. Flin ...5F 83
Caergybi. IOA ...2B 80
Caerlaverock. Per ...2A 136
Caerleon. Newp ...2G 33
Caerllion. Carm ...2G 33
Caerllion. Newp ...2G 33
Caernarfon. Gwyn ...4D 81
Caerphilly. Cphy ...3E 33
Caersws. Powy ...1C 58
Caerwedros. Cdgn ...5C 56
Caerwent. Mon ...2H 33
Caerwys. Flin ...3D 82
Caim. IOA ...2F 81
Caio. Carm ...2G 45
Cairinis. W Isl ...2D 170

Cairisiadar. W Isl ...4C 171
Cairminis. W Isl ...9C 171
Cairnbaan. Arg ...4F 133
Cairnbulg. Abers ...2H 161
Cairncross. Ang ...1D 145
Cairndow. Arg ...2A 134
Cairness. Abers ...2H 161
Cairneyhill. Fife ...1D 128
Cairngarroch. Dum ...5F 109
Cairngorms. High ...3D 151
Cairnhill. Abers ...5D 160
Cairnie. Abers ...4B 160
Cairnorrie. Abers ...4F 161
Cairnryan. Dum ...3F 109
Caister-on-Sea. Norf ...4H 79
Caistor. Linc ...4E 94
Caistor St Edmund. Norf ...5E 79
Caistron. Nmbd ...4D 121
Cakebole. Worc ...3C 60
Calais Street. Suff ...1C 54
Calanais. W Isl ...4E 171
Calbost. W Isl ...6G 171
Calbourne. IOW ...4C 16
Calceby. Linc ...3C 88
Calcot Row. W Ber ...4E 37
Calcott. Kent ...4F 41
Calcott. Shrp ...4G 71
Caldback. Shet ...1H 173
Caldbeck. Cumb ...1E 102
Caldbergh. N Yor ...1C 98
Caldcote. Cambs ...5C 64
(nr. Cambridge)
Caldecote. Cambs ...2A 64
(nr. Peterborough)
Caldecote. Herts ...2C 52
Caldecote. Nptn ...5D 62
Caldecote. Warw ...1A 62
Caldecott. Nptn ...4G 63
Caldecott. Oxon ...2C 36
Caldecott. Rut ...1F 63
Calderbank. N Lan ...3A 128
Calder Bridge. Cumb ...4B 102
Caldercruix. N Lan ...3B 128
Calder Grove. W Yor ...3D 92
Calder Mains. High ...3D 168
Caldermill. S Lan ...5H 127
Calder Vale. Lanc ...5E 97
Calderwood. S Lan ...4H 127
Caldicot. Mon ...3H 33
Caldwell. Derbs ...4G 73
Caldwell. N Yor ...3E 105
Caldy. Mers ...2E 83
Calebrack. Cumb ...1E 103
Calford Green. Suff ...1G 53
Calfsound. Orkn ...4E 172
Calgary. Arg ...3E 139
Califer. Mor ...3E 159
California. Cambs ...2E 65
California. Falk ...2C 128
California. Norf ...4H 79
California. Suff ...1E 55
Calke. Derbs ...3A 74
Callakille. High ...3F 155
Callaly. Nmbd ...4E 121
Callander. Stir ...3F 135
Callaughton. Shrp ...1A 60
Callendoun. Arg ...1E 127
Callestick. Corn ...3B 6
Callington. Corn ...2H 7
Callingwood. Staf ...3F 73
Callow. Here ...2H 47
Callow. Herts ...5D 48
Callow End. Worc ...1D 48
Callow Hill. Wilts ...3F 35
Callow Hill. Worc ...3B 60
(nr. Bewdley)
Callow Hill. Worc ...4E 61
(nr. Redditch)
Calmore. Hants ...1B 16
Calmsden. Glos ...5F 49

Calne. Wilts ...4E 35
Calow. Derbs ...3B 86
Calshot. Hants ...2C 16
Calstock. Corn ...2A 8
Calstone Wellington. Wilts ...5F 35
Calthorpe. Norf ...2D 78
Calthorpe Street. Norf ...3G 79
Calthwaite. Cumb ...5F 113
Calton. Staf ...5F 85
Calveley. Ches E ...5H 83
Calver. Derbs ...3G 85
Calverhall. Shrp ...2A 72
Calverleigh. Devn ...1C 12
Calverley. W Yor ...1C 92
Calvert. Buck ...3E 51
Calverton. Mil ...2F 51
Calverton. Notts ...1D 74
Calvine. Per ...2F 143
Calvo. Cumb ...4C 112
Cam. Glos ...2C 34
Camaghael. High ...1F 141
Camas-luinie. High ...1B 148
Camasnacroise. High ...3C 140
Camastianavaig. High ...5E 155
Camasunary. High ...2D 146
Camault Muir. High ...4H 157
Camb. Shet ...2G 173
Camber. E Sus ...4D 28
Camberley. Surr ...5G 37
Camberwell. G Lon ...3E 39
Camblesforth. N Yor ...2G 93
Cambo. Nmbd ...1D 114
Cambois. Nmbd ...1G 115
Camborne. Corn ...5A 6
Cambourne. Cambs ...5C 64
Cambridge. Cambs ...5D 64
Cambridge. Glos ...5C 48
Cambrose. Corn ...4A 6
Cambus. Clac ...4A 136
Cambusbarron. Stir ...4G 135
Cambuskenneth. Stir ...4H 135
Cambuslang. S Lan ...3H 127
Cambusnethan. N Lan ...4B 128
Cambus o' May. Abers ...4B 152
Camden Town. G Lon ...2D 39
Cameley. Bath ...1B 22
Camelford. Corn ...4B 10
Camelon. Falk ...1B 128
Camelsdale. Surr ...3G 25
Camer's Green. Worc ...2C 48
Camerton. Bath ...1B 22
Camerton. Cumb ...1B 102
Camerton. E Yor ...2F 95
Camghouran. Per ...3C 142
Camlough. New M ...6F 175
Cammachmore. Abers ...4G 153
Cammeringham. Linc ...2G 87
Camore. High ...4E 165
Campbelton. N Ayr ...4C 126
Campbeltown. Arg ...3B 122
Campbeltown Airport. Arg ...3A 122
Cample. Dum ...5A 118
Campmuir. Per ...5B 144
Campsall. S Yor ...3F 93
Campsea Ashe. Suff ...5F 67
Camps End. Cambs ...1G 53
Camp, The. Glos ...5E 49
Campton. C Beds ...2B 52
Camptoun. E Lot ...2B 130
Camptown. Bord ...3A 120
Camrose. Pemb ...2D 42
Camserney. Per ...4F 143
Camster. High ...4E 169
Camus Croise. High ...2E 147
Camuscross. High ...2E 147
Camusdarach. High ...4E 147
Camusnagaul. High ...1E 141
(nr. Fort William)
Camusnagaul. High ...5E 163
(nr. Little Loch Broom)
Camusteel. High ...4G 155
Camusterrach. High ...4G 155
Camusvrachan. Per ...4D 142
Canada. Hants ...1A 16

Canadia. E Sus ...4B 28
Canaston Bridge. Pemb ...3E 43
Candlesby. Linc ...4D 88
Candle Street. Suff ...3C 66
Candy Mill. S Lan ...5D 128
Cane End. Oxon ...4E 37
Canewdon. Essx ...1D 40
Canford Cliffs. Pool ...4F 15
Canford Heath. Pool ...3F 15
Canford Magna. Pool ...3F 15
Cangate. Norf ...4F 79
Canham's Green. Suff ...4C 66
Canholes. Derbs ...3E 85
Canisbay. High ...1F 169
Canley. W Mid ...3H 61
Cann. Dors ...4D 22
Cann Common. Dors ...4D 22
Cannich. High ...5F 157
Cannington. Som ...3F 21
Cannock. Staf ...4D 73
Cannock Wood. Staf ...4E 73
Canonbie. Dum ...2E 113
Canon Bridge. Here ...1H 47
Canon Frome. Here ...1B 48
Canon Pyon. Here ...1H 47
Canons Ashby. Nptn ...5C 62
Canonstown. Corn ...3C 4
Canterbury. Kent ...5F 41
Cantley. Norf ...5F 79
Cantley. S Yor ...4G 93
Cantlop. Shrp ...5H 71
Canton. Card ...4E 33
Cantray. High ...4B 158
Cantraybruich. High ...4B 158
Cantraywood. High ...4B 158
Cantsdam. Fife ...4D 136
Cantsfield. Lanc ...2F 97
Canvey Island. Essx ...2B 40
Canwick. Linc ...4G 87
Canworthy Water. Corn ...3C 10
Caol. High ...1F 141
Caolas. Arg ...4A 138
Caolas. W Isl ...9B 170
Caolas Liubharsaigh. W Isl ...4D 170
Caolas Scalpaigh. W Isl ...8E 171
Caolas Stocinis. W Isl ...8D 171
Caol Ila. Arg ...2C 124
Caol Loch Ailse. High ...1F 147
Caol Reatha. High ...1F 147
Capel. Kent ...1H 27
Capel. Surr ...1C 26
Capel Bangor. Cdgn ...2F 57
Capel Betws Lleucu. Cdgn ...5F 57
Capel Coch. IOA ...2D 80
Capel Curig. Cnwy ...5G 81
Capel Cynon. Cdgn ...1D 45
Capel Dewi. Carm ...3E 45
Capel Dewi. Cdgn ...2E 45
(nr. Aberystwyth)
Capel Dewi. Cdgn ...1E 45
(nr. Llandysul)
Capel Garmon. Cnwy ...5H 81
Capel Green. Suff ...1G 55
Capel Gwyn. IOA ...3C 80
Capel Gwynfe. Carm ...3H 45
Capel Hendre. Carm ...4F 45
Capel Isaac. Carm ...3F 45
Capel Iwan. Carm ...1G 43
Capel-le-Ferne. Kent ...2G 29
Capel Llanilterne. Card ...4D 32
Capel Mawr. IOA ...3D 80
Capel Newydd. Pemb ...1G 43
Capel St Andrew. Suff ...1G 55
Capel St Mary. Suff ...2D 54
Capel Seion. Carm ...4F 45
Capel Seion. Cdgn ...3F 57
Capel Uchaf. Gwyn ...1D 68
Capel-y-ffin. Powy ...2F 47
Capenhurst. Ches W ...3F 83
Capernwray. Lanc ...2E 97
Capheaton. Nmbd ...1D 114
Cappercleuch. Bord ...2E 119
Capplegill. Dum ...4D 118
Capton. Devn ...3E 9
Capton. Som ...3D 20

Caputh. Per ...5H 143
Caradon Town. Corn ...5C 10
Carbis Bay. Corn ...3C 4
Carbost. High ...5C 154
(nr. Loch Harport)
Carbost. High ...4D 154
(nr. Portree)
Carbrook. S Yor ...2A 86
Carbrooke. Norf ...5B 78
Carburton. Notts ...3D 86
Car Colston. Notts ...1E 74
Carcroft. S Yor ...4F 93
Cardenden. Fife ...4E 136
Cardeston. Shrp ...4F 71
Cardewlees. Cumb ...4E 113
Cardiff. Card ...4E 33
Cardiff Airport. V Glam ...5D 32
Cardigan. Cdgn ...1B 44
Cardinal's Green. Cambs ...1G 53
Cardington. Bed ...1A 52
Cardington. Shrp ...1H 59
Cardinham. Corn ...2F 7
Cardno. Abers ...2G 161
Cardow. Mor ...4F 159
Cardross. Arg ...2E 127
Cardurnock. Cumb ...4C 112
Careby. Linc ...4H 75
Careston. Arg ...2E 145
Carew. Pemb ...4E 43
Carew Cheriton. Pemb ...4E 43
Carew Newton. Pemb ...4E 43
Carey. Here ...2A 48
Carfin. N Lan ...4A 128
Carfrae. Bord ...4B 130
Cargate Green. Norf ...4F 79
Cargenbridge. Dum ...2G 111
Cargill. Per ...5A 144
Cargo. Cumb ...4E 113
Cargreen. Corn ...2A 8
Carham. Nmbd ...1C 120
Carhampton. Som ...2D 20
Carharrack. Corn ...4B 6
Carie. Per ...3D 142
(nr. Loch Rannah)
Carie. Per ...5D 142
(nr. Loch Tay)
Carisbrooke. IOW ...4C 16
Cark. Cumb ...2C 96
Carkeel. Corn ...2A 8
Carlabhagh. W Isl ...3E 171
Carland Cross. Corn ...3C 6
Carlbury. Darl ...3F 105
Carlby. Linc ...4H 75
Carlecotes. S Yor ...4B 92
Carleen. Corn ...4D 4
Carlesmoor. N Yor ...2D 98
Carleton. Cumb ...4F 113
(nr. Carlisle)
Carleton. Cumb ...4B 102
(nr. Egremont)
Carleton. Cumb ...2G 103
(nr. Penrith)
Carleton. Lanc ...5C 96
Carleton. N Yor ...5B 98
Carleton. W Yor ...2E 93
Carleton Forehoe. Norf ...5C 78
Carleton Rode. Norf ...1D 66
Carleton St Peter. Norf ...5F 79
Carlidnack. Corn ...4E 5
Carlingcott. Bath ...1B 22
Carlin How. Red C ...3E 107
Carlisle. Cumb ...4F 113
Carloonan. Arg ...2H 133
Carlops. Bord ...4E 129
Carlton. Bed ...5G 63
Carlton. Cambs ...5F 65
Carlton. Leics ...5A 74
Carlton. N Yor ...1A 100
(nr. Helmsley)
Carlton. N Yor ...1C 98
(nr. Middleham)
Carlton. N Yor ...2G 93
(nr. Selby)
Carlton. Notts ...1D 74

Carlton—Chapel Green

Carlton. *S Yor* 3D **92**
Carlton. *Stoc T* 2A **106**
Carlton. *Suff* 4F **67**
Carlton. *W Yor* 2D **92**
Carlton Colville. *Suff* 1H **67**
Carlton Curlieu. *Leics* 1D **62**
Carlton Husthwaite. *N Yor* 2G **99**
Carlton in Cleveland. *N Yor* 4C **106**
Carlton in Lindrick. *Notts* 2C **86**
Carlton-le-Moorland. *Linc* 5G **87**
Carlton Miniott. *N Yor* 1F **99**
Carlton-on-Trent. *Notts* 4F **87**
Carlton Scroop. *Linc* 1G **75**
Carluke. *S Lan* 4B **128**
Carlyon Bay. *Corn* 3E **7**
Carmarthen. *Carm* 4E **45**
Carmel. *Carm* 4F **45**
Carmel. *Flin* 3D **82**
Carmel. *Gwyn* 5D **81**
Carmel. *IOA* 2C **80**
Carmichael. *S Lan* 1B **118**
Carmunnock. *Glas* 4H **127**
Carmyle. *Glas* 3H **127**
Carmyllie. *Ang* 4E **145**
Carnaby. *E Yor* 3F **101**
Carnach. *High* 1C **148**
(nr. Lochcarron)
Carnach. *High* 4E **163**
(nr. Ullapool)
Carnach. *Mor* 4E **159**
Carnach. *W Isl* 8E **171**
Carnachy. *High* 3H **167**
Carnain. *Arg* 3B **124**
Carnais. *W Isl* 4C **171**
Carnan. *Arg* 4B **138**
Carnan. *W Isl* 4C **170**
Carnbee. *Fife* 3H **137**
Carnbo. *Per* 3C **136**
Carn Brea Village. *Corn* 4A **6**
Carndu. *High* 1A **148**
Carne. *Corn* 5D **6**
Carnell. *S Ayr* 1D **116**
Carnforth. *Lanc* 2E **97**
Carn-gorm. *High* 1B **148**
Carnhedryn. *Pemb* 2C **42**
Carnhell Green. *Corn* 3D **4**
Carnie. *Abers* 3F **153**
Carnkie. *Corn* 5B **6**
(nr. Falmouth)
Carnkie. *Corn* 5A **6**
(nr. Redruth)
Carnkief. *Corn* 3B **6**
Carno. *Powy* 1B **58**
Carnock. *Fife* 1D **128**
Carnon Downs. *Corn* 4B **6**
Carnoustie. *Ang* 5E **145**
Carntyne. *Glas* 3H **127**
Carnwath. *S Lan* 5C **128**
Carnyorth. *Corn* 3A **4**
Carol Green. *W Mid* 3G **61**
Carpalla. *Corn* 3D **6**
Carperby. *N Yor* 1C **98**
Carradale. *Arg* 2C **122**
Carragraich. *W Isl* 8D **171**
Carrbridge. *High* 1D **150**
Carr Cross. *Lanc* 3B **90**
Carreglefn. *IOA* 2C **80**
Carrhouse. *N Lin* 4A **94**
Carrick Castle. *Arg* 4A **134**
Carrickfergus. *ME Ant* 3H **175**
Carrick Ho. *Orkn* 4E **172**
Carriden. *Falk* 1D **128**
Carrington. *G Man* 1B **84**
Carrington. *Linc* 5C **88**
Carrington. *Midl* 3G **129**
Carrog. *Cnwy* 1G **69**
Carrog. *Den* 1D **70**
Carron. *Falk* 1B **128**
Carron. *Mor* 4G **159**
Carronbridge. *Dum* 5A **118**
Carronshore. *Falk* 1B **128**
Carrow Hill. *Mon* 2H **33**
Carr Shield. *Nmbd* 5B **114**
Carrutherstown. *Dum* 2C **112**
Carr Vale. *Derbs* 4B **86**
Carrville. *Dur* 5G **115**
Carryduff. *Lis* 4H **175**
Carsaig. *Arg* 1C **132**
Carscreugh. *Dum* 3H **109**
Carsegowan. *Dum* 4B **110**
Carse House. *Arg* 3F **125**
Carseriggan. *Dum* 3A **110**
Carsethorn. *Dum* 4A **112**
Carshalton. *G Lon* 4D **39**
Carsington. *Derbs* 5G **85**
Carskiey. *Arg* 5A **122**
Carsluith. *Dum* 4B **110**
Carsphairn. *Dum* 5E **117**
Carstairs. *S Lan* 5C **128**
Carstairs Junction. *S Lan* 5C **128**
Cartbridge. *Surr* 5B **38**
Carterhaugh. *Ang* 4D **144**
Carter's Clay. *Hants* 4B **24**
Carterton. *Oxon* 5A **50**
Carterway Heads. *Nmbd* 4D **114**
Carthew. *Corn* 3E **6**
Carthorpe. *N Yor* 1F **99**
Cartington. *Nmbd* 4E **121**
Cartland. *S Lan* 5B **128**
Cartmel. *Cumb* 2C **96**
Cartmel Fell. *Cumb* 1D **96**
Cartworth. *W Yor* 4B **92**
Carwath. *Cumb* 5E **112**
Carway. *Carm* 5E **45**
Carwinley. *Cumb* 2F **113**
Cascob. *Powy* 4E **59**
Cas-gwent. *Mon* 2A **34**
Cash Feus. *Fife* 3E **136**
Cashlie. *Per* 4B **142**
Cashmoor. *Dors* 1E **15**
Cas-Mael. *Pemb* 2E **43**
Casnewydd. *Newp* 3G **33**
Cassington. *Oxon* 4C **50**
Cassop. *Dur* 1A **106**
Castell. *Cnwy* 4G **81**
Castell. *Den* 4D **82**
Castell Hendre. *Pemb* 2E **43**
Castell-nedd. *Neat* 2A **32**
Castell Newydd Emlyn. *Carm* 1D **44**
Castell-y-bwch. *Torf* 2F **33**
Casterton. *Cumb* 2F **97**
Castle. *Som* 2A **22**
Castle Acre. *Norf* 4H **77**
Castle Ashby. *Nptn* 5F **63**
Castlebay. *W Isl* 9B **170**
Castle Bolton. *N Yor* 5D **104**
Castle Bromwich. *W Mid* 2F **61**
Castle Bytham. *Linc* 4G **75**
Castlebythe. *Pemb* 2E **43**
Castle Caereinion. *Powy* 5D **70**
Castle Camps. *Cambs* 1G **53**
Castle Carrock. *Cumb* 4G **113**
Castlecary. *N Lan* 2A **128**
Castle Cary. *Som* 3B **22**
Castle Combe. *Wilts* 4D **34**
Castlecraig. *High* 2C **158**
Castledawson. *M Ulst* 3F **175**
Castlederg. *Derr* 3B **174**
Castle Donington. *Leics* 3B **74**
Castle Douglas. *Dum* 3E **111**
Castle Eaton. *Swin* 2G **35**
Castle Eden. *Dur* 1B **106**
Castleford. *W Yor* 2E **93**
Castle Frome. *Here* 1B **48**
Castle Green. *Surr* 4A **38**
Castle Green. *Warw* 3G **61**
Castle Gresley. *Derbs* 4G **73**
Castle Heaton. *Nmbd* 5F **131**
Castle Hedingham. *Essx* 2A **54**
Castle Hill. *Kent* 1A **28**
Castlehill. *Per* 5B **144**
Castlehill. *S Lan* 4B **128**
Castle Hill. *Suff* 1E **55**
Castlehill. *W Dun* 2E **127**
Castle Kennedy. *Dum* 4G **109**
Castle Lachlan. *Arg* 4H **133**
Castlemartin. *Pemb* 5D **42**
Castlemilk. *Glas* 4H **127**
Castlemorris. *Pemb* 1D **42**
Castlemorton. *Worc* 2C **48**
Castle O'er. *Dum* 5E **119**
Castle Park. *N Yor* 3F **107**
Castlerigg. *Cumb* 2D **102**
Castle Rising. *Norf* 3F **77**
Castlerock. *Caus* 1E **174**
Castleside. *Dur* 5D **115**
Castlethorpe. *Mil* 1F **51**
Castleton. *Abers* 4F **151**
Castleton. *Arg* 1G **125**
Castleton. *Derbs* 2F **85**
Castleton. *G Man* 3G **91**
Castleton. *Mor* 1F **151**
Castleton. *Newp* 3F **33**
Castleton. *N Yor* 4D **107**
Castleton. *Per* 2B **136**
Castletown. *Cumb* 1G **103**
Castletown. *Dors* 5B **14**
Castletown. *High* 2D **169**
Castletown. *IOM* 5B **108**
Castletown. *Tyne* 4G **115**
Castlewellan. *New M* 6H **175**
Castley. *N Yor* 5E **99**
Caston. *Norf* 1B **66**
Castor. *Pet* 1A **64**
Caswell. *Swan* 4E **31**
Catacol. *N Ayr* 5H **125**
Catbrook. *Mon* 5A **48**
Catchems End. *Worc* 3B **60**
Catchgate. *Dur* 4E **115**
Catcleugh. *Nmbd* 4B **120**
Catcliffe. *S Yor* 2B **86**
Catcott. *Som* 3G **21**
Caterham. *Surr* 5E **39**
Catfield. *Norf* 3F **79**
Catfield Common. *Norf* 3F **79**
Catfirth. *Shet* 6F **173**
Catford. *G Lon* 3E **39**
Catforth. *Lanc* 1C **90**
Cathcart. *Glas* 3G **127**
Cathedine. *Powy* 3E **47**
Catherine-de-Barnes. *W Mid* 2F **61**
Catherington. *Hants* 1E **17**
Catherston Leweston. *Dors* 3G **13**
Catherton. *Shrp* 3A **60**
Catisfield. *Hants* 2D **16**
Catlodge. *High* 4A **150**
Catlowdy. *Cumb* 2F **113**
Catmore. *W Ber* 3C **36**
Caton. *Devn* 5A **12**
Caton. *Lanc* 3E **97**
Catrine. *E Ayr* 2E **117**
Cat's Ash. *Newp* 2G **33**
Catsfield. *E Sus* 4B **28**
Catsgore. *Som* 4A **22**
Catshill. *Worc* 3D **60**
Cattal. *N Yor* 4G **99**
Cattawade. *Suff* 2E **54**
Catterall. *Lanc* 5E **97**
Catterick. *N Yor* 5F **105**
Catterick Bridge. *N Yor* 5F **105**
Catterick Garrison. *N Yor* 5E **105**
Catterlen. *Cumb* 1F **103**
Catterline. *Abers* 1H **145**
Catterton. *N Yor* 5H **99**
Catteshall. *Surr* 1A **26**
Catthorpe. *Leics* 3C **62**
Cattistock. *Dors* 3A **14**
Catton. *Nmbd* 4B **114**
Catton. *N Yor* 2F **99**
Catwick. *E Yor* 5F **101**
Catworth. *Cambs* 3H **63**
Caudle Green. *Glos* 4E **49**
Caulcott. *Oxon* 3D **50**
Cauldhame. *Stir* 4F **135**
Cauldmill. *Bord* 3H **119**
Cauldon. *Staf* 1E **73**
Cauldon Lowe. *Staf* 1E **73**
Cauldwells. *Abers* 3E **161**
Caulkerbush. *Dum* 4G **111**
Caulside. *Dum* 1F **113**
Caunsall. *Worc* 2C **60**
Caunton. *Notts* 4E **87**
Causewayend. *S Lan* 1C **118**
Causewayhead. *Stir* 4H **135**
Causey Park. *Nmbd* 5F **121**
Caute. *Devn* 1E **11**
Cautley. *Cumb* 5H **103**
Cavendish. *Suff* 1B **54**
Cavendish Bridge. *Leic* 3B **74**
Cavenham. *Suff* 3G **65**
Caversfield. *Oxon* 3D **50**
Caversham. *Read* 4F **37**
Caversham Heights. *Read* 4F **37**
Caverswall. *Staf* 1D **72**
Cawdor. *High* 4C **158**
Cawkwell. *Linc* 2B **88**
Cawood. *N Yor* 1F **93**
Cawsand. *Corn* 3A **8**
Cawston. *Norf* 3D **78**
Cawston. *Warw* 3B **62**
Cawthorne. *N Yor* 1B **100**
Cawthorne. *S Yor* 4C **92**
Cawthorpe. *Linc* 3H **75**
Cawton. *N Yor* 2A **100**
Caxton. *Cambs* 5C **64**
Caynham. *Shrp* 3H **59**
Caythorpe. *Linc* 1G **75**
Caythorpe. *Notts* 1D **74**
Cayton. *N Yor* 1E **101**
Ceallan. *W Isl* 3D **170**
Ceann a Bhàigh. *W Isl* 9C **171**
(on Harris)
Ceann a Bhaigh. *W Isl* 2C **170**
(on North Uist)
Ceann a Bhaigh. *W Isl* 8E **171**
(on Scalpay)
Ceann a Bhaigh. *W Isl* 8D **171**
(on South Harris)
Ceannacroc Lodge. *High* 2E **149**
Ceann a Deas Loch Baghasdail. *W Isl* 7C **170**
Ceann an Leothaid. *High* 5E **147**
Ceann a Tuath Loch Baghasdail. *W Isl* 6C **170**
Ceann Loch Ailleart. *High* 5F **147**
Ceann Loch Muideirt. *High* 1B **140**
Ceann-na-Cleithe. *W Isl* 8D **171**
Ceann Shìphoirt. *W Isl* 6E **171**
Ceann Tarabhaigh. *W Isl* 6E **171**
Cearsiadar. *W Isl* 5F **171**
Ceathramh Meadhanach. *W Isl* 1D **170**
Cefn Berain. *Cnwy* 4B **82**
Cefn-brith. *Cnwy* 5B **82**
Cefn-bryn-brain. *Carm* 4H **45**
Cefn Bychan. *Cphy* 2F **33**
Cefn-bychan. *Flin* 4D **82**
Cefncaeau. *Carm* 3E **31**
Cefn Canol. *Powy* 2E **71**
Cefn Coch. *Powy* 5C **70**
(nr. Llanfair Caereinion)
Cefn-coch. *Powy* 3D **70**
(nr. Llanrhaeadr-ym-Mochnant)
Cefn-coed-y-cymmer. *Mer T* 5D **46**
Cefn Cribwr. *B'end* 3B **32**
Cefn-ddwysarn. *Gwyn* 2B **70**
Cefn Einion. *Shrp* 2E **59**
Cefneithin. *Carm* 4F **45**
Cefn Glas. *B'end* 3B **32**
Cefngorwydd. *Powy* 1C **46**
Cefn Llwyd. *Cdgn* 2F **57**
Cefn-mawr. *Wrex* 1E **71**
Cefn-y-bedd. *Flin* 5F **83**
Cefn-y-coed. *Powy* 1D **58**
Cefn-y-pant. *Carm* 2F **43**
Cegidfa. *Powy* 4E **70**
Ceinewydd. *Cdgn* 5C **56**
Cellan. *Cdgn* 1G **45**
Cellardyke. *Fife* 3H **137**
Cellarhead. *Staf* 1D **72**
Cemaes. *IOA* 1C **80**
Cemmaes. *Powy* 5H **69**
Cemmaes Road. *Powy* 5H **69**
Cenarth. *Cdgn* 1C **44**
Cenin. *Gwyn* 1D **68**
Ceos. *W Isl* 5F **171**
Ceres. *Fife* 2G **137**
Ceri. *Powy* 2D **58**
Cerist. *Powy* 2B **58**
Cerne Abbas. *Dors* 2B **14**
Cerney Wick. *Glos* 2F **35**
Cerrigceinwen. *IOA* 3D **80**
Cerrigydrudion. *Cnwy* 1B **70**
Cess. *Norf* 4G **79**
Cessford. *Bord* 2B **120**
Ceunant. *Gwyn* 4E **81**
Chaceley. *Glos* 2D **48**
Chacewater. *Corn* 4B **6**
Chackmore. *Buck* 2E **51**
Chacombe. *Nptn* 1C **50**
Chadderton. *G Man* 4H **91**
Chaddesden. *Derb* 2A **74**
Chaddesden Common. *Derb* 2A **74**
Chaddesley Corbett. *Worc* 3C **60**
Chaddlehanger. *Devn* 5E **11**
Chaddleworth. *W Ber* 4C **36**
Chadlington. *Oxon* 3B **50**
Chadshunt. *Warw* 5H **61**
Chadstone. *Nptn* 5F **63**
Chad Valley. *W Mid* 2E **61**
Chadwell. *Leics* 3E **75**
Chadwell. *Shrp* 4B **72**
Chadwell Heath. *G Lon* 2F **39**
Chadwell St Mary. *Thur* 3H **39**
Chadwick End. *W Mid* 3G **61**
Chadwick Green. *Mers* 1H **83**
Chaffcombe. *Som* 1G **13**
Chafford Hundred. *Thur* 3H **39**
Chagford. *Devn* 4H **11**
Chailey. *E Sus* 4E **27**
Chainbridge. *Cambs* 5D **76**
Chain Bridge. *Linc* 1C **76**
Chainhurst. *Kent* 1B **28**
Chalbury. *Dors* 2F **15**
Chalbury Common. *Dors* 2F **15**
Chaldon. *Surr* 5E **39**
Chaldon Herring. *Dors* 4C **14**
Chale. *IOW* 5C **16**
Chale Green. *IOW* 5C **16**
Chalfont Common. *Buck* 1B **38**
Chalfont St Giles. *Buck* 1A **38**
Chalfont St Peter. *Buck* 2B **38**
Chalford. *Glos* 5D **49**
Chalgrove. *Oxon* 2E **37**
Chalk. *Kent* 3A **40**
Chalk End. *Essx* 4G **53**
Chalk Hill. *Glos* 3G **49**
Challaborough. *Devn* 4C **8**
Challacombe. *Devn* 2G **19**
Challister. *Shet* 5G **173**
Challoch. *Dum* 3A **110**
Challock. *Kent* 5E **40**
Chalton. *C Beds* 5A **64**
(nr. Bedford)
Chalton. *C Beds* 3A **52**
(nr. Luton)
Chalton. *Hants* 1F **17**
Chalvington. *E Sus* 5G **27**
Champany. *Falk* 2D **128**
Chance Inn. *Fife* 2F **137**
Chancery. *Cdgn* 3E **57**
Chandler's Cross. *Herts* 1B **38**
Chandler's Cross. *Worc* 2C **48**
Chandler's Ford. *Hants* 4C **24**
Chanlockfoot. *Dum* 4G **117**
Channel's End. *Bed* 5A **64**
Channel Tunnel. *Kent* 2F **29**
Channerwick. *Shet* 9F **173**
Chantry. *Som* 2C **22**
Chantry. *Suff* 1E **55**
Chapel. *Cumb* 1D **102**
Chapel. *Fife* 4E **137**
Chapel Allerton. *Som* 1H **21**
Chapel Allerton. *W Yor* 1C **92**
Chapel Amble. *Corn* 1D **6**
Chapel Brampton. *Nptn* 4E **63**
Chapelbridge. *Cambs* 1B **64**
Chapel Chorlton. *Staf* 2C **72**
Chapel Cleeve. *Som* 2D **20**
Chapel End. *C Beds* 1A **52**
Chapel-en-le-Frith. *Derbs* 2E **85**
Chapelfield. *Abers* 2G **145**
Chapelgate. *Linc* 3D **76**
Chapel Green. *Warw* 2G **61**
(nr. Coventry)

Chapel Green—Church Brough

Chapel Green. *Warw* 4B **62**
(nr. Southam)
Chapel Haddlesey. *N Yor* 2F **93**
Chapelhall. *N Lan* 3A **128**
Chapel Hill. *Abers* 5H **161**
Chapel Hill. *Linc* 5B **88**
Chapel Hill. *Mon* 5A **48**
Chapelhill. *Per* 1E **136**
(nr. Glencarse)
Chapelhill. *Per* 5H **143**
(nr. Harrietfield)
Chapelknowe. *Dum* 2E **112**
Chapel Lawn. *Shrp* 3F **59**
Chapel le Dale. *N Yor* 2G **97**
Chapel Milton. *Derbs* 2E **85**
Chapel of Garioch. *Abers* 1E **152**
Chapel Row. *W Ber* 5D **36**
Chapels. *Cumb* 1B **96**
Chapel St Leonards. *Linc* 3E **89**
Chapel Stile. *Cumb* 4E **102**
Chapelthorne. *W Yor* 3D **92**
Chapelton. *Ang* 4F **145**
Chapelton. *Devn* 4F **19**
Chapelton. *High* 2D **150**
(nr. Grantown-on-Spey)
Chapelton. *High* 3H **157**
(nr. Inverness)
Chapelton. *S Lan* 5H **127**
Chapeltown. *Bkbn* 3F **91**
Chapel Town. *Corn* 3C **6**
Chapeltown. *Mor* 1G **151**
Chapeltown. *S Yor* 1A **86**
Chapmanslade. *Wilts* 2D **22**
Chapmans Well. *Devn* 3D **10**
Chapmore End. *Herts* 4D **52**
Chappel. *Essx* 3B **54**
Chard. *Som* 2G **13**
Chard Junction. *Dors* 2G **13**
Chardstock. *Devn* 2G **13**
Charfield. *S Glo* 2C **34**
Charing. *Kent* 1D **28**
Charing Heath. *Kent* 1D **28**
Charing Hill. *Kent* 5D **40**
Charingworth. *Glos* 2H **49**
Charlbury. *Oxon* 4B **50**
Charlcombe. *Bath* 5C **34**
Charlcutt. *Wilts* 4E **35**
Charlecote. *Warw* 5G **61**
Charles. *Devn* 3G **19**
Charlesfield. *Dum* 3C **112**
Charleshill. *Surr* 2G **25**
Charleston. *Ang* 4C **144**
Charleston. *Ren* 3F **127**
Charlestown. *Aber* 3G **153**
Charlestown. *Abers* 2H **161**
Charlestown. *Corn* 3E **7**
Charlestown. *Dors* 5B **14**
Charlestown. *Fife* 1D **128**
Charlestown. *G Man* 4G **91**
Charlestown. *High* 1H **155**
(nr. Gairloch)
Charlestown. *High* 4A **158**
(nr. Inverness)
Charlestown. *W Yor* 2H **91**
Charlestown of Aberlour. *Mor* 4G **159**
Charles Tye. *Suff* 5C **66**
Charlesworth. *Derbs* 1E **85**
Charlton. *G Lon* 3F **39**
Charlton. *Hants* 2B **24**
Charlton. *Herts* 3B **52**
Charlton. *Nptn* 2D **50**
Charlton. *Nmbd* 1B **114**
Charlton. *Oxon* 3C **36**
Charlton. *Som* 1B **22**
(nr. Radstock)
Charlton. *Som* 2B **22**
(nr. Shepton Mallet)
Charlton. *Som* 4F **21**
(nr. Taunton)
Charlton. *Telf* 4H **71**
Charlton. *W Sus* 1G **17**
Charlton. *Wilts* 3E **35**
(nr. Malmesbury)
Charlton. *Wilts* 1G **23**
(nr. Pewsey)
Charlton. *Wilts* 4G **23**
(nr. Salisbury)
Charlton. *Wilts* 4E **23**
(nr. Shaftesbury)
Charlton. *Worc* 1F **49**
(nr. Evesham)
Charlton. *Worc* 3C **60**
(nr. Stourport-on-Severn)
Charlton Abbots. *Glos* 3F **49**
Charlton Adam. *Som* 4A **22**
Charlton Down. *Dors* 3B **14**
Charlton Horethorne. *Som* 4B **22**
Charlton Kings. *Glos* 3E **49**
Charlton Mackrell. *Som* 4A **22**
Charlton Marshall. *Dors* 2E **15**
Charlton Musgrove. *Som* 4C **22**
Charlton-on-Otmoor. *Oxon* 4D **50**
Charlton on the Hill. *Dors* 2D **15**
Charlwood. *Hants* 3E **25**
Charlwood. *Surr* 1D **26**
Charlynch. *Som* 3F **21**
Charminster. *Dors* 3B **14**
Charmouth. *Dors* 3G **13**
Charndon. *Buck* 3E **51**
Charney Bassett. *Oxon* 2B **36**
Charnock Green. *Lanc* 3D **90**
Charnock Richard. *Lanc* 3D **90**
Charsfield. *Suff* 5E **67**
Chart Corner. *Kent* 5B **40**
Charter Alley. *Hants* 1D **24**
Charterhouse. *Som* 1H **21**
Charterville Allotments. *Oxon* 4B **50**
Chartham. *Kent* 5F **41**
Chartham Hatch. *Kent* 5F **41**
Chartridge. *Buck* 5H **51**
Chart Sutton. *Kent* 5B **40**
Chart, The. *Kent* 5F **39**
Charvil. *Wok* 4F **37**
Charwelton. *Nptn* 5C **62**
Chase Terrace. *Staf* 5E **73**
Chasetown. *Staf* 5E **73**
Chastleton. *Oxon* 3H **49**
Chasty. *Devn* 2D **10**
Chatburn. *Lanc* 5G **97**
Chatcull. *Staf* 2B **72**
Chatham. *Medw* 4B **40**
Chatham Green. *Essx* 4H **53**
Chathill. *Nmbd* 2F **121**
Chatley. *Worc* 4C **60**
Chattenden. *Medw* 3B **40**
Chatteris. *Cambs* 2C **64**
Chattisham. *Suff* 1D **54**
Chatton. *Nmbd* 2E **121**
Chatwall. *Shrp* 1H **59**
Chaulden. *Herts* 5A **52**
Chaul End. *C Beds* 3A **52**
Chawleigh. *Devn* 1H **11**
Chawley. *Oxon* 5C **50**
Chawston. *Bed* 5A **64**
Chawton. *Hants* 3F **25**
Chaxhill. *Glos* 4C **48**
Cheadle. *G Man* 2C **84**
Cheadle. *Staf* 1E **73**
Cheadle Hulme. *G Man* 2C **84**
Cheam. *Surr* 4D **38**
Cheapside. *Wind* 4A **38**
Chearsley. *Buck* 4F **51**
Chebsey. *Staf* 3C **72**
Checkendon. *Oxon* 3E **37**
Checkley. *Ches E* 1B **72**
Checkley. *Here* 2A **48**
Checkley. *Staf* 2E **73**
Chedburgh. *Suff* 5G **65**
Cheddar. *Som* 1H **21**
Cheddington. *Buck* 4H **51**
Cheddleton. *Staf* 5D **84**
Cheddon Fitzpaine. *Som* 4F **21**
Chedglow. *Wilts* 2E **35**
Chedgrave. *Norf* 1F **67**
Chedington. *Dors* 2H **13**
Chediston. *Suff* 3F **67**
Chediston Green. *Suff* 3F **67**
Chedworth. *Glos* 4F **49**
Chedzoy. *Som* 3G **21**
Cheeseman's Green. *Kent* 2E **29**
Cheetham Hill. *G Man* 4G **91**
Cheglinch. *Devn* 2F **19**
Cheldon. *Devn* 1H **11**
Chelford. *Ches E* 3C **84**
Chellaston. *Derb* 2A **74**
Chellington. *Bed* 5G **63**
Chelmarsh. *Shrp* 2B **60**
Chelmick. *Shrp* 1G **59**
Chelmondiston. *Suff* 2F **55**
Chelmorton. *Derbs* 4F **85**
Chelmsford. *Essx* 5H **53**
Chelsea. *G Lon* 3D **38**
Chelsfield. *G Lon* 4F **39**
Chelsham. *Surr* 5E **39**
Chelston. *Som* 4E **21**
Chelsworth. *Suff* 1C **54**
Cheltenham. *Glos* 3E **49**
Chelveston. *Nptn* 4G **63**
Chelvey. *N Som* 5H **33**
Chelwood. *Bath* 5B **34**
Chelwood Common. *E Sus* 3F **27**
Chelwood Gate. *E Sus* 3F **27**
Chelworth. *Wilts* 2E **35**
Chelworth Lower Green. *Wilts* 2F **35**
Chelworth Upper Green. *Wilts* 2F **35**
Chelynch. *Som* 2B **22**
Cheney Longville. *Shrp* 2G **59**
Chenies. *Buck* 1B **38**
Chepstow. *Mon* 2A **34**
Chequerfield. *W Yor* 2E **93**
Chequers Corner. *Norf* 5D **77**
Cherhill. *Wilts* 4F **35**
Cherington. *Glos* 2E **35**
Cherington. *Warw* 2A **50**
Cheriton. *Devn* 2H **19**
Cheriton. *Hants* 4D **24**
Cheriton. *Kent* 2G **29**
Cheriton. *Pemb* 5D **43**
Cheriton. *Swan* 3D **30**
Cheriton Bishop. *Devn* 3A **12**
Cheriton Cross. *Devn* 3A **12**
Cheriton Fitzpaine. *Devn* 2B **12**
Cherrington. *Telf* 3A **72**
Cherrybank. *Per* 1D **136**
Cherry Burton. *E Yor* 5D **101**
Cherry Green. *Herts* 3D **52**
Cherry Hinton. *Cambs* 5D **65**
Cherry Willingham. *Linc* 3H **87**
Chertsey. *Surr* 4B **38**
Cheselbourne. *Dors* 3C **14**
Chesham. *Buck* 5H **51**
Chesham. *G Man* 3G **91**
Chesham Bois. *Buck* 1A **38**
Cheshunt. *Herts* 5D **52**
Cheslyn Hay. *Staf* 5D **73**
Chessetts Wood. *Warw* 3F **61**
Chessington. *G Lon* 4C **38**
Chester. *Ches W* 4G **83**
Chesterblade. *Som* 2B **22**
Chesterfield. *Derbs* 3A **86**
Chesterfield. *Staf* 5F **73**
Chesterhope. *Nmbd* 1B **114**
Chester-le-Street. *Dur* 4F **115**
Chester Moor. *Dur* 5F **115**
Chesters. *Bord* 3A **120**
Chesterton. *Cambs* 4D **64**
(nr. Cambridge)
Chesterton. *Cambs* 1A **64**
(nr. Peterborough)
Chesterton. *Glos* 5F **49**
Chesterton. *Oxon* 3D **50**
Chesterton. *Shrp* 1B **60**
Chesterton. *Staf* 1C **72**
Chesterton Green. *Warw* 5H **61**
Chesterwood. *Nmbd* 3B **114**
Chestfield. *Kent* 4F **41**
Cheston. *Devn* 3C **8**
Cheswardine. *Shrp* 2B **72**
Cheswell. *Telf* 4B **72**
Cheswick. *Nmbd* 5G **131**
Cheswick Green. *W Mid* 3F **61**
Chetnole. *Dors* 2B **14**
Chettiscombe. *Devn* 1C **12**
Chettisham. *Cambs* 2E **65**
Chettle. *Dors* 1E **15**
Chetton. *Shrp* 1A **60**
Chetwode. *Buck* 3E **51**
Chetwynd Aston. *Telf* 4B **72**
Cheveley. *Cambs* 4F **65**
Chevening. *Kent* 5F **39**
Chevington. *Suff* 5G **65**
Chevithorne. *Devn* 1C **12**
Chew Magna. *Bath* 5A **34**
Chew Moor. *G Man* 4E **91**
Chew Stoke. *Bath* 5A **34**
Chewton Keynsham. *Bath* 5B **34**
Chewton Mendip. *Som* 1A **22**
Chichacott. *Devn* 3G **11**
Chicheley. *Mil* 1H **51**
Chichester. *W Sus* 2G **17**
Chickerell. *Dors* 4B **14**
Chickering. *Suff* 3E **66**
Chicklade. *Wilts* 3E **23**
Chicksands. *C Beds* 2B **52**
Chickward. *Here* 5E **59**
Chidden. *Hants* 1E **17**
Chiddingfold. *Surr* 2A **26**
Chiddingly. *E Sus* 4G **27**
Chiddingstone. *Kent* 1G **27**
Chiddingstone Causeway. *Kent* 1G **27**
Chiddingstone Hoath. *Kent* 1F **27**
Chideock. *Dors* 3H **13**
Chidgley. *Som* 3D **20**
Chidham. *W Sus* 2F **17**
Chieveley. *W Ber* 4C **36**
Chignal St James. *Essx* 5G **53**
Chignal Smealy. *Essx* 4G **53**
Chigwell. *Essx* 1F **39**
Chigwell Row. *Essx* 1F **39**
Chilbolton. *Hants* 2B **24**
Chilcomb. *Hants* 4D **24**
Chilcombe. *Dors* 3A **14**
Chilcompton. *Som* 1B **22**
Chilcote. *Leics* 4G **73**
Childer Thornton. *Ches W* 3F **83**
Child Okeford. *Dors* 1D **14**
Childrey. *Oxon* 3B **36**
Child's Ercall. *Shrp* 3A **72**
Childswickham. *Worc* 2F **49**
Childwall. *Mers* 2G **83**
Childwickbury. *Herts* 4B **52**
Chilfrome. *Dors* 3A **14**
Chilgrove. *W Sus* 1G **17**
Chilham. *Kent* 5E **41**
Chilhampton. *Wilts* 3F **23**
Chilla. *Devn* 2E **11**
Chilland. *Hants* 3D **24**
Chillaton. *Devn* 4E **11**
Chillenden. *Kent* 5G **41**
Chillerton. *IOW* 4C **16**
Chillesford. *Suff* 5F **67**
Chillingham. *Nmbd* 2E **121**
Chillington. *Devn* 4D **9**
Chillington. *Som* 1G **13**
Chilmark. *Wilts* 3E **23**
Chilmington Green. *Kent* 1D **28**
Chilson. *Oxon* 4B **50**
Chilsworthy. *Corn* 5E **11**
Chilsworthy. *Devn* 2D **10**
Chiltern Green. *C Beds* 4B **52**
Chilthorne Domer. *Som* 1A **14**
Chilton. *Buck* 4E **51**
Chilton. *Devn* 2B **12**
Chilton. *Dur* 2F **105**
Chilton. *Oxon* 3C **36**
Chilton Candover. *Hants* 2D **24**
Chilton Cantelo. *Som* 4A **22**
Chilton Foliat. *Wilts* 4B **36**
Chilton Lane. *Dur* 1A **106**
Chilton Polden. *Som* 3G **21**
Chilton Street. *Suff* 1A **54**
Chilton Trinity. *Som* 3F **21**
Chilwell. *Notts* 2C **74**
Chilworth. *Hants* 1C **16**
Chilworth. *Surr* 1B **26**
Chimney. *Oxon* 5B **50**
Chimney Street. *Suff* 1H **53**
Chineham. *Hants* 1E **25**
Chingford. *G Lon* 1E **39**
Chinley. *Derbs* 2E **85**
Chinnor. *Oxon* 5F **51**
Chipley. *Som* 4E **20**
Chipnall. *Shrp* 2B **72**
Chippenham. *Cambs* 4F **65**
Chippenham. *Wilts* 4E **35**
Chipperfield. *Herts* 5A **52**
Chipping. *Herts* 2D **52**
Chipping. *Lanc* 5F **97**
Chipping Campden. *Glos* 2G **49**
Chipping Hill. *Essx* 4B **54**
Chipping Norton. *Oxon* 3B **50**
Chipping Ongar. *Essx* 5F **53**
Chipping Sodbury. *S Glo* 3C **34**
Chipping Warden. *Nptn* 1C **50**
Chipstable. *Som* 4D **20**
Chipstead. *Kent* 5G **39**
Chipstead. *Surr* 5D **38**
Chirbury. *Shrp* 1E **59**
Chirk. *Wrex* 2E **71**
Chirmorie. *S Ayr* 2H **109**
Chirnside. *Bord* 4E **131**
Chirnsidebridge. *Bord* 4E **131**
Chirton. *Wilts* 1F **23**
Chisbridge Cross. *Buck* 3G **37**
Chisbury. *Wilts* 5A **36**
Chiselborough. *Som* 1H **13**
Chiseldon. *Swin* 4G **35**
Chiselhampton. *Oxon* 2D **36**
Chiserley. *W Yor* 2A **92**
Chislehurst. *G Lon* 3F **39**
Chislet. *Kent* 4G **41**
Chiswell. *Dors* 5B **14**
Chiswell Green. *Herts* 5B **52**
Chiswick. *G Lon* 3D **38**
Chisworth. *Derbs* 1D **85**
Chitcombe. *E Sus* 3C **28**
Chithurst. *W Sus* 4G **25**
Chittering. *Cambs* 4D **65**
Chitterley. *Devn* 2C **12**
Chitterne. *Wilts* 2E **23**
Chittlehamholt. *Devn* 4G **19**
Chittlehampton. *Devn* 4G **19**
Chittoe. *Wilts* 5E **35**
Chivelstone. *Devn* 5D **9**
Chivenor. *Devn* 3F **19**
Chobham. *Surr* 4A **38**
Cholderton. *Wilts* 2H **23**
Cholesbury. *Buck* 5H **51**
Chollerford. *Nmbd* 2C **114**
Chollerton. *Nmbd* 2C **114**
Cholsey. *Oxon* 3D **36**
Cholstrey. *Here* 5G **59**
Chop Gate. *N Yor* 5C **106**
Choppington. *Nmbd* 1F **115**
Chopwell. *Tyne* 4E **115**
Chorley. *Ches E* 5H **83**
Chorley. *Lanc* 3D **90**
Chorley. *Shrp* 2A **60**
Chorley. *Staf* 4E **73**
Chorleywood. *Herts* 1B **38**
Chorlton. *Ches E* 5B **84**
Chorlton-cum-Hardy. *G Man* 1C **84**
Chorlton Lane. *Ches W* 1G **71**
Choulton. *Shrp* 2F **59**
Chrishall. *Essx* 2E **53**
Christchurch. *Cambs* 1D **65**
Christchurch. *Dors* 3G **15**
Christchurch. *Glos* 4A **48**
Christian Malford. *Wilts* 4E **35**
Christleton. *Ches W* 4G **83**
Christmas Common. *Oxon* 2F **37**
Christon. *N Som* 1G **21**
Christon Bank. *Nmbd* 2G **121**
Christow. *Devn* 4B **12**
Chryston. *N Lan* 2H **127**
Chuck Hatch. *E Sus* 2F **27**
Chudleigh. *Devn* 5B **12**
Chudleigh Knighton. *Devn* 5B **12**
Chulmleigh. *Devn* 1G **11**
Chunal. *Derbs* 1E **85**
Church. *Lanc* 2F **91**
Churcham. *Glos* 4C **48**
Church Aston. *Telf* 4B **72**
Church Brampton. *Nptn* 4E **62**
Church Brough. *Cumb* 3A **104**

Cononley—Craigend

Cononley. *N Yor* 5B **98**
Cononsyth. *Ang* 4E **145**
Conordan. *High* 5E **155**
Consall. *Staf* 1D **73**
Consett. *Dur* 4E **115**
Constable Burton. *N Yor* 5E **105**
Constantine. *Corn* 4E **5**
Constantine Bay. *Corn* 1C **6**
Contin. *High* 3G **157**
Contullich. *High* 1A **158**
Conwy. *Cnwy* 3G **81**
Conyer. *Kent* 4D **40**
Conyer's Green. *Suff* 4A **66**
Cooden. *E Sus* 5B **28**
Cooil. *IOM* 4C **108**
Cookbury. *Devn* 2E **11**
Cookbury Wick. *Devn* 2D **11**
Cookham. *Wind* 3G **37**
Cookham Dean. *Wind* 3G **37**
Cookham Rise. *Wind* 3G **37**
Cookhill. *Worc* 5E **61**
Cookley. *Suff* 3F **67**
Cookley. *Worc* 2C **60**
Cookley Green. *Oxon* 2E **37**
Cookney. *Abers* 4F **153**
Cooksbridge. *E Sus* 4F **27**
Cooksey Green. *Worc* 4D **60**
Cookshill. *Staf* 1D **72**
Cooksmill Green. *Essx* 5G **53**
Cookstown. *M Ulst* 4E **175**
Coolham. *W Sus* 3C **26**
Cooling. *Medw* 3B **40**
Cooling Street. *Medw* 3B **40**
Coombe. *Corn* 1C **10**
(nr. Bude)
Coombe. *Corn* 3D **6**
(nr. St Austell)
Coombe. *Corn* 4C **6**
(nr. Truro)
Coombe. *Devn* 3E **12**
(nr. Sidmouth)
Coombe. *Devn* 5C **12**
(nr. Teignmouth)
Coombe. *Glos* 2C **34**
Coombe. *Hants* 4E **25**
Coombe. *Wilts* 1G **23**
Coombe Bissett. *Wilts* 4G **23**
Coombe Hill. *Glos* 3D **49**
Coombe Keynes. *Dors* 4D **14**
Coombes. *W Sus* 5C **26**
Coopersale Common. *Essx* 5E **53**
Coopersale Street. *Essx* 5E **53**
Cooper's Corner. *Kent* 1F **27**
Cooper Street. *Kent* 5H **41**
Cootham. *W Sus* 4B **26**
Copalder Corner. *Cambs* 1C **64**
Copdock. *Suff* 1E **54**
Copford. *Essx* 3C **54**
Copford Green. *Essx* 3C **54**
Copgrove. *N Yor* 3F **99**
Copister. *Shet* 4F **173**
Cople. *Bed* 1B **52**
Copley. *Dur* 2D **105**
Coplow Dale. *Derbs* 3F **85**
Copmanthorpe. *York* 5H **99**
Copp. *Lanc* 1C **90**
Coppathorne. *Corn* 2C **10**
Coppenhall. *Ches E* 5B **84**
Coppenhall. *Staf* 4D **72**
Coppenhall Moss. *Ches E* 5B **84**
Copperhouse. *Corn* 3C **4**
Coppicegate. *Shrp* 2B **60**
Coppingford. *Cambs* 2A **64**
Copplestone. *Devn* 2A **12**
Coppull. *Lanc* 3D **90**
Coppull Moor. *Lanc* 3D **90**
Copsale. *W Sus* 3C **26**
Copshaw Holm. *Bord* 1F **113**
Copster Green. *Lanc* 1E **91**
Copston Magna. *Warw* 2B **62**
Copt Green. *Warw* 4F **61**
Copthall Green. *Essx* 5E **53**
Copt Heath. *W Mid* 3F **61**
Copt Hewick. *N Yor* 2F **99**
Copthill. *Dur* 5B **114**
Copthorne. *W Sus* 2E **27**
Coptiviney. *Shrp* 2G **71**
Copy's Green. *Norf* 2B **78**
Copythorne. *Hants* 1B **16**
Corbridge. *Nmbd* 3C **114**
Corby. *Nptn* 2F **63**
Corby Glen. *Linc* 3G **75**
Cordon. *N Ayr* 2E **123**
Coreley. *Shrp* 3A **60**
Corfe. *Som* 1F **13**
Corfe Castle. *Dors* 4E **15**
Corfe Mullen. *Dors* 3E **15**
Corfton. *Shrp* 2G **59**
Corgarff. *Abers* 3G **151**
Corhampton. *Hants* 4E **24**
Corlae. *Dum* 5F **117**
Corlannau. *Neat* 2A **32**
Corley. *Warw* 2H **61**
Corley Ash. *Warw* 2G **61**
Corley Moor. *Warw* 2G **61**
Cormiston. *S Lan* 1C **118**
Cornaa. *IOM* 3D **108**
Cornaigbeg. *Arg* 4A **138**
Cornaigmore. *Arg* 2D **138**
(on Coll)
Cornaigmore. *Arg* 4A **138**
(on Tiree)
Corner Row. *Lanc* 1C **90**
Corney. *Cumb* 5C **102**
Cornforth. *Dur* 1A **106**
Cornhill. *Abers* 3C **160**
Cornhill. *High* 4C **164**
Cornhill-on-Tweed. *Nmbd* 1C **120**
Cornholme. *W Yor* 2H **91**
Cornish Hall End. *Essx* 2G **53**
Cornquoy. *Orkn* 7E **172**
Cornriggs. *Dur* 5B **114**
Cornsay. *Dur* 5E **115**
Cornsay Colliery. *Dur* 5E **115**
Corntown. *High* 3H **157**
Corntown. *V Glam* 4C **32**
Cornwell. *Oxon* 3A **50**
Cornwood. *Devn* 3C **8**
Cornworthy. *Devn* 3E **9**
Corpach. *High* 1E **141**
Corpusty. *Norf* 3D **78**
Corra. *Dum* 3F **111**
Corran. *High* 2E **141**
(nr. Arnisdale)
Corran. *High* 3A **148**
(nr. Fort William)
Corrany. *IOM* 3D **108**
Corribeg. *High* 1D **141**
Corrie. *N Ayr* 5B **126**
Corrie Common. *Dum* 1D **112**
Corriecravie. *N Ayr* 3D **122**
Corriekinloch. *High* 1A **164**
Corriemoillie. *High* 2F **157**
Corrievarkie Lodge. *Per* 1C **142**
Corrievorrie. *High* 1B **150**
Corrigall. *Orkn* 6C **172**
Corrimony. *High* 5F **157**
Corringham. *Linc* 1F **87**
Corringham. *Thur* 2B **40**
Corris. *Gwyn* 5G **69**
Corris Uchaf. *Gwyn* 5G **69**
Corrour Shooting Lodge. *High* 2B **142**
Corry. *High* 1E **147**
Corrybrough. *High* 1C **150**
Corrygills. *N Ayr* 2E **123**
Corry of Ardnagrask. *High* 4H **157**
Corsback. *High* 1E **169**
(nr. Dunnet)
Corsback. *High* 3E **169**
(nr. Halkirk)
Corscombe. *Dors* 2A **14**
Corse. *Abers* 4D **160**
Corse. *Glos* 3C **48**
Corsehill. *Abers* 3G **161**
Corse Lawn. *Worc* 2D **48**
Corse of Kinnoir. *Abers* 4C **160**
Corsham. *Wilts* 4D **34**
Corsley. *Wilts* 2D **22**
Corsley Heath. *Wilts* 2D **22**
Corsock. *Dum* 2E **111**
Corston. *Bath* 5B **34**
Corston. *Wilts* 3E **35**
Corstorphine. *Edin* 2F **129**
Cortachy. *Ang* 3C **144**
Corton. *Suff* 1H **67**
Corton. *Wilts* 2E **23**
Corton Denham. *Som* 4B **22**
Corwar House. *S Ayr* 1H **109**
Corwen. *Den* 1C **70**
Coryates. *Dors* 4B **14**
Coryton. *Devn* 4E **11**
Coryton. *Thur* 2B **40**
Cosby. *Leics* 1C **62**
Coscote. *Oxon* 3D **36**
Coseley. *W Mid* 1D **60**
Cosgrove. *Nptn* 1F **51**
Cosham. *Port* 2E **17**
Cosheston. *Pemb* 4E **43**
Coskills. *N Lin* 3D **94**
Cosmeston. *V Glam* 5E **33**
Cossall. *Notts* 1B **74**
Cossington. *Leics* 4D **74**
Cossington. *Som* 2G **21**
Costa. *Orkn* 5C **172**
Costessey. *Norf* 4D **78**
Costock. *Notts* 3C **74**
Coston. *Leics* 3F **75**
Coston. *Norf* 5C **78**
Cote. *Oxon* 5B **50**
Cotebrook. *Ches W* 4H **83**
Cotehill. *Cumb* 4F **113**
Cotes. *Cumb* 1D **97**
Cotes. *Leics* 3C **74**
Cotes. *Staf* 2C **72**
Cotesbach. *Leics* 2C **62**
Cotes Heath. *Staf* 2C **72**
Cotford St Luke. *Som* 4E **21**
Cotgrave. *Notts* 2D **74**
Cothall. *Abers* 2F **153**
Cotham. *Notts* 1E **75**
Cothelstone. *Som* 3E **21**
Cotheridge. *Worc* 5B **60**
Cotherstone. *Dur* 3D **104**
Cothill. *Oxon* 2C **36**
Cotland. *Mon* 5A **48**
Cotleigh. *Devn* 2F **13**
Cotmanhay. *Derbs* 1B **74**
Coton. *Cambs* 5D **64**
Coton. *Nptn* 3D **62**
Coton. *Staf* 3C **72**
(nr. Gnosall)
Coton. *Staf* 2D **73**
(nr. Stone)
Coton. *Staf* 5F **73**
(nr. Tamworth)
Coton Clanford. *Staf* 3C **72**
Coton Hayes. *Staf* 2D **73**
Coton Hill. *Shrp* 4G **71**
Coton in the Clay. *Staf* 3F **73**
Coton in the Elms. *Derbs* 4G **73**
Cotonwood. *Shrp* 2H **71**
Cotonwood. *Staf* 3C **72**
Cott. *Devn* 2D **9**
Cott. *Orkn* 5F **172**
Cottam. *E Yor* 3D **101**
Cottam. *Lanc* 1D **90**
Cottam. *Notts* 3F **87**
Cottartown. *High* 5E **159**
Cottarville. *Nptn* 4E **63**
Cottenham. *Cambs* 4D **64**
Cotterdale. *N Yor* 5B **104**
Cottered. *Herts* 3D **52**
Cotterstock. *Nptn* 1H **63**
Cottesbrooke. *Nptn* 3E **62**
Cottesmore. *Rut* 4G **75**
Cotteylands. *Devn* 1C **12**
Cottingham. *E Yor* 1D **94**
Cottingham. *Nptn* 1F **63**
Cottingley. *W Yor* 1B **92**
Cottisford. *Oxon* 2D **50**
Cotton. *Staf* 1E **73**
Cotton. *Suff* 4C **66**
Cotton End. *Bed* 1A **52**
Cottown. *Abers* 4F **161**
Cotts. *Devn* 2A **8**
Cotwalton. *Staf* 2D **72**
Couch's Mill. *Corn* 3F **7**
Coughton. *Here* 3A **48**
Coughton. *Warw* 4E **61**
Coulags. *High* 4B **156**
Coulby Newham. *Midd* 3C **106**
Coulderton. *Cumb* 4A **102**
Coulin Lodge. *High* 3C **156**
Coull. *Abers* 3C **152**
Coulport. *Arg* 1D **126**
Coulsdon. *G Lon* 5D **39**
Coulston. *Wilts* 1E **23**
Coulter. *S Lan* 1C **118**
Coultershaw Bridge. *W Sus* 4A **26**
Coultings. *Som* 2F **21**
Coulton. *N Yor* 2A **100**
Cound. *Shrp* 5H **71**
Coundon. *Dur* 2F **105**
Coundon Grange. *Dur* 2F **105**
Countersett. *N Yor* 1B **98**
Countess. *Wilts* 2G **23**
Countess Cross. *Essx* 2B **54**
Countesthorpe. *Leics* 1C **62**
Countisbury. *Devn* 2H **19**
Coupar Angus. *Per* 4B **144**
Coupe Green. *Lanc* 2D **90**
Coupland. *Cumb* 3A **104**
Coupland. *Nmbd* 1D **120**
Cour. *Arg* 5G **125**
Courance. *Dum* 5C **118**
Court-at-Street. *Kent* 2E **29**
Courteachan. *High* 4E **147**
Courteenhall. *Nptn* 5E **63**
Court Henry. *Carm* 3F **45**
Courtsend. *Essx* 1E **41**
Courtway. *Som* 3F **21**
Cousland. *Midl* 3G **129**
Cousley Wood. *E Sus* 2A **28**
Coustonn. *Arg* 2B **126**
Cove. *Arg* 1D **126**
Cove. *Devn* 1C **12**
Cove. *Hants* 1G **25**
Cove. *High* 4C **162**
Cove. *Bord* 2D **130**
Cove Bay. *Aber* 3G **153**
Covehithe. *Suff* 2H **67**
Coven. *Staf* 5D **72**
Coveney. *Cambs* 2D **65**
Covenham St Bartholomew. *Linc* 1C **88**
Covenham St Mary. *Linc* 1C **88**
Coven Heath. *Staf* 5D **72**
Coventry. *W Mid* 3H **61**
Coverack. *Corn* 5E **5**
Coverham. *N Yor* 1D **98**
Covesea. *Mor* 1F **159**
Covingham. *Swin* 3G **35**
Covington. *Cambs* 3H **63**
Covington. *S Lan* 1B **118**
Cowan Bridge. *Lanc* 2F **97**
Cowan Head. *Cumb* 5F **103**
Cowbar. *Red C* 3E **107**
Cowbeech. *E Sus* 4H **27**
Cowbit. *Linc* 4B **76**
Cowbridge. *V Glam* 4C **32**
Cowden. *Kent* 1F **27**
Cowdenbeath. *Fife* 4D **136**
Cowdenburn. *Bord* 4F **129**
Cowdenend. *Fife* 4D **136**
Cowers Lane. *Derbs* 1H **73**
Cowes. *IOW* 3C **16**
Cowesby. *N Yor* 1G **99**
Cowfold. *W Sus* 3D **26**
Cowfords. *Mor* 2H **159**
Cowgill. *Cumb* 1G **97**
Cowie. *Abers* 5F **153**
Cowie. *Stir* 1B **128**
Cowlam. *E Yor* 3D **100**
Cowley. *Devn* 3C **12**
Cowley. *Glos* 4E **49**
Cowley. *G Lon* 2B **38**
Cowley. *Oxon* 5D **50**
Cowley. *Staf* 4C **72**
Cowleymoor. *Devn* 1C **12**
Cowling. *Lanc* 3D **90**
Cowling. *N Yor* 1E **99**
(nr. Bedale)
Cowling. *N Yor* 5B **98**
(nr. Glusburn)
Cowlinge. *Suff* 5G **65**
Cowmes. *W Yor* 3B **92**
Cowpe. *Lanc* 2G **91**
Cowpen. *Nmbd* 1F **115**
Cowpen Bewley. *Stoc T* 2B **106**
Cowplain. *Hants* 1E **17**
Cowshill. *Dur* 5B **114**
Cowslip Green. *N Som* 5H **33**
Cowstrandburn. *Fife* 4C **136**
Cowthorpe. *N Yor* 4G **99**
Coxall. *Here* 3F **59**
Coxbank. *Ches E* 1A **72**
Coxbench. *Derbs* 1A **74**
Cox Common. *Suff* 2G **67**
Coxford. *Norf* 3H **77**
Coxgreen. *Staf* 2C **60**
Cox Green. *Surr* 2B **26**
Cox Green. *Tyne* 4G **115**
Coxheath. *Kent* 5B **40**
Coxhoe. *Dur* 1A **106**
Coxley. *Som* 2A **22**
Coxwold. *N Yor* 2H **99**
Coychurch. *B'end* 3C **32**
Coylton. *S Ayr* 3D **116**
Coylumbridge. *High* 2D **150**
Coynach. *Abers* 3B **152**
Coynachie. *Abers* 5B **160**
Coytrahen. *B'end* 3B **32**
Crabbs Cross. *Worc* 4E **61**
Crabgate. *Norf* 3C **78**
Crab Orchard. *Dors* 2F **15**
Crabtree. *W Sus* 3D **26**
Crabtree Green. *Wrex* 1F **71**
Crackaig. *High* 2G **165**
Crackenthorpe. *Cumb* 2H **103**
Crackington Haven. *Corn* 3B **10**
Crackley. *Staf* 5C **84**
Crackley. *Warw* 3G **61**
Crackleybank. *Shrp* 4B **72**
Crackpot. *N Yor* 5C **104**
Cracoe. *N Yor* 3B **98**
Craddock. *Devn* 1D **12**
Cradhlastadh. *W Isl* 4C **171**
Cradley. *Here* 1C **48**
Cradley. *W Mid* 2D **60**
Cradoc. *Powy* 2D **46**
Crafthole. *Corn* 3H **7**
Crafton. *Buck* 4G **51**
Cragabus. *Arg* 5B **124**
Crag Foot. *Lanc* 2D **97**
Craggan. *High* 1E **151**
Cragganmore. *Mor* 5F **159**
Cragganvallie. *High* 5H **157**
Craggie. *High* 2F **165**
Craggiemore. *High* 5B **158**
Cragg Vale. *W Yor* 2A **92**
Craghead. *Dur* 4F **115**
Crai. *Powy* 3B **46**
Craibstone. *Aber* 2F **153**
Craichie. *Ang* 4E **145**
Craig. *Arg* 5E **141**
Craig. *Dum* 2D **111**
Craig. *High* 4C **156**
(nr. Achnashellach)
Craig. *High* 2G **155**
(nr. Lower Diabaig)
Craig. *High* 5H **155**
(nr. Stromeferry)
Craiganour Lodge. *Per* 3D **142**
Craigavon. *Arm* 5F **175**
Craigbrack. *Arg* 4A **134**
Craig-cefn-parc. *Swan* 5G **45**
Craigdallie. *Per* 1E **137**
Craigdam. *Abers* 5F **161**
Craigdarroch. *E Ayr* 4F **117**
Craigdarroch. *High* 3G **157**
Craigdhu. *High* 4G **157**
Craigearn. *Abers* 2E **152**
Craigellachie. *Mor* 4G **159**
Craigend. *Per* 1D **136**

Darra. *Abers* ...4E 161
Darracott. *Devn* ...3E 19
Darras Hall. *Nmbd* ...2E 115
Darrington. *W Yor* ...2E 93
Darrow Green. *Norf* ...2E 67
Darsham. *Suff* ...4G 67
Dartfield. *Abers* ...3H 161
Dartford. *Kent* ...3G 39
Dartford-Thurrock River Crossing.
 Kent ...3G 39
Dartington. *Devn* ...2D 9
Dartmeet. *Devn* ...5G 11
Dartmoor. *Devn* ...4F 11
Dartmouth. *Devn* ...3E 9
Darton. *S Yor* ...3D 92
Darvel. *E Ayr* ...1E 117
Darwen. *Bkbn* ...2E 91
Dassels. *Herts* ...3D 53
Datchet. *Wind* ...3A 38
Datchworth. *Herts* ...4C 52
Datchworth Green. *Herts* ...4C 52
Daubhill. *G Man* ...4F 91
Dauntsey. *Wilts* ...3E 35
Dauntsey Green. *Wilts* ...3E 35
Dauntsey Lock. *Wilts* ...3E 35
Dava. *Mor* ...5E 159
Davenham. *Ches W* ...3A 84
Daventry. *Nptn* ...4C 62
Davidson's Mains. *Edin* ...2F 129
Davidston. *High* ...2B 158
Davidstow. *Corn* ...4B 10
David's Well. *Powy* ...3C 58
Davington. *Dum* ...4E 119
Daviot. *Abers* ...1E 153
Daviot. *High* ...5B 158
Davyhulme. *G Man* ...1B 84
Daw Cross. *N Yor* ...4E 99
Dawdon. *Dur* ...5H 115
Dawesgreen. *Surr* ...1D 26
Dawley. *Telf* ...5A 72
Dawlish. *Devn* ...5C 12
Dawlish Warren. *Devn* ...5C 12
Dawn. *Cnwy* ...3A 82
Daws Heath. *Essx* ...2C 40
Dawshill. *Worc* ...5C 60
Daw's House. *Corn* ...4D 10
Dawsmere. *Linc* ...2D 76
Dayhills. *Staf* ...2D 72
Dayhouse Bank. *Worc* ...3D 60
Daylesford. *Glos* ...3H 49
Daywall. *Shrp* ...2E 71
Ddol. *Flin* ...3D 82
Ddol Cownwy. *Powy* ...4C 70
Deadman's Cross. *C Beds* ...1B 52
Deadwater. *Nmbd* ...5A 120
Deaf Hill. *Dur* ...1A 106
Deal. *Kent* ...5H 41
Dean. *Cumb* ...2B 102
Dean. *Devn* ...2G 19
 (nr. Combe Martin)
Dean. *Devn* ...2H 19
 (nr. Lynton)
Dean. *Dors* ...1E 15
Dean. *Hants* ...1D 16
 (nr. Bishop's Waltham)
Dean. *Hants* ...3C 24
 (nr. Winchester)
Dean. *Oxon* ...3B 50
Dean. *Som* ...2B 22
Dean Bank. *Dur* ...1F 105
Deanburnhaugh. *Bord* ...3F 119
Dean Cross. *Devn* ...2F 19
Deane. *Hants* ...1D 24
Deanich Lodge. *High* ...5A 164
Deanland. *Dors* ...1E 15
Deanlane End. *W Sus* ...1F 17
Dean Park. *Shrp* ...4A 60
Dean Prior. *Devn* ...2D 8
Dean Row. *Ches E* ...2C 84
Deans. *W Lot* ...3D 128
Deanscales. *Cumb* ...2B 102
Deanshanger. *Nptn* ...1F 51
Deanston. *Stir* ...3G 135
Dearham. *Cumb* ...1B 102
Dearne Valley. *S Yor* ...4D 93

Debach. *Suff* ...5E 67
Debden. *Essx* ...2F 53
Debden Green. *Essx* ...1F 39
 (nr. Loughton)
Debden Green. *Essx* ...2F 53
 (nr. Saffron Walden)
Debenham. *Suff* ...4D 66
Dechmont. *W Lot* ...2D 128
Deddington. *Oxon* ...2C 50
Dedham. *Essx* ...2D 54
Dedham Heath. *Essx* ...2D 54
Deebank. *Abers* ...4D 152
Deene. *Nptn* ...1G 63
Deenethorpe. *Nptn* ...1G 63
Deepcar. *S Yor* ...1G 85
Deepcut. *Surr* ...5A 38
Deepdale. *Cumb* ...1G 97
Deepdale. *N Lin* ...3D 94
Deepdale. *N Yor* ...2A 98
Deeping Gate. *Pet* ...5A 76
Deeping St James. *Linc* ...4A 76
Deeping St Nicholas. *Linc* ...4B 76
Deerhill. *Mor* ...3B 160
Deerhurst. *Glos* ...3D 48
Deerhurst Walton. *Glos* ...3D 49
Deerness. *Orkn* ...7E 172
Defford. *Worc* ...1E 49
Defynnog. *Powy* ...3C 46
Deganwy. *Cnwy* ...3G 81
Deighton. *N Yor* ...4A 106
Deighton. *W Yor* ...3B 92
Deighton. *York* ...5A 100
Deiniolen. *Gwyn* ...4E 81
Delabole. *Corn* ...4A 10
Delamere. *Ches W* ...4H 83
Delfour. *High* ...3C 150
Dellifure. *High* ...5E 159
Dell, The. *Suff* ...1G 67
Delly End. *Oxon* ...4B 50
Delph. *G Man* ...4H 91
Delves. *Dur* ...5E 115
Delves, The. *W Mid* ...1E 61
Delvin End. *Essx* ...2A 54
Dembleby. *Linc* ...2H 75
Demelza. *Corn* ...2D 6
Denaby Main. *S Yor* ...1B 86
Denbeath. *Fife* ...4F 137
Denbigh. *Den* ...4C 82
Denbury. *Devn* ...2E 9
Denby. *Derbs* ...1A 74
Denby Common. *Derbs* ...1B 74
Denby Dale. *W Yor* ...4C 92
Denchworth. *Oxon* ...2B 36
Dendron. *Cumb* ...2B 96
Deneside. *Dur* ...5H 115
Denford. *Nptn* ...3G 63
Dengie. *Essx* ...5C 54
Denham. *Buck* ...2B 38
Denham. *Suff* ...4G 65
 (nr. Bury St Edmunds)
Denham. *Suff* ...3D 66
 (nr. Eye)
Denham Green. *Buck* ...2B 38
Denham Street. *Suff* ...3D 66
Denhead. *Abers* ...5G 161
 (nr. Ellon)
Denhead. *Abers* ...3G 161
 (nr. Strichen)
Denhead. *Fife* ...2G 137
Denholm. *Bord* ...3H 119
Denholme. *W Yor* ...1A 92
Denholme Clough. *W Yor* ...1A 92
Denholme Gate. *W Yor* ...1A 92
Denio. *Gwyn* ...2C 68
Denmead. *Hants* ...1E 17
Dennington. *Suff* ...4E 67
Denny. *Falk* ...1B 128
Denny End. *Cambs* ...4D 65
Dennyloanhead. *Falk* ...1B 128
Den of Lindores. *Fife* ...2E 137
Denshaw. *G Man* ...3H 91
Denside. *Abers* ...4F 153
Denston. *Suff* ...5G 65

Denstone. *Staf* ...1F 73
Denstroude. *Kent* ...4F 41
Dent. *Cumb* ...1G 97
Den, The. *N Ayr* ...4E 127
Denton. *Cambs* ...2A 64
Denton. *Darl* ...3F 105
Denton. *E Sus* ...5F 27
Denton. *G Man* ...1D 84
Denton. *Kent* ...1G 29
Denton. *Linc* ...2F 75
Denton. *Norf* ...2E 67
Denton. *Nptn* ...5F 63
Denton. *N Yor* ...5D 98
Denton. *Oxon* ...5D 50
Denver. *Norf* ...5F 77
Denwick. *Nmbd* ...3G 121
Deopham. *Norf* ...5C 78
Deopham Green. *Norf* ...1C 66
Depden. *Suff* ...5G 65
Depden Green. *Suff* ...5G 65
Deptford. *G Lon* ...3E 39
Deptford. *Wilts* ...3F 23
Derby. *Derb* ...2A 74
Derbyhaven. *IOM* ...5B 108
Derculich. *Per* ...3F 143
Dereham. *Norf* ...4B 78
Deri. *Cphy* ...5E 47
Derril. *Devn* ...2D 10
Derringstone. *Kent* ...1G 29
Derrington. *Shrp* ...1A 60
Derrington. *Staf* ...3C 72
Derriton. *Devn* ...2D 10
Derry. *Derr* ...2C 174
Derryguaig. *Arg* ...5F 139
Derry Hill. *Wilts* ...4E 35
Derrythorpe. *N Lin* ...4B 94
Dersingham. *Norf* ...2F 77
Dervaig. *Arg* ...3F 139
Derwen. *Den* ...5C 82
Derwen Gam. *Cdgn* ...5D 56
Derwenlas. *Powy* ...1G 57
Desborough. *Nptn* ...2F 63
Desford. *Leics* ...5B 74
Detchant. *Nmbd* ...1E 121
Dethick. *Derbs* ...5H 85
Detling. *Kent* ...5B 40
Deuchar. *Ang* ...2D 144
Deuddwr. *Powy* ...4E 71
Devauden. *Mon* ...2H 33
Devil's Bridge. *Cdgn* ...3G 57
Devitts Green. *Warw* ...1G 61
Devizes. *Wilts* ...5F 35
Devonport. *Plym* ...3A 8
Devonside. *Clac* ...4B 136
Devoran. *Corn* ...5B 6
Dewartown. *Midl* ...3G 129
Dewlish. *Dors* ...3C 14
Dewsall Court. *Here* ...2H 47
Dewsbury. *W Yor* ...2C 92
Dexbeer. *Devn* ...2C 10
Dhoon. *IOM* ...3D 108
Dhoor. *IOM* ...2D 108
Dhowin. *IOM* ...1D 108
Dial Green. *W Sus* ...3A 26
Dial Post. *W Sus* ...4C 26
Dibberford. *Dors* ...2H 13
Dibden. *Hants* ...2C 16
Dibden Purlieu. *Hants* ...2C 16
Dickleburgh. *Norf* ...2D 66
Didbrook. *Glos* ...2F 49
Didcot. *Oxon* ...2D 36
Diddington. *Cambs* ...4A 64
Diddlebury. *Shrp* ...2H 59
Didley. *Here* ...2H 47
Didling. *W Sus* ...1G 17
Didmarton. *Glos* ...3D 34
Didsbury. *G Man* ...1C 84
Didworthy. *Devn* ...2C 8
Digby. *Linc* ...5H 87
Digg. *High* ...2D 154
Diggle. *G Man* ...4A 92
Digmoor. *Lanc* ...4C 90
Digswell. *Herts* ...4C 52
Dihewyd. *Cdgn* ...5D 56
Dilham. *Norf* ...3F 79

Dilhorne. *Staf* ...1D 72
Dillarburn. *S Lan* ...5B 128
Dillington. *Cambs* ...4A 64
Dilston. *Nmbd* ...3C 114
Dilton Marsh. *Wilts* ...2D 22
Dilwyn. *Here* ...5G 59
Dimmer. *Som* ...3B 22
Dimple. *G Man* ...3F 91
Dinas. *Carm* ...1G 43
Dinas. *Gwyn* ...5D 81
 (nr. Caernarfon)
Dinas. *Gwyn* ...2B 68
 (nr. Tudweiliog)
Dinas Cross. *Pemb* ...1E 43
Dinas Dinlle. *Gwyn* ...5D 80
Dinas Mawddwy. *Gwyn* ...4A 70
Dinas Powys. *V Glam* ...4E 33
Dinbych. *Den* ...4C 82
Dinbych-y-Pysgod. *Pemb* ...4F 43
Dinckley. *Lanc* ...1E 91
Dinder. *Som* ...2A 22
Dinedor. *Here* ...2A 48
Dinedor Cross. *Here* ...2A 48
Dingestow. *Mon* ...4H 47
Dingle. *Mers* ...2F 83
Dingleden. *Kent* ...2C 28
Dingleton. *Bord* ...1H 119
Dingley. *Nptn* ...2E 63
Dingwall. *High* ...3H 157
Dinmael. *Cnwy* ...1C 70
Dinnet. *Abers* ...4B 152
Dinnington. *Som* ...1H 13
Dinnington. *S Yor* ...2C 86
Dinnington. *Tyne* ...2F 115
Dinorwig. *Gwyn* ...4E 81
Dinton. *Buck* ...4F 51
Dinton. *Wilts* ...3F 23
Dinworthy. *Devn* ...1D 10
Dipley. *Hants* ...1F 25
Dippen. *Arg* ...2B 122
Dippenhall. *Surr* ...2G 25
Dippertown. *Devn* ...4E 11
Dippin. *N Ayr* ...3E 123
Dipple. *S Ayr* ...4B 116
Dipton. *Dur* ...4E 115
Dirleton. *E Lot* ...1B 130
Dirt Pot. *Nmbd* ...5B 114
Discoed. *Powy* ...4E 59
Diseworth. *Leics* ...3B 74
Dishes. *Orkn* ...5F 172
Dishforth. *N Yor* ...2F 99
Disley. *Ches E* ...2D 85
Diss. *Norf* ...3D 66
Disserth. *Powy* ...5C 58
Distington. *Cumb* ...2B 102
Ditchampton. *Wilts* ...3F 23
Ditcheat. *Som* ...3B 22
Ditchingham. *Norf* ...1F 67
Ditchling. *E Sus* ...4E 27
Ditteridge. *Wilts* ...5D 34
Dittisham. *Devn* ...3E 9
Ditton. *Hal* ...2G 83
Ditton. *Kent* ...5B 40
Ditton Green. *Cambs* ...5F 65
Ditton Priors. *Shrp* ...2A 60
Divach. *High* ...1G 149
Dixonfield. *High* ...2D 168
Dixton. *Glos* ...2E 49
Dixton. *Mon* ...4A 48
Dizzard. *Corn* ...3B 10
Doagh. *Ant* ...3G 175
Dobcross. *G Man* ...4H 91
Dobs Hill. *Flin* ...4F 83
Dobson's Bridge. *Shrp* ...2G 71
Dobwalls. *Corn* ...2G 7
Doccombe. *Devn* ...4A 12
Dochgarroch. *High* ...4A 158
Docking. *Norf* ...2G 77
Docklow. *Here* ...5H 59
Dockray. *Cumb* ...2E 103
Doc Penfro. *Pemb* ...4D 42
Dodbrooke. *Devn* ...4D 8
Doddenham. *Worc* ...5B 60
Doddinghurst. *Essx* ...1G 39

Doddington. *Cambs* ...1C 64
Doddington. *Kent* ...5D 40
Doddington. *Linc* ...3G 87
Doddington. *Nmbd* ...1D 121
Doddington. *Shrp* ...3A 60
Doddiscombsleigh. *Devn* ...4B 12
Doddshill. *Norf* ...2G 77
Dodford. *Nptn* ...4D 62
Dodford. *Worc* ...3D 60
Dodington. *Som* ...2E 21
Dodington. *S Glo* ...4C 34
Dodleston. *Ches W* ...4F 83
Dods Leigh. *Staf* ...2E 73
Dodworth. *S Yor* ...4D 92
Doe Lea. *Derbs* ...4B 86
Dogdyke. *Linc* ...5B 88
Dogmersfield. *Hants* ...1F 25
Dogsthorpe. *Pet* ...5B 76
Dog Village. *Devn* ...3C 12
Dolanog. *Powy* ...4C 70
Dolau. *Powy* ...4D 58
Dolau. *Rhon* ...3D 32
Dolbenmaen. *Gwyn* ...1E 69
Dolfach. *Powy* ...3B 72
Dol-fâch. *Powy* ...5B 70
 (nr. Llanbrynmair)
Dolfach. *Powy* ...3B 58
 (nr. Llanidloes)
Dolfor. *Powy* ...2D 58
Dolgarrog. *Cnwy* ...4G 81
Dolgellau. *Gwyn* ...4G 69
Dolgoch. *Gwyn* ...5F 69
Dol-gran. *Carm* ...2E 45
Dolhelfa. *Powy* ...3B 58
Doll. *High* ...3F 165
Dollar. *Clac* ...4B 136
Dolley Green. *Powy* ...4E 59
Dollingstown. *Arm* ...5G 175
Dollwen. *Cdgn* ...2F 57
Dolphin. *Flin* ...3D 82
Dolphingstone. *E Lot* ...2G 129
Dolphinholme. *Lanc* ...4E 97
Dolphinton. *S Lan* ...5E 129
Dolton. *Devn* ...1F 11
Dolwen. *Cnwy* ...3A 82
Dolwyddelan. *Cnwy* ...5G 81
Dol-y-Bont. *Cdgn* ...2F 57
Dolyhir. *Powy* ...5E 59
Domgay. *Powy* ...4E 71
Donaghadee. *N Dwn* ...4J 175
Doncaster. *S Yor* ...4F 93
Donhead St Andrew. *Wilts* ...4E 23
Donhead St Mary. *Wilts* ...4E 23
Doniford. *Som* ...2D 20
Donington. *Linc* ...2B 76
Donington. *Shrp* ...5C 72
Donington Eaudike. *Linc* ...2B 76
Donington le Heath. *Leics* ...4B 74
Donington on Bain. *Linc* ...2B 88
Donington South Ing. *Linc* ...2B 76
Donisthorpe. *Leics* ...4H 73
Donkey Street. *Kent* ...2F 29
Donkey Town. *Surr* ...4A 38
Donna Nook. *Linc* ...1D 88
Donnington. *Glos* ...3G 49
Donnington. *Here* ...2C 48
Donnington. *Shrp* ...5H 71
Donnington. *Telf* ...4B 72
Donnington. *W Ber* ...5C 36
Donnington. *W Sus* ...2G 17
Donyatt. *Som* ...1G 13
Doomsday Green. *W Sus* ...3C 26
Doonfoot. *S Ayr* ...3C 116
Doonholm. *S Ayr* ...3C 116
Dorback Lodge. *High* ...2E 151
Dorchester. *Dors* ...3B 14
Dorchester on Thames. *Oxon* ...2D 36
Dordon. *Warw* ...5G 73
Dore. *S Yor* ...2H 85
Dores. *High* ...5H 157
Dorking. *Surr* ...1C 26
Dorking Tye. *Suff* ...2C 54
Dormansland. *Surr* ...1F 27
Dormans Park. *Surr* ...1E 27
Dormanstown. *Red C* ...2C 106

Dormington—Dunston

Dormington. *Here* 1A 48
Dormston. *Worc* 5D 61
Dorn. *Glos* 2H 49
Dorney. *Buck* 3A 38
Dornie. *High* 1A 148
Dornoch. *High* 5E 165
Dornock. *Dum* 3D 112
Dorrery. *High* 3C 168
Dorridge. *W Mid* 3F 61
Dorrington. *Linc* 5H 87
Dorrington. *Shrp* 5G 71
Dorsington. *Warw* 1G 49
Dorstone. *Here* 1G 47
Dorton. *Buck* 4E 51
Dosthill. *Staf* 5G 73
Dotham. *IOA* 3C 80
Dottery. *Dors* 3H 13
Doublebois. *Corn* 2F 7
Dougarie. *N Ayr* 2C 122
Doughton. *Glos* 2D 35
Douglas. *IOM* 4C 108
Douglas. *S Lan* 1H 117
Douglastown. *Ang* 4D 144
Douglas Water. *S Lan* 1A 118
Doulting. *Som* 2B 22
Dounby. *Orkn* 5B 172
Doune. *High* 2C 150
(nr. Kingussie)
Doune. *High* 3B 164
(nr. Lairg)
Doune. *Stir* 3G 135
Dounie. *High* 4C 164
(nr. Bonar Bridge)
Dounie. *High* 5D 164
(nr. Tain)
Dounreay. *High* 2B 168
Doura. *N Ayr* 5E 127
Dousland. *Devn* 2B 8
Dovaston. *Shrp* 3F 71
Dove Holes. *Derbs* 3E 85
Dovenby. *Cumb* 1B 102
Dover. *Kent* 1H 29
Dovercourt. *Essx* 2F 55
Doverdale. *Worc* 4C 60
Doveridge. *Derbs* 2F 73
Doversgreen. *Surr* 1D 26
Dowally. *Per* 4H 143
Dowbridge. *Lanc* 1C 90
Dowdeswell. *Glos* 4F 49
Dowlais. *Mer T* 5D 46
Dowland. *Devn* 1F 11
Dowlands. *Devn* 3F 13
Dowles. *Worc* 3B 60
Dowlesgreen. *Wok* 5G 37
Dowlish Wake. *Som* 1G 13
Downall Green. *Mers* 4D 90
Down Ampney. *Glos* 2G 35
Downderry. *Corn* 3H 7
(nr. Looe)
Downderry. *Corn* 3D 6
(nr. St Austell)
Downe. *G Lon* 4F 39
Downend. *IOW* 4D 16
Downend. *S Glo* 4B 34
Downend. *W Ber* 4C 36
Down Field. *Cambs* 3F 65
Downfield. *D'dee* 5C 144
Downgate. *Corn* 5D 10
(nr. Kelly Bray)
Downgate. *Corn* 5C 10
(nr. Upton Cross)
Downham. *Essx* 1B 40
Downham. *Lanc* 5G 97
Downham. *Nmbd* 1C 120
Downham Market. *Norf* 5F 77
Down Hatherley. *Glos* 3D 48
Downhead. *Som* 2B 22
(nr. Frome)
Downhead. *Som* 4A 22
(nr. Yeovil)
Downholland Cross. *Lanc* 4B 90
Downholme. *N Yor* 5E 105
Downies. *Abers* 4G 153
Downley. *Buck* 2G 37
Downpatrick. *New M* 5H 175
Down St Mary. *Devn* 2H 11
Downside. *Som* 1B 22
(nr. Chilcompton)
Downside. *Som* 2B 22
(nr. Shepton Mallet)
Downside. *Surr* 5C 38
Down, The. *Shrp* 1A 60
Down Thomas. *Devn* 3B 8
Downton. *Hants* 3A 16
Downton. *Wilts* 4G 23
Downton on the Rock. *Here* 3G 59
Dowsby. *Linc* 3A 76
Dowsdale. *Linc* 4B 76
Dowthwaitehead. *Cumb* 2E 103
Doxey. *Staf* 3D 72
Doxford. *Nmbd* 2F 121
Doynton. *S Glo* 4C 34
Drabblegate. *Norf* 3E 78
Draethen. *Cphy* 3F 33
Draffan. *S Lan* 5A 128
Dragonby. *N Lin* 3C 94
Dragons Green. *W Sus* 3C 26
Drakelow. *Worc* 2C 60
Drakemyre. *N Ayr* 4D 126
Drakes Broughton. *Worc* 1E 49
Drakes Cross. *Worc* 3E 61
Drakewalls. *Corn* 5E 11
Draperstown. *M Ulst* 3E 174
Draughton. *Nptn* 3E 63
Draughton. *N Yor* 4C 98
Drax. *N Yor* 2G 93
Draycot. *Oxon* 5E 51
Draycote. *Warw* 3B 62
Draycot Foliat. *Swin* 4G 35
Draycott. *Derbs* 2B 74
Draycott. *Glos* 2G 49
Draycott. *Shrp* 1C 60
Draycott. *Som* 1H 21
(nr. Cheddar)
Draycott. *Som* 4A 22
(nr. Yeovil)
Draycott. *Worc* 1D 48
Draycott in the Clay. *Staf* 3F 73
Draycott in the Moors. *Staf* 1D 73
Drayford. *Devn* 1A 12
Drayton. *Leics* 1F 63
Drayton. *Linc* 2B 76
Drayton. *Norf* 4D 78
Drayton. *Nptn* 4C 62
Drayton. *Oxon* 2C 36
(nr. Abingdon)
Drayton. *Oxon* 1C 50
(nr. Banbury)
Drayton. *Port* 2E 17
Drayton. *Som* 4H 21
Drayton. *Warw* 5F 61
Drayton. *Worc* 3D 60
Drayton Bassett. *Staf* 5F 73
Drayton Beauchamp. *Buck* 4H 51
Drayton Parslow. *Buck* 3G 51
Drayton St Leonard. *Oxon* 2D 36
Drebley. *N Yor* 4C 98
Dreenhill. *Pemb* 3D 42
Drefach. *Carm* 4F 45
(nr. Meidrim)
Drefach. *Carm* 2D 44
(nr. Newcastle Emlyn)
Drefach. *Carm* 2G 43
(nr. Tumble)
Drefach. *Cdgn* 1E 45
Dreghorn. *N Ayr* 1C 116
Drellingore. *Kent* 1G 29
Drem. *E Lot* 2B 130
Dreumasdal. *W Isl* 5C 170
Drewsteignton. *Devn* 3H 11
Driby. *Linc* 3C 88
Driffield. *E Yor* 4E 101
Driffield. *Glos* 2F 35
Drift. *Corn* 4B 4
Drigg. *Cumb* 5B 102
Drighlington. *W Yor* 2C 92
Drimnin. *High* 3G 139
Drimpton. *Dors* 2H 13
Dringhoe. *E Yor* 4F 101
Drinisiadar. *W Isl* 8D 171
Drinkstone. *Suff* 4B 66
Drinkstone Green. *Suff* 4B 66
Drointon. *Staf* 3E 73
Droitwich Spa. *Worc* 4C 60
Droman. *High* 3B 166
Dromore. *Arm* 5G 175
Dromore. *Ferm* 4C 174
Dron. *Per* 2D 136
Dronfield. *Derbs* 3A 86
Dronfield Woodhouse. *Derbs* 3H 85
Drongan. *E Ayr* 3D 116
Dronley. *Ang* 5C 144
Droop. *Dors* 2C 14
Drope. *V Glam* 4E 32
Droxford. *Hants* 1E 16
Droylsden. *G Man* 1C 84
Druggers End. *Worc* 2C 48
Druid. *Den* 1C 70
Druid's Heath. *W Mid* 5E 73
Druidston. *Pemb* 3C 42
Druim. *High* 3D 158
Druimarbin. *High* 1E 141
Druim Fhearna. *High* 2E 147
Druimindarroch. *High* 5E 147
Druim Saighdinis. *W Isl* 2D 170
Drum. *Per* 3C 136
Drumaness. *New M* 5H 175
Drumbeg. *High* 5B 166
Drumblade. *Abers* 4C 160
Drumbuie. *Dum* 1C 110
Drumbuie. *High* 5G 155
Drumburgh. *Cumb* 4D 112
Drumburn. *Dum* 3A 112
Drumchapel. *Glas* 2G 127
Drumchardine. *High* 4H 157
Drumchork. *High* 5C 162
Drumclog. *S Lan* 1F 117
Drumeldrie. *Fife* 3G 137
Drumelzier. *Bord* 1D 118
Drumfearn. *High* 2E 147
Drumgask. *High* 4A 150
Drumgelloch. *N Lan* 3A 128
Drumgley. *Ang* 3D 144
Drumguish. *High* 4B 150
Drumin. *Mor* 5F 159
Drumindorsair. *High* 4G 157
Drumlamford House. *S Ayr* 2H 109
Drumlasie. *Abers* 3D 152
Drumlemble. *Arg* 4A 122
Drumlithie. *Abers* 5E 153
Drummoddie. *Dum* 5A 110
Drummond. *High* 2A 158
Drummore. *Dum* 5E 109
Drummuir. *Mor* 4A 160
Drumnadrochit. *High* 5H 157
Drumnagorrach. *Mor* 3C 160
Drumnakilly. *Ferm* 4D 174
Drumoak. *Abers* 4E 153
Drumrunie. *High* 3F 163
Drumry. *W Dun* 2G 127
Drums. *Abers* 1G 153
Drumsleet. *Dum* 2G 111
Drumsmittal. *High* 4A 158
Drums of Park. *Abers* 3C 160
Drumsturdy. *Ang* 5D 145
Drumtochty Castle. *Abers* 5D 152
Drumuie. *High* 4D 154
Drumuillie. *High* 1D 150
Drumvaich. *Stir* 3F 135
Drumwhindle. *Abers* 5G 161
Drunkendub. *Ang* 4F 145
Drury. *Flin* 4E 83
Drury Square. *Norf* 4B 78
Drybeck. *Cumb* 3H 103
Drybridge. *Mor* 2B 160
Drybridge. *N Ayr* 1C 116
Drybrook. *Glos* 4B 48
Drybrook. *Here* 4A 48
Dryburgh. *Bord* 1H 119
Dry Doddington. *Linc* 1F 75
Dry Drayton. *Cambs* 4C 64
Drym. *Corn* 3D 4
Drymen. *Stir* 1F 127
Drymuir. *Abers* 4G 161
Drynachan Lodge. *High* 5C 158
Drynie Park. *High* 3H 157
Drynoch. *High* 5D 154
Dry Sandford. *Oxon* 5C 50
Dryslwyn. *Carm* 3F 45
Dry Street. *Essx* 2A 40
Dryton. *Shrp* 5H 71
Dubford. *Abers* 2E 161
Dubiton. *Abers* 3D 160
Dubton. *Ang* 3E 145
Duchally. *High* 2A 164
Duck End. *Essx* 3G 53
Duckington. *Ches W* 5G 83
Ducklington. *Oxon* 5B 50
Duckmanton. *Derbs* 3B 86
Duck Street. *Hants* 2B 24
Dudbridge. *Glos* 5D 48
Duddenhoe End. *Essx* 2E 53
Duddingston. *Edin* 2F 129
Duddington. *Nptn* 5G 75
Duddleswell. *E Sus* 3F 27
Duddo. *Nmbd* 5F 131
Duddon. *Ches W* 4H 83
Duddon Bridge. *Cumb* 1A 96
Dudleston. *Shrp* 2F 71
Dudleston Heath. *Shrp* 2F 71
Dudley. *Tyne* 2F 115
Dudley. *W Mid* 2D 60
Dudston. *Shrp* 1E 59
Dudwells. *Pemb* 2D 42
Duffield. *Derbs* 1H 73
Duffryn. *Neat* 2B 32
Dufftown. *Mor* 4H 159
Duffus. *Mor* 2F 159
Dufton. *Cumb* 2H 103
Duggleby. *N Yor* 3C 100
Duirinish. *High* 5G 155
Duisdalemore. *High* 2E 147
Duisdeil Mòr. *High* 2E 147
Duisky. *High* 1E 141
Dukesfield. *Nmbd* 4C 114
Dukestown. *Blae* 5E 47
Dukinfield. *G Man* 1D 84
Dulas. *IOA* 2D 81
Dulcote. *Som* 2A 22
Dulford. *Devn* 2D 12
Dull. *Per* 4F 143
Dullatur. *N Lan* 2A 128
Dullingham. *Cambs* 5F 65
Dullingham Ley. *Cambs* 5F 65
Dulnain Bridge. *High* 1D 151
Duloe. *Bed* 4A 64
Duloe. *Corn* 3G 7
Dulverton. *Som* 4C 20
Dulwich. *G Lon* 3E 39
Dumbarton. *W Dun* 2F 127
Dumbleton. *Glos* 2F 49
Dumfin. *Arg* 1E 127
Dumfries. *Dum* 2A 112
Dumgoyne. *Stir* 1G 127
Dummer. *Hants* 2D 24
Dumpford. *W Sus* 4G 25
Dun. *Ang* 2F 145
Dunagoil. *Arg* 4B 126
Dunalastair. *Per* 3E 142
Dunan. *High* 1D 147
Dunball. *Som* 2G 21
Dunbar. *E Lot* 2C 130
Dunbeath. *High* 5D 168
Dunbeg. *Arg* 5C 140
Dunblane. *Stir* 3G 135
Dunbog. *Fife* 2E 137
Dunbridge. *Hants* 4B 24
Duncanston. *Abers* 1C 152
Duncanston. *High* 3H 157
Dun Charlabhaigh. *W Isl* 3D 171
Dunchideock. *Devn* 4B 12
Dunchurch. *Warw* 3B 62
Duncote. *Nptn* 5D 62
Duncow. *Dum* 1A 112
Duncrievie. *Per* 3D 136
Duncton. *W Sus* 4A 26
Dundee. *D'dee* 5D 144
Dundee Airport. *D'dee* 1F 137
Dundon. *Som* 3H 21
Dundonald. *Lis* 4H 175
Dundonald. *S Ayr* 1C 116
Dundonnell. *High* 5E 163
Dundraw. *Cumb* 5D 112
Dundreggan. *High* 2F 149
Dundrennan. *Dum* 5E 111
Dundridge. *Hants* 1D 16
Dundrum. *New M* 6H 175
Dundry. *N Som* 5A 34
Dunecht. *Abers* 3E 153
Dunfermline. *Fife* 1D 129
Dunford Bridge. *S Yor* 4B 92
Dungannon. *M Ulst* 4E 174
Dungate. *Kent* 5D 40
Dunge. *Wilts* 1D 23
Dungeness. *Kent* 4E 29
Dungiven. *Caus* 2D 174
Dungworth. *S Yor* 2G 85
Dunham-on-the-Hill. *Ches W* 3G 83
Dunham-on-Trent. *Notts* 3F 87
Dunhampton. *Worc* 4C 60
Dunham Town. *G Man* 2B 84
Dunham Woodhouses. *G Man* 2B 84
Dunholme. *Linc* 3H 87
Dunino. *Fife* 2H 137
Dunipace. *Falk* 1B 128
Dunira. *Per* 1G 135
Dunkeld. *Per* 4H 143
Dunkerton. *Bath* 1C 22
Dunkeswell. *Devn* 2E 13
Dunkeswick. *N Yor* 5F 99
Dunkirk. *Kent* 5E 41
Dunkirk. *S Glo* 3C 34
Dunkirk. *Staf* 5C 84
Dunkirk. *Wilts* 5E 35
Dunk's Green. *Kent* 5H 39
Dunlappie. *Ang* 2E 145
Dunley. *Hants* 1C 24
Dunley. *Worc* 4B 60
Dunlichity Lodge. *High* 5A 158
Dunlop. *E Ayr* 5F 127
Dunloy. *Caus* 2F 175
Dunmaglass Lodge. *High* 1H 149
Dunmore. *Arg* 3F 125
Dunmore. *Falk* 1B 128
Dunmore. *High* 4H 157
Dunmurry. *Bel* 4G 175
Dunnet. *High* 1E 169
Dunnichen. *Ang* 4E 145
Dunning. *Per* 2C 136
Dunnington. *E Yor* 4F 101
Dunnington. *Warw* 5E 61
Dunnington. *York* 4A 100
Dunningwell. *Cumb* 1A 96
Dunnockshaw. *Lanc* 2G 91
Dunoon. *Arg* 2C 126
Dunphail. *Mor* 4E 159
Dunragit. *Dum* 4G 109
Dunrostan. *Arg* 1F 125
Duns. *Bord* 4D 130
Dunsby. *Linc* 3A 76
Dunscar. *G Man* 3F 91
Dunscore. *Dum* 1F 111
Dunscroft. *S Yor* 4G 93
Dunsdale. *Red C* 3D 106
Dunsden Green. *Oxon* 4F 37
Dunsfold. *Surr* 2B 26
Dunsford. *Devn* 4B 12
Dunshalt. *Fife* 2E 137
Dunshillock. *Abers* 4G 161
Dunsley. *N Yor* 3F 107
Dunsley. *Staf* 2C 60
Dunsmore. *Buck* 5G 51
Dunsop Bridge. *Lanc* 4F 97
Dunstable. *C Beds* 3A 52
Dunstal. *Staf* 3E 73
Dunstall. *Staf* 3F 73
Dunstall Green. *Suff* 4G 65
Dunstall Hill. *W Mid* 5D 72
Dunstan. *Nmbd* 3G 121
Dunster. *Som* 2C 20
Duns Tew. *Oxon* 3C 50
Dunston. *Linc* 4H 87
Dunston. *Norf* 5E 79
Dunston. *Staf* 4D 72
Dunston. *Tyne* 3F 115

Dunstone—East Lyng

Dunstone. Devn 3B 8
Dunston Heath. Staf 4D 72
Dunsville. S Yor 4G 93
Dunswell. E Yor 1D 94
Dunsyre. S Lan 5D 128
Dunterton. Devn 5D 11
Duntisbourne Abbots. Glos 5E 49
Duntisbourne Leer. Glos 5E 49
Duntisbourne Rouse. Glos 5E 49
Duntish. Dors 2B 14
Duntocher. W Dun 2F 127
Dunton. Buck 3G 51
Dunton. C Beds 1C 52
Dunton. Norf 2A 78
Dunton Bassett. Leics 1C 62
Dunton Green. Kent 5G 39
Dunton Patch. Norf 2A 78
Duntulm. High 1D 154
Dunure. S Ayr 3B 116
Dunvant. Swan 3E 31
Dunvegan. High 4B 154
Dunwich. Suff 3G 67
Dunwood. Staf 5D 84
Durdar. Cumb 4F 113
Durgates. E Sus 2H 27
Durham. Dur 5F 115
Durham Tees Valley Airport. Darl 3A 106
Durisdeer. Dum 4A 118
Durisdeermill. Dum 4A 118
Durkar. W Yor 3D 92
Durleigh. Som 3F 21
Durley. Hants 1D 16
Durley. Wilts 5H 35
Durley Street. Hants 1D 16
Durlow Common. Here 2B 48
Durnamuck. High 4E 163
Durness. High 2E 166
Durno. Abers 1E 152
Durns Town. Hants 3A 16
Duror. High 3D 141
Durran. Arg 3G 133
Durran. High 2D 169
Durrant Green. Kent 2C 28
Durrants. Hants 1F 17
Durrington. W Sus 5C 26
Durrington. Wilts 2G 23
Dursley. Glos 2C 34
Dursley Cross. Glos 4B 48
Durston. Som 4F 21
Durweston. Dors 2D 14
Dury. Shet 6F 173
Duston. Nptn 4E 63
Duthil. High 1D 150
Dutlas. Powy 3E 58
Duton Hill. Essx 3G 53
Dutson. Corn 4D 10
Dutton. Ches W 3H 83
Duxford. Cambs 1E 53
Duxford. Oxon 2B 36
Dwygyfylchi. Cnwy 3G 81
Dwyran. IOA 4D 80
Dyce. Aber 2F 153
Dyffryn. B'end 2B 32
Dyffryn. Carm 2H 43
Dyffryn. Pemb 1D 42
Dyffryn. V Glam 4D 32
Dyffryn Ardudwy. Gwyn 3E 69
Dyffryn Castell. Cdgn 2G 57
Dyffryn Ceidrych. Carm 3H 45
Dyffryn Cellwen. Neat 5B 46
Dyke. Linc 3A 76
Dyke. Mor 3D 159
Dykehead. Ang 2C 144
Dykehead. N Lan 3B 128
Dykehead. Stir 4E 135
Dykend. Ang 3B 144
Dykesfield. Cumb 4E 112
Dylife. Powy 1A 58
Dymchurch. Kent 3F 29
Dymock. Glos 2C 48
Dyrham. S Glo 4C 34
Dysart. Fife 4F 137
Dyserth. Den 3C 82

E

Eachwick. Nmbd 2E 115
Eadar Dha Fhadhail. W Isl 4C 171
Eagland Hill. Lanc 5D 96
Eagle. Linc 4F 87
Eagle Barnsdale. Linc 4F 87
Eagle Moor. Linc 4F 87
Eaglescliffe. Stoc T 3B 106
Eaglesfield. Cumb 2B 102
Eaglesfield. Dum 2D 112
Eaglesham. E Ren 4G 127
Eaglethorpe. Nptn 1H 63
Eagley. G Man 3F 91
Eairy. IOM 4B 108
Eakley Lanes. Mil 5F 63
Eakring. Notts 4D 86
Ealand. N Lin 3A 94
Ealing. G Lon 2C 38
Eallabus. Arg 3B 124
Eals. Nmbd 4H 113
Eamont Bridge. Cumb 2G 103
Earby. Lanc 5B 98
Earcroft. Bkbn 2E 91
Eardington. Shrp 1B 60
Eardisland. Here 5G 59
Eardisley. Here 1G 47
Eardiston. Shrp 3F 71
Eardiston. Worc 4A 60
Earith. Cambs 3C 64
Earlais. High 2C 154
Earle. Nmbd 2D 121
Earlesfield. Linc 2G 75
Earlestown. Mers 1H 83
Earley. Wok 4F 37
Earlham. Norf 5D 78
Earlish. High 2C 154
Earls Barton. Nptn 4F 63
Earls Colne. Essx 3B 54
Earls Common. Worc 5D 60
Earl's Croome. Worc 1D 48
Earlsdon. W Mid 3H 61
Earlsferry. Fife 3G 137
Earlsford. Abers 5F 161
Earl's Green. Suff 4C 66
Earlsheaton. W Yor 2C 92
Earl Shilton. Leics 1B 62
Earl Soham. Suff 4E 67
Earl Sterndale. Derbs 4E 85
Earlston. E Ayr 1D 116
Earlston. Bord 1H 119
Earl Stonham. Suff 5D 66
Earlstoun. Dum 1D 110
Earlswood. Mon 2H 33
Earlswood. Warw 3F 61
Earlyvale. Bord 4F 129
Earnley. W Sus 3G 17
Earsairidh. W Isl 9C 170
Earsdon. Tyne 2G 115
Earsham. Norf 2F 67
Earsham Street. Suff 3E 67
Earswick. York 4A 100
Eartham. W Sus 5A 26
Earthcott Green. S Glo 3B 34
Easby. N Yor 4C 106 (nr. Great Ayton)
Easby. N Yor 4E 105 (nr. Richmond)
Easdale. Arg 2E 133
Easebourne. W Sus 4G 25
Easenhall. Warw 3B 62
Eashing. Surr 1A 26
Easington. Buck 4E 51
Easington. Dur 5H 115
Easington. E Yor 3G 95
Easington. Nmbd 1F 121
Easington. Oxon 2C 50 (nr. Banbury)
Easington. Oxon 2E 37 (nr. Watlington)
Easington. Red C 3E 107
Easington Colliery. Dur 5H 115
Easington Lane. Tyne 5G 115
Easingwold. N Yor 2H 99
Eassie. Ang 4C 144
Eassie and Nevay. Ang 4C 144
East Aberthaw. V Glam 5D 32
Eastacombe. Devn 4F 19
Eastacott. Devn 4G 19
East Allington. Devn 4D 8
East Anstey. Devn 4B 20
East Anton. Hants 2B 24
East Appleton. N Yor 5F 105
East Ardsley. W Yor 2D 92
East Ashley. Devn 1G 11
East Ashling. W Sus 2G 17
East Aston. Hants 2C 24
East Ayton. N Yor 1D 101
East Barkwith. Linc 2A 88
East Barnby. N Yor 3F 107
East Barnet. G Lon 1D 39
East Barns. E Lot 2D 130
East Barsham. Norf 2B 78
East Beach. W Sus 3G 17
East Beckham. Norf 2D 78
East Bedfont. G Lon 3B 38
East Bennan. N Ayr 3D 123
East Bergholt. Suff 2D 54
East Bierley. W Yor 2C 92
East Bilney. Norf 4B 78
East Blatchington. E Sus 5F 27
East Bloxworth. Dors 3D 15
East Boldre. Hants 2B 16
East Bolton. Nmbd 3F 121
Eastbourne. Darl 3F 105
Eastbourne. E Sus 5H 27
East Brent. Som 1G 21
East Bridge. Suff 4G 67
East Bridgford. Notts 1D 74
East Briscoe. Dur 3C 104
East Buckland. Devn 3G 19 (nr. Barnstaple)
East Buckland. Devn 4C 8 (nr. Thurlestone)
East Budleigh. Devn 4D 12
Eastburn. W Yor 5C 98
East Burnham. Buck 2A 38
East Burrafirth. Shet 6E 173
East Burton. Dors 4D 14
Eastbury. Herts 1B 38
Eastbury. W Ber 4B 36
East Butsfield. Dur 5E 115
East Butterleigh. Devn 2C 12
East Butterwick. N Lin 4B 94
Eastby. N Yor 4C 98
East Calder. W Lot 3D 129
East Carleton. Norf 5D 78
East Carlton. Nptn 2F 63
East Carlton. W Yor 5E 98
East Chaldon. Dors 4C 14
East Challow. Oxon 3B 36
East Charleton. Devn 4D 8
East Chelborough. Dors 2A 14
East Chiltington. E Sus 4E 27
East Chinnock. Som 1H 13
East Chisenbury. Wilts 1G 23
Eastchurch. Kent 3D 40
East Clandon. Surr 5B 38
East Claydon. Buck 3F 51
East Clevedon. N Som 4H 33
East Clyne. High 3F 165
East Clyth. High 5E 169
East Coker. Som 1A 14
Eastcombe. Glos 5D 49
East Combe. Som 3E 21
East Common. N Yor 1G 93
East Compton. Som 2B 22
East Cornworthy. Devn 3E 9
Eastcote. G Lon 2C 38
Eastcote. Nptn 5D 62
Eastcote. W Mid 3F 61
Eastcott. Corn 1C 10
Eastcott. Wilts 1F 23
East Cottingwith. E Yor 5B 100
Eastcourt. Wilts 5H 35 (nr. Pewsey)
Eastcourt. Wilts 2E 35 (nr. Tetbury)
East Cowes. IOW 3D 16
East Cowick. E Yor 2G 93
East Cowton. N Yor 4A 106
East Cramlington. Nmbd 2F 115
East Cranmore. Som 2B 22
East Creech. Dors 4E 15
East Croachy. High 1A 150
East Dean. E Sus 5G 27
East Dean. Glos 3B 48
East Dean. Hants 4A 24
East Dean. W Sus 4A 26
East Down. Devn 2G 19
East Drayton. Notts 3E 87
East Dundry. N Som 5A 34
East Ella. Hull 2D 94
East End. Cambs 3C 64
East End. Dors 3E 15
East End. E Yor 4F 101 (nr. Ulrome)
East End. E Yor 2F 95 (nr. Withernsea)
East End. Hants 3B 16 (nr. Lymington)
East End. Hants 5C 36 (nr. Newbury)
East End. Herts 3E 53
East End. Kent 3D 40 (nr. Minster)
East End. Kent 2C 28 (nr. Tenterden)
East End. N Som 4H 33
East End. Oxon 4B 50
East End. Som 1A 22
East End. Suff 2E 54
Easter Ardross. High 1A 158
Easter Balgedie. Per 3D 136
Easter Balmoral. Abers 4G 151
Easter Brae. High 2A 158
Easter Buckieburn. Stir 1A 128
Easter Bush. Midl 3F 129
Easter Compton. S Glo 3A 34
Easter Fearn. High 5D 164
Easter Galcantray. High 4C 158
Eastergate. W Sus 5A 26
Easterhouse. Glas 3H 127
Easter Howgate. Midl 3F 129
Easter Kinkell. High 3H 157
Easter Lednathie. Ang 2C 144
Easter Ogil. Ang 2D 144
Easter Ord. Abers 3F 153
Easter Quarff. Shet 8F 173
Easter Rhynd. Per 2D 136
Easter Skeld. Shet 7E 173
Easter Suddie. High 3A 158
Easterton. Wilts 1F 23
Eastertown. Som 1G 21
Easter Tulloch. Abers 1G 145
East Everleigh. Wilts 1H 23
East Farleigh. Kent 5B 40
East Farndon. Nptn 2E 62
East Ferry. Linc 1F 87
Eastfield. N Lan 3B 128 (nr. Caldercruix)
Eastfield. N Lan 3B 128 (nr. Harthill)
Eastfield. N Yor 1E 101
Eastfield. S Lan 3H 127
Eastfield Hall. Nmbd 4G 121
East Fortune. E Lot 2B 130
East Garforth. W Yor 1E 93
East Garston. W Ber 4B 36
Eastgate. Dur 1C 104
Eastgate. Norf 3D 78
East Ginge. Oxon 3C 36
East Gores. Essx 3B 54
East Goscote. Leics 4D 74
East Grafton. Wilts 5A 36
East Green. Suff 5F 65
East Grimstead. Wilts 4H 23
East Grinstead. W Sus 2E 27
East Guldeford. E Sus 3D 28
East Haddon. Nptn 4D 62
East Hagbourne. Oxon 3D 36
East Halton. N Lin 2E 95
East Ham. G Lon 2F 39
Eastham. Mers 2F 83
Eastham. Worc 4A 60
Eastham Ferry. Mers 2F 83
Easthampstead. Brac 5G 37
Easthampton. Here 4G 59
East Hanney. Oxon 2C 36
East Hanningfield. Essx 5A 54
East Hardwick. W Yor 3E 93
East Harling. Norf 2B 66
East Harlsey. N Yor 5B 106
East Harnham. Wilts 4G 23
East Harptree. Bath 1A 22
East Hartford. Nmbd 2F 115
East Harting. W Sus 1G 17
East Hatch. Wilts 4E 23
East Hatley. Cambs 5B 64
Easthaugh. Norf 4C 78
East Hauxwell. N Yor 5E 105
East Haven. Ang 5E 145
Eastheath. Wok 5G 37
East Heckington. Linc 1A 76
East Hedleyhope. Dur 5E 115
East Helmsdale. High 2H 165
East Hendred. Oxon 3C 36
East Heslerton. N Yor 2D 100
East Hoathly. E Sus 4G 27
East Holme. Dors 4D 15
Easthope. Shrp 1H 59
Easthorpe. Essx 3C 54
Easthorpe. Leics 2F 75
East Horrington. Som 2A 22
East Horsley. Surr 5B 38
East Horton. Nmbd 1E 121
Easthouses. Midl 3G 129
East Howe. Bour 3F 15
East Huntspill. Som 2G 21
East Hyde. C Beds 4B 52
East Ilsley. W Ber 3C 36
Eastington. Devn 2H 11
Eastington. Glos 4G 49 (nr. Northleach)
Eastington. Glos 5C 48 (nr. Stonehouse)
East Keal. Linc 4C 88
East Kennett. Wilts 5G 35
East Keswick. W Yor 5F 99
East Kilbride. S Lan 4H 127
East Kirkby. Linc 4C 88
East Knapton. N Yor 2C 100
East Knighton. Dors 4D 14
East Knowstone. Devn 4B 20
East Knoyle. Wilts 3D 23
East Kyloe. Nmbd 1E 121
East Lambrook. Som 1H 13
East Langdon. Kent 1H 29
East Langton. Leics 1E 63
East Langwell. High 3E 164
East Lavant. W Sus 2G 17
East Lavington. W Sus 4A 26
East Layton. N Yor 4E 105
Eastleach Martin. Glos 5H 49
Eastleach Turville. Glos 5G 49
East Leake. Notts 3C 74
East Learmouth. Nmbd 1C 120
Eastleigh. Devn 4E 19 (nr. Bideford)
East Leigh. Devn 2G 11 (nr. Crediton)
East Leigh. Devn 3C 8 (nr. Modbury)
Eastleigh. Hants 1C 16
East Lexham. Norf 4A 78
East Lilburn. Nmbd 2E 121
Eastling. Kent 5D 40
East Linton. E Lot 2B 130
East Liss. Hants 4F 25
East Lockinge. Oxon 3C 36
East Looe. Corn 3G 7
East Lound. N Lin 1E 87
East Lulworth. Dors 4D 14
East Lutton. N Yor 3D 100
East Lydford. Som 3A 22
East Lyng. Som 4G 21

East Mains—Elstone

East Mains. *Abers* 4D **152**
East Malling. *Kent* 5B **40**
East Marden. *W Sus* 1G **17**
East Markham. *Notts* 3E **87**
East Marton. *N Yor* 4B **98**
East Meon. *Hants* 4E **25**
East Mersea. *Essx* 4D **54**
East Mey. *High* 1F **169**
East Midlands Airport. *Leics* 3B **74**
East Molesey. *Surr* 4C **38**
Eastmoor. *Norf* 5G **77**
East Morden. *Dors* 3E **15**
East Morton. *W Yor* 5D **98**
East Ness. *N Yor* 2A **100**
East Newton. *E Yor* 1F **95**
East Newton. *N Yor* 2A **100**
Eastney. *Port* 3E **17**
Eastnor. *Here* 2C **48**
East Norton. *Leics* 5E **75**
East Nynehead. *Som* 4E **21**
East Oakley. *Hants* 1D **24**
Eastoft. *N Lin* 3B **94**
East Ogwell. *Devn* 5B **12**
Easton. *Cambs* 3A **64**
Easton. *Cumb* 4D **112**
(nr. Burgh by Sands)
Easton. *Cumb* 2F **113**
(nr. Longtown)
Easton. *Devn* 4H **11**
Easton. *Dors* 5B **14**
Easton. *Hants* 3D **24**
Easton. *Linc* 3G **75**
Easton. *Norf* 4D **78**
Easton. *Som* 2A **22**
Easton. *Suff* 5E **67**
Easton. *Wilts* 4D **35**
Easton Grey. *Wilts* 3D **35**
Easton-in-Gordano. *N Som* 4A **34**
Easton Maudit. *Nptn* 5F **63**
Easton on the Hill. *Nptn* 5H **75**
Easton Royal. *Wilts* 5H **35**
East Orchard. *Dors* 1D **14**
East Ord. *Nmbd* 4F **131**
East Panson. *Devn* 3D **10**
East Peckham. *Kent* 1A **28**
East Pennard. *Som* 3A **22**
East Perry. *Cambs* 4A **64**
East Pitcorthie. *Fife* 3H **137**
East Portlemouth. *Devn* 5D **8**
East Prawle. *Devn* 5D **9**
East Preston. *W Sus* 5B **26**
East Putford. *Devn* 1D **10**
East Quantoxhead. *Som* 2E **21**
East Rainton. *Tyne* 5G **115**
East Ravendale. *NE Lin* 1B **88**
East Raynham. *Norf* 3A **78**
Eastrea. *Cambs* 1B **64**
East Rhidorroch Lodge. *High* 4G **163**
Eastriggs. *Dum* 3D **112**
East Rigton. *W Yor* 5F **99**
Eastrington. *E Yor* 2A **94**
East Rounton. *N Yor* 4B **106**
East Row. *N Yor* 3F **107**
East Rudham. *Norf* 3H **77**
East Runton. *Norf* 1D **78**
East Ruston. *Norf* 3F **79**
Eastry. *Kent* 5H **41**
East Saltoun. *E Lot* 3A **130**
East Shaws. *Dur* 3D **105**
East Shefford. *W Ber* 4B **36**
Eastshore. *Shet* 10E **173**
East Sleekburn. *Nmbd* 1F **115**
East Somerton. *Norf* 4G **79**
East Stockwith. *Linc* 1E **87**
East Stoke. *Dors* 4D **14**
East Stoke. *Notts* 1E **75**
East Stoke. *Som* 1H **13**
East Stour. *Dors* 4D **22**
East Stourmouth. *Kent* 4G **41**
East Stowford. *Devn* 4G **19**
East Stratton. *Hants* 2D **24**
East Studdal. *Kent* 1H **29**
East Taphouse. *Corn* 2F **7**
East-the-Water. *Devn* 4E **19**
East Thirston. *Nmbd* 5F **121**
East Tilbury. *Thur* 3A **40**
East Tisted. *Hants* 3F **25**
East Torrington. *Linc* 2A **88**
East Tuddenham. *Norf* 4C **78**
East Tytherley. *Hants* 4A **24**
East Tytherton. *Wilts* 4E **35**
East Village. *Devn* 2B **12**
Eastville. *Linc* 5D **88**
East Wall. *Shrp* 1H **59**
East Walton. *Norf* 4G **77**
East Week. *Devn* 3G **11**
Eastwell. *Leics* 3E **75**
East Wellow. *Hants* 4B **24**
East Wemyss. *Fife* 4F **137**
East Whitburn. *W Lot* 3C **128**
Eastwick. *Herts* 4E **53**
Eastwick. *Shet* 4E **173**
East Williamston. *Pemb* 4E **43**
East Winch. *Norf* 4F **77**
East Winterslow. *Wilts* 3H **23**
East Wittering. *W Sus* 3F **17**
East Witton. *N Yor* 1D **98**
Eastwood. *Notts* 1B **74**
Eastwood. *S'end* 2C **40**
East Woodburn. *Nmbd* 1C **114**
Eastwood End. *Cambs* 1D **64**
East Woodhay. *Hants* 5C **36**
East Woodlands. *Som* 2C **22**
East Worldham. *Hants* 3F **25**
East Worlington. *Devn* 1A **12**
East Wretham. *Norf* 1B **66**
East Youlstone. *Devn* 1C **10**
Eathorpe. *Warw* 4A **62**
Eaton. *Ches E* 4C **84**
Eaton. *Ches W* 4H **83**
Eaton. *Leics* 3E **75**
Eaton. *Norf* 2F **77**
(nr. Heacham)
Eaton. *Norf* 5E **78**
(nr. Norwich)
Eaton. *Notts* 3E **86**
Eaton. *Oxon* 5C **50**
Eaton. *Shrp* 2F **59**
(nr. Bishop's Castle)
Eaton. *Shrp* 2H **59**
(nr. Church Stretton)
Eaton Bishop. *Here* 2H **47**
Eaton Bray. *C Beds* 3H **51**
Eaton Constantine. *Shrp* 5H **71**
Eaton Hastings. *Oxon* 2A **36**
Eaton Socon. *Cambs* 5A **64**
Eaton upon Tern. *Shrp* 3A **72**
Eau Brink. *Norf* 4E **77**
Eaves Green. *W Mid* 2G **61**
Ebberley Hill. *Devn* 1F **11**
Ebberston. *N Yor* 1C **100**
Ebbesbourne Wake. *Wilts* 4E **23**
Ebblake. *Dors* 2G **15**
Ebbsfleet. *Kent* 3H **39**
Ebbw Vale. *Blae* 5E **47**
Ebchester. *Dur* 4E **115**
Ebernoe. *W Sus* 3A **26**
Ebford. *Devn* 4C **12**
Ebley. *Glos* 5D **48**
Ebnal. *Ches W* 1G **71**
Ebrington. *Glos* 1G **49**
Ecchinswell. *Hants* 1D **24**
Ecclefechan. *Dum* 2C **112**
Eccles. *G Man* 1B **84**
Eccles. *Kent* 4B **40**
Eccles. *Bord* 5D **130**
Ecclesall. *S Yor* 2H **85**
Ecclesfield. *S Yor* 1A **86**
Eccles Green. *Here* 1G **47**
Eccleshall. *Staf* 3C **72**
Eccleshill. *W Yor* 1B **92**
Ecclesmachan. *W Lot* 2D **128**
Eccles on Sea. *Norf* 3G **79**
Eccles Road. *Norf* 1C **66**
Eccleston. *Ches W* 4G **83**
Eccleston. *Lanc* 3D **90**
Eccleston. *Mers* 1G **83**
Eccup. *W Yor* 5E **99**
Echt. *Abers* 3E **153**
Eckford. *Bord* 2B **120**
Eckington. *Derbs* 3B **86**
Eckington. *Worc* 1E **49**
Ecton. *Nptn* 4F **63**
Edale. *Derbs* 2F **85**
Eday Airport. *Orkn* 4E **172**
Edburton. *W Sus* 4D **26**
Edderside. *Cumb* 5C **112**
Edderton. *High* 5E **164**
Eddington. *Kent* 4F **41**
Eddington. *W Ber* 5B **36**
Eddleston. *Bord* 5F **129**
Eddlewood. *S Lan* 4A **128**
Edenbridge. *Kent* 1F **27**
Edendonich. *Arg* 1A **134**
Edenfield. *Lanc* 3F **91**
Edenhall. *Cumb* 1G **103**
Edenham. *Linc* 3H **75**
Edensor. *Derbs* 4G **85**
Edentaggart. *Arg* 4C **134**
Edenthorpe. *S Yor* 4G **93**
Eden Vale. *Dur* 1B **106**
Edern. *Gwyn* 2B **68**
Edgarley. *Som* 3A **22**
Edgbaston. *W Mid* 2E **61**
Edgcott. *Buck* 3E **51**
Edgcott. *Som* 3B **20**
Edge. *Glos* 5D **48**
Edge. *Shrp* 5F **71**
Edgebolton. *Shrp* 3H **71**
Edge End. *Glos* 4A **48**
Edgefield. *Norf* 2C **78**
Edgefield Street. *Norf* 2C **78**
Edge Green. *Ches W* 5G **83**
Edgehead. *Midl* 3G **129**
Edgeley. *Shrp* 1H **71**
Edgeside. *Lanc* 2G **91**
Edgeworth. *Glos* 5E **49**
Edgiock. *Worc* 4E **61**
Edgmond. *Telf* 4B **72**
Edgmond Marsh. *Telf* 3B **72**
Edgton. *Shrp* 2F **59**
Edgware. *G Lon* 1C **38**
Edgworth. *Bkbn* 3F **91**
Edinbane. *High* 3C **154**
Edinburgh. *Edin* 2F **129**
Edinburgh Airport. *Edin* 2E **129**
Edingale. *Staf* 4G **73**
Edingley. *Notts* 5D **86**
Edingthorpe. *Norf* 2F **79**
Edington. *Som* 3G **21**
Edington. *Wilts* 1E **23**
Edingworth. *Som* 1G **21**
Edistone. *Devn* 4C **18**
Edithmead. *Som* 2G **21**
Edith Weston. *Rut* 5G **75**
Edlaston. *Derbs* 1F **73**
Edlesborough. *Buck* 4H **51**
Edlingham. *Nmbd* 4F **121**
Edlington. *Linc* 3B **88**
Edmondsham. *Dors* 1F **15**
Edmondsley. *Dur* 5F **115**
Edmondthorpe. *Leics* 4F **75**
Edmonstone. *Orkn* 5E **172**
Edmonton. *Corn* 1D **6**
Edmonton. *G Lon* 1E **39**
Edmundbyers. *Dur* 4D **114**
Ednam. *Bord* 1B **120**
Ednaston. *Derbs* 1G **73**
Edney Common. *Essx* 5G **53**
Edrom. *Bord* 4E **131**
Edstaston. *Shrp* 2H **71**
Edstone. *Warw* 4F **61**
Edwalton. *Notts* 2C **74**
Edwardstone. *Suff* 1C **54**
Edwardsville. *Mer T* 2D **32**
Edwinsford. *Carm* 2G **45**
Edwinstowe. *Notts* 4D **86**
Edworth. *C Beds* 1C **52**
Edwyn Ralph. *Here* 5A **60**
Edzell. *Ang* 2F **145**
Efail-fach. *Neat* 2A **32**
Efail Isaf. *Rhon* 3D **32**
Efailnewydd. *Gwyn* 2C **68**
Efail-rhyd. *Powy* 3D **70**
Efailwen. *Carm* 2F **43**
Efenechtyd. *Den* 5D **82**
Effingham. *Surr* 5C **38**
Effingham Common. *Surr* 5C **38**
Effirth. *Shet* 6E **173**
Efflinch. *Staf* 4F **73**
Efford. *Devn* 2B **12**
Efstigarth. *Shet* 2F **173**
Egbury. *Hants* 1C **24**
Egdon. *Worc* 5D **60**
Egerton. *G Man* 3F **91**
Egerton. *Kent* 1D **28**
Egerton Forstal. *Kent* 1C **28**
Eggborough. *N Yor* 2F **93**
Eggbuckland. *Plym* 3A **8**
Eggesford. *Devn* 1G **11**
Eggington. *C Beds* 3H **51**
Egginton. *Derbs* 3G **73**
Egglescliffe. *Stoc T* 3B **106**
Eggleston. *Dur* 2C **104**
Egham. *Surr* 3B **38**
Egham Hythe. *Surr* 3B **38**
Egleton. *Rut* 5F **75**
Eglingham. *Nmbd* 3F **121**
Eglinton. *Derr* 1D **174**
Egloshayle. *Corn* 5A **10**
Egloskerry. *Corn* 4C **10**
Eglwysbach. *Cnwy* 3H **81**
Eglwys-Brewis. *V Glam* 5D **32**
Eglwys Fach. *Cdgn* 1F **57**
Eglwyswrw. *Pemb* 1F **43**
Egmanton. *Notts* 4E **87**
Egmere. *Norf* 2B **78**
Egremont. *Cumb* 3B **102**
Egremont. *Mers* 1F **83**
Egton. *N Yor* 4F **107**
Egton Bridge. *N Yor* 4F **107**
Egypt. *Buck* 2A **38**
Egypt. *Hants* 2C **24**
Eight Ash Green. *Essx* 3C **54**
Eight Mile Burn. *Midl* 4E **129**
Eignaig. *High* 4B **140**
Eilanreach. *High* 2G **147**
Eildon. *Bord* 1H **119**
Eileanach Lodge. *High* 2H **157**
Eilean Fhlodaigh. *W Isl* 3D **170**
Eilean Iarmain. *High* 2F **147**
Einacleit. *W Isl* 5D **171**
Eisgein. *W Isl* 6F **171**
Eisingrug. *Gwyn* 2F **69**
Elan Village. *Powy* 4B **58**
Elberton. *S Glo* 3B **34**
Elbridge. *W Sus* 5A **26**
Elburton. *Plym* 3B **8**
Elcho. *Per* 1D **136**
Elcombe. *Swin* 3G **35**
Elcot. *W Ber* 5B **36**
Eldernell. *Cambs* 1C **64**
Eldersfield. *Worc* 2D **48**
Elderslie. *Ren* 3F **127**
Elder Street. *Essx* 2F **53**
Eldon. *Dur* 2F **105**
Eldroth. *N Yor* 3G **97**
Eldwick. *W Yor* 5D **98**
Elfhowe. *Cumb* 5F **103**
Elford. *Nmbd* 1F **121**
Elford. *Staf* 4F **73**
Elford Closes. *Cambs* 3D **65**
Elgin. *Mor* 2G **159**
Elgol. *High* 2D **146**
Elham. *Kent* 1F **29**
Elie. *Fife* 3G **137**
Eling. *Hants* 1B **16**
Eling. *W Ber* 4D **36**
Elishaw. *Nmbd* 5C **120**
Elizafield. *Dum* 2B **112**
Elkesley. *Notts* 3D **86**
Elkington. *Nptn* 3D **62**
Elkins Green. *Essx* 5G **53**
Elkstone. *Glos* 4E **49**
Ellan. *High* 1C **150**
Elland. *W Yor* 2B **92**
Ellary. *Arg* 2F **125**
Ellastone. *Staf* 1F **73**
Ellbridge. *Corn* 2A **8**
Ellel. *Lanc* 4D **97**
Ellemford. *Bord* 3D **130**
Ellenabeich. *Arg* 2E **133**
Ellenborough. *Cumb* 1B **102**
Ellenbrook. *Herts* 5C **52**
Ellenhall. *Staf* 3C **72**
Ellen's Green. *Surr* 2B **26**
Ellerbeck. *N Yor* 5B **106**
Ellerburn. *N Yor* 1C **100**
Ellerby. *N Yor* 3E **107**
Ellerdine. *Telf* 3A **72**
Ellerdine Heath. *Telf* 3A **72**
Ellerhayes. *Devn* 2C **12**
Elleric. *Arg* 4E **141**
Ellerker. *E Yor* 2C **94**
Ellerton. *E Yor* 1H **93**
Ellerton. *N Yor* 5F **105**
Ellerton. *Shrp* 3B **72**
Ellesborough. *Buck* 5G **51**
Ellesmere. *Shrp* 2G **71**
Ellesmere Port. *Ches W* 3G **83**
Ellingham. *Hants* 2G **15**
Ellingham. *Norf* 1F **67**
Ellingham. *Nmbd* 2F **121**
Ellingstring. *N Yor* 1D **98**
Ellington. *Cambs* 3A **64**
Ellington. *Nmbd* 5G **121**
Ellington Thorpe. *Cambs* 3A **64**
Elliot. *Ang* 5F **145**
Ellisfield. *Hants* 2E **25**
Ellishadder. *High* 2E **155**
Ellistown. *Leics* 4B **74**
Ellon. *Abers* 5G **161**
Ellonby. *Cumb* 1F **103**
Ellough. *Suff* 2G **67**
Elloughton. *E Yor* 2C **94**
Ellwood. *Glos* 5A **48**
Elm. *Cambs* 5D **76**
Elmbridge. *Glos* 4D **48**
Elmbridge. *Worc* 4D **60**
Elmdon. *Essx* 2E **53**
Elmdon. *W Mid* 2F **61**
Elmdon Heath. *W Mid* 2F **61**
Elmesthorpe. *Leics* 1B **62**
Elmfield. *IOW* 3E **16**
Elm Hill. *Dors* 4D **22**
Elmhurst. *Staf* 4F **73**
Elmley Castle. *Worc* 1E **49**
Elmley Lovett. *Worc* 4C **60**
Elmore. *Glos* 4C **48**
Elmore Back. *Glos* 4C **48**
Elm Park. *G Lon* 2G **39**
Elmscott. *Devn* 4C **18**
Elmsett. *Suff* 1D **54**
Elmstead. *Essx* 3D **54**
Elmstead Heath. *Essx* 3D **54**
Elmstead Market. *Essx* 3D **54**
Elmsted. *Kent* 1F **29**
Elmstone. *Kent* 4G **41**
Elmstone Hardwicke. *Glos* 3E **49**
Elmswell. *E Yor* 4D **101**
Elmswell. *Suff* 4B **66**
Elmton. *Derbs* 3C **86**
Elphin. *High* 2G **163**
Elphinstone. *E Lot* 2G **129**
Elrick. *Abers* 3F **153**
Elrick. *Mor* 1B **152**
Elrig. *Dum* 5A **110**
Elsdon. *Nmbd* 5D **120**
Elsecar. *S Yor* 1A **86**
Elsenham. *Essx* 3F **53**
Elsfield. *Oxon* 4D **50**
Elsham. *N Lin* 3D **94**
Elsing. *Norf* 4C **78**
Elslack. *N Yor* 5B **98**
Elsrickle. *S Lan* 5D **128**
Elstead. *Surr* 1A **26**
Elsted. *W Sus* 1G **17**
Elsted Marsh. *W Sus* 4G **25**
Elsthorpe. *Linc* 3H **75**
Elstob. *Dur* 2A **106**
Elston. *Devn* 2A **12**
Elston. *Lanc* 1E **90**
Elston. *Notts* 1E **75**
Elston. *Wilts* 2F **23**
Elstone. *Devn* 1G **11**

Elstow—Farr

Elstow. *Bed* 1A 52
Elstree. *Herts* 1C 38
Elstronwick. *E Yor* 1F 95
Elswick. *Lanc* 1C 90
Elswick. *Tyne* 3F 115
Elsworth. *Cambs* 4C 64
Elterwater. *Cumb* 4E 103
Eltham. *G Lon* 3F 39
Eltisley. *Cambs* 5B 64
Elton. *Cambs* 1H 63
Elton. *Ches W* 3G 83
Elton. *Derbs* 4G 85
Elton. *Glos* 4C 48
Elton. *G Man* 3F 91
Elton. *Here* 3G 59
Elton. *Notts* 2E 75
Elton. *Stoc T* 3B 106
Elton Green. *Ches W* 3G 83
Eltringham. *Nmbd* 3D 115
Elvanfoot. *S Lan* 3B 118
Elvaston. *Derbs* 2B 74
Elveden. *Suff* 3H 65
Elvetham Heath. *Hants* 1F 25
Elvingston. *E Lot* 2A 130
Elvington. *Kent* 5G 41
Elvington. *York* 5B 100
Elwick. *Hart* 1B 106
Elwick. *Nmbd* 1F 121
Elworth. *Ches E* 4B 84
Elworth. *Dors* 4A 14
Elworthy. *Som* 3D 20
Ely. *Cambs* 2E 65
Ely. *Card* 4E 33
Emberton. *Mil* 1G 51
Embleton. *Cumb* 1C 102
Embleton. *Dur* 2B 106
Embleton. *Nmbd* 2G 121
Embo. *High* 4F 165
Emborough. *Som* 1B 22
Embo Street. *High* 4F 165
Embsay. *N Yor* 4C 98
Emery Down. *Hants* 2A 16
Emley. *W Yor* 3C 92
Emmbrook. *Wok* 5F 37
Emmer Green. *Read* 4F 37
Emmington. *Oxon* 5F 51
Emneth. *Norf* 5D 77
Emneth Hungate. *Norf* 5E 77
Empingham. *Rut* 5G 75
Empshott. *Hants* 3F 25
Emsworth. *Hants* 2F 17
Enborne. *W Ber* 5C 36
Enborne Row. *W Ber* 5C 36
Enchmarsh. *Shrp* 1H 59
Enderby. *Leics* 1C 62
Endmoor. *Cumb* 1E 97
Endon. *Staf* 5D 84
Endon Bank. *Staf* 5D 84
Enfield. *G Lon* 1E 39
Enfield Wash. *G Lon* 1E 39
Enford. *Wilts* 1G 23
Engine Common. *S Glo* 3B 34
Englefield. *W Ber* 4E 37
Englefield Green. *Surr* 3A 38
Englesea-brook. *Ches E* 5B 84
English Bicknor. *Glos* 4A 48
Englishcombe. *Bath* 5C 34
English Frankton. *Shrp* 3G 71
Enham Alamein. *Hants* 2B 24
Enmore. *Som* 3F 21
Ennerdale Bridge. *Cumb* 3B 102
Enniscaven. *Corn* 3D 6
Enniskillen. *Ferm* 5B 174
Enoch. *Dum* 4A 118
Enochdhu. *Per* 2H 143
Ensay. *Arg* 4E 139
Ensbury. *Bour* 3F 15
Ensdon. *Shrp* 4G 71
Ensis. *Devn* 4F 19
Enson. *Staf* 3D 72
Enstone. *Oxon* 3B 50
Enterkinfoot. *Dum* 4A 118
Enville. *Staf* 2C 60
Eolaigearraidh. *W Isl* 8C 170
Eorabus. *Arg* 1A 132
Eoropaidh. *W Isl* 1H 171
Epney. *Glos* 4C 48
Epperstone. *Notts* 1D 74
Epping. *Essx* 5E 53
Epping Green. *Essx* 5E 53
Epping Green. *Herts* 5C 52
Epping Upland. *Essx* 5E 53
Eppleby. *N Yor* 3E 105
Eppleworth. *E Yor* 1D 94
Epsom. *Surr* 4D 38
Epwell. *Oxon* 1B 50
Epworth. *N Lin* 4A 94
Epworth Turbary. *N Lin* 4A 94
Erbistock. *Wrex* 1F 71
Erbusaig. *High* 1F 147
Erchless Castle. *High* 4G 157
Erdington. *W Mid* 1F 61
Eredine. *Arg* 3G 133
Eriboll. *High* 3E 167
Ericstane. *Dum* 3C 118
Eridge Green. *E Sus* 2G 27
Erines. *Arg* 2G 125
Eriswell. *Suff* 3G 65
Erith. *G Lon* 3G 39
Erlestoke. *Wilts* 1E 23
Ermine. *Linc* 3G 87
Ermington. *Devn* 3C 8
Ernesettle. *Plym* 3A 8
Erpingham. *Norf* 2D 78
Erriottwood. *Kent* 5D 40
Errogie. *High* 1H 149
Errol. *Per* 1E 137
Errol Station. *Per* 1E 137
Erskine. *Ren* 2F 127
Erskine Bridge. *Ren* 2F 127
Ervie. *Dum* 3F 109
Erwarton. *Suff* 2F 55
Erwood. *Powy* 1D 46
Eryholme. *N Yor* 4A 106
Eryrys. *Den* 5E 82
Escalls. *Corn* 4A 4
Escomb. *Dur* 1E 105
Escrick. *N Yor* 5A 100
Esgair. *Carm* 3D 45
(nr. Carmarthen)
Esgair. *Carm* 3G 43
(nr. St Clears)
Esgairgeiliog. *Powy* 5G 69
Esh. *Dur* 5E 115
Esher. *Surr* 4C 38
Esholt. *W Yor* 5D 98
Eshott. *Nmbd* 5G 121
Eshton. *N Yor* 4B 98
Esh Winning. *Dur* 5E 115
Eskadale. *High* 5G 157
Eskbank. *Midl* 3G 129
Eskdale Green. *Cumb* 4C 102
Eskdalemuir. *Dum* 5E 119
Eskham. *Linc* 1C 88
Esknish. *Arg* 3B 124
Esk Valley. *N Yor* 4F 107
Eslington Hall. *Nmbd* 3E 121
Esprick. *Lanc* 1C 90
Essendine. *Rut* 4H 75
Essendon. *Herts* 5C 52
Essich. *High* 5A 158
Essington. *Staf* 5D 72
Eston. *Red C* 3C 106
Estover. *Plym* 3B 8
Eswick. *Shet* 6F 173
Etal. *Nmbd* 1D 120
Etchilhampton. *Wilts* 5F 35
Etchingham. *E Sus* 3B 28
Etchinghill. *Kent* 2F 29
Etchinghill. *Staf* 4E 73
Etherley Dene. *Dur* 2E 105
Ethie Haven. *Ang* 4F 145
Etling Green. *Norf* 4C 78
Etloe. *Glos* 5B 48
Eton. *Wind* 3A 38
Eton Wick. *Wind* 3A 38
Etteridge. *High* 4A 150
Ettersgill. *Dur* 2B 104
Ettiley Heath. *Ches E* 4B 84
Ettington. *Warw* 1A 50
Etton. *E Yor* 5D 101
Etton. *Pet* 5A 76
Ettrick. *Bord* 3E 119
Ettrickbridge. *Bord* 2F 119
Etwall. *Derbs* 2G 73
Eudon Burnell. *Shrp* 2B 60
Eudon George. *Shrp* 2A 60
Euston. *Suff* 3A 66
Euxton. *Lanc* 3D 90
Evanstown. *B'end* 3C 32
Evanton. *High* 2A 158
Evedon. *Linc* 1H 75
Evelix. *High* 4E 165
Evendine. *Here* 1C 48
Evenjobb. *Powy* 4E 59
Evenley. *Nptn* 2D 50
Evenlode. *Glos* 3H 49
Even Swindon. *Swin* 3G 35
Evenwood. *Dur* 2E 105
Evenwood Gate. *Dur* 2E 105
Everbay. *Orkn* 5F 172
Evercreech. *Som* 3B 22
Everdon. *Nptn* 5C 62
Everingham. *E Yor* 5C 100
Everleigh. *Wilts* 1H 23
Everley. *N Yor* 1D 100
Eversholt. *C Beds* 2H 51
Evershot. *Dors* 2A 14
Eversley. *Hants* 5F 37
Eversley Centre. *Hants* 5F 37
Eversley Cross. *Hants* 5F 37
Everthorpe. *E Yor* 1C 94
Everton. *C Beds* 5B 64
Everton. *Hants* 3A 16
Everton. *Mers* 1F 83
Everton. *Notts* 1D 86
Evertown. *Dum* 2E 113
Evesbatch. *Here* 1B 48
Evesham. *Worc* 1F 49
Evington. *Leic* 5D 74
Ewden Village. *S Yor* 1G 85
Ewdness. *Shrp* 1B 60
Ewell. *Surr* 4D 38
Ewell Minnis. *Kent* 1G 29
Ewelme. *Oxon* 2E 37
Ewen. *Glos* 2F 35
Ewenny. *V Glam* 4C 32
Ewerby. *Linc* 1A 76
Ewes. *Dum* 5F 119
Ewesley. *Nmbd* 5E 121
Ewhurst. *Surr* 1B 26
Ewhurst Green. *E Sus* 3B 28
Ewhurst Green. *Surr* 2B 26
Ewlo. *Flin* 4E 83
Ewloe. *Flin* 4E 83
Ewood Bridge. *Lanc* 2F 91
Eworthy. *Devn* 3E 11
Ewshot. *Hants* 1G 25
Ewyas Harold. *Here* 3G 47
Exbourne. *Devn* 2G 11
Exbury. *Hants* 2C 16
Exceat. *E Sus* 5G 27
Exebridge. *Som* 4C 20
Exelby. *N Yor* 1E 99
Exeter. *Devn* 3C 12
Exeter International Airport.
Devn 3D 12
Exford. *Som* 3B 20
Exfords Green. *Shrp* 5G 71
Exhall. *Warw* 5F 61
Exlade Street. *Oxon* 3E 37
Exminster. *Devn* 4C 12
Exmoor. *Som* 3B 20
Exmouth. *Devn* 4D 12
Exnaboe. *Shet* 10E 173
Exning. *Suff* 4F 65
Exton. *Devn* 4C 12
Exton. *Hants* 4E 24
Exton. *Rut* 4G 75
Exton. *Som* 3C 20
Exwick. *Devn* 3C 12
Eyam. *Derbs* 3G 85
Eydon. *Nptn* 5C 62
Eye. *Here* 4G 59
Eye. *Pet* 5B 76
Eye. *Suff* 3D 66
Eye Green. *Pet* 5B 76
Eyemouth. *Bord* 3F 131
Eyeworth. *C Beds* 1C 52
Eyhorne Street. *Kent* 5C 40
Eyke. *Suff* 5F 67
Eynesbury. *Cambs* 5A 64
Eynort. *High* 1B 146
Eynsford. *Kent* 4G 39
Eynsham. *Oxon* 5C 50
Eyre. *High* 3D 154
(on Isle of Skye)
Eyre. *High* 5E 155
(on Raasay)
Eythorne. *Kent* 1G 29
Eyton. *Here* 4G 59
Eyton. *Shrp* 2F 59
(nr. Bishop's Castle)
Eyton. *Shrp* 4F 71
(nr. Shrewsbury)
Eyton. *Wrex* 1F 71
Eyton on Severn. *Shrp* 5H 71
Eyton upon the Weald Moors.
Telf 4A 72

F

Faccombe. *Hants* 1B 24
Faceby. *N Yor* 4B 106
Faddiley. *Ches E* 5H 83
Fadmoor. *N Yor* 1A 100
Fagwyr. *Swan* 5G 45
Faichem. *High* 3E 149
Faifley. *W Dun* 2G 127
Fail. *S Ayr* 2D 116
Failand. *N Som* 4A 34
Failford. *S Ayr* 2D 116
Failsworth. *G Man* 4H 91
Fairbourne. *Gwyn* 4F 69
Fairbourne Heath. *Kent* 5C 40
Fairburn. *N Yor* 2E 93
Fairfield. *Derbs* 3E 85
Fairfield. *Kent* 3D 28
Fairfield. *Worc* 3D 60
(nr. Bromsgrove)
Fairfield. *Worc* 1F 49
(nr. Evesham)
Fairford. *Glos* 5G 49
Fair Green. *Norf* 4F 77
Fair Hill. *Cumb* 1G 103
Fairhill. *S Lan* 4A 128
Fair Isle Airport. *Shet* 1B 172
Fairlands. *Surr* 5A 38
Fairlie. *N Ayr* 4D 126
Fairlight. *E Sus* 4C 28
Fairlight Cove. *E Sus* 4C 28
Fairmile. *Devn* 3D 12
Fairmile. *Surr* 4C 38
Fairmilehead. *Edin* 3F 129
Fair Oak. *Devn* 1D 12
Fair Oak. *Hants* 1C 16
(nr. Eastleigh)
Fair Oak. *Hants* 5D 36
(nr. Kingsclere)
Fairoak. *Staf* 2B 72
Fair Oak Green. *Hants* 5E 37
Fairseat. *Kent* 4H 39
Fairstead. *Essx* 4A 54
Fairstead. *Norf* 4F 77
Fairwarp. *E Sus* 3F 27
Fairwater. *Card* 4E 33
Fairy Cross. *Devn* 4E 19
Fakenham. *Norf* 3B 78
Fakenham Magna. *Suff* 3B 66
Fala. *Midl* 3H 129
Fala Dam. *Midl* 3H 129
Falcon. *Here* 2B 48
Faldingworth. *Linc* 2H 87
Falfield. *S Glo* 2B 34
Falkenham. *Suff* 2F 55
Falkirk. *Falk* 1B 128
Falkland. *Fife* 3E 137
Fallin. *Stir* 4H 135
Fallowfield. *G Man* 1C 84
Falmer. *E Sus* 5E 27
Falmouth. *Corn* 5C 6
Falsgrave. *N Yor* 1E 101
Falstone. *Nmbd* 1A 114
Fanagmore. *High* 4B 166
Fancott. *C Beds* 3A 52
Fanellan. *High* 4G 157
Fangdale Beck. *N Yor* 5C 106
Fangfoss. *E Yor* 4B 100
Fankerton. *Falk* 1A 128
Fanmore. *Arg* 4F 139
Fanner's Green. *Essx* 4G 53
Fannich Lodge. *High* 2E 156
Fans. *Bord* 5C 130
Farcet. *Cambs* 1B 64
Far Cotton. *Nptn* 5E 63
Fareham. *Hants* 2D 16
Farewell. *Staf* 4E 73
Far Forest. *Worc* 3B 60
Farforth. *Linc* 3C 88
Far Green. *Glos* 5C 48
Far Hoarcross. *Staf* 3F 73
Faringdon. *Oxon* 2A 36
Farington. *Lanc* 2D 90
Farlam. *Cumb* 4G 113
Farleigh. *N Som* 5H 33
Farleigh. *Surr* 4E 39
Farleigh Hungerford. *Som* 1D 22
Farleigh Wallop. *Hants* 2E 24
Farleigh Wick. *Wilts* 5D 34
Farlesthorpe. *Linc* 3D 88
Farleton. *Cumb* 1E 97
Farleton. *Lanc* 3E 97
Farley. *High* 4G 157
Farley. *N Som* 4H 33
Farley. *Shrp* 5F 71
(nr. Shrewsbury)
Farley. *Shrp* 5A 72
(nr. Telford)
Farley. *Staf* 1E 73
Farley. *Wilts* 4H 23
Farley Green. *Suff* 5G 65
Farley Green. *Surr* 1B 26
Farley Hill. *Wok* 5F 37
Farley's End. *Glos* 4C 48
Farlington. *N Yor* 3A 100
Farlington. *Port* 2E 17
Farlow. *Shrp* 2A 60
Farmborough. *Bath* 5B 34
Farmcote. *Glos* 3F 49
Farmcote. *Shrp* 1B 60
Farmington. *Glos* 4G 49
Far Moor. *G Man* 4D 90
Farmoor. *Oxon* 5C 50
Farmtown. *Mor* 3C 160
Farnah Green. *Derbs* 1H 73
Farnborough. *G Lon* 4F 39
Farnborough. *Hants* 1G 25
Farnborough. *Warw* 1C 50
Farnborough. *W Ber* 3C 36
Farncombe. *Surr* 1A 26
Farndish. *Bed* 4G 63
Farndon. *Ches W* 5G 83
Farndon. *Notts* 5E 87
Farnell. *Ang* 3F 145
Farnham. *Dors* 1E 15
Farnham. *Essx* 3E 53
Farnham. *N Yor* 3F 99
Farnham. *Suff* 4F 67
Farnham. *Surr* 2G 25
Farnham Common. *Buck* 2A 38
Farnham Green. *Essx* 3E 53
Farnham Royal. *Buck* 2A 38
Farnhill. *N Yor* 5C 98
Farningham. *Kent* 4G 39
Farnley. *N Yor* 5E 98
Farnley Tyas. *W Yor* 3B 92
Farnsfield. *Notts* 5D 86
Farnworth. *G Man* 4F 91
Farnworth. *Hal* 2H 83
Far Oakridge. *Glos* 5E 49
Farr. *High* 2H 167
(nr. Bettyhill)
Farr. *High* 5A 158
(nr. Inverness)

Farr. High .....3C 150 (nr. Kingussie)
Farraline. High 1H 149
Farringdon. Devn 3D 12
Farrington. Dors 1D 14
Farrington Gurney. Bath 1B 22
Far Sawrey. Cumb 5E 103
Farsley. W Yor 1C 92
Farthinghoe. Nptn 2D 50
Farthingstone. Nptn 5D 62
Farthorpe. Linc 3B 88
Fartown. W Yor 3B 92
Farway. Devn 3E 13
Fasag. High 3A 156
Fascadale. High 1G 139
Fasnacloich. Arg 4E 141
Fassfern. High 1E 141
Fatfield. Tyne 4G 115
Faugh. Cumb 4G 113
Fauld. Staf 3F 73
Fauldhouse. W Lot 3C 128
Faulkbourne. Essx 4A 54
Faulkland. Som 1C 22
Fauls. Shrp 2H 71
Faverdale. Darl 3F 105
Faversham. Kent 4E 40
Fawdington. N Yor 2G 99
Fawfieldhead. Staf 4E 85
Fawkham Green. Kent 4G 39
Fawler. Oxon 4B 50
Fawley. Buck 3F 37
Fawley. Hants 2C 16
Fawley. W Ber 3B 36
Fawley Chapel. Here 3A 48
Fawton. Corn 2F 7
Faxfleet. E Yor 2B 94
Faygate. W Sus 2D 26
Fazakerley. Mers 1F 83
Fazeley. Staf 5F 73
Feagour. High 4H 149
Fearann Dhomhnaill. High 3E 147
Fearby. N Yor 1D 98
Fearn. High 1C 158
Fearnan. Per 4E 142
Fearnbeg. High 3G 155
Fearnhead. Warr 1A 84
Fearnmore. High 2G 155
Featherstone. Staf 5D 72
Featherstone. W Yor 2E 93
Featherstone Castle. Nmbd 3H 113
Feckenham. Worc 4E 61
Feering. Essx 3B 54
Feetham. N Yor 5C 104
Feizor. N Yor 3G 97
Felbridge. Surr 2E 27
Felbrigg. Norf 2E 78
Felcourt. Surr 1E 27
Felden. Herts 5A 52
Felhampton. Shrp 2G 59
Felindre. Carm .....3F 45 (nr. Llandeilo)
Felindre. Carm .....2G 45 (nr. Llandovery)
Felindre. Carm .....2D 44 (nr. Newcastle Emlyn)
Felindre. Powy 2D 58
Felindre. Swan 5G 45
Felindre Farchog. Pemb 1F 43
Felinfach. Cdgn 5E 57
Felinfach. Powy 2D 46
Felinfoel. Carm 5F 45
Felingwmisaf. Carm 3F 45
Felingwmuchaf. Carm 3F 45
Felin Newydd. Powy .....5C 70 (nr. Newtown)
Felin Newydd. Powy .....2E 46 (nr. Oswestry)
Felin Wnda. Cdgn 1D 44
Felinwynt. Cdgn 5B 56
Felixkirk. N Yor 1G 99
Felixstowe. Suff 2F 55
Felixstowe Ferry. Suff 2G 55
Felkington. Nmbd 5F 131
Fell End. Cumb 5A 104
Felling. Tyne 3F 115

Fell Side. Cumb 1E 102
Felmersham. Bed 5G 63
Felmingham. Norf 3E 79
Felpham. W Sus 3H 17
Felsham. Suff 5B 66
Felsted. Essx 3G 53
Feltham. G Lon 3C 38
Felthamhill. Surr 3B 38
Felthorpe. Norf 4D 78
Felton. Here 1A 48
Felton. N Som 5A 34
Felton. Nmbd 4F 121
Felton Butler. Shrp 4F 71
Feltwell. Norf 1G 65
Fenay Bridge. W Yor 3B 92
Fence. Lanc 1G 91
Fence Houses. Tyne 4G 115
Fencott. Oxon 4D 50
Fen Ditton. Cambs 4D 65
Fen Drayton. Cambs 4C 64
Fen End. Linc 3B 76
Fen End. W Mid 3G 61
Fenham. Nmbd 5G 131
Fenham. Tyne 3F 115
Fenhouses. Linc 1B 76
Feniscowles. Bkbn 2E 91
Feniton. Devn 3D 12
Fenn Green. Shrp 2B 60
Fenn's Bank. Wrex 2H 71
Fenn Street. Medw 3B 40
Fenny Bentley. Derbs 5F 85
Fenny Bridges. Devn 3E 12
Fenny Compton. Warw 5B 62
Fenny Drayton. Leics 1H 61
Fenny Stratford. Mil 2G 51
Fenrother. Nmbd 5F 121
Fenstanton. Cambs 4C 64
Fen Street. Norf 1C 66
Fenton. Cambs 3C 64
Fenton. Cumb 4G 113
Fenton. Linc .....5F 87 (nr. Caythorpe)
Fenton. Linc .....1D 120 (nr. Saxilby)
Fenton. Nmbd 1D 120
Fenton. Notts 2E 87
Fenton. Stoke 1C 72
Fentonadle. Corn 5A 10
Fenton Barns. E Lot 1B 130
Fenwick. E Ayr 5F 127
Fenwick. Nmbd .....5G 131 (nr. Berwick-upon-Tweed)
Fenwick. Nmbd .....2D 114 (nr. Hexham)
Fenwick. S Yor 3F 93
Feochaig. Arg 4B 122
Feock. Corn 5C 6
Feolin Ferry. Arg 3C 124
Feorlan. Arg 5A 122
Ferindonald. High 3E 147
Feriniquarrie. High 3A 154
Fern. Ang 2D 145
Ferndale. Rhon 2C 32
Ferndown. Dors 2F 15
Ferness. High 4D 158
Fernham. Oxon 2A 36
Fernhill. W Sus 1E 27
Fernhill Heath. Worc 5C 60
Fernhurst. W Sus 4G 25
Fernieflatt. Abers 1H 145
Ferniegair. S Lan 4A 128
Fernilea. High 5C 154
Fernilee. Derbs 3E 85
Ferrensby. N Yor 3F 99
Ferriby Sluice. N Lin 2C 94
Ferrybridge. W Yor 2E 93
Ferryden. Ang 3G 145
Ferryhill. Aber 3G 153
Ferryhill. Dur 1F 105
Ferryhill Station. Dur 1A 106
Ferryside. Carm 4D 44
Fersfield. Norf 2C 66

Fersit. High 1A 142
Feshiebridge. High 3C 150
Fetcham. Surr 5C 38
Fetterangus. Abers 3G 161
Fettercairn. Abers 1F 145
Fewcott. Oxon 3D 50
Fewston. N Yor 4D 98
Ffairfach. Carm 3G 45
Ffair Rhos. Cdgn 4G 57
Ffaldybrenin. Carm 1G 45
Ffarmers. Carm 1G 45
Ffawyddog. Powy 4F 47
Fflodun. Powy 5E 71
Ffont-y-gari. V Glam 5D 32
Fforest. Carm 5F 45
Fforest-fach. Swan 3F 31
Fforest Goch. Neat 5H 45
Ffostrasol. Cdgn 1D 44
Ffos-y-ffin. Cdgn 4D 56
Ffrith. Flin 5E 83
Ffwl-y-mwn. V Glam 5D 32
Ffynnongroyw. Flin 2D 82
Ffynnon Gynydd. Powy 1E 47
Ffynnon-oer. Cdgn 5E 57
Fiag Lodge. High 1B 164
Fidden. Arg 2B 132
Fiddington. Glos 2E 49
Fiddington. Som 2F 21
Fiddleford. Dors 1D 14
Fiddlers Hamlet. Essx 5E 53
Field. Staf 2E 73
Field Assarts. Oxon 4B 50
Field Broughton. Cumb 1C 96
Field Dalling. Norf 2C 78
Fieldhead. Cumb 1F 103
Field Head. Leics 5B 74
Fifehead Magdalen. Dors 4C 22
Fifehead Neville. Dors 1C 14
Fifehead St Quintin. Dors 1C 14
Fife Keith. Mor 3B 160
Fifield. Oxon 4H 49
Fifield. Wilts 1G 23
Fifield. Wind 3A 38
Fifield Bavant. Wilts 4F 23
Figheldean. Wilts 2G 23
Filby. Norf 4G 79
Filey. N Yor 1F 101
Filford. Dors 3H 13
Filgrave. Mil 1G 51
Filkins. Oxon 5H 49
Filleigh. Devn .....1H 11 (nr. Crediton)
Filleigh. Devn .....4G 19 (nr. South Molton)
Fillingham. Linc 2G 87
Fillongley. Warw 2G 61
Filton. S Glo 4B 34
Fimber. E Yor 3C 100
Finavon. Ang 3D 145
Fincham. Norf 5F 77
Finchampstead. Wok 5F 37
Finchdean. Hants 1F 17
Finchfield. Essx 2G 53
Finchley. G Lon 1D 38
Findern. Derbs 2H 73
Findhorn. Mor 2E 159
Findhorn Bridge. High 1C 150
Findochty. Mor 2B 160
Findo Gask. Per 1C 136
Findon. Abers 4G 153
Findon. W Sus 5C 26
Findon Mains. High 2A 158
Findon Valley. W Sus 5C 26
Finedon. Nptn 3G 63
Fingal Street. Suff 3E 66
Fingest. Buck 2F 37
Finghall. N Yor 1D 98
Fingland. Cumb 4D 112
Fingland. Dum 3G 117
Finglesham. Kent 5H 41
Fingringhoe. Essx 3D 54
Finiskaig. High 4A 148
Finmere. Oxon 2E 51

Finnart. Per 3C 142
Finningham. Suff 4C 66
Finningley. S Yor 1D 86
Finnygaud. Abers 3D 160
Finsbury. G Lon 2E 39
Finstall. Worc 4D 61
Finsthwaite. Cumb 1C 96
Finstock. Oxon 4B 50
Finstown. Orkn 6C 172
Fintry. Abers 3E 161
Fintry. D'dee 5D 144
Fintry. Stir 1H 127
Finwood. Warw 4F 61
Finzean. Abers 4D 152
Fionnphort. Arg 2B 132
Fionnsabhagh. W Isl 9C 171
Firbeck. S Yor 2C 86
Firby. N Yor .....1E 99 (nr. Bedale)
Firby. N Yor .....3B 100 (nr. Malton)
Firgrove. G Man 3H 91
Firle. E Sus 5F 27
Firsby. Linc 4D 88
Firsdown. Wilts 3H 23
First Coast. High 4D 162
Firth. Shet 4F 173
Fir Tree. Dur 1E 105
Fishbourne. IOW 3D 16
Fishbourne. W Sus 2G 17
Fishburn. Dur 1A 106
Fishcross. Clac 4A 136
Fisherford. Abers 5D 160
Fisherrow. E Lot 2G 129
Fisher's Pond. Hants 4C 24
Fisher's Row. Lanc 5D 96
Fisherstreet. W Sus 2A 26
Fisherton. High 3B 158
Fisherton. S Ayr 3B 116
Fisherton de la Mere. Wilts 3E 23
Fishguard. Pemb 1D 42
Fishlake. S Yor 3G 93
Fishley. Norf 4G 79
Fishnish. Arg 4A 140
Fishpond Bottom. Dors 3G 13
Fishponds. Bris 4B 34
Fishpool. Glos 3B 48
Fishpool. G Man 3G 91
Fishpools. Powy 4D 58
Fishtoft. Linc 1C 76
Fishtoft Drove. Linc 1C 76
Fishwick. Bord 4F 131
Fiskavaig. High 5C 154
Fiskerton. Linc 3H 87
Fiskerton. Notts 5E 87
Fitch. Shet 7E 173
Fittleton. Wilts 2G 23
Fittleworth. W Sus 4B 26
Fitton End. Cambs 4D 76
Fitz. Shrp 4G 71
Fitzhead. Som 4E 20
Fitzwilliam. W Yor 3E 93
Fiunary. High 4A 140
Five Ash Down. E Sus 3F 27
Five Ashes. E Sus 3G 27
Five Bells. Som 2D 20
Five Bridges. Here 1B 48
Five Lane Ends. Lanc 4E 97
Fivelanes. Corn 4C 10
Fivemiletown. M Ulst 5C 174
Five Oak Green. Kent 1H 27
Five Oaks. W Sus 3B 26
Five Roads. Carm 5E 45
Five Ways. Warw 3G 61
Flack's Green. Essx 4A 54
Flackwell Heath. Buck 3G 37
Fladbury. Worc 1E 49
Fladda. Shet 3E 173
Fladdabister. Shet 8F 173
Flagg. Derbs 4F 85
Flamborough. E Yor 2G 101
Flamstead. Herts 4A 52

Flansham. W Sus 5A 26
Flasby. N Yor 4B 98
Flash. Staf 4E 85
Flashader. High 3C 154
Flatt, The. Cumb 2G 113
Flaunden. Herts 5A 52
Flawborough. Notts 1E 75
Flawith. N Yor 3G 99
Flax Bourton. N Som 5A 34
Flaxby. N Yor 4F 99
Flaxholme. Derbs 1H 73
Flaxley. Glos 4B 48
Flaxley Green. Staf 4E 73
Flaxpool. Som 3E 21
Flaxton. N Yor 3A 100
Fleck. Shet 10E 173
Fleckney. Leics 1D 62
Flecknoe. Warw 4C 62
Fledborough. Notts 3F 87
Fleet. Dors 4B 14
Fleet. Hants .....1G 25 (nr. Farnborough)
Fleet. Hants .....2F 17 (nr. South Hayling)
Fleet. Linc 3C 76
Fleet Hargate. Linc 3C 76
Fleetville. Herts 5B 52
Fleetwood. Lanc 5C 96
Fleggburgh. Norf 4G 79
Fleisirin. W Isl 4H 171
Flemingston. V Glam 5D 32
Flemington. S Lan .....3H 127 (nr. Glasgow)
Flemington. S Lan .....5A 128 (nr. Strathaven)
Flempton. Suff 4H 65
Fleoideabhagh. W Isl 9C 171
Fletcher's Green. Kent 1G 27
Fletchertown. Cumb 5D 112
Fletching. E Sus 3F 27
Fleuchary. High 4E 165
Flexbury. Corn 2C 10
Flexford. Surr 1A 26
Flimby. Cumb 1B 102
Flimwell. E Sus 2B 28
Flint. Flin 3E 83
Flintham. Notts 1E 75
Flint Mountain. Flin 3E 83
Flinton. E Yor 1F 95
Flintsham. Here 5F 59
Flishinghurst. Kent 2B 28
Flitcham. Norf 3G 77
Flitton. C Beds 2A 52
Flitwick. C Beds 2A 52
Flixborough. N Lin 3B 94
Flixton. G Man 1B 84
Flixton. N Yor 2E 101
Flixton. Suff 2F 67
Flockton. W Yor 3C 92
Flodden. Nmbd 1D 120
Flodigarry. High 1D 154
Flood's Ferry. Cambs 1C 64
Floodkburgh. Cumb 2C 96
Flordon. Norf 1D 66
Flore. Nptn 4D 62
Flotterton. Nmbd 4E 121
Flowton. Suff 1D 54
Flushing. Abers 4H 161
Flushing. Corn 5C 6
Fluxton. Devn 3D 12
Flyford Flavell. Worc 5D 61
Fobbing. Thur 2B 40
Fochabers. Mor 3H 159
Fochriw. Cphy 5E 46
Fockerby. N Lin 3B 94
Fodderty. High 3H 157
Foddington. Som 4A 22
Foel. Powy 4B 70
Foffarty. Ang 4D 144
Foggathorpe. E Yor 1A 94
Fogo. Bord 5D 130
Fogorig. Bord 5D 130
Foindle. High 4B 166
Folda. Ang 2A 144
Fole. Staf 2E 73

Foleshill—Fylingthorpe

Foleshill. *W Mid* 2A **62**
Foley Park. *Worc* 3C **60**
Folke. *Dors* 1B **14**
Folkestone. *Kent* 2G **29**
Folkingham. *Linc* 2H **75**
Folkington. *E Sus* 5G **27**
Folksworth. *Cambs* 2A **64**
Folkton. *N Yor* 2E **101**
Folla Rule. *Abers* 5E **161**
Follifoot. *N Yor* 4F **99**
Folly Cross. *Devn* 2E **11**
Folly Gate. *Devn* 3F **11**
Folly, The. *Herts* 4B **52**
Fonmon. *V Glam* 5D **32**
Fonthill Bishop. *Wilts* 3E **23**
Fonthill Gifford. *Wilts* 3E **23**
Fontmell Magna. *Dors* 1D **14**
Fontwell. *W Sus* 5A **26**
Font-y-gary. *V Glam* 5D **32**
Foodieash. *Fife* 2F **137**
Foolow. *Derbs* 3F **85**
Footdee. *Aber* 3G **153**
Footherley. *Staf* 5F **73**
Foots Cray. *G Lon* 3F **39**
Forbestown. *Abers* 2A **152**
Force Forge. *Cumb* 5E **103**
Force Mills. *Cumb* 5E **103**
Forcett. *N Yor* 3E **105**
Ford. *Arg* 3F **133**
Ford. *Buck* 5F **51**
Ford. *Derbs* 2B **86**
Ford. *Devn* 4E **19**
(nr. Bideford)
Ford. *Devn* 3C **8**
(nr. Holbeton)
Ford. *Devn* 4D **9**
(nr. Salcombe)
Ford. *Glos* 3F **49**
Ford. *Nmbd* 1D **120**
Ford. *Plym* 3A **8**
Ford. *Shrp* 4G **71**
Ford. *Som* 1A **22**
(nr. Wells)
Ford. *Som* 4D **20**
(nr. Wiveliscombe)
Ford. *Staf* 5E **85**
Ford. *W Sus* 5B **26**
Ford. *Wilts* 4D **34**
(nr. Chippenham)
Ford. *Wilts* 3G **23**
(nr. Salisbury)
Forda. *Devn* 3E **19**
Ford Barton. *Devn* 1C **12**
Fordcombe. *Kent* 1G **27**
Fordell. *Fife* 1E **129**
Forden. *Powy* 5E **71**
Ford End. *Essx* 4G **53**
Forder Green. *Devn* 2D **9**
Ford Green. *Lanc* 5D **97**
Fordham. *Cambs* 3F **65**
Fordham. *Essx* 3C **54**
Fordham. *Norf* 1F **65**
Fordham Heath. *Essx* 3C **54**
Ford Heath. *Shrp* 4G **71**
Fordhouses. *W Mid* 5D **72**
Fordie. *Per* 1G **135**
Fordingbridge. *Hants* 1G **15**
Fordington. *Linc* 3D **88**
Fordon. *E Yor* 2E **101**
Fordoun. *Abers* 1G **145**
Ford Street. *Essx* 3C **54**
Ford Street. *Som* 1E **13**
Fordton. *Devn* 3B **12**
Fordwells. *Oxon* 4B **50**
Fordwich. *Kent* 5F **41**
Fordyce. *Abers* 2C **160**
Forebridge. *Staf* 3D **72**
Foremark. *Derbs* 3H **73**
Forest. *N Yor* 4F **105**
Forestburn Gate. *Nmbd* 5E **121**
Foresterseat. *Mor* 3F **159**
Forest Green. *Glos* 2D **34**
Forest Green. *Surr* 1C **26**
Forest Hall. *Cumb* 4G **103**
Forest Head. *Cumb* 4G **113**
Forest Hill. *Oxon* 5D **50**
Forest-in-Teesdale. *Dur* 2B **104**
Forest Lodge. *Per* 1G **143**
Forest Mill. *Clac* 4B **136**
Forest Row. *E Sus* 2F **27**
Forestside. *W Sus* 1F **17**
Forest Town. *Notts* 4C **86**
Forfar. *Ang* 3D **144**
Forgandenny. *Per* 2C **136**
Forge. *Powy* 1G **57**
Forge Side. *Torf* 5F **47**
Forge, The. *Here* 5F **59**
Forgewood. *N Lan* 4A **128**
Forgie. *Mor* 3A **160**
Forgue. *Abers* 4D **160**
Formby. *Mers* 4B **90**
Forncett End. *Norf* 1D **66**
Forncett St Mary. *Norf* 1D **66**
Forncett St Peter. *Norf* 1D **66**
Forneth. *Per* 4H **143**
Fornham All Saints. *Suff* 4H **65**
Fornham St Martin. *Suff* 4A **66**
Forres. *Mor* 3E **159**
Forrestfield. *N Lan* 3B **128**
Forrest Lodge. *Dum* 1C **110**
Forsbrook. *Staf* 1D **72**
Forse. *High* 5E **169**
Forsinard. *High* 4A **168**
Forss. *High* 2C **168**
Forstal, The. *Kent* 2E **29**
Forston. *Dors* 3B **14**
Fort Augustus. *High* 3F **149**
Forteviot. *Per* 2C **136**
Fort George. *High* 3B **158**
Forth. *S Lan* 4C **128**
Forthampton. *Glos* 2D **48**
Forthay. *Glos* 2C **34**
Forth Road Bridge. *Fife* 2E **129**
Fortingall. *Per* 4E **143**
Fort Matilda. *Inv* 2D **126**
Forton. *Hants* 2C **24**
Forton. *Lanc* 4D **97**
Forton. *Shrp* 4G **71**
Forton. *Som* 2G **13**
Forton. *Staf* 3B **72**
Forton Heath. *Shrp* 4G **71**
Fortrie. *Abers* 4D **160**
Fortrose. *High* 3B **158**
Fortuneswell. *Dors* 5B **14**
Fort William. *High* 1F **141**
Forty Green. *Buck* 1A **38**
Forty Hill. *G Lon* 1E **39**
Forward Green. *Suff* 5C **66**
Fosbury. *Wilts* 1B **24**
Foscot. *Oxon* 3H **49**
Fosdyke. *Linc* 2C **76**
Foss. *Per* 3E **143**
Fossebridge. *Glos* 4F **49**
Foster Street. *Essx* 5E **53**
Foston. *Derbs* 2F **73**
Foston. *Leics* 1D **62**
Foston. *Linc* 1F **75**
Foston. *N Yor* 3A **100**
Foston on the Wolds. *E Yor* 4F **101**
Fotherby. *Linc* 1C **88**
Fothergill. *Cumb* 1B **102**
Fotheringhay. *Nptn* 1H **63**
Foubister. *Orkn* 7E **172**
Foula Airport. *Shet* 8A **173**
Foul Anchor. *Cambs* 4D **76**
Foulbridge. *Cumb* 5F **113**
Foulden. *Norf* 1G **65**
Foulden. *Bord* 4F **131**
Foul Mile. *E Sus* 4H **27**
Foulridge. *Lanc* 5A **98**
Foulsham. *Norf* 3C **78**
Fountainhall. *Bord* 5H **129**
Four Alls, The. *Shrp* 2A **72**
Four Ashes. *Staf* 5D **72**
(nr. Cannock)
Four Ashes. *Staf* 2C **60**
(nr. Kinver)
Four Ashes. *Suff* 3C **66**
Four Crosses. *Powy* 5C **70**
(nr. Llanerfyl)
Four Crosses. *Powy* 4E **71**
(nr. Llanymynech)
Four Crosses. *Staf* 5D **72**
Four Elms. *Kent* 1F **27**
Four Forks. *Som* 3F **21**
Four Gotes. *Cambs* 4D **76**
Four Lane End. *S Yor* 4C **92**
Four Lane Ends. *Lanc* 4E **97**
Four Lanes. *Corn* 5A **6**
Fourlanes End. *Ches E* 5C **84**
Four Marks. *Hants* 3E **25**
Four Mile Bridge. *IOA* 3B **80**
Four Oaks. *E Sus* 3C **28**
Four Oaks. *Glos* 3B **48**
Four Oaks. *W Mid* 2G **61**
Four Roads. *Carm* 5E **45**
Four Roads. *IOM* 5B **108**
Fourstones. *Nmbd* 3B **114**
Four Throws. *Kent* 3B **28**
Fovant. *Wilts* 4F **23**
Foveran. *Abers* 1G **153**
Fowey. *Corn* 3F **7**
Fowlershill. *Abers* 2G **153**
Fowley Common. *Warr* 1A **84**
Fowlis. *Ang* 5C **144**
Fowlis Wester. *Per* 1B **136**
Fowlmere. *Cambs* 1E **53**
Fownhope. *Here* 2A **48**
Fox Corner. *Surr* 5A **38**
Foxcote. *Glos* 4F **49**
Foxcote. *Som* 1C **22**
Foxdale. *IOM* 4B **108**
Foxearth. *Essx* 1B **54**
Foxfield. *Cumb* 1B **96**
Foxham. *Wilts* 4E **35**
Fox Hatch. *Essx* 1G **39**
Foxhole. *Corn* 3D **6**
Foxholes. *N Yor* 2E **101**
Foxhunt Green. *E Sus* 4G **27**
Fox Lane. *Hants* 1G **25**
Foxley. *Norf* 3C **78**
Foxley. *Nptn* 5D **62**
Foxley. *Wilts* 3D **35**
Foxlydiate. *Worc* 4E **61**
Fox Street. *Essx* 3D **54**
Foxt. *Staf* 1E **73**
Foxton. *Cambs* 1E **53**
Foxton. *Dur* 2A **106**
Foxton. *Leics* 2D **62**
Foxton. *N Yor* 5B **106**
Foxup. *N Yor* 2A **98**
Foxwist Green. *Ches W* 4A **84**
Foxwood. *Shrp* 3A **60**
Foy. *Here* 3A **48**
Foyers. *High* 1G **149**
Foynesfield. *High* 3C **158**
Fraddam. *Corn* 3C **4**
Fraddon. *Corn* 3D **6**
Fradley. *Staf* 4F **73**
Fradley South. *Staf* 4F **73**
Fradswell. *Staf* 2D **73**
Fraisthorpe. *E Yor* 3F **101**
Framfield. *E Sus* 3F **27**
Framingham Earl. *Norf* 5E **79**
Framingham Pigot. *Norf* 5E **79**
Framlingham. *Suff* 4E **67**
Frampton. *Dors* 3B **14**
Frampton. *Linc* 2C **76**
Frampton Cotterell. *S Glo* 3B **34**
Frampton Mansell. *Glos* 5E **49**
Frampton on Severn. *Glos* 5C **48**
Frampton West End. *Linc* 1B **76**
Framsden. *Suff* 5D **66**
Framwellgate Moor. *Dur* 5F **115**
Franche. *Worc* 3C **60**
Frandley. *Ches W* 3A **84**
Frankby. *Mers* 2E **83**
Frankfort. *Norf* 3F **79**
Frankley. *Worc* 2D **61**
Frank's Bridge. *Powy* 5D **58**
Frankton. *Warw* 3B **62**
Frankwell. *Shrp* 4G **71**
Frant. *E Sus* 2G **27**
Fraserburgh. *Abers* 2G **161**
Frating Green. *Essx* 3D **54**
Fratton. *Port* 2E **17**
Freathy. *Corn* 3A **8**
Freckenham. *Suff* 3F **65**
Freckleton. *Lanc* 2C **90**
Freeby. *Leics* 3F **75**
Freefolk Priors. *Hants* 2C **24**
Freehay. *Staf* 1E **73**
Freeland. *Oxon* 4C **50**
Freester. *Shet* 6F **173**
Freethorpe. *Norf* 5G **79**
Freiston. *Linc* 1C **76**
Freiston Shore. *Linc* 1C **76**
Fremington. *Devn* 3F **19**
Fremington. *N Yor* 5D **104**
Frenchay. *S Glo* 4B **34**
Frenchbeer. *Devn* 4G **11**
Frenich. *Stir* 3D **134**
Frensham. *Surr* 2G **25**
Frenze. *Norf* 2D **66**
Fresgoe. *High* 2B **168**
Freshfield. *Mers* 4A **90**
Freshford. *Bath* 5C **34**
Freshwater. *IOW* 4B **16**
Freshwater Bay. *IOW* 4B **16**
Freshwater East. *Pemb* 5E **43**
Fressingfield. *Suff* 3E **67**
Freston. *Suff* 2E **55**
Freswick. *High* 2F **169**
Fretherne. *Glos* 5C **48**
Frettenham. *Norf* 4E **79**
Freuchie. *Fife* 3E **137**
Freystrop. *Pemb* 3D **42**
Friar's Gate. *E Sus* 2F **27**
Friar Waddon. *Dors* 4B **14**
Friday Bridge. *Cambs* 5D **76**
Friday Street. *E Sus* 5H **27**
Friday Street. *Surr* 1C **26**
Fridaythorpe. *E Yor* 4C **100**
Friden. *Derbs* 4F **85**
Friern Barnet. *G Lon* 1D **39**
Friesthorpe. *Linc* 2H **87**
Frieston. *Linc* 1G **75**
Frieth. *Buck* 2F **37**
Friezeland. *Notts* 5B **86**
Frilford. *Oxon* 2C **36**
Frilsham. *W Ber* 4D **36**
Frimley. *Surr* 1G **25**
Frimley Green. *Surr* 1G **25**
Frindsbury. *Medw* 4B **40**
Fring. *Norf* 2G **77**
Fringford. *Oxon* 3E **50**
Frinsted. *Kent* 5C **40**
Frinton-on-Sea. *Essx* 4F **55**
Friockheim. *Ang* 4E **145**
Friog. *Gwyn* 4F **69**
Frisby. *Leics* 5E **74**
Frisby on the Wreake. *Leics* 4D **74**
Friskney. *Linc* 5D **88**
Friskney Eaudyke. *Linc* 5D **88**
Friston. *E Sus* 5G **27**
Friston. *Suff* 4G **67**
Fritchley. *Derbs* 5A **86**
Fritham. *Hants* 1H **15**
Frith Bank. *Linc* 1C **76**
Frith Common. *Worc* 4A **60**
Frithelstock. *Devn* 1E **11**
Frithelstock Stone. *Devn* 1E **11**
Frithsden. *Herts* 5A **52**
Frithville. *Linc* 5C **88**
Frittenden. *Kent* 1C **28**
Frittiscombe. *Devn* 4E **9**
Fritton. *Norf* 5G **79**
(nr. Great Yarmouth)
Fritton. *Norf* 1E **67**
(nr. Long Stratton)
Fritwell. *Oxon* 3D **50**
Frizinghall. *W Yor* 1B **92**
Frizington. *Cumb* 3B **102**
Frobost. *W Isl* 6C **170**
Frocester. *Glos* 5C **48**
Frochas. *Powy* 5D **70**
Frodesley. *Shrp* 5H **71**
Frodingham. *N Lin* 3C **94**
Frodsham. *Ches W* 3H **83**
Froggatt. *Derbs* 3G **85**
Froghall. *Staf* 1E **73**
Frogham. *Hants* 1G **15**
Frogham. *Kent* 5G **41**
Frogmore. *Devn* 4D **8**
Frogmore. *Hants* 5G **37**
Frogmore. *Herts* 5B **52**
Frognall. *Linc* 4A **76**
Frogshall. *Norf* 2E **79**
Frogwell. *Corn* 2H **7**
Frolesworth. *Leics* 1C **62**
Frome. *Som* 2C **22**
Fromefield. *Som* 2C **22**
Frome St Quintin. *Dors* 2A **14**
Fromes Hill. *Here* 1B **48**
Fron. *Gwyn* 2C **68**
Fron. *Powy* 4C **58**
(nr. Llandrindod Wells)
Fron. *Powy* 1D **58**
(nr. Newtown)
Fron. *Powy* 5E **71**
(nr. Welshpool)
Froncysyllte. *Wrex* 1E **71**
Frongoch. *Gwyn* 2B **70**
Fron Isaf. *Wrex* 1E **71**
Fronoleu. *Gwyn* 2G **69**
Frosterley. *Dur* 1D **104**
Frotoft. *Orkn* 5D **172**
Froxfield. *C Beds* 2H **51**
Froxfield. *Wilts* 5A **36**
Froxfield Green. *Hants* 4F **25**
Fryern Hill. *Hants* 4C **24**
Fryerning. *Essx* 5G **53**
Fryton. *N Yor* 2A **100**
Fugglestone St Peter.
Wilts 3G **23**
Fulbeck. *Linc* 5G **87**
Fulbourn. *Cambs* 5E **65**
Fulbrook. *Oxon* 4A **50**
Fulflood. *Hants* 3C **24**
Fulford. *Som* 4F **21**
Fulford. *Staf* 2D **72**
Fulford. *York* 5A **100**
Fulham. *G Lon* 3D **38**
Fulking. *W Sus* 4D **26**
Fuller's Moor. *Ches W* 5G **83**
Fuller Street. *Essx* 4H **53**
Fullerton. *Hants* 3B **24**
Fulletby. *Linc* 3B **88**
Full Sutton. *E Yor* 4B **100**
Fullwood. *E Ayr* 4F **127**
Fulmer. *Buck* 2A **38**
Fulmodestone. *Norf* 2B **78**
Fulnetby. *Linc* 3H **87**
Fulney. *Linc* 3B **76**
Fulstow. *Linc* 1C **88**
Fulthorpe. *Stoc T* 2B **106**
Fulwell. *Tyne* 4G **115**
Fulwood. *Lanc* 1D **90**
Fulwood. *Notts* 5B **86**
Fulwood. *Som* 1F **13**
Fulwood. *S Yor* 2G **85**
Fundenhall. *Norf* 1D **66**
Funtington. *W Sus* 2G **17**
Funtley. *Hants* 2D **16**
Funzie. *Shet* 2H **173**
Furley. *Devn* 2F **13**
Furnace. *Arg* 3H **133**
Furnace. *Carm* 5F **45**
Furnace. *Cdgn* 1F **57**
Furner's Green. *E Sus* 3F **27**
Furness Vale. *Derbs* 2E **85**
Furneux Pelham. *Herts* 3E **53**
Furzebrook. *Dors* 4E **15**
Furzehill. *Devn* 2H **19**
Furzehill. *Dors* 2F **15**
Furzeley Corner. *Hants* 1E **17**
Furzey Lodge. *Hants* 2B **16**
Furzley. *Hants* 1A **16**
Fyfield. *Essx* 5F **53**
Fyfield. *Glos* 5H **49**
Fyfield. *Hants* 2A **24**
Fyfield. *Oxon* 2C **36**
Fyfield. *Wilts* 5G **35**
Fylde, The. *Lanc* 1B **90**
Fylingthorpe. *N Yor* 4G **107**

Fyning. W Sus ...4G 25
Fyvie. Abers ...5E 161

G

Gabhsann bho Dheas. W Isl ...2G 171
Gabhsann bho Thuath. W Isl ...2G 171
Gabroc Hill. E Ayr ...4F 127
Gadbrook. Surr ...1D 26
Gaddesby. Leics ...4D 74
Gadfa. IOA ...2D 80
Gadgirth. S Ayr ...2D 116
Gaer. Powy ...3E 47
Gaerwen. IOA ...3D 81
Gagingwell. Oxon ...3C 50
Gaick Lodge. High ...5B 150
Gailey. Staf ...4D 72
Gainford. Dur ...3E 105
Gainsborough. Linc ...1F 87
Gainsborough. Suff ...1E 55
Gainsford End. Essx ...2H 53
Gairletter. Arg ...1C 126
Gairloch. Abers ...3E 153
Gairloch. High ...1H 155
Gairlochy. High ...5D 148
Gairney Bank. Per ...4D 136
Gairnshiel Lodge. Abers ...3G 151
Gaisgill. Cumb ...4H 103
Gaitsgill. Cumb ...5E 113
Galashiels. Bord ...1G 119
Galgate. Lanc ...4D 97
Galhampton. Som ...4B 22
Gallatown. Fife ...4E 137
Galley Common. Warw ...1H 61
Galleyend. Essx ...5H 53
Galleywood. Essx ...5H 53
Gallin. Per ...4C 142
Gallowfauld. Ang ...4D 144
Gallowhill. E Dun ...2H 127
Gallowhill. Per ...5A 144
Gallowhill. Ren ...3F 127
Gallowhills. Abers ...3H 161
Gallows Green. Staf ...1E 73
Gallows Green. Worc ...4D 60
Gallowstree Common. Oxon ...3E 37
Galltair. High ...1G 147
Gallt Melyd. Den ...2C 82
Galmington. Som ...4F 21
Galmisdale. High ...5C 146
Galmpton. Devn ...4C 8
Galmpton. Torb ...3E 9
Galmpton Warborough. Torb ...3E 9
Galphay. N Yor ...2E 99
Galston. E Ayr ...1D 117
Galton. Dors ...4C 14
Galtrigill. High ...3A 154
Gamblesby. Cumb ...1H 103
Gamelsby. Cumb ...4D 112
Gamesley. Derbs ...1E 85
Gamlingay. Cambs ...5B 64
Gamlingay Cinques. Cambs ...5B 64
Gamlingay Great Heath. Cambs ...5B 64
Gammaton. Devn ...4E 19
Gammersgill. N Yor ...1C 98
Gamston. Notts ...2D 74
(nr. Nottingham)
Gamston. Notts ...3E 86
(nr. Retford)
Ganarew. Here ...4A 48
Ganavan. Arg ...5C 140
Ganborough. Glos ...3G 49
Gang. Corn ...2H 7
Ganllwyd. Gwyn ...3G 69
Gannochy. Ang ...1E 145
Gannochy. Per ...1D 136
Gansclet. High ...4F 169
Ganstead. E Yor ...1E 95
Ganthorpe. N Yor ...2A 100
Ganton. N Yor ...2D 101
Gants Hill. G Lon ...2F 39
Gappah. Devn ...5B 12
Garafad. High ...2D 155
Garboldisham. Norf ...2C 66
Garden City. Flin ...4F 83

Gardeners Green. Wok ...5G 37
Gardenstown. Abers ...2F 161
Garden Village. S Yor ...1G 85
Garden Village. Swan ...3E 31
Garderhouse. Shet ...7E 173
Gardham. E Yor ...5D 100
Gardie. Shet ...5C 173
(on Papa Stour)
Gardie. Shet ...1H 173
(on Unst)
Gardie Ho. Shet ...7F 173
Gare Hill. Som ...2C 22
Garelochhead. Arg ...4B 134
Garford. Oxon ...2C 36
Garforth. W Yor ...1E 93
Gargrave. N Yor ...4B 98
Gargunnock. Stir ...4G 135
Garleffin. S Ayr ...1F 109
Garlieston. Dum ...5B 110
Garlinge Green. Kent ...5F 41
Garlogie. Abers ...3E 153
Garmelow. Staf ...3B 72
Garmond. Abers ...3F 161
Garmondsway. Dur ...1A 106
Garmony. Arg ...4A 140
Garmouth. Mor ...2H 159
Garmston. Shrp ...5A 72
Garnant. Carm ...4G 45
Garndiffaith. Torf ...5F 47
Garndolbenmaen. Gwyn ...1D 69
Garnett Bridge. Cumb ...5G 103
Garnfadryn. Gwyn ...2B 68
Garnkirk. N Lan ...3H 127
Garnlydan. Blae ...4E 47
Garnsgate. Linc ...3D 76
Garnswllt. Swan ...5G 45
Garn-yr-erw. Torf ...4F 47
Garrabost. W Isl ...4H 171
Garrallan. E Ayr ...3E 117
Garras. Corn ...4E 5
Garreg. Gwyn ...1F 69
Garrigill. Cumb ...5A 114
Garriston. N Yor ...5E 105
Garrogie Lodge. High ...2H 149
Garros. High ...2D 155
Garsdale. Cumb ...1G 97
Garsdale Head. Cumb ...5A 104
Garsdon. Wilts ...3E 35
Garshall Green. Staf ...2D 72
Garsington. Oxon ...5D 50
Garstang. Lanc ...5D 97
Garston. Mers ...2G 83
Garswood. Mers ...1H 83
Gartcosh. N Lan ...3H 127
Garth. B'end ...2B 32
Garth. Cdgn ...2F 57
Garth. Gwyn ...2E 69
Garth. IOM ...4C 108
Garth. Powy ...1C 46
(nr. Builth Wells)
Garth. Powy ...3E 59
(nr. Knighton)
Garth. Shet ...6D 173
(nr. Sandness)
Garth. Shet ...6F 173
(nr. Skellister)
Garth. Wrex ...1E 71
Garthamlock. Glas ...3H 127
Garthbrengy. Powy ...2D 46
Gartheli. Cdgn ...5E 57
Garthmyl. Powy ...1D 58
Garthorpe. Leics ...3F 75
Garthorpe. N Lin ...3B 94
Garth Owen. Powy ...1D 58
Garth Row. Cumb ...5G 103
Gartly. Abers ...5C 160
Gartmore. Stir ...4E 135
Gartness. N Lan ...3A 128
Gartness. Stir ...1G 127
Gartocharn. W Dun ...1F 127
Garton. E Yor ...1F 95
Garton-on-the-Wolds. E Yor ...4D 101
Gartsherrie. N Lan ...3A 128
Gartymore. High ...2H 165

Garvagh. Caus ...2E 175
Garvald. E Lot ...2B 130
Garvamore. High ...4H 149
Garvard. Arg ...4A 132
Garvault. High ...5H 167
Garve. High ...2F 157
Garvestone. Norf ...5C 78
Garvie. Arg ...4H 133
Garvock. Abers ...1G 145
Garvock. Inv ...2D 126
Garway. Here ...3H 47
Garway Common. Here ...3H 47
Garway Hill. Here ...3H 47
Garwick. Linc ...1A 76
Gaskan. High ...1C 140
Gasper. Wilts ...3C 22
Gastard. Wilts ...5D 35
Gasthorpe. Norf ...2B 66
Gatcombe. IOW ...4C 16
Gateacre. Mers ...2G 83
Gatebeck. Cumb ...1E 97
Gate Burton. Linc ...2F 87
Gateforth. N Yor ...2F 93
Gatehead. E Ayr ...1C 116
Gate Helmsley. N Yor ...4A 100
Gatehouse. Nmbd ...1A 114
Gatehouse of Fleet. Dum ...4D 110
Gatelawbridge. Dum ...5B 118
Gateley. Norf ...3B 78
Gatenby. N Yor ...1F 99
Gatesgarth. Cumb ...3C 102
Gateshead. Tyne ...3F 115
Gatesheath. Ches W ...4G 83
Gateside. Ang ...4D 144
(nr. Forfar)
Gateside. Ang ...4C 144
(nr. Kirriemuir)
Gateside. Fife ...3D 136
Gateside. N Ayr ...4E 127
Gathurst. G Man ...4D 90
Gatley. G Man ...2C 84
Gatton. Surr ...5D 39
Gattonside. Bord ...1H 119
Gatwick (London) Airport.
W Sus ...1D 27
Gaufron. Powy ...4B 58
Gaulby. Leics ...5D 74
Gauldry. Fife ...1F 137
Gaultree. Norf ...5D 77
Gaunt's Common. Dors ...2F 15
Gaunt's Earthcott. S Glo ...3B 34
Gautby. Linc ...3A 88
Gavinton. Bord ...4D 130
Gawber. S Yor ...4D 92
Gawcott. Buck ...2E 51
Gawsworth. Ches E ...4C 84
Gawthorpe. W Yor ...2C 92
Gawthrop. Cumb ...1F 97
Gawthwaite. Cumb ...1B 96
Gay Bowers. Essx ...5A 54
Gaydon. Warw ...5A 62
Gayfield. Orkn ...2D 172
Gayhurst. Mil ...1G 51
Gayle. N Yor ...1A 98
Gayles. N Yor ...4E 105
Gay Street. W Sus ...3B 26
Gayton. Mers ...2E 83
Gayton. Norf ...4G 77
Gayton. Nptn ...5E 62
Gayton. Staf ...3D 73
Gayton le Marsh. Linc ...2D 88
Gayton le Wold. Linc ...2B 88
Gayton Thorpe. Norf ...4G 77
Gaywood. Norf ...3F 77
Gazeley. Suff ...4G 65
Geanies. High ...1C 158
Gearraidh Bhaltos. W Isl ...6C 170
Gearraidh Bhaird. W Isl ...6F 171
Gearraidh ma Monadh. W Isl ...7C 170
Gearraidh na h-Aibhne. W Isl ...4E 171
Geary. High ...2B 154
Geddes. High ...3C 158
Gedding. Suff ...5B 66
Geddington. Nptn ...2F 63
Gedintailor. High ...5E 155

Gedling. Notts ...1D 74
Gedney. Linc ...3D 76
Gedney Broadgate. Linc ...3D 76
Gedney Drove End. Linc ...3D 76
Gedney Dyke. Linc ...3D 76
Gedney Hill. Linc ...4C 76
Gee Cross. G Man ...1D 84
Geeston. Rut ...5G 75
Geilston. Arg ...2E 127
Geirinis. W Isl ...4C 170
Geldeston. Norf ...1F 67
Gell. Cnwy ...4A 82
Gelli. Pemb ...2E 43
Gelli. Rhon ...2C 32
Gellifor. Den ...4D 82
Gelligaer. Cphy ...2E 33
Gellilydan. Gwyn ...2F 69
Gellinudd. Neat ...5H 45
Gellyburn. Per ...5H 143
Gellywen. Carm ...2G 43
Gelston. Dum ...4E 111
Gelston. Linc ...1G 75
Gembling. E Yor ...4F 101
Gentleshaw. Staf ...4E 73
Geocrab. W Isl ...8D 171
George Best Belfast City Airport.
Bel ...4H 175
George Green. Buck ...2A 38
Georgeham. Devn ...3E 19
George Nympton. Devn ...4H 19
Georgetown. Blae ...5E 47
Georgetown. Ren ...3F 127
Georth. Orkn ...5C 172
Gerlan. Gwyn ...4F 81
Germansweek. Devn ...3E 11
Germoe. Corn ...4C 4
Gerrans. Corn ...5C 6
Gerrard's Bromley. Staf ...2B 72
Gerrards Cross. Buck ...2A 38
Gerston. High ...3D 168
Gestingthorpe. Essx ...2B 54
Gethsemane. Pemb ...1A 44
Geuffordd. Powy ...4E 70
Gibraltar. Buck ...4F 51
Gibraltar. Linc ...5E 89
Gibraltar. Suff ...5D 66
Gibsmere. Notts ...1E 74
Giddeahall. Wilts ...4D 34
Gidea Park. G Lon ...2G 39
Gidleigh. Devn ...4G 11
Giffnock. E Ren ...4G 127
Giffordland. E Lot ...3B 130
Gifford. N Ayr ...5D 126
Giffordtown. Fife ...2E 137
Giggetty. Staf ...1C 60
Giggleswick. N Yor ...3H 97
Gignog. Pemb ...2C 42
Gilberdyke. E Yor ...2B 94
Gilbert's End. Worc ...1D 48
Gilbert's Green. Warw ...3F 61
Gilchriston. E Lot ...3A 130
Gilcrux. Cumb ...1C 102
Gildersome. W Yor ...2C 92
Gildingwells. S Yor ...2C 86
Gilesgate Moor. Dur ...5F 115
Gileston. V Glam ...5D 32
Gilfach. Cphy ...2E 33
Gilfach Goch. Rhon ...3C 32
Gilfachreda. Cdgn ...5D 56
Gilford. Arm ...5F 175
Gilgarran. Cumb ...2B 102
Gillamoor. N Yor ...5D 107
Gillan. Corn ...4E 5
Gillar's Green. Mers ...1G 83
Gillbank. Cumb ...3B 154
Gilling East. N Yor ...2A 100
Gillingham. Dors ...4D 22
Gillingham. Medw ...4B 40
Gillingham. Norf ...1G 67
Gilling West. N Yor ...4E 105
Gillock. High ...3E 169
Gillow Heath. Staf ...5C 84

Gills. High ...1F 169
Gill's Green. Kent ...2B 28
Gilmanscleuch. Bord ...2F 119
Gilmerton. Edin ...3F 129
Gilmerton. Per ...1A 136
Gilmilnrigg. Dur ...3C 104
Gilmonby. Dur ...3C 104
Gilmorton. Leics ...2C 62
Gilsland. Nmbd ...3H 113
Gilsland Spa. Cumb ...3H 113
Gilston. Midl ...4H 129
Giltbrook. Notts ...1B 74
Gilwern. Mon ...4F 47
Gimingham. Norf ...2E 79
Giosla. W Isl ...5D 171
Gipping. Suff ...4C 66
Gipsey Bridge. Linc ...1B 76
Gipton. W Yor ...1D 92
Girdle Toll. N Ayr ...5E 127
Girlsta. Shet ...6F 173
Girsby. N Yor ...4A 106
Girthon. Dum ...4D 110
Girton. Cambs ...4D 64
Girton. Notts ...4F 87
Girvan. S Ayr ...5A 116
Gisburn. Lanc ...5H 97
Gisleham. Suff ...2H 67
Gislingham. Suff ...3C 66
Gissing. Norf ...2D 66
Gittisham. Devn ...3E 13
Gladestry. Powy ...5E 59
Gladsmuir. E Lot ...2A 130
Glaichbea. High ...5H 157
Glais. Swan ...5H 45
Glaisdale. N Yor ...4E 107
Glame. Arg ...4E 155
Glamis. Arg ...4C 144
Glanaman. Carm ...4G 45
Glan-Conwy. Cnwy ...5H 81
Glandford. Norf ...1C 78
Glan Duar. Carm ...1F 45
Glandwr. Blae ...5F 47
Glandwr. Pemb ...2F 43
Glan-Dwyfach. Gwyn ...1D 69
Glandy Cross. Carm ...2F 43
Glandyfi. Cdgn ...1F 57
Glangrwyney. Powy ...4F 47
Glanmule. Powy ...1D 58
Glanrhyd. Gwyn ...2B 68
Glanrhyd. Pemb ...1B 44
(nr. Cardigan)
Glan-rhyd. Pemb ...1F 43
(nr. Crymych)
Glan-rhyd. Powy ...5A 46
Glanton. Nmbd ...3E 121
Glanton Pyke. Nmbd ...3E 121
Glanvilles Wootton. Dors ...2B 14
Glan-y-don. Flin ...3D 82
Glan-y-nant. Powy ...2B 58
Glan-yr-afon. Gwyn ...1C 70
Glan-yr-afon. Gwyn ...2F 81
Glan-yr-afon. IOA ...2F 81
Glan-yr-afon. Powy ...5C 70
Glan-y-wern. Gwyn ...2F 69
Glapthorn. Nptn ...1H 63
Glapwell. Derbs ...4B 86
Glas Aird. Arg ...4A 132
Glas-allt Shiel. Abers ...5G 151
Glasbury. Powy ...2E 47
Glaschoil. High ...5E 159
Glascoed. Den ...3B 82
Glascoed. Mon ...5G 47
Glascote. Staf ...5G 73
Glascwm. Powy ...5D 58
Glasfryn. Cnwy ...5B 82
Glasgow. Glas ...3G 127
Glasgow Airport. Ren ...3F 127
Glasgow Prestwick Airport.
S Ayr ...2C 116
Glashvin. High ...2D 154
Glasinfryn. Gwyn ...4E 81
Glas na Cardaich. High ...4E 147
Glasnacardoch. High ...4E 147
Glasnakille. High ...2D 146
Glaspwll. Powy ...1G 57
Glassburn. High ...5F 157
Glassenbury. Kent ...2B 28

Glasserton—Gratton

Glasserton. Dum 5B 110
Glassford. S Lan 5A 128
Glassgreen. Mor 2G 159
Glasshouse. Glos 3C 48
Glasshouses. N Yor 3D 98
Glasson. Cumb 3D 112
Glasson. Lanc 4D 96
Glassonby. Cumb 1G 103
Glasterlaw. Ang 3E 145
Glaston. Rut 5F 75
Glastonbury. Som 3H 21
Glatton. Cambs 2A 64
Glazebrook. Warr 1A 84
Glazebury. Warr 1A 84
Glazeley. Shrp 2B 60
Gleadless. S Yor 2A 86
Gleadsmoss. Ches E 4C 84
Gleann Dail bho Dheas. W Isl 7C 170
Gleann Tholastaidh. W Isl 3H 171
Gleann Uige. High 1A 140
Gleaston. Cumb 2B 96
Glecknabae. Arg 3B 126
Gledrid. Shrp 2E 71
Gleiniant. Powy 1B 58
Glemsford. Suff 1B 54
Glen. Dum 4C 110
Glenancross. High 4E 147
Glen Auldyn. IOM 2D 108
Glenavy. Lis 4G 175
Glenbarr. Arg 2A 122
Glenbeg. High 2G 139
Glen Bernisdale. High 4D 154
Glenbervie. Abers 5E 153
Glenboig. N Lan 3A 128
Glenborrodale. High 2A 140
Glenbranter. Arg 4A 134
Glenbreck. Bord 2C 118
Glenbrein Lodge. High 2G 149
Glenbrittle. High 1C 146
Glenbuchat Lodge. Abers 2H 151
Glenbuck. E Ayr 2G 117
Glenburn. Ren 3F 127
Glencalvie Lodge. High 5B 164
Glencaple. Dum 3A 112
Glencarron Lodge. High 3C 156
Glencarse. Per 1D 136
Glencassley Castle. High 3B 164
Glencat. Abers 4C 152
Glencoe. High 3F 141
Glen Cottage. High 5E 147
Glencraig. Fife 4D 136
Glendale. High 4A 154
Glendevon. Per 3B 136
Glendoebeg. High 3G 149
Glendoick. Per 1E 136
Glendoune. S Ayr 5A 116
Glenduckie. Fife 2E 137
Gleneagles. Per 3B 136
Glenegedale. Arg 4B 124
Glenegedale Lots. Arg 4B 124
Glenelg. High 2G 147
Glenernie. Mor 4E 159
Glenesslin. Dum 1F 111
Glenfarg. Per 2D 136
Glenfarquhar Lodge. Abers 5E 152
Glenferness Mains. High 4D 158
Glenfeshie Lodge. High 4C 150
Glenfiddich Lodge. Mor 5H 159
Glenfield. Leics 5C 74
Glenfinnan. High 5B 148
Glenfintaig Lodge. High 5E 148
Glenfoot. Per 2D 136
Glenfyne Lodge. Arg 2B 134
Glengap. Dum 4D 110
Glengarnock. N Ayr 4E 126
Glengolly. High 2D 168
Glengorm Castle. Arg 3F 139
Glengrasco. High 4D 154
Glenhead Farm. Ang 2B 144
Glenholm. Bord 1D 118
Glen House. Bord 1E 119
Glenhurich. High 2C 140
Glenkerry. Bord 3E 119
Glenkiln. Dum 2F 111
Glenkindie. Abers 2B 152
Glenkinglass Lodge. Arg 5F 141
Glenkirk. Bord 2C 118
Glenlean. Arg 1B 126
Glenlee. Dum 1D 110
Glenleraig. High 5B 166
Glenlichorn. Per 2G 135
Glenlivet. Mor 1F 151
Glenlochar. Dum 3E 111
Glenlochsie Lodge. Per 1H 143
Glenluce. Dum 4G 109
Glenmarksie. High 3F 157
Glenmassan. Arg 1C 126
Glenmavis. N Lan 3A 128
Glen Maye. IOM 4B 108
Glenmazeran Lodge. High 1B 150
Glenmidge. Dum 1F 111
Glen Mona. IOM 3D 108
Glenmore. High 2G 139
(nr. Glenborrodale)
Glenmore. High 3D 151
(nr. Kingussie)
Glenmore. High 4D 154
(on Isle of Skye)
Glenmoy. Ang 2D 144
Glennoe. Arg 5E 141
Glen of Coachford. Abers 4B 160
Glenogil. Ang 2D 144
Glen Parva. Leics 1C 62
Glenprosen Village. Ang 2C 144
Glenree. N Ayr 3D 122
Glenridding. Cumb 3E 103
Glenrosa. N Ayr 2E 123
Glenrothes. Fife 3E 137
Glensanda. High 4C 140
Glensaugh. Abers 1F 145
Glenshero Lodge. High 4H 149
Glensluain. Arg 4H 133
Glenstockadale. Dum 3F 109
Glenstriven. Arg 2B 126
Glen Tanar House. Abers 4B 152
Glentham. Linc 1H 87
Glenton. Abers 1D 152
Glentress. Bord 1E 119
Glentromie Lodge. High 4B 150
Glentrool Lodge. Dum 1B 110
Glentrool Village. Dum 2A 110
Glentruim House. High 4A 150
Glentworth. Linc 2G 87
Glenuig. High 1A 140
Glen Village. Falk 2B 128
Glen Vine. IOM 4C 108
Glenwhilly. Dum 2G 109
Glenzierfoot. Dum 2E 113
Glespin. S Lan 2H 117
Gletness. Shet 6F 173
Glewstone. Here 3A 48
Glib Cheois. W Isl 5F 171
Glinton. Pet 5A 76
Glooston. Leics 1E 63
Glossop. Derbs 1E 85
Gloster Hill. Nmbd 4G 121
Gloucester. Glos 4D 48
Gloucestershire Airport. Glos 3D 49
Gloup. Shet 1G 173
Glusburn. N Yor 5C 98
Glutt Lodge. High 5B 168
Glutton Bridge. Staf 4E 85
Gluvian. Corn 2D 6
Glympton. Oxon 3C 50
Glyn. Cnwy 3A 82
Glynarthen. Cdgn 1D 44
Glynbrochan. Powy 2B 58
Glyn Ceiriog. Wrex 2E 70
Glyncoch. Rhon 2D 32
Glyncorrwg. Neat 2B 32
Glynde. E Sus 5F 27
Glyndebourne. E Sus 4F 27
Glyndyfrdwy. Den 1D 70
Glyn Ebwy. Blae 5E 47
Glynllan. B'end 3C 32
Glyn-neath. Neat 5B 46
Glynogwr. B'end 3C 32
Glyntaff. Rhon 3D 32
Glyntawe. Powy 4B 46
Glynteg. Carm 2D 44
Gnosall. Staf 3C 72
Gnosall Heath. Staf 3C 72
Goadby. Leics 1E 63
Goadby Marwood. Leics 3E 75
Goatacre. Wilts 4F 35
Goathill. Dors 1B 14
Goathland. N Yor 4F 107
Goathurst. Som 3F 21
Goathurst Common. Kent 5F 39
Goat Lees. Kent 1E 28
Gobernuisgach Lodge. High 4E 167
Gobernuisgeach. High 5B 168
Gobhaig. W Isl 7C 171
Gobowen. Shrp 2F 71
Godalming. Surr 1A 26
Goddard's Corner. Suff 4E 67
Goddard's Green. Kent 2C 28
(nr. Benenden)
Goddard's Green. Kent 2B 28
(nr. Cranbrook)
Goddards Green. W Sus 3D 27
Godford Cross. Devn 2E 13
Godleybrook. Staf 1D 73
Godmanchester. Cambs 3B 64
Godmanstone. Dors 3B 14
Godmersham. Kent 5E 41
Godolphin Cross. Corn 3D 4
Godre'r-graig. Neat 5A 46
Godshill. Hants 1G 15
Godshill. IOW 4D 16
Godstone. Staf 2E 73
Godstone. Surr 5E 39
Goetre. Mon 5G 47
Goff's Oak. Herts 5D 52
Gogar. Edin 2E 129
Goginan. Cdgn 2F 57
Golan. Gwyn 1E 69
Golant. Corn 3F 7
Golberdon. Corn 5D 10
Golborne. G Man 1A 84
Golcar. W Yor 3A 92
Goldcliff. Newp 3G 33
Golden Cross. E Sus 4G 27
Golden Green. Kent 1H 27
Golden Grove. Carm 4F 45
Golden Grove. N Yor 4F 107
Golden Hill. Pemb 2D 43
Goldenhill. Stoke 5C 84
Golden Pot. Hants 2F 25
Golden Valley. Glos 3E 49
Golders Green. G Lon 2D 38
Goldhanger. Essx 5C 54
Gold Hill. Norf 1E 65
Golding. Shrp 5H 71
Goldington. Bed 5H 63
Goldsborough. N Yor 4F 99
(nr. Harrogate)
Goldsborough. N Yor 3F 107
(nr. Whitby)
Goldsithney. Corn 3C 4
Goldstone. Kent 4G 41
Goldstone. Shrp 3B 72
Goldthorpe. S Yor 4E 93
Goldworthy. Devn 4D 19
Golfa. Powy 3D 70
Gollanfield. High 3C 158
Gollinglith Foot. N Yor 1D 98
Golsoncott. Som 3D 20
Golspie. High 4F 165
Gomeldon. Wilts 3G 23
Gomersal. W Yor 2C 92
Gometra House. Arg 4E 139
Gomshall. Surr 1B 26
Gonalston. Notts 1D 74
Gonerby Hill Foot. Linc 2G 75
Gonfirth. Shet 5E 173
Good Easter. Essx 4G 53
Gooderstone. Norf 5G 77
Goodleigh. Devn 3G 19
Goodmanham. E Yor 5C 100
Goodmayes. G Lon 2F 39
Goodnestone. Kent 5G 41
(nr. Aylesham)
Goodnestone. Kent 4E 41
(nr. Faversham)
Goodrich. Here 4A 48
Goodrington. Torb 3E 9
Goodshaw. Lanc 2G 91
Goodshaw Fold. Lanc 2G 91
Goodstone. Devn 5A 12
Goodwick. Pemb 1D 42
Goodworth Clatford. Hants 2B 24
Goole. E Yor 2H 93
Goom's Hill. Worc 5E 61
Goonabarn. Corn 3D 6
Goonbell. Corn 4B 6
Goonhavern. Corn 3B 6
Goonvrea. Corn 4B 6
Goose Green. Cumb 1E 97
Goose Green. S Glo 3C 34
Gooseham. Corn 1C 10
Goosewell. Plym 3B 8
Goosey. Oxon 2B 36
Goosnargh. Lanc 1D 90
Goostrey. Ches E 3B 84
Gorcott Hill. Warw 4E 61
Gord. Shet 9F 173
Gordon. Bord 5C 130
Gordonbush. High 3F 165
Gordonstown. Abers 3C 160
(nr. Cornhill)
Gordonstown. Abers 5E 160
(nr. Fyvie)
Gorebridge. Midl 3G 129
Gorefield. Cambs 4D 76
Gores. Wilts 1G 23
Gorgie. Edin 2F 129
Goring. Oxon 3E 36
Goring-by-Sea. W Sus 5C 26
Goring Heath. Oxon 4E 37
Gorleston-on-Sea. Norf 5H 79
Gornalwood. W Mid 1D 60
Gorran Churchtown. Corn 4D 6
Gorran Haven. Corn 4E 6
Gorran High Lanes. Corn 4D 6
Gors. Cdgn 3F 57
Gorsedd. Flin 3D 82
Gorseinon. Swan 3E 31
Gorseness. Orkn 6D 172
Gorseybank. Derbs 5G 85
Gorsgoch. Cdgn 5D 57
Gorslas. Carm 4F 45
Gorsley. Glos 3B 48
Gorsley Common. Here 3B 48
Gorstan. High 2F 157
Gorstella. Ches W 4F 83
Gorsty Common. Here 2H 47
Gorsty Hill. Staf 3F 73
Gortantaoid. Arg 2B 124
Gorteneorn. High 2A 140
Gortenfern. High 2A 140
Gorton. G Man 1C 84
Gosbeck. Suff 5D 66
Gosberton. Linc 2B 76
Gosberton Cheal. Linc 3B 76
Gosberton Clough. Linc 3A 76
Goseley Dale. Derbs 3H 73
Gosfield. Essx 3A 54
Gosford. Oxon 4D 50
Gosforth. Cumb 4B 102
Gosforth. Tyne 3F 115
Gosmore. Herts 3B 52
Gospel End Village. Staf 1C 60
Gosport. Hants 3E 16
Gossabrough. Shet 3G 173
Gossington. Glos 5C 48
Gossops Green. W Sus 2D 26
Goswick. Nmbd 5G 131
Gotham. Notts 2C 74
Gotherington. Glos 3E 49
Gott. Arg 4B 138
Gott. Shet 7F 173
Goudhurst. Kent 2B 28
Goulceby. Linc 3B 88
Gourdon. Abers 1H 145
Gourock. Inv 2D 126
Govan. Glas 3G 127
Govanhill. Glas 3G 127
Goverton. Notts 1E 74
Goveton. Devn 4D 8
Govilon. Mon 4F 47
Gowanhill. Abers 2H 161
Gowdall. E Yor 2G 93
Gowerton. Swan 3E 31
Gowkhall. Fife 1D 128
Gowthorpe. E Yor 4B 100
Goxhill. E Yor 5F 101
Goxhill. N Lin 2E 94
Goxhill Haven. N Lin 2E 94
Goytre. Neat 3A 32
Grabhair. W Isl 6F 171
Graby. Linc 3H 75
Graffham. W Sus 4A 26
Grafham. Cambs 4A 64
Grafham. Surr 1B 26
Grafton. Here 2H 47
Grafton. N Yor 3G 99
Grafton. Oxon 5A 50
Grafton. Shrp 4G 71
Grafton. Worc 2E 49
(nr. Evesham)
Grafton. Worc 4H 59
(nr. Leominster)
Grafton Flyford. Worc 5D 60
Grafton Regis. Nptn 1F 51
Grafton Underwood. Nptn 2G 63
Grafty Green. Kent 1C 28
Graianrhyd. Den 5E 82
Graig. Carm 5E 45
Graig. Cnwy 3H 81
Graig. Den 3C 82
Graig-fechan. Den 5D 82
Graig Penllyn. V Glam 4C 32
Grain. Medw 3C 40
Grainsby. Linc 1B 88
Grainthorpe. Linc 1C 88
Grainthorpe Fen. Linc 1C 88
Graiselound. N Lin 1E 87
Gramasdail. W Isl 3D 170
Grampound. Corn 4D 6
Grampound Road. Corn 3D 6
Granborough. Buck 3F 51
Granby. Notts 2E 75
Grandborough. Warw 4B 62
Grandpont. Oxon 5D 50
Grandtully. Per 3G 143
Grange. Cumb 3D 102
Grange. E Ayr 1D 116
Grange. Here 3G 59
Grange. Mers 2E 82
Grange. Per 1E 137
Grange Crossroads. Mor 3B 160
Grange Hill. Essx 1F 39
Grangemill. Derbs 5G 85
Grange Moor. W Yor 3C 92
Grangemouth. Falk 1C 128
Grange of Lindores. Fife 2E 137
Grange-over-Sands. Cumb 2D 96
Grangepans. Falk 1D 128
Grange, The. N Yor 5C 106
Grangetown. Card 4E 33
Grangetown. Red C 2C 106
Grange Villa. Dur 4F 115
Granish. High 2C 150
Gransmoor. E Yor 4F 101
Granston. Pemb 1C 42
Grantchester. Cambs 5D 64
Grantham. Linc 2G 75
Grantley. N Yor 3E 99
Grantlodge. Abers 2E 152
Granton. Edin 2F 129
Grantown-on-Spey. High 1E 151
Grantshouse. Bord 3E 130
Grappenhall. Warr 2A 84
Grasby. Linc 4D 94
Grasmere. Cumb 4E 103
Grasscroft. G Man 4H 91
Grassendale. Mers 2F 83
Grassgarth. Cumb 5E 113
Grassholme. Dur 2C 104
Grassington. N Yor 3C 98
Grassmoor. Derbs 4B 86
Grassthorpe. Notts 4E 87
Grateley. Hants 2A 24
Gratton. Devn 1D 11

Gratton—Grinshill

Gratton. *Staf* 5D **84**
Gratwich. *Staf* 2E **73**
Graveley. *Cambs* 4B **64**
Graveley. *Herts* 3C **52**
Gravelhill. *Shrp* 4G **71**
Gravel Hole. *G Man* 4H **91**
Gravelly Hill. *W Mid* 1F **61**
Graven. *Shet* 4F **173**
Graveney. *Kent* 4E **41**
Gravesend. *Kent* 3H **39**
Grayingham. *Linc* 1G **87**
Grayrigg. *Cumb* 5G **103**
Grays. *Thur* 3H **39**
Grayshott. *Hants* 3G **25**
Grayson Green. *Cumb* 2A **102**
Grayswood. *Surr* 2A **26**
Graythorp. *Hart* 2C **106**
Grazeley. *Wok* 5E **37**
Grealin. *High* 2E **155**
Greasbrough. *S Yor* 1B **86**
Greasby. *Mers* 2E **83**
Great Abington. *Cambs* 1F **53**
Great Addington. *Nptn* 3G **63**
Great Alne. *Warw* 5F **61**
Great Altcar. *Lanc* 4B **90**
Great Amwell. *Herts* 4D **52**
Great Asby. *Cumb* 3H **103**
Great Ashfield. *Suff* 4B **66**
Great Ayton. *N Yor* 3C **106**
Great Baddow. *Essx* 5H **53**
Great Bardfield. *Essx* 2G **53**
Great Barford. *Bed* 5A **64**
Great Barr. *W Mid* 1E **61**
Great Barrington. *Glos* 4H **49**
Great Barrow. *Ches W* 4G **83**
Great Barton. *Suff* 4A **66**
Great Barugh. *N Yor* 2B **100**
Great Bavington. *Nmbd* 1C **114**
Great Bealings. *Suff* 1F **55**
Great Bedwyn. *Wilts* 5A **36**
Great Bentley. *Essx* 3E **54**
Great Billing. *Nptn* 4F **63**
Great Bircham. *Norf* 2G **77**
Great Blakenham. *Suff* 5D **66**
Great Blencow. *Cumb* 1F **103**
Great Bolas. *Telf* 3A **72**
Great Bookham. *Surr* 5C **38**
Great Bosullow. *Corn* 3B **4**
Great Bourton. *Oxon* 1C **50**
Great Bowden. *Leics* 2E **63**
Great Bradley. *Suff* 5F **65**
Great Braxted. *Essx* 4B **54**
Great Bricett. *Suff* 5C **66**
Great Brickhill. *Buck* 2H **51**
Great Bridgeford. *Staf* 3C **72**
Great Brington. *Nptn* 4D **62**
Great Bromley. *Essx* 3D **54**
Great Broughton. *Cumb* 1B **102**
Great Broughton. *N Yor* 4C **106**
Great Budworth. *Ches W* 3A **84**
Great Burdon. *Darl* 3A **106**
Great Burstead. *Essx* 1A **40**
Great Busby. *N Yor* 4C **106**
Great Canfield. *Essx* 4F **53**
Great Carlton. *Linc* 2D **88**
Great Casterton. *Rut* 5G **75**
Great Chalfield. *Wilts* 5D **34**
Great Chart. *Kent* 1D **28**
Great Chatwell. *Staf* 4B **72**
Great Chesterford. *Essx* 1F **53**
Great Cheverell. *Wilts* 1E **23**
Great Chilton. *Dur* 1F **105**
Great Chishill. *Cambs* 2E **53**
Great Clacton. *Essx* 4E **55**
Great Cliff. *W Yor* 3D **92**
Great Clifton. *Cumb* 2B **102**
Great Coates. *NE Lin* 3F **95**
Great Comberton. *Worc* 1E **49**
Great Corby. *Cumb* 4F **113**
Great Cornard. *Suff* 1B **54**
Great Cowden. *E Yor* 5G **101**
Great Coxwell. *Oxon* 2A **36**
Great Crakehall. *N Yor* 5F **105**
Great Cransley. *Nptn* 3F **63**
Great Cressingham. *Norf* 5A **78**
Great Crosby. *Mers* 4B **90**
Great Cubley. *Derbs* 2F **73**
Great Dalby. *Leics* 4E **75**
Great Doddington. *Nptn* 4F **63**
Great Doward. *Here* 4A **48**
Great Dunham. *Norf* 4A **78**
Great Dunmow. *Essx* 3G **53**
Great Durnford. *Wilts* 3G **23**
Great Easton. *Essx* 3G **53**
Great Easton. *Leics* 1F **63**
Great Eccleston. *Lanc* 5D **96**
Great Edstone. *N Yor* 1B **100**
Great Ellingham. *Norf* 1C **66**
Great Elm. *Som* 2C **22**
Great Eppleton. *Tyne* 5G **115**
Great Eversden. *Cambs* 5C **64**
Great Fencote. *N Yor* 5F **105**
Great Finborough. *Suff* 5C **66**
Greatford. *Linc* 4H **75**
Great Fransham. *Norf* 4A **78**
Great Gaddesden. *Herts* 4A **52**
Great Gate. *Staf* 1E **73**
Great Gidding. *Cambs* 2A **64**
Great Givendale. *E Yor* 4C **100**
Great Glemham. *Suff* 4F **67**
Great Glen. *Leics* 1D **62**
Great Gonerby. *Linc* 2F **75**
Great Gransden. *Cambs* 5B **64**
Great Green. *Norf* 2E **67**
Great Green. *Suff* 5B **66**
(nr. Lavenham)
Great Green. *Suff* 3D **66**
(nr. Palgrave)
Great Habton. *N Yor* 2B **100**
Great Hale. *Linc* 1A **76**
Great Hallingbury. *Essx* 4F **53**
Greatham. *Hants* 3F **25**
Greatham. *Hart* 2B **106**
Greatham. *W Sus* 4B **26**
Great Hampden. *Buck* 5G **51**
Great Harrowden. *Nptn* 3F **63**
Great Harwood. *Lanc* 1F **91**
Great Haseley. *Oxon* 5E **51**
Great Hatfield. *E Yor* 5F **101**
Great Haywood. *Staf* 3D **73**
Great Heath. *W Mid* 2H **61**
Great Heck. *N Yor* 2F **93**
Great Henny. *Essx* 2B **54**
Great Hinton. *Wilts* 1E **23**
Great Hockham. *Norf* 1B **66**
Great Holland. *Essx* 4F **55**
Great Horkesley. *Essx* 2C **54**
Great Hormead. *Herts* 2E **53**
Great Horton. *W Yor* 1B **92**
Great Horwood. *Buck* 2F **51**
Great Houghton. *Nptn* 5E **63**
Great Houghton. *S Yor* 4E **93**
Great Hucklow. *Derbs* 3F **85**
Great Kelk. *E Yor* 4F **101**
Great Kendale. *E Yor* 3E **101**
Great Kimble. *Buck* 5G **51**
Great Kingshill. *Buck* 2G **37**
Great Langdale. *Cumb* 4D **102**
Great Langton. *N Yor* 5F **105**
Great Leighs. *Essx* 4H **53**
Great Limber. *Linc* 4E **95**
Great Linford. *Mil* 1G **51**
Great Livermere. *Suff* 3A **66**
Great Longstone. *Derbs* 3G **85**
Great Lumley. *Dur* 5F **115**
Great Lyth. *Shrp* 5G **71**
Great Malvern. *Worc* 1C **48**
Great Maplestead. *Essx* 2B **54**
Great Marton. *Bkpl* 1B **90**
Great Massingham. *Norf* 3G **77**
Great Melton. *Norf* 5D **78**
Great Milton. *Oxon* 5E **51**
Great Missenden. *Buck* 5G **51**
Great Mitton. *Lanc* 1F **91**
Great Mongeham. *Kent* 5H **41**
Great Moulton. *Norf* 1D **66**
Great Munden. *Herts* 3D **52**
Great Musgrave. *Cumb* 3A **104**
Great Ness. *Shrp* 4F **71**
Great Notley. *Essx* 3H **53**
Great Oak. *Mon* 5G **47**
Great Oakley. *Essx* 3E **55**
Great Oakley. *Nptn* 2F **63**
Great Offley. *Herts* 3B **52**
Great Ormside. *Cumb* 3A **104**
Great Orton. *Cumb* 4E **113**
Great Ouseburn. *N Yor* 3G **99**
Great Oxendon. *Nptn* 2E **63**
Great Oxney Green. *Essx* 5G **53**
Great Parndon. *Essx* 5E **53**
Great Paxton. *Cambs* 4B **64**
Great Plumpton. *Lanc* 1B **90**
Great Plumstead. *Norf* 4F **79**
Great Ponton. *Linc* 2G **75**
Great Potheridge. *Devn* 1F **11**
Great Preston. *W Yor* 2E **93**
Great Raveley. *Cambs* 2B **64**
Great Rissington. *Glos* 4G **49**
Great Rollright. *Oxon* 2B **50**
Great Ryburgh. *Norf* 3B **78**
Great Ryle. *Nmbd* 3E **121**
Great Ryton. *Shrp* 5G **71**
Great Saling. *Essx* 3H **53**
Great Salkeld. *Cumb* 1G **103**
Great Sampford. *Essx* 2G **53**
Great Sankey. *Warr* 2H **83**
Great Saredon. *Staf* 5D **72**
Great Saxham. *Suff* 4G **65**
Great Shefford. *W Ber* 4B **36**
Great Shelford. *Cambs* 5D **64**
Great Shoddesden. *Hants* 2A **24**
Great Smeaton. *N Yor* 4A **106**
Great Snoring. *Norf* 2B **78**
Great Somerford. *Wilts* 3E **35**
Great Stainton. *Darl* 2A **106**
Great Stambridge. *Essx* 1C **40**
Great Staughton. *Cambs* 4A **64**
Great Steeping. *Linc* 4D **88**
Great Stonar. *Kent* 5H **41**
Greatstone-on-Sea. *Kent* 3E **29**
Great Strickland. *Cumb* 2G **103**
Great Stukeley. *Cambs* 3B **64**
Great Sturton. *Linc* 3B **88**
Great Sutton. *Ches W* 3F **83**
Great Sutton. *Shrp* 2H **59**
Great Swinburne. *Nmbd* 2C **114**
Great Tew. *Oxon* 3B **50**
Great Tey. *Essx* 3B **54**
Great Thirkleby. *N Yor* 2G **99**
Great Thorness. *IOW* 3C **16**
Great Thurlow. *Suff* 5F **65**
Great Torr. *Devn* 4C **8**
Great Torrington. *Devn* 1E **11**
Great Tosson. *Nmbd* 4E **121**
Great Totham North. *Essx* 4B **54**
Great Totham South. *Essx* 4B **54**
Great Tows. *Linc* 1B **88**
Great Urswick. *Cumb* 2B **96**
Great Wakering. *Essx* 2D **40**
Great Waldingfield. *Suff* 1C **54**
Great Walsingham. *Norf* 2B **78**
Great Waltham. *Essx* 4G **53**
Great Warley. *Essx* 1G **39**
Great Washbourne. *Glos* 2E **49**
Great Wenham. *Suff* 2D **54**
Great Whelnetham. *Suff* 5A **66**
Great Whittington. *Nmbd* 2D **114**
Great Wigborough. *Essx* 4C **54**
Great Wilbraham. *Cambs* 5E **65**
Great Wilne. *Derbs* 2B **74**
Great Wishford. *Wilts* 3F **23**
Great Witchingham. *Norf* 3D **78**
Great Witcombe. *Glos* 4E **49**
Great Witley. *Worc* 4B **60**
Great Wolford. *Warw* 2H **49**
Greatworth. *Nptn* 1D **50**
Great Wratting. *Suff* 1G **53**
Great Wymondley. *Herts* 3C **52**
Great Wyrley. *Staf* 5D **73**
Great Wytheford. *Shrp* 4H **71**
Great Yarmouth. *Norf* 5H **79**
Great Yeldham. *Essx* 2A **54**
Grebby. *Linc* 4D **88**
Greeba Castle. *IOM* 3C **108**
Greenbank. *Shet* 1G **173**
Greenbottom. *Corn* 4B **6**
Greenburn. *W Lot* 3C **128**
Greencroft. *Dur* 4E **115**
Greendown. *Som* 1A **22**
Greendykes. *Nmbd* 2E **121**
Green End. *Bed* 1A **52**
(nr. Bedford)
Green End. *Bed* 4A **64**
(nr. St Neots)
Green End. *Herts* 2D **52**
(nr. Buntingford)
Green End. *Herts* 3D **52**
(nr. Stevenage)
Green End. *N Yor* 4F **107**
Green End. *Warw* 2G **61**
Greenfield. *Arg* 4B **134**
Greenfield. *C Beds* 2A **52**
Greenfield. *Flin* 3D **82**
Greenfield. *G Man* 4H **91**
Greenfield. *Oxon* 2F **37**
Greenfoot. *N Lan* 3A **128**
Greenford. *G Lon* 2C **38**
Greengairs. *N Lan* 2A **128**
Greengate. *Norf* 4C **78**
Greengill. *Cumb* 1C **102**
Greenhalgh. *Lanc* 1C **90**
Greenham. *Dors* 2H **13**
Greenham. *Som* 4D **20**
Greenham. *W Ber* 5C **36**
Green Hammerton. *N Yor* 4G **99**
Greenhaugh. *Nmbd* 1A **114**
Greenhead. *Nmbd* 3H **113**
Green Heath. *Staf* 4D **73**
Greenhill. *Dum* 2C **112**
Greenhill. *Falk* 2B **128**
Greenhill. *Kent* 4F **41**
Greenhill. *S Yor* 2H **85**
Greenhill. *Worc* 3C **60**
Greenhills. *N Ayr* 4E **127**
Greenhithe. *Kent* 3G **39**
Greenholm. *E Ayr* 1E **117**
Greenhow Hill. *N Yor* 3D **98**
Greenigoe. *Orkn* 7D **172**
Greenland. *High* 2E **169**
Greenland Mains. *High* 2E **169**
Greenlands. *Worc* 4E **61**
Green Lane. *Shrp* 3A **72**
Green Lane. *Warw* 4E **61**
Greenlaw. *Bord* 5D **130**
Greenlea. *Dum* 2B **112**
Greenloaning. *Per* 3H **135**
Greenmount. *G Man* 3F **91**
Greenmow. *Shet* 9F **173**
Greenock. *Inv* 2D **126**
Greenock Mains. *E Ayr* 2F **117**
Greenodd. *Cumb* 1C **96**
Green Ore. *Som* 1A **22**
Greenrow. *Cumb* 4C **112**
Greens. *Abers* 4F **161**
Greensgate. *Norf* 4D **78**
Greenside. *Tyne* 3E **115**
Greensidehill. *Nmbd* 3D **121**
Greens Norton. *Nptn* 1E **51**
Greenstead Green. *Essx* 3B **54**
Greensted Green. *Essx* 5F **53**
Green Street. *Herts* 1C **38**
Green Street. *Suff* 3D **66**
Green Street Green. *G Lon* 4F **39**
Green Street Green. *Kent* 3G **39**
Greenstreet Green. *Suff* 1D **54**
Green, The. *Cumb* 1A **96**
Green, The. *Wilts* 3D **22**
Green Tye. *Herts* 4E **53**
Greenwall. *Orkn* 7E **172**
Greenway. *Pemb* 1E **43**
Greenway. *V Glam* 4D **32**
Greenwell. *Cumb* 4G **113**
Greenwich. *G Lon* 3E **39**
Greet. *Glos* 2F **49**
Greete. *Shrp* 3H **59**
Greetham. *Linc* 3C **88**
Greetham. *Rut* 4G **75**
Greetland. *W Yor* 2A **92**
Gregson Lane. *Lanc* 2D **90**
Grein. *W Isl* 8B **170**
Greinetobht. *W Isl* 1D **170**
Greinton. *Som* 3H **21**
Gremista. *Shet* 7F **173**
Grenaby. *IOM* 4B **108**
Grendon. *Nptn* 4F **63**
Grendon. *Warw* 1G **61**
Grendon Common. *Warw* 1G **61**
Grendon Green. *Here* 5H **59**
Grendon Underwood. *Buck* 3E **51**
Grenofen. *Devn* 5E **11**
Grenoside. *S Yor* 1H **85**
Greosabhagh. *W Isl* 8D **171**
Gresford. *Wrex* 5F **83**
Gresham. *Norf* 2D **78**
Greshornish. *High* 3C **154**
Gressenhall. *Norf* 4B **78**
Gressingham. *Lanc* 3E **97**
Greta Bridge. *Dur* 3D **105**
Gretna. *Dum* 3E **112**
Gretna Green. *Dum* 3E **112**
Gretton. *Glos* 2F **49**
Gretton. *Nptn* 1G **63**
Gretton. *Shrp* 1H **59**
Grewelthorpe. *N Yor* 2E **99**
Greyabbey. *N Dwn* 4J **175**
Greygarth. *N Yor* 2D **98**
Grey Green. *N Lin* 4A **94**
Greylake. *Som* 3G **21**
Greysouthen. *Cumb* 2B **102**
Greysteel. *Caus* 1D **174**
Greystoke. *Cumb* 1F **103**
Greystoke Gill. *Cumb* 2F **103**
Greystone. *Ang* 4E **145**
Greystones. *S Yor* 2H **85**
Greywell. *Hants* 1F **25**
Griais. *W Isl* 3G **171**
Grianan. *W Isl* 4G **171**
Gribthorpe. *E Yor* 1A **94**
Gribun. *Arg* 5F **139**
Griff. *Warw* 2A **62**
Griffithstown. *Torf* 2F **33**
Griffydam. *Leics* 4B **74**
Griggs Green. *Hants* 3G **25**
Grimbister. *Orkn* 6C **172**
Grimeford Village. *Lanc* 3E **90**
Grimeston. *Orkn* 6C **172**
Grimethorpe. *S Yor* 4E **93**
Griminis. *W Isl* 3C **170**
(on Benbecula)
Griminis. *W Isl* 1C **170**
(on North Uist)
Grimister. *Shet* 2F **173**
Grimley. *Worc* 4C **60**
Grimness. *Orkn* 8D **172**
Grimoldby. *Linc* 2C **88**
Grimpo. *Shrp* 3F **71**
Grimsargh. *Lanc* 1D **90**
Grimsbury. *Oxon* 1C **50**
Grimsby. *NE Lin* 4F **95**
Grimscote. *Nptn* 5D **62**
Grimscott. *Corn* 2C **10**
Grimshaw. *Bkbn* 2F **91**
Grimshaw Green. *Lanc* 3C **90**
Grimsthorpe. *Linc* 3H **75**
Grimston. *E Yor* 1F **95**
Grimston. *Leics* 3D **74**
Grimston. *Norf* 3G **77**
Grimston. *York* 4A **100**
Grimstone. *Dors* 3B **14**
Grimstone End. *Suff* 4B **66**
Grinacombe Moor. *Devn* 3E **11**
Grindale. *E Yor* 2F **101**
Grindhill. *Devn* 3E **11**
Grindiscol. *Shet* 8F **173**
Grindle. *Shrp* 5B **72**
Grindleford. *Derbs* 3G **85**
Grindleton. *Lanc* 5G **97**
Grindley. *Staf* 3E **73**
Grindley Brook. *Shrp* 1H **71**
Grindlow. *Derbs* 3F **85**
Grindon. *Nmbd* 5F **131**
Grindon. *Staf* 5E **85**
Gringley on the Hill. *Notts* 1E **87**
Grinsdale. *Cumb* 4E **113**
Grinshill. *Shrp* 3H **71**

Grinton—Hanbury

Grinton. N Yor 5D 104
Griomsidar. W Isl 5G 171
Grishipoll. Arg 3C 138
Grisling Common. E Sus 3F 27
Gristhorpe. N Yor 1E 101
Griston. Norf 1B 66
Gritley. Orkn 7E 172
Grittenham. Wilts 3F 35
Grittleton. Wilts 3D 34
Grizebeck. Cumb 1B 96
Grizedale. Cumb 5E 103
Grobister. Orkn 5F 172
Grobsness. Shet 5E 173
Groby. Leics 5C 74
Groes. Cnwy 4C 82
Groes. Neat 3A 32
Groes-faen. Rhon 3D 32
Groesffordd. Gwyn 2B 68
Groesffordd. Powy 3D 46
Groeslon. Gwyn 5D 81
Groes-lwyd. Powy 4E 70
Groes-wen. Cphy 3E 33
Grogport. Arg 5G 125
Groigearraidh. W Isl 4C 170
Gromford. Suff 5F 67
Gronant. Flin 2C 82
Groombridge. E Sus 2G 27
Grosmont. Mon 3H 47
Grosmont. N Yor 4F 107
Groton. Suff 1C 54
Grove. Dors 5B 14
Grove. Kent 4G 41
Grove. Notts 3E 87
Grove. Oxon 2B 36
Grovehill. E Yor 1D 94
Grove Park. G Lon 3F 39
Grovesend. Swan 5F 45
Grove, The. Dum 2A 112
Grove, The. Worc 1D 48
Grub Street. Staf 3B 72
Grudie. High 2F 157
Gruids. High 3C 164
Gruinard House. High 4D 162
Gruinart. Arg 3A 124
Grulinbeg. Arg 3A 124
Gruline. Arg 4G 139
Grummore. High 5G 167
Grundisburgh. Suff 5E 66
Gruting. Shet 7D 173
Grutness. Shet 10F 173
Gualachulain. High 4F 141
Gualin House. High 3D 166
Guardbridge. Fife 2G 137
Guarlford. Worc 1D 48
Guay. Per 4H 143
Gubblecote. Herts 4H 51
Guestling Green. E Sus 4C 28
Guestling Thorn. E Sus 4C 28
Guestwick. Norf 3C 78
Guestwick Green. Norf 3C 78
Guide. Bkbn 2F 91
Guide Post. Nmbd 1F 115
Guilden Down. Shrp 2F 59
Guilden Morden. Cambs 1C 52
Guilden Sutton. Ches W 4G 83
Guildford. Surr 1A 26
Guildtown. Per 5A 144
Guilsborough. Nptn 3D 62
Guilsfield. Powy 4E 70
Guineaford. Devn 3F 19
Guisborough. Red C 3D 106
Guiseley. W Yor 5D 98
Guist. Norf 3B 78
Guiting Power. Glos 3F 49
Gulberwick. Shet 8F 173
Gullane. E Lot 1A 130
Gulling Green. Suff 5H 65
Gulval. Corn 3B 4
Gulworthy. Devn 5E 11
Gumfreston. Pemb 4F 43
Gumley. Leics 1D 62
Gunby. E Yor 1H 93
Gunby. Linc 3G 75
Gundleton. Hants 3E 24
Gun Green. Kent 2B 28
Gun Hill. E Sus 4G 27
Gunn. Devn 3G 19
Gunnerside. N Yor 5C 104
Gunnerton. Nmbd 2C 114
Gunness. N Lin 3B 94
Gunnislake. Corn 5E 11
Gunnista. Shet 7F 173
Gunsgreenhill. Bord 3F 131
Gunstone. Staf 5C 72
Gunthorpe. Norf 2C 78
Gunthorpe. N Lin 1F 87
Gunthorpe. Notts 1D 74
Gunthorpe. Pet 5A 76
Gunville. IOW 4C 16
Gupworthy. Som 3C 20
Gurnard. IOW 3C 16
Gurney Slade. Som 2B 22
Gurnos. Powy 5A 46
Gussage All Saints. Dors 1F 15
Gussage St Andrew. Dors 1E 15
Gussage St Michael. Dors 1E 15
Guston. Kent 1H 29
Gutcher. Shet 2G 173
Guthram Gowt. Linc 3A 76
Guthrie. Ang 3E 145
Guyhirn. Cambs 5D 76
Guyhirn Gull. Cambs 5C 76
Guy's Head. Linc 3D 77
Guy's Marsh. Dors 4D 22
Guyzance. Nmbd 4G 121
Gwaelod-y-garth. Card 3E 32
Gwaenynog Bach. Den 4C 82
Gwaenysgor. Flin 2C 82
Gwalchmai. IOA 3C 80
Gwastad. Pemb 2E 43
Gwaun-Cae-Gurwen. Neat 4H 45
Gwaun-y-bara. Cphy 3E 33
Gwbert. Cdgn 1B 44
Gweek. Corn 4E 5
Gwehelog. Mon 5G 47
Gwenddwr. Powy 1D 46
Gwennap. Corn 4B 6
Gwenter. Corn 5E 5
Gwernaffield. Flin 4E 82
Gwernesney. Mon 5H 47
Gwernogle. Carm 2F 45
Gwern-y-go. Powy 1E 58
Gwernymynydd. Flin 4E 82
Gwersyllt. Wrex 5F 83
Gwespyr. Flin 2D 82
Gwinear. Corn 3C 4
Gwithian. Corn 2C 4
Gwredog. IOA 2D 80
Gwyddelwern. Den 1C 70
Gwyddgrug. Carm 2E 45
Gwynfryn. Wrex 5E 83
Gwystre. Powy 4C 58
Gwytherin. Cnwy 4A 82
Gyfelia. Wrex 1F 71
Gyffin. Cnwy 3G 81

H

Haa of Houlland. Shet 1G 173
Habberley. Shrp 5G 71
Habblesthorpe. Notts 2E 87
Habergham. Lanc 1G 91
Habin. W Sus 4G 25
Habrough. NE Lin 3E 95
Haceby. Linc 2H 75
Hacheston. Suff 5F 67
Hackenthorpe. S Yor 2B 86
Hackford. Norf 5C 78
Hackforth. N Yor 5F 105
Hackland. Orkn 5C 172
Hackleton. Nptn 5F 63
Hackman's Gate. Worc 3C 60
Hackness. N Yor 5G 107
Hackness. Orkn 8C 172
Hackney. G Lon 2E 39
Hackthorn. Linc 2G 87
Hackthorpe. Cumb 2G 103
Haclait. W Isl 4D 170
Haconby. Linc 3A 76
Hadden. Bord 1B 120
Haddenham. Buck 5F 51
Haddenham. Cambs 3D 64
Haddenham End. Cambs 3D 64
Haddington. E Lot 2B 130
Haddington. Linc 4G 87
Haddiscoe. Norf 1G 67
Haddo. Abers 5F 161
Haddon. Cambs 1A 64
Hademore. Staf 5F 73
Hadfield. Derbs 1E 85
Hadham Cross. Herts 4E 53
Hadham Ford. Herts 3E 53
Hadleigh. Essx 2C 40
Hadleigh. Suff 1D 54
Hadleigh Heath. Suff 1C 54
Hadley. Telf 4A 72
Hadley. Worc 4C 60
Hadley End. Staf 3F 73
Hadley Wood. G Lon 1D 38
Hadlow. Kent 1H 27
Hadlow Down. E Sus 3G 27
Hadnall. Shrp 3H 71
Hadstock. Essx 1F 53
Hadston. Nmbd 4G 121
Hady. Derbs 3A 86
Hadzor. Worc 4D 60
Haffenden Quarter. Kent 1C 28
Haggate. Lanc 1G 91
Haggbeck. Cumb 2F 113
Haggersta. Shet 7E 173
Haggerston. Nmbd 5G 131
Haggrister. Shet 4E 173
Hagley. Here 1A 48
Hagley. Worc 2D 60
Hagnaby. Linc 4C 88
Hagworthingham. Linc 4C 88
Haigh. G Man 4E 90
Haigh Moor. W Yor 2C 92
Haighton Green. Lanc 1D 90
Haile. Cumb 4B 102
Hailes. Glos 2F 49
Hailey. Herts 4D 52
Hailey. Oxon 4B 50
Hailsham. E Sus 5G 27
Hail Weston. Cambs 4A 64
Hainault. G Lon 1F 39
Hainford. Norf 4E 78
Hainton. Linc 2A 88
Hainworth. W Yor 1A 92
Haisthorpe. E Yor 3F 101
Hakin. Pemb 4C 42
Halam. Notts 5D 86
Halbeath. Fife 1E 129
Halberton. Devn 1D 12
Halcro. High 2E 169
Hale. Cumb 2E 97
Hale. G Man 2B 84
Hale. Hal 2G 83
Hale. Hants 1G 15
Hale. Surr 2G 25
Hale Bank. Hal 2G 83
Halebarns. G Man 2B 84
Hales. Norf 1F 67
Hales. Staf 2B 72
Halesgate. Linc 3C 76
Hales Green. Derbs 1F 73
Halesowen. W Mid 2D 60
Hale Street. Kent 1A 28
Halesworth. Suff 3F 67
Halewood. Mers 2G 83
Halford. Shrp 2G 59
Halford. Warw 1A 50
Halfpenny. Cumb 1E 97
Halfpenny Furze. Carm 3G 43
Halfpenny Green. Staf 1C 60
Halfway. Carm 2G 45
Halfway. Powy 2B 46
Halfway. S Yor 2B 86
Halfway. W Ber 5C 36
Halfway House. Shrp 4F 71
Halfway Houses. Kent 3D 40
Halgabron. Corn 4A 10
Halifax. W Yor 2A 92
Halistra. High 3B 154
Halket. E Ayr 4F 127
Halkirk. High 3D 168
Halkyn. Flin 3E 82
Hall. E Ren 4F 127
Hallam Fields. Derbs 1B 74
Halland. E Sus 4G 27
Hallands, The. N Lin 2D 94
Hallaton. Leics 1E 63
Hallatrow. Bath 1B 22
Hallbank. Cumb 5H 103
Hallbankgate. Cumb 4G 113
Hall Dunnerdale. Cumb 5D 102
Hallen. S Glo 3A 34
Hall End. Bed 1A 52
Hallgarth. Dur 5G 115
Hall Green. Ches E 5C 84
Hall Green. Norf 2D 66
Hall Green. W Mid 2F 61
Hall Green. W Yor 3D 92
Hall Green. Wrex 1G 71
Halliburton. Bord 5C 130
Hallin. High 3B 154
Halling. Medw 4B 40
Hallington. Linc 2C 88
Hallington. Nmbd 2C 114
Halloughton. Notts 5D 86
Hallow. Worc 5C 60
Hallow Heath. Worc 5C 60
Hallowsgate. Ches W 4H 83
Hallsands. Devn 5E 9
Hall's Green. Herts 3C 52
Hallspill. Devn 4E 19
Hallthwaites. Cumb 1A 96
Hall Waberthwaite. Cumb 5C 102
Hallwood Green. Glos 2B 48
Hallworthy. Corn 4B 10
Hallyne. Bord 5E 129
Halmer End. Staf 1C 72
Halmond's Frome. Here 1B 48
Halmore. Glos 5B 48
Halnaker. W Sus 5A 26
Halsall. Lanc 3B 90
Halse. Nptn 1D 50
Halse. Som 4E 21
Halsetown. Corn 3C 4
Halsham. E Yor 2F 95
Halsinger. Devn 3F 19
Halstead. Essx 2B 54
Halstead. Kent 4F 39
Halstead. Leics 5E 75
Halstock. Dors 2A 14
Halsway. Som 3E 21
Haltcliff Bridge. Cumb 1E 103
Haltham. Linc 4B 88
Haltoft End. Linc 1C 76
Halton. Buck 5G 51
Halton. Hal 2H 83
Halton. Lanc 3E 97
Halton. Nmbd 3C 114
Halton. W Yor 1D 92
Halton. Wrex 2F 71
Halton East. N Yor 4C 98
Halton Fenside. Linc 4D 88
Halton Gill. N Yor 2A 98
Halton Holegate. Linc 4D 88
Halton Lea Gate. Nmbd 4H 113
Halton Moor. W Yor 1D 92
Halton Shields. Nmbd 3D 114
Halton West. N Yor 4H 97
Haltwhistle. Nmbd 3A 114
Halvergate. Norf 5G 79
Halwell. Devn 3D 9
Halwill. Devn 3E 11
Halwill Junction. Devn 3E 11
Ham. Devn 2F 13
Ham. Glos 2B 34
Ham. G Lon 3C 38
Ham. High 1E 169
Ham. Kent 5H 41
Ham. Plym 3A 8
Ham. Shet 8A 173
Ham. Som 1F 13
(nr. Ilminster)
Ham. Som 4F 21
(nr. Taunton)
Ham. Som 4E 21
(nr. Wellington)
Ham. Wilts 5B 36
Hambleden. Buck 3F 37
Hambledon. Hants 1E 17
Hambledon. Surr 2A 26
Hamble-le-Rice. Hants 2C 16
Hambleton. Lanc 5C 96
Hambleton. N Yor 1F 93
Hambridge. Som 4G 21
Hambrook. S Glo 4B 34
Hambrook. W Sus 2F 17
Ham Common. Dors 4D 22
Hameringham. Linc 4C 88
Hamerton. Cambs 3A 64
Ham Green. Here 1C 48
Ham Green. Kent 4C 40
Ham Green. N Som 4A 34
Ham Green. Worc 4E 61
Ham Hill. Kent 4A 40
Hamilton. Leics 5D 74
Hamilton. S Lan 4A 128
Hamister. Shet 5G 173
Hammer. W Sus 3G 25
Hammersmith. G Lon 3D 38
Hammerwich. Staf 5E 73
Hammerwood. E Sus 2F 27
Hammill. Kent 5G 41
Hammond Street. Herts 5D 52
Hammoon. Dors 1D 14
Hamnavoe. Shet 3D 173
(nr. Braehoulland)
Hamnavoe. Shet 8E 173
(nr. Burland)
Hamnavoe. Shet 4F 173
(nr. Lunna)
Hamnavoe. Shet 3F 173
(on Yell)
Hamp. Som 3G 21
Hampden Park. E Sus 5G 27
Hampen. Glos 4F 49
Hamperden End. Essx 2F 53
Hamperley. Shrp 2G 59
Hampnett. Glos 4F 49
Hampole. S Yor 3F 93
Hampreston. Dors 3F 15
Hampstead. G Lon 2D 38
Hampstead Norreys. W Ber 4D 36
Hampsthwaite. N Yor 4E 99
Hampton. Devn 3F 13
Hampton. G Lon 3C 38
Hampton. Kent 4F 41
Hampton. Shrp 2B 60
Hampton. Swin 2G 35
Hampton. Worc 1F 49
Hampton Bishop. Here 2A 48
Hampton Fields. Glos 2D 35
Hampton Hargate. Pet 1A 64
Hampton Heath. Ches W 1H 71
Hampton in Arden. W Mid 2G 61
Hampton Loade. Shrp 2B 60
Hampton Lovett. Worc 4C 60
Hampton Lucy. Warw 5G 61
Hampton Magna. Warw 4G 61
Hampton on the Hill. Warw 4G 61
Hampton Poyle. Oxon 4D 50
Hampton Wick. G Lon 4C 38
Hamptworth. Wilts 1H 15
Hamrow. Norf 3B 78
Hamsey. E Sus 4F 27
Hamsey Green. Surr 5E 39
Hamstall Ridware. Staf 4F 73
Hamstead. IOW 3C 16
Hamstead. W Mid 1E 61
Hamstead Marshall. W Ber 5C 36
Hamsterley. Dur 4E 115
(nr. Consett)
Hamsterley. Dur 1E 105
(nr. Wolsingham)
Hamsterley Mill. Dur 4E 115
Hamstreet. Kent 2E 28
Ham Street. Som 3A 22
Hamworthy. Pool 3E 15
Hanbury. Staf 3F 73
Hanbury. Worc 4D 60

Hickling—Hoggrill's End

Hickling. *Notts* 3D **74**
Hickling Green. *Norf* 3G **79**
Hickling Heath. *Norf* 3G **79**
Hickstead. *W Sus* 3D **26**
Hidcote Bartrim. *Glos* 1G **49**
Hidcote Boyce. *Glos* 1G **49**
Higford. *Shrp* 5B **72**
High Ackworth. *W Yor* 3E **93**
Higham. *Derbs* 5A **86**
Higham. *Kent* 3B **40**
Higham. *Lanc* 1G **91**
Higham. *S Yor* 4D **92**
Higham. *Suff* 2D **54**
(nr. Ipswich)
Higham. *Suff* 4G **65**
(nr. Newmarket)
Higham Dykes. *Nmbd* 2E **115**
Higham Ferrers. *Nptn* 4G **63**
Higham Gobion. *C Beds* 2B **52**
Higham on the Hill. *Leics* 1A **62**
Highampton. *Devn* 2E **11**
Higham Wood. *Kent* 1H **27**
High Angerton. *Nmbd* 1D **115**
High Auldgirth. *Dum* 1G **111**
High Bankhill. *Cumb* 5G **113**
High Banton. *N Lan* 1A **128**
High Barnet. *G Lon* 1D **38**
High Beech. *Essx* 1F **39**
High Bentham. *N Yor* 3F **97**
High Bickington. *Devn* 4G **19**
High Biggins. *Cumb* 2E **97**
High Birkwith. *N Yor* 2H **97**
High Blantyre. *S Lan* 4H **127**
High Bonnybridge. *Falk* 2B **128**
High Borrans. *Cumb* 4F **103**
High Bradfield. *S Yor* 1G **85**
High Bray. *Devn* 3G **19**
Highbridge. *Cumb* 5E **113**
Highbridge. *High* 5E **148**
Highbridge. *Som* 2G **21**
Highbrook. *W Sus* 2E **27**
High Brooms. *Kent* 1G **27**
High Bullen. *Devn* 4F **19**
Highburton. *W Yor* 3B **92**
Highbury. *Som* 2B **22**
High Buston. *Nmbd* 4G **121**
High Callerton. *Nmbd* 2E **115**
High Carlingill. *Cumb* 4H **103**
High Catton. *E Yor* 4B **100**
High Church. *Nmbd* 1E **115**
Highclere. *Hants* 5C **36**
Highcliffe. *Dors* 3H **15**
High Cogges. *Oxon* 5B **50**
High Common. *Norf* 5B **78**
High Coniscliffe. *Darl* 3F **105**
High Crosby. *Cumb* 4F **113**
High Cross. *Hants* 4F **25**
High Cross. *Herts* 4D **52**
High Easter. *Essx* 4G **53**
High Eggborough. *N Yor* 2F **93**
High Ellington. *N Yor* 1D **98**
Higher Alham. *Som* 2B **22**
Higher Ansty. *Dors* 2C **14**
Higher Ashton. *Devn* 4B **12**
Higher Ballam. *Lanc* 1B **90**
Higher Bartle. *Lanc* 1D **90**
Higher Bockhampton. *Dors* 3C **14**
Higher Bojewyan. *Corn* 3A **4**
High Ercall. *Telf* 4H **71**
Higher Cheriton. *Devn* 2E **12**
Higher Clovelly. *Devn* 4D **18**
Higher Compton. *Plym* 3A **8**
Higher Dean. *Devn* 2D **8**
Higher Dinting. *Derbs* 1E **85**
Higher Dunstone. *Devn* 5H **11**
Higher End. *G Man* 4D **90**
Higherford. *Lanc* 5A **98**
Higher Gabwell. *Devn* 2F **9**
Higher Halstock Leigh. *Dors* 2A **14**
Higher Heysham. *Lanc* 3D **96**
Higher Hurdsfield. *Ches E* 3D **84**
Higher Kingcombe. *Dors* 3A **14**
Higher Kinnerton. *Flin* 4F **83**
Higher Melcombe. *Dors* 2C **14**
Higher Penwortham. *Lanc* 2D **90**
Higher Porthpean. *Corn* 3E **7**
Higher Poynton. *Ches E* 2D **84**
Higher Shotton. *Flin* 4F **83**
Higher Shurlach. *Ches W* 3A **84**
Higher Slade. *Devn* 2F **19**
Higher Tale. *Devn* 2D **12**
Highertown. *Corn* 4C **6**
Higher Town. *IOS* 1B **4**
Higher Town. *Som* 2C **20**
Higher Vexford. *Som* 3E **20**
Higher Walton. *Lanc* 2D **90**
Higher Walton. *Warr* 2H **83**
Higher Whatcombe. *Dors* 2D **14**
Higher Wheelton. *Lanc* 2E **90**
Higher Whiteleigh. *Corn* 3C **10**
Higher Whitley. *Ches W* 2A **84**
Higher Wincham. *Ches W* 3A **84**
Higher Wraxall. *Dors* 2A **14**
Higher Wych. *Wrex* 1G **71**
Higher Yalberton. *Torb* 3E **9**
High Etherley. *Dur* 2E **105**
High Ferry. *Linc* 1C **76**
Highfield. *E Yor* 1H **93**
Highfield. *N Ayr* 4E **126**
Highfield. *Tyne* 4E **115**
Highfields Caldecote. *Cambs* 5C **64**
High Garrett. *Essx* 3A **54**
Highgate. *G Lon* 2D **39**
Highgate. *N Ayr* 4E **127**
Highgate. *Powy* 1D **58**
High Grange. *Dur* 1E **105**
High Green. *Cumb* 4F **103**
High Green. *Norf* 5D **78**
High Green. *Shrp* 2B **60**
High Green. *S Yor* 1H **85**
High Green. *W Yor* 3B **92**
High Green. *Worc* 1D **49**
Highgreen Manor. *Nmbd* 5C **120**
High Halden. *Kent* 2C **28**
High Halstow. *Medw* 3B **40**
High Ham. *Som* 3H **21**
High Harrington. *Cumb* 2B **102**
High Haswell. *Dur* 5G **115**
High Hatton. *Shrp* 3A **72**
High Hawsker. *N Yor* 4G **107**
High Hesket. *Cumb* 5F **113**
High Hesleden. *Dur* 1B **106**
High Hoyland. *S Yor* 3C **92**
High Hunsley. *E Yor* 1C **94**
High Hurstwood. *E Sus* 3F **27**
High Hutton. *N Yor* 3B **100**
High Ireby. *Cumb* 1D **102**
High Keil. *Arg* 5A **122**
High Kelling. *Norf* 2D **78**
High Kilburn. *N Yor* 2H **99**
High Knipe. *Cumb* 3G **103**
High Lands. *Dur* 2E **105**
Highlands, The. *Shrp* 2A **60**
Highlane. *Ches E* 4C **84**
Highlane. *Derbs* 2B **86**
High Lane. *G Man* 2D **84**
High Lane. *Here* 4A **60**
High Laver. *Essx* 5F **53**
Highlaws. *Cumb* 5C **112**
Highleadon. *Glos* 3C **48**
High Legh. *Ches E* 2B **84**
Highleigh. *W Sus* 3G **17**
High Leven. *Stoc T* 3B **106**
Highley. *Shrp* 2B **60**
High Littleton. *Bath* 1B **22**
High Longthwaite. *Cumb* 5D **112**
High Lorton. *Cumb* 2C **102**
High Marishes. *N Yor* 2C **100**
High Marnham. *Notts* 3F **87**
High Melton. *S Yor* 4F **93**
High Mickley. *Nmbd* 3D **115**
Highmoor. *Cumb* 5D **112**
High Moor. *Lanc* 3D **90**
Highmoor. *Oxon* 3F **37**
Highmoor Cross. *Oxon* 3F **37**
Highmoor Hill. *Mon* 3H **33**
Highnam. *Glos* 4C **48**
High Newport. *Tyne* 4G **115**
High Newton. *Cumb* 1D **96**
High Newton-by-the-Sea. *Nmbd* 2G **121**
High Nibthwaite. *Cumb* 1B **96**
High Offley. *Staf* 3B **72**
High Ongar. *Essx* 5F **53**
High Onn. *Staf* 4C **72**
High Orchard. *Glos* 4D **48**
High Park. *Mers* 3B **90**
High Roding. *Essx* 4G **53**
High Row. *Cumb* 1E **103**
High Salvington. *W Sus* 5C **26**
High Scales. *Cumb* 5C **112**
High Shaw. *N Yor* 5B **104**
High Shincliffe. *Dur* 5F **115**
High Side. *Cumb* 1D **102**
High Spen. *Tyne* 3E **115**
Highsted. *Kent* 4D **40**
High Stoop. *Dur* 5E **115**
High Street. *Corn* 3D **6**
High Street. *Suff* 5G **67**
(nr. Aldeburgh)
High Street. *Suff* 2F **67**
(nr. Bungay)
High Street. *Suff* 3G **67**
(nr. Yoxford)
Highstreet Green. *Essx* 2A **54**
High Street Green. *Suff* 5C **66**
Highstreet Green. *Surr* 2A **26**
Hightae. *Dum* 2B **112**
High Throston. *Hart* 1B **106**
Hightown. *Ches E* 4C **84**
Hightown. *Mers* 4A **90**
High Town. *Staf* 4D **73**
Hightown Green. *Suff* 5B **66**
High Toynton. *Linc* 4B **88**
High Trewhitt. *Nmbd* 4E **121**
High Valleyfield. *Fife* 1D **128**
Highway. *Here* 1H **47**
Highweek. *Devn* 5B **12**
High Westwood. *Dur* 4E **115**
Highwood. *Staf* 2E **73**
Highwood. *Worc* 4A **60**
High Worsall. *N Yor* 4A **106**
Highworth. *Swin* 2H **35**
High Wray. *Cumb* 5E **103**
High Wych. *Herts* 4E **53**
High Wycombe. *Buck* 2G **37**
Hilborough. *Norf* 5H **77**
Hilcott. *Wilts* 1G **23**
Hildenborough. *Kent* 1G **27**
Hildersham. *Cambs* 1F **53**
Hilderstone. *Staf* 2D **72**
Hilderthorpe. *E Yor* 3F **101**
Hilfield. *Dors* 2B **14**
Hilgay. *Norf* 1F **65**
Hill. *S Glo* 2B **34**
Hill. *Warw* 4B **62**
Hill. *Worc* 1E **49**
Hillam. *N Yor* 2F **93**
Hillbeck. *Cumb* 3A **104**
Hillberry. *IOM* 4C **108**
Hillborough. *Kent* 4G **41**
Hillbourne. *Pool* 3F **15**
Hillbrae. *Abers* 4D **160**
(nr. Aberchirder)
Hillbrae. *Abers* 1E **153**
(nr. Inverurie)
Hillbrae. *Abers* 5F **161**
(nr. Methlick)
Hill Brow. *Hants* 4F **25**
Hillbutts. *Dors* 2E **15**
Hillclifflane. *Derbs* 1G **73**
Hillcommon. *Som* 4E **21**
Hill Deverill. *Wilts* 2D **22**
Hilldyke. *Linc* 1C **76**
Hill End. *Dur* 1D **104**
Hillend. *Fife* 1E **129**
(nr. Inverkeithing)
Hill End. *Fife* 4C **136**
(nr. Saline)
Hillend. *N Lan* 3B **128**
Hill End. *N Yor* 4C **98**
Hillend. *Shrp* 1C **60**
Hillend. *Swan* 3D **30**
Hillersland. *Glos* 4A **48**
Hillerton. *Devn* 3H **11**
Hillesden. *Buck* 3E **51**
Hillesley. *Glos* 3C **34**
Hillfarrance. *Som* 4E **21**
Hill Gate. *Here* 3H **47**
Hill Green. *Essx* 2E **53**
Hillgreen. *W Ber* 4C **36**
Hillhead. *Abers* 5C **160**
Hill Head. *Hants* 2D **16**
Hillhead. *S Ayr* 3D **116**
Hillhead. *Torb* 3F **9**
Hillhead of Auchentumb. *Abers* 3G **161**
Hilliard's Cross. *Staf* 4F **73**
Hilliclay. *High* 2D **168**
Hillingdon. *G Lon* 2B **38**
Hillington. *Glas* 3G **127**
Hillington. *Norf* 3G **77**
Hillmorton. *Warw* 3C **62**
Hill of Beath. *Fife* 4D **136**
Hill of Fearn. *High* 1C **158**
Hill of Fiddes. *Abers* 1G **153**
Hill of Keillor. *Ang* 4B **144**
Hill of Overbrae. *Abers* 2F **161**
Hill Ridware. *Staf* 4E **73**
Hillsborough. *Lis* 5G **175**
Hillsborough. *S Yor* 1H **85**
Hillside. *Abers* 4G **153**
Hillside. *Ang* 2G **145**
Hillside. *Devn* 2D **8**
Hillside. *Mers* 3B **90**
Hillside. *Orkn* 5C **172**
Hillside. *Shet* 5F **173**
Hillside. *Shrp* 2A **60**
Hill Side. *W Yor* 3B **92**
Hillside. *Worc* 4B **60**
Hillside of Prieston. *Ang* 5C **144**
Hill Somersal. *Derbs* 2F **73**
Hillstown. *Derbs* 4B **86**
Hillstreet. *Hants* 1B **16**
Hillswick. *Shet* 4D **173**
Hill, The. *Cumb* 1A **96**
Hill Top. *Dur* 2C **104**
(nr. Barnard Castle)
Hill Top. *Dur* 5F **115**
(nr. Durham)
Hill Top. *Dur* 4E **115**
(nr. Stanley)
Hill View. *Dors* 3E **15**
Hillwell. *Shet* 10E **173**
Hill Wootton. *Warw* 4H **61**
Hillyland. *Per* 1C **136**
Hilmarton. *Wilts* 4F **35**
Hilperton. *Wilts* 1D **22**
Hilperton Marsh. *Wilts* 1D **22**
Hilsea. *Port* 2E **17**
Hilston. *E Yor* 1F **95**
Hiltingbury. *Hants* 4C **24**
Hilton. *Cambs* 4B **64**
Hilton. *Cumb* 2A **104**
Hilton. *Derbs* 2G **73**
Hilton. *Dors* 2C **14**
Hilton. *Dur* 2E **105**
Hilton. *High* 5E **165**
Hilton. *Shrp* 1B **60**
Hilton. *Staf* 5E **73**
Hilton. *Stoc T* 3B **106**
Hilton of Cadboll. *High* 1C **158**
Himbleton. *Worc* 5D **60**
Himley. *Staf* 1C **60**
Hincaster. *Cumb* 1E **97**
Hinchcliffe Mill. *W Yor* 4B **92**
Hinchwick. *Glos* 3G **49**
Hinckley. *Leics* 1B **62**
Hinderclay. *Suff* 3C **66**
Hinderwell. *N Yor* 3E **107**
Hindford. *Shrp* 2F **71**
Hindhead. *Surr* 3G **25**
Hindley. *G Man* 4E **90**
Hindley. *Nmbd* 4D **114**
Hindley Green. *G Man* 4E **91**
Hindlip. *Worc* 5C **60**
Hindolveston. *Norf* 3C **78**
Hindon. *Wilts* 3E **23**
Hindringham. *Norf* 2B **78**
Hingham. *Norf* 5C **78**
Hinksford. *Staf* 2C **60**
Hinstock. *Shrp* 3A **72**
Hintlesham. *Suff* 1D **54**
Hinton. *Hants* 3H **15**
Hinton. *Here* 2G **47**
Hinton. *Nptn* 5C **62**
Hinton. *Shrp* 5G **71**
Hinton. *S Glo* 4C **34**
Hinton Ampner. *Hants* 4D **24**
Hinton Blewett. *Bath* 1A **22**
Hinton Charterhouse. *Bath* 1C **22**
Hinton-in-the-Hedges. *Nptn* 2D **50**
Hinton Martell. *Dors* 2F **15**
Hinton on the Green. *Worc* 1F **49**
Hinton Parva. *Swin* 3H **35**
Hinton St George. *Som* 1H **13**
Hinton St Mary. *Dors* 1C **14**
Hinton Waldrist. *Oxon* 2B **36**
Hints. *Shrp* 3A **60**
Hints. *Staf* 5F **73**
Hinwick. *Bed* 4G **63**
Hinxhill. *Kent* 1E **29**
Hinxton. *Cambs* 1E **53**
Hinxworth. *Herts* 1C **52**
Hipley. *Hants* 1E **16**
Hipperholme. *W Yor* 2B **92**
Hipsburn. *Nmbd* 3G **121**
Hipswell. *N Yor* 5E **105**
Hiraeth. *Carm* 2F **43**
Hirn. *Abers* 3E **153**
Hirnant. *Powy* 3C **70**
Hirst. *N Lan* 3B **128**
Hirst. *Nmbd* 1F **115**
Hirst Courtney. *N Yor* 2G **93**
Hirwaen. *Den* 4D **82**
Hirwaun. *Rhon* 5C **46**
Hiscott. *Devn* 4F **19**
Histon. *Cambs* 4D **64**
Hitcham. *Suff* 5B **66**
Hitchin. *Herts* 3B **52**
Hittisleigh. *Devn* 3H **11**
Hittisleigh Barton. *Devn* 3H **11**
Hive. *E Yor* 1B **94**
Hixon. *Staf* 3E **73**
Hoaden. *Kent* 5G **41**
Hoar Cross. *Staf* 3F **73**
Hoarwithy. *Here* 3A **48**
Hoath. *Kent* 4G **41**
Hobarris. *Shrp* 3F **59**
Hobbister. *Orkn* 7C **172**
Hobbles Green. *Suff* 5G **65**
Hobbs Cross. *Essx* 1F **39**
Hobkirk. *Bord* 3H **119**
Hobson. *Dur* 4E **115**
Hoby. *Leics* 4D **74**
Hockering. *Norf* 4C **78**
Hockering Heath. *Norf* 4C **78**
Hockerton. *Notts* 5E **86**
Hockley. *Essx* 1C **40**
Hockley. *Staf* 5G **73**
Hockley. *W Mid* 3G **61**
Hockley Heath. *W Mid* 3F **61**
Hockliffe. *C Beds* 3H **51**
Hockwold cum Wilton. *Norf* 2G **65**
Hockworthy. *Devn* 1D **12**
Hoddesdon. *Herts* 5D **52**
Hoddlesden. *Bkbn* 2F **91**
Hoddomcross. *Dum* 2C **112**
Hodgeston. *Pemb* 5E **43**
Hodley. *Powy* 1D **58**
Hodnet. *Shrp* 3A **72**
Hodsoll Street. *Kent* 4H **39**
Hodson. *Swin* 3G **35**
Hodthorpe. *Derbs* 3C **86**
Hoe. *Norf* 4B **78**
Hoe Gate. *Hants* 1E **17**
Hoe, The. *Plym* 3A **8**
Hoff. *Cumb* 3H **103**
Hoffleet Stow. *Linc* 2B **76**
Hogaland. *Shet* 4E **173**
Hogben's Hill. *Kent* 5E **41**
Hoggard's Green. *Suff* 5A **66**
Hoggeston. *Buck* 3G **51**
Hoggrill's End. *Warw* 1G **61**

Houghton-le-Spring—Ingon

Houghton-le-Spring. *Tyne* 4G 115
Houghton on the Hill. *Leics* 5D 74
Houghton Regis. *C Beds* 3A 52
Houghton St Giles. *Norf* 2B 78
Houlland. *Shet* 6E 173
(on Mainland)
Houlland. *Shet* 4G 173
(on Yell)
Houlsyke. *N Yor* 4E 107
Hound. *Hants* 2C 16
Hound Green. *Hants* 1F 25
Houndslow. *Bord* 5C 130
Houndsmoor. *Som* 4E 21
Houndwood. *Bord* 3E 131
Hounsdown. *Hants* 1B 16
Hounslow. *G Lon* 3C 38
Housabister. *Shet* 6F 173
Housay. *Shet* 4H 173
Househill. *High* 3C 158
Housetter. *Shet* 3E 173
Houss. *Shet* 8E 173
Houston. *Ren* 3F 127
Housty. *High* 5D 168
Houton. *Orkn* 7C 172
Hove. *Brig* 5D 27
Hoveringham. *Notts* 1D 74
Hoveton. *Norf* 4F 79
Hovingham. *N Yor* 2A 100
How. *Cumb* 4G 113
How Caple. *Here* 2B 48
Howden. *E Yor* 2H 93
Howden-le-Wear. *Dur* 1E 105
Howe. *High* 2F 169
Howe. *Norf* 5E 79
Howe. *N Yor* 1F 99
Howe Green. *Essx* 5H 53
(nr. Chelmsford)
Howegreen. *Essx* 5B 54
(nr. Maldon)
Howe Green. *Warw* 2H 61
Howell. *Linc* 1A 76
How End. *C Beds* 1A 52
Howe of Teuchar. *Abers* 4E 161
Howes. *Dum* 3C 112
Howe Street. *Essx* 4G 53
(nr. Chelmsford)
Howe Street. *Essx* 2G 53
(nr. Finchingfield)
Howe, The. *Cumb* 1D 96
Howe, The. *IOM* 5A 108
Howey. *Powy* 5C 58
Howgate. *Midl* 4F 129
Howgill. *Lanc* 5H 97
Howgill. *N Yor* 4C 98
How Green. *Kent* 1F 27
How Hill. *Norf* 4F 79
Howick. *Nmbd* 3G 121
Howle. *Telf* 3A 72
Howle Hill. *Here* 3B 48
Howleigh. *Som* 1F 13
Howlett End. *Essx* 2F 53
Howley. *Som* 2F 13
Howley. *Warr* 2A 84
Hownam. *Bord* 3B 120
Howsham. *N Lin* 4D 94
Howsham. *N Yor* 3B 100
Howtel. *Nmbd* 1C 120
Howt Green. *Kent* 4C 40
Howton. *Here* 3H 47
Howwood. *Ren* 3E 127
Hoxne. *Suff* 3D 66
Hoylake. *Mers* 2E 82
Hoyland. *S Yor* 4D 92
Hoylandswaine. *S Yor* 4C 92
Hoyle. *W Sus* 4A 26
Hubberholme. *N Yor* 2B 98
Hubberston. *Pemb* 4C 42
Hubbert's Bridge. *Linc* 1B 76
Huby. *N Yor* 5E 99
(nr. Harrogate)
Huby. *N Yor* 3H 99
(nr. York)
Hucclecote. *Glos* 4D 48
Hucking. *Kent* 5C 40
Hucknall. *Notts* 1C 74
Huddersfield. *W Yor* 3B 92
Huddington. *Worc* 5D 60
Huddlesford. *Staf* 5F 73
Hudswell. *N Yor* 4E 105
Huggate. *E Yor* 4C 100
Hugglescote. *Leics* 4B 74
Hughenden Valley. *Buck* 2G 37
Hughley. *Shrp* 1H 59
Hughton. *High* 4G 157
Hugh Town. *IOS* 1B 4
Hugus. *Corn* 4B 6
Huish. *Devn* 1F 11
Huish. *Wilts* 5G 35
Huish Champflower. *Som* 4D 20
Huish Episcopi. *Som* 4H 21
Huisinis. *W Isl* 6B 171
Hulcote. *Nptn* 1F 51
Hulcott. *Buck* 4G 51
Hulham. *Devn* 4D 12
Hull. *Hull* 2E 94
Hulland. *Derbs* 1G 73
Hulland Moss. *Derbs* 1G 73
Hulland Ward. *Derbs* 1G 73
Hullavington. *Wilts* 3D 35
Hullbridge. *Essx* 1C 40
Hulme. *G Man* 1C 84
Hulme. *Staf* 1D 72
Hulme End. *Staf* 5F 85
Hulme Walfield. *Ches E* 4C 84
Hulverstone. *IOW* 4B 16
Hulver Street. *Suff* 2G 67
Humber. *Devn* 5C 12
Humber. *Here* 5H 59
Humber Bridge. *N Lin* 2D 94
Humberside Airport. *N Lin* 3D 94
Humberston. *NE Lin* 4G 95
Humberstone. *Leic* 5D 74
Humbie. *E Lot* 3A 130
Humbleton. *E Yor* 1F 95
Humbleton. *Nmbd* 2D 121
Humby. *Linc* 2H 75
Hume. *Bord* 5D 130
Humshaugh. *Nmbd* 2C 114
Huna. *High* 1F 169
Huncoat. *Lanc* 1F 91
Huncote. *Leics* 1C 62
Hundall. *Derbs* 3A 86
Hunderthwaite. *Dur* 2C 104
Hundleby. *Linc* 4C 88
Hundle Houses. *Linc* 5B 88
Hundleton. *Pemb* 4D 42
Hundon. *Suff* 1H 53
Hundred Acres. *Hants* 1D 16
Hundred House. *Powy* 5D 58
Hundred, The. *Here* 4H 59
Hungarton. *Leics* 5D 74
Hungerford. *Hants* 1G 15
Hungerford. *Shrp* 2H 59
Hungerford. *Som* 2D 20
Hungerford. *W Ber* 5B 36
Hungerford Newtown. *W Ber* 4B 36
Hunger Hill. *G Man* 4E 91
Hungerton. *Linc* 2F 75
Hungladder. *High* 1C 154
Hungryhatton. *Shrp* 3A 72
Hunmanby. *N Yor* 2E 101
Hunmanby Sands. *N Yor* 2F 101
Hunningham. *Warw* 4A 62
Hunnington. *Worc* 2D 60
Hunny Hill. *IOW* 4C 16
Hunsdon. *Herts* 4E 53
Hunsdonbury. *Herts* 4E 53
Hunsingore. *N Yor* 4G 99
Hunslet. *W Yor* 1D 92
Hunslet Carr. *W Yor* 1D 92
Hunsonby. *Cumb* 1G 103
Hunspow. *High* 1E 169
Hunstanton. *Norf* 1F 77
Hunstanworth. *Dur* 5C 114
Hunston. *Suff* 4B 66
Hunston. *W Sus* 2G 17
Hunstrete. *Bath* 5B 34
Hunt End. *Worc* 4E 61
Hunterfield. *Midl* 3G 129
Hunters Forstal. *Kent* 4F 41
Hunter's Quay. *Arg* 2C 126
Huntham. *Som* 4G 21
Hunthill Lodge. *Ang* 1D 144
Huntingdon. *Cambs* 3B 64
Huntingfield. *Suff* 3F 67
Huntingford. *Dors* 4D 22
Huntington. *Ches W* 4G 83
Huntington. *E Lot* 2A 130
Huntington. *Here* 5E 59
Huntington. *Staf* 4D 72
Huntington. *Telf* 5A 72
Huntington. *York* 4A 100
Huntingtower. *Per* 1C 136
Huntley. *Glos* 4C 48
Huntley. *Staf* 1E 73
Huntly. *Abers* 5C 160
Huntlywood. *Bord* 5C 130
Hunton. *Hants* 3C 24
Hunton. *Kent* 1B 28
Hunton. *N Yor* 5E 105
Hunton Bridge. *Herts* 1B 38
Hunt's Corner. *Norf* 2C 66
Huntscott. *Som* 2C 20
Hunt's Cross. *Mers* 2G 83
Hunts Green. *Warw* 1F 61
Huntsham. *Devn* 4D 20
Huntshaw. *Devn* 4F 19
Huntspill. *Som* 2G 21
Huntstile. *Som* 3F 21
Huntworth. *Som* 3G 21
Hunwick. *Dur* 1E 105
Hunworth. *Norf* 2C 78
Hurcott. *Som* 1G 13
(nr. Ilminster)
Hurcott. *Som* 4A 22
(nr. Somerton)
Hurdcott. *Wilts* 3G 23
Hurdley. *Powy* 1E 59
Hurdsfield. *Ches E* 3D 84
Hurlet. *Glas* 3G 127
Hurley. *Warw* 1G 61
Hurley. *Wind* 3G 37
Hurlford. *E Ayr* 1D 116
Hurliness. *Orkn* 9B 172
Hurlston Green. *Lanc* 3C 90
Hurn. *Dors* 3G 15
Hursey. *Dors* 2H 13
Hursley. *Hants* 4C 24
Hurst. *G Man* 4H 91
Hurst. *N Yor* 4D 104
Hurst. *Som* 1H 13
Hurst. *Wok* 4F 37
Hurstbourne Priors. *Hants* 2C 24
Hurstbourne Tarrant. *Hants* 1B 24
Hurst Green. *Ches E* 1H 71
Hurst Green. *E Sus* 3B 28
Hurst Green. *Essx* 4D 54
Hurst Green. *Lanc* 1E 91
Hurst Green. *Surr* 5E 39
Hurstley. *Here* 1G 47
Hurstpierpoint. *W Sus* 4D 27
Hurstway Common. *Here* 1G 47
Hurst Wickham. *W Sus* 4D 27
Hurstwood. *Lanc* 1G 91
Hurtmore. *Surr* 1A 26
Hurworth-on-Tees. *Darl* 3A 106
Hurworth Place. *Darl* 4F 105
Hury. *Dur* 3C 104
Husbands Bosworth. *Leics* 2D 62
Husborne Crawley. *C Beds* 2H 51
Husthwaite. *N Yor* 2H 99
Hutcherleigh. *Devn* 3D 9
Hut Green. *N Yor* 2F 93
Huthwaite. *Notts* 5B 86
Huttoft. *Linc* 3E 89
Hutton. *Cumb* 2F 103
Hutton. *E Yor* 4E 101
Hutton. *Essx* 1H 39
Hutton. *Lanc* 2C 90
Hutton. *N Som* 1G 21
Hutton. *Bord* 4F 131
Hutton Bonville. *N Yor* 4A 106
Hutton Buscel. *N Yor* 1D 100
Hutton Conyers. *N Yor* 2F 99
Hutton Cranswick. *E Yor* 4E 101
Hutton End. *Cumb* 1F 103
Hutton Gate. *Red C* 3C 106
Hutton Henry. *Dur* 1B 106
Hutton-le-Hole. *N Yor* 1B 100
Hutton Magna. *Dur* 3E 105
Hutton Mulgrave. *N Yor* 4F 107
Hutton Roof. *Cumb* 2E 97
(nr. Kirkby Lonsdale)
Hutton Roof. *Cumb* 1E 103
(nr. Penrith)
Hutton Rudby. *N Yor* 4B 106
Huttons Ambo. *N Yor* 3B 100
Hutton Sessay. *N Yor* 2G 99
Hutton Village. *Red C* 3D 106
Hutton Wandesley. *N Yor* 4H 99
Huxham. *Devn* 3C 12
Huxham Green. *Som* 3A 22
Huxley. *Ches W* 4H 83
Huxter. *Shet* 6C 173
(on Mainland)
Huxter. *Shet* 5G 173
(on Whalsay)
Huyton. *Mers* 1G 83
Hwlffordd. *Pemb* 3D 42
Hycemoor. *Cumb* 1A 96
Hyde. *Glos* 5D 49
(nr. Stroud)
Hyde. *Glos* 3F 49
(nr. Winchcombe)
Hyde. *G Man* 1D 84
Hyde Heath. *Buck* 5H 51
Hyde Lea. *Staf* 4D 72
Hyde Park. *S Yor* 4F 93
Hydestile. *Surr* 1A 26
Hyndford Bridge. *S Lan* 5C 128
Hynish. *Arg* 5A 138
Hyssington. *Powy* 1F 59
Hythe. *Hants* 2C 16
Hythe. *Kent* 2F 29
Hythe End. *Wind* 3B 38
Hythie. *Abers* 3H 161
Hyton. *Cumb* 1A 96

I

Ianstown. *Mor* 2B 160
Iarsiadar. *W Isl* 4D 171
Ibberton. *Dors* 2C 14
Ible. *Derbs* 5G 85
Ibrox. *Glas* 3G 127
Ibsley. *Hants* 2G 15
Ibstock. *Leics* 4B 74
Ibstone. *Buck* 2F 37
Ibthorpe. *Hants* 1B 24
Iburndale. *N Yor* 4F 107
Ibworth. *Hants* 1D 24
Icelton. *N Som* 5G 33
Ichrachan. *Arg* 5E 141
Ickburgh. *Norf* 1H 65
Ickenham. *G Lon* 2B 38
Ickenthwaite. *Cumb* 1C 96
Ickford. *Buck* 5E 51
Ickham. *Kent* 5G 41
Ickleford. *Herts* 2B 52
Icklesham. *E Sus* 4C 28
Ickleton. *Cambs* 1E 53
Icklingham. *Suff* 3G 65
Ickwell. *C Beds* 1B 52
Icomb. *Glos* 3H 49
Idbury. *Oxon* 4H 49
Iddesleigh. *Devn* 2F 11
Ide. *Devn* 3B 12
Ideford. *Devn* 5B 12
Ide Hill. *Kent* 5F 39
Iden. *E Sus* 3D 28
Iden Green. *Kent* 2C 28
(nr. Benenden)
Iden Green. *Kent* 2B 28
(nr. Goudhurst)
Idle. *W Yor* 1B 92
Idless. *Corn* 4C 6
Idlicote. *Warw* 1A 50
Idmiston. *Wilts* 3G 23
Idole. *Carm* 4E 45
Idridgehay. *Derbs* 1G 73
Idrigill. *High* 2C 154
Idstone. *Oxon* 3A 36
Iffley. *Oxon* 5D 50
Ifield. *W Sus* 2D 26
Ifieldwood. *W Sus* 2D 26
Ifold. *W Sus* 2B 26
Iford. *E Sus* 5F 27
Ifton Heath. *Shrp* 2F 71
Ightfield. *Shrp* 2H 71
Ightham. *Kent* 5G 39
Iken. *Suff* 5G 67
Ilam. *Staf* 5F 85
Ilchester. *Som* 4A 22
Ilderton. *Nmbd* 2E 121
Ilford. *G Lon* 2F 39
Ilford. *Som* 1G 13
Ilfracombe. *Devn* 2F 19
Ilkeston. *Derbs* 1B 74
Ilketshall St Andrew. *Suff* 2F 67
Ilketshall St Lawrence. *Suff* 2F 67
Ilketshall St Margaret. *Suff* 2F 67
Ilkley. *W Yor* 5D 98
Illand. *Corn* 5C 10
Illey. *W Mid* 2D 61
Illidge Green. *Ches E* 4B 84
Illington. *Norf* 2B 66
Illingworth. *W Yor* 2A 92
Illogan. *Corn* 4A 6
Illogan Highway. *Corn* 4A 6
Illston on the Hill. *Leics* 1E 62
Ilmer. *Buck* 5F 51
Ilmington. *Warw* 1H 49
Ilminster. *Som* 1G 13
Ilsington. *Devn* 5A 12
Ilsington. *Dors* 3C 14
Ilston. *Swan* 3E 31
Ilton. *N Yor* 2D 98
Ilton. *Som* 1G 13
Imachar. *N Ayr* 5G 125
Imber. *Wilts* 2E 23
Immingham. *NE Lin* 3E 95
Immingham Dock. *NE Lin* 3F 95
Impington. *Cambs* 4D 64
Ince. *Ches W* 3G 83
Ince Blundell. *Mers* 4B 90
Ince-in-Makerfield. *G Man* 4D 90
Inchbae Lodge. *High* 2G 157
Inchbare. *Ang* 2F 145
Inchberry. *Mor* 3H 159
Inchbraoch. *Ang* 3G 145
Inchbrook. *Glos* 5D 48
Incheril. *High* 2C 156
Inchinnan. *Ren* 3F 127
Inchlaggan. *High* 3D 148
Inchmichael. *Per* 1E 137
Inchnadamph. *High* 1G 163
Inchree. *High* 2E 141
Inchture. *Per* 1E 137
Inchyra. *Per* 1D 136
Indian Queens. *Corn* 3D 6
Ingatestone. *Essx* 1H 39
Ingbirchworth. *S Yor* 4C 92
Ingestre. *Staf* 3D 73
Ingham. *Linc* 2G 87
Ingham. *Norf* 3F 79
Ingham. *Suff* 3A 66
Ingham Corner. *Norf* 3F 79
Ingleborough. *Norf* 4D 76
Ingleby. *Derbs* 3H 73
Ingleby Arncliffe. *N Yor* 4B 106
Ingleby Barwick. *Stoc T* 3B 106
Ingleby Greenhow. *N Yor* 4C 106
Ingleigh Green. *Devn* 2G 11
Inglemire. *Hull* 1D 94
Inglesbatch. *Bath* 5C 34
Ingleton. *Dur* 2E 105
Ingleton. *N Yor* 2F 97
Inglewhite. *Lanc* 5E 97
Ingoe. *Nmbd* 2D 114
Ingol. *Lanc* 1D 90
Ingoldisthorpe. *Norf* 2F 77
Ingoldmells. *Linc* 4E 89
Ingoldsby. *Linc* 2H 75
Ingon. *Warw* 5G 61

Ingram—Kerridge

Ingram. *Nmbd* 3E 121
Ingrave. *Essx* 1H 39
Ingrow. *W Yor* 1A 92
Ings. *Cumb* 5F 103
Ingst. *S Glo* 3A 34
Ingthorpe. *Rut* 5G 75
Ingworth. *Norf* 3D 78
Inkberrow. *Worc* 5E 61
Inkford. *Worc* 3E 61
Inkpen. *W Ber* 5B 36
Inkstack. *High* 1E 169
Innellan. *Arg* 3C 126
Inner Hope. *Devn* 5C 8
Innerleith. *Fife* 2E 137
Innerleithen. *Bord* 1F 119
Innerleven. *Fife* 3F 137
Innermessan. *Dum* 3F 109
Innerwick. *E Lot* 2D 130
Innerwick. *Per* 4C 142
Innsworth. *Glos* 3D 48
Insch. *Abers* 1D 152
Insh. *High* 3C 150
Inshegra. *High* 3C 166
Inshore. *High* 1D 166
Inskip. *Lanc* 1C 90
Instow. *Devn* 3E 19
Intwood. *Norf* 5D 78
Inver. *Abers* 4G 151
Inver. *High* 5F 165
Inver. *Per* 4H 143
Inverailort. *High* 5F 147
Inveralligin. *High* 3H 155
Inverallochy. *Abers* 2H 161
Inveramsay. *Abers* 1E 153
Inveran. *High* 4C 164
Inveraray. *Arg* 3H 133
Inverarish. *High* 5E 155
Inverarity. *Ang* 4D 144
Inverarnan. *Stir* 2C 134
Inverarnie. *High* 5A 158
Inverbeg. *Arg* 4C 134
Inverbervie. *Abers* 1H 145
Inverboyndie. *Abers* 2D 160
Invercassley. *High* 3B 164
Invercharnan. *High* 4F 141
Inverchoran. *High* 3E 157
Invercreran. *Arg* 4E 141
Inverdruie. *High* 2D 150
Inverebrie. *Abers* 5G 161
Invereck. *Arg* 1C 126
Inveresk. *E Lot* 2G 129
Inveresragan. *Arg* 5D 141
Inverey. *Abers* 5E 151
Inverfarigaig. *High* 1H 149
Invergarry. *High* 3F 149
Invergeldie. *Per* 1G 135
Invergordon. *High* 2B 158
Invergowrie. *Per* 5C 144
Inverguseran. *High* 3F 147
Inverharroch. *Mor* 5A 160
Inverie. *High* 3F 147
Inverinan. *Arg* 2G 133
Inverinate. *High* 1B 148
Inverkeilor. *Ang* 4F 145
Inverkeithing. *Fife* 1E 129
Inverkeithny. *Abers* 4D 160
Inverkip. *Inv* 2D 126
Inverkirkaig. *High* 2E 163
Inverlael. *High* 5F 163
Inverliever Lodge. *Arg* 3F 133
Inverliver. *Arg* 5E 141
Inverlochlarig. *Stir* 2D 134
Inverlochy. *High* 1F 141
Inverlussa. *Arg* 1E 125
Inver Mallie. *High* 5D 148
Invermarkie. *Abers* 5B 160
Invermoriston. *High* 2G 149
Invernaver. *High* 2H 167
Inverneil House. *Arg* 1G 125
Inverness. *High* 4A 158
Inverness Airport. *High* 3B 158
Invernettie. *Abers* 4H 161
Inverpolly Lodge. *High* 2E 163
Inverquhomery. *Abers* 4H 161
Inverroy. *High* 5E 149
Inversanda. *High* 3D 140
Invershiel. *High* 2B 148
Invershin. *High* 4C 164
Invershore. *High* 5E 169
Inversnaid. *Stir* 3C 134
Inverugie. *Abers* 4H 161
Inveruglas. *Arg* 3C 134
Inverurie. *Abers* 1E 153
Invervar. *Per* 4D 142
Inverythan. *Abers* 4E 161
Inwardleigh. *Devn* 3F 11
Inworth. *Essx* 4B 54
Iochdar. *W Isl* 4C 170
Iping. *W Sus* 4G 25
Ipplepen. *Devn* 2E 9
Ipsden. *Oxon* 3E 37
Ipstones. *Staf* 1E 73
Ipswich. *Suff* 1E 55
Irby. *Mers* 2E 83
Irby in the Marsh. *Linc* 4D 88
Irby upon Humber. *NE Lin* 4E 95
Irchester. *Nptn* 4G 63
Ireby. *Cumb* 1D 102
Ireby. *Lanc* 2F 97
Ireland. *Shet* 9E 173
Ireleth. *Cumb* 2B 96
Ireshopeburn. *Dur* 1B 104
Ireton Wood. *Derbs* 1G 73
Irlam. *G Man* 1B 84
Irnham. *Linc* 3H 75
Iron Acton. *S Glo* 3B 34
Iron Bridge. *Cambs* 1D 65
Ironbridge. *Telf* 5A 72
Iron Cross. *Warw* 5E 61
Ironville. *Derbs* 5B 86
Irstead. *Norf* 3F 79
Irthington. *Cumb* 3F 113
Irthlingborough. *Nptn* 3G 63
Irton. *N Yor* 1E 101
Irvine. *N Ayr* 1C 116
Irvine Mains. *N Ayr* 1C 116
Irvinestown. *Ferm* 5B 174
Isabella Pit. *Nmbd* 1G 115
Isauld. *High* 2B 168
Isbister. *Orkn* 6C 172
Isbister. *Shet* 2E 173 (on Mainland)
Isbister. *Shet* 5G 173 (on Whalsay)
Isfield. *E Sus* 4F 27
Isham. *Nptn* 3F 63
Island Carr. *N Lin* 4C 94
Islay Airport. *Arg* 4B 124
Isle Abbotts. *Som* 4G 21
Isle Brewers. *Som* 4G 21
Isleham. *Cambs* 3F 65
Isle of Man Airport. *IOM* 5B 108
Isle of Thanet. *Kent* 4H 41
Isle of Whithorn. *Dum* 5B 110
Isle of Wight. *IOW* 4C 16
Isleornsay. *High* 2F 147
Islesburgh. *Shet* 5E 173
Isles of Scilly (St Mary's) Airport. *IOS* 1B 4
Islesteps. *Dum* 2A 112
Isleworth. *G Lon* 3C 38
Isley Walton. *Leics* 3B 74
Islibhig. *W Isl* 5B 171
Islington. *G Lon* 2E 39
Islington. *Telf* 3B 72
Islip. *Nptn* 3G 63
Islip. *Oxon* 4D 50
Islwyn. *Cphy* 2F 33
Isombridge. *Telf* 4A 72
Istead Rise. *Kent* 4H 39
Itchen. *Sotn* 1C 16
Itchen Abbas. *Hants* 3D 24
Itchen Stoke. *Hants* 3D 24
Itchingfield. *W Sus* 3C 26
Itchington. *S Glo* 3B 34
Itlaw. *Abers* 3D 160
Itteringham. *Norf* 2D 78
Itteringham Common. *Norf* 3D 78
Itton. *Devn* 3G 11
Itton Common. *Mon* 2H 33
Ivegill. *Cumb* 5F 113
Ivelet. *N Yor* 5C 104
Iverchaolain. *Arg* 2B 126
Iver Heath. *Buck* 2B 38
Iveston. *Dur* 4E 115
Ivetsey Bank. *Staf* 4C 72
Ivinghoe. *Buck* 4H 51
Ivinghoe Aston. *Buck* 4H 51
Ivington. *Here* 5G 59
Ivington Green. *Here* 5G 59
Ivybridge. *Devn* 3C 8
Ivychurch. *Kent* 3E 29
Ivy Hatch. *Kent* 5G 39
Ivy Todd. *Norf* 5A 78
Iwade. *Kent* 4D 40
Iwerne Courtney. *Dors* 1D 14
Iwerne Minster. *Dors* 1D 14
Ixworth. *Suff* 3B 66
Ixworth Thorpe. *Suff* 3B 66

J

Jackfield. *Shrp* 5A 72
Jack Hill. *N Yor* 4D 98
Jacksdale. *Notts* 5B 86
Jackton. *S Lan* 4G 127
Jacobstow. *Corn* 3B 10
Jacobstowe. *Devn* 2F 11
Jacobswell. *Surr* 5A 38
Jameston. *Pemb* 5E 43
Jamestown. *Dum* 5F 119
Jamestown. *Fife* 1E 129
Jamestown. *High* 3G 157
Jamestown. *W Dun* 1E 127
Janetstown. *High* 2C 168 (nr. Thurso)
Janetstown. *High* 3F 169 (nr. Wick)
Jarrow. *Tyne* 3G 115
Jarvis Brook. *E Sus* 3G 27
Jasper's Green. *Essx* 3H 53
Jaywick. *Essx* 4E 55
Jedburgh. *Bord* 2A 120
Jeffreyston. *Pemb* 4E 43
Jemimaville. *High* 2B 158
Jenkins Park. *High* 3F 149
Jersey Marine. *Neat* 3G 31
Jesmond. *Tyne* 3F 115
Jevington. *E Sus* 5G 27
Jingle Street. *Mon* 4H 47
Jockey End. *Herts* 4A 52
Jodrell Bank. *Ches E* 3B 84
Johnby. *Cumb* 1F 103
John o' Gaunts. *W Yor* 2D 92
John o' Groats. *High* 1F 169
John's Cross. *E Sus* 3B 28
Johnshaven. *Abers* 2G 145
Johnson Street. *Norf* 4F 79
Johnston. *Pemb* 3D 42
Johnstone. *Ren* 3F 127
Johnstonebridge. *Dum* 5C 118
Johnstown. *Carm* 4E 45
Johnstown. *Wrex* 1F 71
Joppa. *Edin* 2G 129
Joppa. *S Ayr* 3D 116
Jordan Green. *Norf* 3C 78
Jordans. *Buck* 1A 38
Jordanston. *Pemb* 1D 42
Jump. *S Yor* 4D 93
Jumpers Common. *Dors* 3G 15
Juniper. *Nmbd* 4C 114
Juniper Green. *Edin* 3E 129
Jurby East. *IOM* 2C 108
Jurby West. *IOM* 2C 108
Jury's Gap. *E Sus* 4D 28

K

Kaber. *Cumb* 3A 104
Kaimend. *S Lan* 5C 128
Kaimes. *Edin* 3F 129
Kaimrig End. *Bord* 5D 129
Kames. *Arg* 2A 126
Kames. *E Ayr* 2F 117
Kea. *Corn* 4C 6
Keadby. *N Lin* 3B 94
Keady. *Arm* 6E 175
Keal Cotes. *Linc* 4C 88
Kearsley. *G Man* 4F 91
Kearsney. *Kent* 1G 29
Kearstwick. *Cumb* 1F 97
Kearton. *N Yor* 5C 104
Kearvaig. *High* 1C 166
Keasden. *N Yor* 3G 97
Keason. *Corn* 2H 7
Keckwick. *Hal* 2H 83
Keddington. *Linc* 2C 88
Keddington Corner. *Linc* 2C 88
Kedington. *Suff* 1H 53
Kedleston. *Derbs* 1H 73
Kedlock Feus. *Fife* 2F 137
Keekle. *Cumb* 3B 102
Keelby. *Linc* 3E 95
Keele. *Staf* 1C 72
Keeley Green. *Bed* 1A 52
Keeston. *Pemb* 3D 42
Keevil. *Wilts* 1E 23
Kegworth. *Leics* 3B 74
Kehelland. *Corn* 2D 4
Keig. *Abers* 2D 152
Keighley. *W Yor* 5C 98
Keilarsbrae. *Clac* 4A 136
Keillmore. *Arg* 1E 125
Keillor. *Per* 4B 144
Keillour. *Per* 1B 136
Keills. *Arg* 3C 124
Keiloch. *Abers* 4F 151
Keils. *Arg* 3D 124
Keinton Mandeville. *Som* 3A 22
Keir Mill. *Dum* 5A 118
Keirsleywell Row. *Nmbd* 4A 114
Keisby. *Linc* 3H 75
Keisley. *Cumb* 2A 104
Keiss. *High* 2F 169
Keith. *Mor* 3B 160
Keith Inch. *Abers* 4H 161
Kelbrook. *Lanc* 5B 98
Kelby. *Linc* 1H 75
Keld. *Cumb* 3G 103
Keld. *N Yor* 4B 104
Keldholme. *N Yor* 1B 100
Kelfield. *N Lin* 4B 94
Kelfield. *N Yor* 1F 93
Kelham. *Notts* 5E 87
Kellacott. *Devn* 4E 11
Kellan. *Arg* 4G 139
Kellas. *Ang* 5D 144
Kellas. *Mor* 3F 159
Kellaton. *Devn* 5E 9
Kelleth. *Cumb* 4H 103
Kelling. *Norf* 1C 78
Kellingley. *N Yor* 2F 93
Kellington. *N Yor* 2F 93
Kelloe. *Dur* 1A 106
Kelloholm. *Dum* 3G 117
Kells. *Cumb* 3A 102
Kells. *ME Ant* 3G 175
Kelly. *Devn* 4D 11
Kelly Bray. *Corn* 5D 10
Kelmarsh. *Nptn* 3E 63
Kelmscott. *Oxon* 2H 35
Kelsale. *Suff* 4F 67
Kelsall. *Ches W* 4H 83
Kelshall. *Herts* 2D 52
Kelsick. *Cumb* 4C 112
Kelso. *Bord* 1B 120
Kelstedge. *Derbs* 4H 85
Kelstern. *Linc* 1B 88
Kelsterton. *Flin* 3E 83
Kelston. *Bath* 5C 34
Keltneyburn. *Per* 4E 143
Kelton. *Dum* 2A 112
Kelton Hill. *Dum* 4E 111
Kelty. *Fife* 4D 136
Kelvedon. *Essx* 4B 54
Kelvedon Hatch. *Essx* 1G 39
Kelvinside. *Glas* 3G 127
Kelynack. *Corn* 3A 4
Kemback. *Fife* 2G 137
Kemberton. *Shrp* 5B 72
Kemble. *Glos* 2E 35
Kemerton. *Worc* 2E 49
Kemeys Commander. *Mon* 5G 47
Kemnay. *Abers* 2E 153
Kempe's Corner. *Kent* 1E 29
Kempley. *Glos* 3B 48
Kempley Green. *Glos* 3B 48
Kempsey. *Worc* 1D 48
Kempsford. *Glos* 2G 35
Kemps Green. *Warw* 3F 61
Kempshott. *Hants* 2E 24
Kempston. *Bed* 1A 52
Kempston Hardwick. *Bed* 1A 52
Kempton. *Shrp* 2F 59
Kemp Town. *Brig* 5E 27
Kemsing. *Kent* 5G 39
Kemsley. *Kent* 4D 40
Kenardington. *Kent* 2D 28
Kenchester. *Here* 1H 47
Kencot. *Oxon* 5A 50
Kendal. *Cumb* 5G 103
Kendleshire. *S Glo* 4B 34
Kendray. *S Yor* 4D 92
Kenfig. *B'end* 3B 32
Kenfig Hill. *B'end* 3B 32
Kengharair. *Arg* 4F 139
Kenilworth. *Warw* 3G 61
Kenknock. *Stir* 5B 142
Kenley. *G Lon* 5E 39
Kenley. *Shrp* 5H 71
Kenmore. *High* 3G 155
Kenmore. *Per* 4E 143
Kenn. *Devn* 4C 12
Kenn. *N Som* 5H 33
Kennacraig. *Arg* 3G 125
Kenneggy Downs. *Corn* 4C 4
Kennerleigh. *Devn* 2B 12
Kennet. *Clac* 4B 136
Kennethmont. *Abers* 1C 152
Kennett. *Cambs* 4G 65
Kennford. *Devn* 4C 12
Kenninghall. *Norf* 2C 66
Kennington. *Kent* 1E 28
Kennington. *Oxon* 5D 50
Kennoway. *Fife* 3F 137
Kennyhill. *Suff* 3F 65
Kennythorpe. *N Yor* 3B 100
Kenovay. *Arg* 4A 138
Kensaleyre. *High* 3D 154
Kensington. *G Lon* 3D 38
Kenstone. *Shrp* 3H 71
Kensworth. *C Beds* 4A 52
Kensworth Common. *C Beds* 4A 52
Kentallen. *High* 3E 141
Kentchurch. *Here* 3H 47
Kentford. *Suff* 4G 65
Kentisbeare. *Devn* 2D 12
Kentisbury. *Devn* 2G 19
Kentisbury Ford. *Devn* 2G 19
Kentmere. *Cumb* 4F 103
Kenton. *Devn* 4C 12
Kenton. *G Lon* 2C 38
Kenton. *Suff* 4D 66
Kenton Bankfoot. *Tyne* 3F 115
Kentra. *High* 2A 140
Kentrigg. *Cumb* 5G 103
Kents Bank. *Cumb* 2C 96
Kent's Green. *Glos* 3C 48
Kent's Oak. *Hants* 4B 24
Kent Street. *E Sus* 4B 28
Kent Street. *Kent* 5A 40
Kent Street. *W Sus* 3D 26
Kenwick. *Shrp* 2G 71
Kenwyn. *Corn* 4C 6
Kenyon. *Warr* 1A 84
Keoldale. *High* 2D 166
Keppoch. *High* 1B 148
Kepwick. *N Yor* 5B 106
Keresley. *W Mid* 2H 61
Keresley Newland. *Warw* 2H 61
Keristal. *IOM* 4C 108
Kerne Bridge. *Here* 4A 48
Kerridge. *Ches E* 3D 84

Lagg—Leegomery

Lagg. *N Ayr* 3D **122**
Laggan. *Arg* 4A **124**
Laggan. *High* 4E **149**
(nr. Fort Augustus)
Laggan. *High* 4A **150**
(nr. Newtonmore)
Laggan. *Mor* 5H **159**
Lagganlia. *High* 3C **150**
Lagganulva. *Arg* 4F **139**
Laglingarten. *Arg* 3A **134**
Lagness. *W Sus* 2G **17**
Laid. *High* 3E **166**
Laide. *High* 4C **162**
Laigh Fenwick. *E Ayr* 5F **127**
Laindon. *Essx* 2A **40**
Lairg. *High* 3C **164**
Lairg Muir. *High* 3C **164**
Laithes. *Cumb* 1F **103**
Laithkirk. *Dur* 2C **104**
Lake. *Devn* 3F **19**
Lake. *IOW* 4D **16**
Lake. *Wilts* 3G **23**
Lake District. *Cumb* 3E **103**
Lakenham. *Norf* 5E **79**
Lakenheath. *Suff* 2G **65**
Lakesend. *Norf* 1E **65**
Lakeside. *Cumb* 1C **96**
Laleham. *Surr* 4B **38**
Laleston. *B'end* 3B **32**
Lamancha. *Bord* 4F **129**
Lamarsh. *Essx* 2B **54**
Lamas. *Norf* 3E **79**
Lamb Corner. *Essx* 2D **54**
Lambden. *Bord* 5D **130**
Lamberhead Green. *G Man* 4D **90**
Lamberhurst. *Kent* 2A **28**
Lamberhurst Quarter. *Kent* 2A **28**
Lamberton. *Bord* 4F **131**
Lambeth. *G Lon* 3E **39**
Lambfell Moar. *IOM* 3B **108**
Lambhill. *Glas* 3G **127**
Lambley. *Nmbd* 4H **113**
Lambley. *Notts* 1D **74**
Lambourn. *W Ber* 4B **36**
Lambourne End. *Essx* 1F **39**
Lambourn Woodlands. *W Ber* 4B **36**
Lambrook. *Som* 4F **21**
Lambs Green. *Dors* 3E **15**
Lambs Green. *W Sus* 2D **26**
Lambston. *Pemb* 3D **42**
Lamellion. *Corn* 2G **7**
Lamerton. *Devn* 5E **11**
Lamesley. *Tyne* 4F **115**
Laminess. *Orkn* 4F **172**
Lamington. *High* 1B **158**
Lamington. *S Lan* 1B **118**
Lamlash. *N Ayr* 2E **123**
Lamonby. *Cumb* 1F **103**
Lamorick. *Corn* 2E **7**
Lamorna. *Corn* 4B **4**
Lamorran. *Corn* 4C **6**
Lampeter. *Cdgn* 1F **45**
Lampeter Velfrey. *Pemb* 3F **43**
Lamphey. *Pemb* 4E **43**
Lamplugh. *Cumb* 2B **102**
Lamport. *Nptn* 3E **63**
Lamyatt. *Som* 3B **22**
Lana. *Devn* 3D **10**
(nr. Ashwater)
Lana. *Devn* 2D **10**
(nr. Holsworthy)
Lanark. *S Lan* 5B **128**
Lanarth. *Corn* 4E **5**
Lancaster. *Lanc* 3D **97**
Lanchester. *Dur* 5E **115**
Lancing. *W Sus* 5C **26**
Landbeach. *Cambs* 4D **65**
Landcross. *Devn* 4E **19**
Landerberry. *Abers* 3E **153**
Landford. *Wilts* 1A **16**
Land Gate. *G Man* 4D **90**
Landhallow. *High* 5D **169**
Landimore. *Swan* 3D **30**
Landkey. *Devn* 3F **19**
Landkey Newland. *Devn* 3F **19**
Landore. *Swan* 3F **31**
Landport. *Port* 2E **17**
Landrake. *Corn* 2H **7**
Landscove. *Devn* 2D **9**
Land's End (St Just) Airport.
Corn 4A **4**
Landshipping. *Pemb* 3E **43**
Landulph. *Corn* 2A **8**
Landywood. *Staf* 5D **73**
Lane. *Corn* 2C **6**
Laneast. *Corn* 4C **10**
Lane Bottom. *Lanc* 1G **91**
Lane End. *Buck* 2G **37**
Lane End. *Hants* 4D **24**
Lane End. *IOW* 4E **17**
Lane End. *Wilts* 2D **22**
Lane Ends. *Derbs* 2G **73**
Lane Ends. *Dur* 1E **105**
Lane Ends. *Lanc* 4G **97**
Laneham. *Notts* 3F **87**
Lanehead. *Dur* 5B **114**
(nr. Cowshill)
Lane Head. *Dur* 3E **105**
(nr. Hutton Magna)
Lane Head. *Dur* 2D **105**
(nr. Woodland)
Lane Head. *G Man* 1A **84**
Lanehead. *Nmbd* 1A **114**
Lane Head. *W Yor* 4B **92**
Lane Heads. *Lanc* 1C **90**
Lanercost. *Cumb* 3G **113**
Laneshaw Bridge. *Lanc* 5B **98**
Laney Green. *Staf* 5D **72**
Langais. *W Isl* 2D **170**
Langal. *High* 2B **140**
Langar. *Notts* 2E **74**
Langbank. *Ren* 2E **127**
Langbar. *N Yor* 4C **98**
Langburnshiels. *Bord* 4H **119**
Langcliffe. *N Yor* 3H **97**
Langdale End. *N Yor* 5G **107**
Langdon. *Corn* 3C **10**
Langdon Beck. *Dur* 1B **104**
Langdon Cross. *Corn* 4D **10**
Langdon Hills. *Essx* 2A **40**
Langdown. *Hants* 2C **16**
Langdyke. *Fife* 3F **137**
Langenhoe. *Essx* 4D **54**
Langford. *C Beds* 1B **52**
Langford. *Devn* 2D **12**
Langford. *Essx* 5B **54**
Langford. *Notts* 5F **87**
Langford. *Oxon* 5H **49**
Langford. *Som* 4F **21**
Langford Budville. *Som* 4E **20**
Langham. *Dors* 4C **22**
Langham. *Essx* 2D **54**
Langham. *Norf* 1C **78**
Langham. *Rut* 4F **75**
Langham. *Suff* 4B **66**
Langho. *Lanc* 1F **91**
Langholm. *Dum* 1E **113**
Langland. *Swan* 4F **31**
Langleeford. *Nmbd* 2D **120**
Langley. *Ches E* 3D **84**
Langley. *Derbs* 1B **74**
Langley. *Essx* 2E **53**
Langley. *Glos* 3F **49**
Langley. *Hants* 2C **16**
Langley. *Herts* 3C **52**
Langley. *Kent* 5C **40**
Langley. *Nmbd* 3B **114**
Langley. *Slo* 3B **38**
Langley. *Som* 4D **20**
Langley. *Warw* 4F **61**
Langley. *W Sus* 4G **25**
Langley Burrell. *Wilts* 4E **35**
Langleybury. *Herts* 5A **52**
Langley Common. *Derbs* 2G **73**
Langley Green. *Derbs* 2G **73**
Langley Green. *Norf* 5F **79**
Langley Green. *Warw* 4F **61**
Langley Green. *W Sus* 2D **26**
Langley Heath. *Kent* 5C **40**
Langley Marsh. *Som* 4D **20**
Langley Moor. *Dur* 5F **115**
Langley Park. *Dur* 5F **115**
Langley Street. *Norf* 5F **79**
Langney. *E Sus* 5H **27**
Langold. *Notts* 2C **86**
Langore. *Corn* 4C **10**
Langport. *Som* 4H **21**
Langrick. *Linc* 1B **76**
Langridge. *Bath* 5C **34**
Langridgeford. *Devn* 4F **19**
Langrigg. *Cumb* 5C **112**
Langrish. *Hants* 4F **25**
Langsett. *S Yor* 4C **92**
Langshaw. *Bord* 1H **119**
Langstone. *Hants* 2F **17**
Langthorne. *N Yor* 5F **105**
Langthorpe. *N Yor* 3F **99**
Langthwaite. *N Yor* 4D **104**
Langtoft. *E Yor* 3E **101**
Langtoft. *Linc* 4A **76**
Langton. *Dur* 3E **105**
Langton. *Linc* 4B **88**
(nr. Horncastle)
Langton. *Linc* 3C **88**
(nr. Spilsby)
Langton. *N Yor* 3B **100**
Langton by Wragby. *Linc* 3A **88**
Langton Green. *Kent* 2G **27**
Langton Herring. *Dors* 4B **14**
Langton Long Blandford. *Dors* 2D **15**
Langton Matravers. *Dors* 5E **15**
Langtree. *Devn* 1E **11**
Langwathby. *Cumb* 1G **103**
Langwith. *Derbs* 3C **86**
Langworth. *Linc* 3H **87**
Lanivet. *Corn* 2E **7**
Lanjeth. *Corn* 3D **6**
Lank. *Corn* 5A **10**
Lanlivery. *Corn* 3E **7**
Lanner. *Corn* 5B **6**
Lanreath. *Corn* 3F **7**
Lansallos. *Corn* 3F **7**
Lansdown. *Bath* 5C **34**
Lansdown. *Glos* 3E **49**
Lanteglos Highway. *Corn* 3F **7**
Lanton. *Nmbd* 1D **120**
Lanton. *Bord* 2A **120**
Lapford. *Devn* 2H **11**
Lapford Cross. *Devn* 2H **11**
Laphroaig. *Arg* 5B **124**
Lapley. *Staf* 4C **72**
Lapworth. *Warw* 3F **61**
Larachbeg. *High* 4A **140**
Larbert. *Falk* 1B **128**
Larden Green. *Ches E* 5H **83**
Larel. *High* 3D **169**
Largie. *Abers* 5D **160**
Largiemore. *Arg* 1H **125**
Largoward. *Fife* 3G **137**
Largs. *N Ayr* 4D **126**
Largue. *Abers* 4D **160**
Largybeg. *N Ayr* 3E **123**
Largymeanoch. *N Ayr* 3E **123**
Largymore. *N Ayr* 3E **123**
Larkfield. *Inv* 2D **126**
Larkfield. *Kent* 5B **40**
Larkhall. *Bath* 5C **34**
Larkhall. *S Lan* 4A **128**
Larkhill. *Wilts* 2G **23**
Larling. *Norf* 2B **66**
Larne. *ME Ant* 2H **175**
Larport. *Here* 2A **48**
Lartington. *Dur* 3D **104**
Lary. *Abers* 3H **151**
Lasham. *Hants* 2E **25**
Lashenden. *Kent* 1C **28**
Lasswade. *Midl* 3G **129**
Lastingham. *N Yor* 5E **107**
Latchford. *Herts* 3D **53**
Latchford. *Oxon* 5E **51**
Latchingdon. *Essx* 5B **54**
Latchley. *Corn* 5E **11**
Latchmere Green. *Hants* 1E **25**
Lathbury. *Mil* 1G **51**
Latheron. *High* 5D **169**
Latheronwheel. *High* 5D **169**
Lathom. *Lanc* 4C **90**
Lathones. *Fife* 3G **137**
Latimer. *Buck* 1B **38**
Latteridge. *S Glo* 3B **34**
Lattiford. *Som* 4B **22**
Latton. *Wilts* 2F **35**
Laudale House. *High* 3B **140**
Lauder. *Bord* 5B **130**
Laugharne. *Carm* 3H **43**
Laughterton. *Linc* 3F **87**
Laughton. *E Sus* 4G **27**
Laughton. *Leics* 2D **62**
Laughton. *Linc* 1F **87**
(nr. Gainsborough)
Laughton. *Linc* 2H **75**
(nr. Grantham)
Laughton Common. *S Yor* 2C **86**
Laughton en le Morthen. *S Yor* 2C **86**
Launcells. *Corn* 2C **10**
Launceston. *Corn* 4D **10**
Launcherley. *Som* 2A **22**
Launton. *Oxon* 3E **50**
Laurencekirk. *Abers* 1G **145**
Laurieston. *Dum* 3D **111**
Laurieston. *Falk* 2C **128**
Lavendon. *Mil* 5G **63**
Lavenham. *Suff* 1C **54**
Laverhay. *Dum* 5D **118**
Laversdale. *Cumb* 3F **113**
Laverstock. *Wilts* 3G **23**
Laverstoke. *Hants* 2C **24**
Laverton. *Glos* 2F **49**
Laverton. *N Yor* 2E **99**
Laverton. *Som* 1C **22**
Lavister. *Wrex* 5F **83**
Law. *S Lan* 4B **128**
Lawers. *Per* 5D **142**
Lawford. *Essx* 2D **54**
Lawhitton. *Corn* 4D **10**
Lawkland. *N Yor* 3G **97**
Lawley. *Telf* 5A **72**
Lawnhead. *Staf* 3C **72**
Lawrenny. *Pemb* 4E **43**
Lawshall. *Suff* 5A **66**
Lawton. *Here* 5G **59**
Laxey. *IOM* 3D **108**
Laxfield. *Suff* 3E **67**
Laxfirth. *Shet* 6F **173**
Laxo. *Shet* 5F **173**
Laxton. *E Yor* 2A **94**
Laxton. *Nptn* 1G **63**
Laxton. *Notts* 4E **86**
Laycock. *W Yor* 5C **98**
Layer Breton. *Essx* 4C **54**
Layer-de-la-Haye. *Essx* 3C **54**
Layer Marney. *Essx* 4C **54**
Layland's Green. *W Ber* 5B **36**
Laymore. *Dors* 2G **13**
Laysters Pole. *Here* 4H **59**
Layter's Green. *Buck* 1A **38**
Laytham. *E Yor* 1H **93**
Lazenby. *Red C* 3C **106**
Lazonby. *Cumb* 1G **103**
Lea. *Derbs* 5H **85**
Lea. *Here* 3B **48**
Lea. *Linc* 2F **87**
Lea. *Shrp* 2F **59**
(nr. Bishop's Castle)
Lea. *Shrp* 5G **71**
(nr. Shrewsbury)
Lea. *Wilts* 3E **35**
Leabrooks. *Derbs* 5B **86**
Leac a Li. *W Isl* 8D **171**
Leachd. *Arg* 4H **133**
Leachkin. *High* 4A **158**
Leachpool. *Pemb* 3D **42**
Leadburn. *Midl* 4F **129**
Leadenham. *Linc* 5G **87**
Leaden Roding. *Essx* 4F **53**
Leaderfoot. *Bord* 1H **119**
Leadgate. *Cumb* 5A **114**
Leadgate. *Dur* 4E **115**
Leadgate. *Nmbd* 4E **115**
Leadhills. *S Lan* 3A **118**
Leadingcross Green. *Kent* 5C **40**
Lea End. *Worc* 3E **61**
Leafield. *Oxon* 4B **50**
Leagrave. *Lutn* 3A **52**
Lea Hall. *W Mid* 2F **61**
Lea Heath. *Staf* 3E **73**
Leake. *N Yor* 5B **106**
Leake Common Side. *Linc* 5C **88**
Leake Fold Hill. *Linc* 5D **88**
Leake Hurn's End. *Linc* 1D **76**
Lealholm. *N Yor* 4E **107**
Lealt. *Arg* 4D **132**
Lealt. *High* 2E **155**
Leam. *Derbs* 3G **85**
Lea Marston. *Warw* 1G **61**
Leamington Hastings. *Warw* 4B **62**
Leamington Spa, Royal.
Warw 4H **61**
Leamonsley. *Staf* 5F **73**
Leamside. *Dur* 5G **115**
Leargybreck. *Arg* 2D **124**
Lease Rigg. *N Yor* 4F **107**
Leasgill. *Cumb* 1D **97**
Leasingham. *Linc* 1H **75**
Leasingthorne. *Dur* 1F **105**
Leasowe. *Mers* 1E **83**
Leatherhead. *Surr* 5C **38**
Leathley. *N Yor* 5E **99**
Leaths. *Dum* 3E **111**
Leaton. *Shrp* 4G **71**
Leaton. *Telf* 4A **72**
Lea Town. *Lanc* 1C **90**
Leaveland. *Kent* 5E **40**
Leavenheath. *Suff* 2C **54**
Leavening. *N Yor* 3B **100**
Leaves Green. *G Lon* 4F **39**
Lea Yeat. *Cumb* 1G **97**
Leazes. *Dur* 4E **115**
Lebberston. *N Yor* 1E **101**
Lechlade on Thames. *Glos* 2H **35**
Leck. *Lanc* 2F **97**
Leckford. *Hants* 3B **24**
Leckfurin. *High* 3H **167**
Leckgruinart. *Arg* 3A **124**
Leckhampstead. *Buck* 2F **51**
Leckhampstead. *W Ber* 4C **36**
Leckhampstead Street. *W Ber* 4C **36**
Leckhampton. *Glos* 4E **49**
Leckmelm. *High* 4F **163**
Leckwith. *V Glam* 4E **33**
Leconfield. *E Yor* 5E **101**
Ledaig. *Arg* 5D **140**
Ledburn. *Buck* 3H **51**
Ledbury. *Here* 2C **48**
Ledgemoor. *Here* 5G **59**
Ledgowan. *High* 3D **156**
Ledicot. *Here* 4G **59**
Ledmore. *High* 2G **163**
Lednabirichen. *High* 4E **165**
Lednagullin. *High* 2A **168**
Ledsham. *Ches W* 3F **83**
Ledsham. *W Yor* 2E **93**
Ledston. *W Yor* 2E **93**
Ledstone. *Devn* 4D **8**
Ledwell. *Oxon* 3C **50**
Lee. *Devn* 2E **19**
(nr. Ilfracombe)
Lee. *Devn* 4B **20**
(nr. South Molton)
Lee. *G Lon* 3E **39**
Lee. *Hants* 1B **16**
Lee. *Lanc* 4E **97**
Lee. *Shrp* 2G **71**
Leeans. *Shet* 7E **173**
Leebotten. *Shet* 9F **173**
Leebotwood. *Shrp* 1G **59**
Lee Brockhurst. *Shrp* 3H **71**
Leece. *Cumb* 3B **96**
Leechpool. *Mon* 3A **34**
Lee Clump. *Buck* 5H **51**
Leeds. *Kent* 5C **40**
Leeds. *W Yor* 1C **92**
Leeds Bradford Airport. *W Yor* 5E **99**
Leedstown. *Corn* 3D **4**
Leegomery. *Telf* 4A **72**

Little Crosby—Llanfaes

Little Crosby. *Mers* 4B **90**
Little Crosthwaite. *Cumb* 2D **102**
Little Cubley. *Derbs* 2F **73**
Little Dalby. *Leics* 4E **75**
Little Dawley. *Telf* 5A **72**
Littledean. *Glos* 4B **48**
Little Dens. *Abers* 4H **161**
Little Dewchurch. *Here* 2A **48**
Little Ditton. *Cambs* 5F **65**
Little Down. *Hants* 1B **24**
Little Downham. *Cambs* 2E **65**
Little Drayton. *Shrp* 2A **72**
Little Driffield. *E Yor* 4E **101**
Little Dunham. *Norf* 4A **78**
Little Dunkeld. *Per* 4H **143**
Little Dunmow. *Essx* 3G **53**
Little Easton. *Essx* 3G **53**
Little Eaton. *Derbs* 1A **74**
Little Eccleston. *Lanc* 5D **96**
Little Ellingham. *Norf* 1C **66**
Little Elm. *Som* 2C **22**
Little End. *Essx* 5F **53**
Little Everdon. *Nptn* 5C **62**
Little Eversden. *Cambs* 5C **64**
Little Faringdon. *Oxon* 5H **49**
Little Fencote. *N Yor* 5F **105**
Little Fenton. *N Yor* 1F **93**
Littleferry. *High* 4F **165**
Little Fransham. *Norf* 4B **78**
Little Gaddesden. *Herts* 4H **51**
Little Garway. *Here* 3H **47**
Little Gidding. *Cambs* 2A **64**
Little Glemham. *Suff* 5F **67**
Little Glenshee. *Per* 5G **143**
Little Gransden. *Cambs* 5B **64**
Little Green. *Suff* 3C **66**
Little Green. *Wrex* 1G **71**
Little Grimsby. *Linc* 1C **88**
Little Habton. *N Yor* 2B **100**
Little Hadham. *Herts* 3E **53**
Little Hale. *Linc* 1A **76**
Little Hallingbury. *Essx* 4E **53**
Littleham. *Devn* 4E **19**
(nr. Bideford)
Littleham. *Devn* 4D **12**
(nr. Exmouth)
Little Hampden. *Buck* 5G **51**
Littlehampton. *W Sus* 5B **26**
Little Haresfield. *Glos* 5D **48**
Little Harrowden. *Nptn* 3F **63**
Little Haseley. *Oxon* 5E **51**
Little Hatfield. *E Yor* 5F **101**
Little Hautbois. *Norf* 3E **79**
Little Haven. *Pemb* 3C **42**
Little Hay. *Staf* 5F **73**
Little Hayfield. *Derbs* 2E **85**
Little Haywood. *Staf* 3E **73**
Little Heath. *W Mid* 2H **61**
Little Heck. *N Yor* 2F **93**
Littlehempston. *Devn* 2E **9**
Little Herbert's. *Glos* 4E **49**
Little Hereford. *Here* 4H **59**
Little Horkesley. *Essx* 2C **54**
Little Hormead. *Herts* 3D **53**
Little Horsted. *E Sus* 4F **27**
Little Horton. *W Yor* 1B **92**
Little Horwood. *Buck* 2F **51**
Little Houghton. *Nptn* 5F **63**
Littlehoughton. *Nmbd* 3G **121**
Little Houghton. *S Yor* 4E **93**
Little Hucklow. *Derbs* 3F **85**
Little Hulton. *G Man* 4F **91**
Little Irchester. *Nptn* 4G **63**
Little Kelk. *E Yor* 3E **101**
Little Kimble. *Buck* 5G **51**
Little Kineton. *Warw* 5H **61**
Little Kingshill. *Buck* 2G **37**
Little Langdale. *Cumb* 4E **102**
Little Langford. *Wilts* 3F **23**
Little Laver. *Essx* 5F **53**
Little Lawford. *Warw* 3B **62**
Little Leigh. *Ches W* 3A **84**
Little Leighs. *Essx* 4H **53**
Little Leven. *E Yor* 5E **101**
Little Lever. *G Man* 4F **91**
Little Linford. *Mil* 1G **51**
Little London. *Buck* 4E **51**
Little London. *E Sus* 4G **27**
Little London. *Hants* 2B **24**
(nr. Andover)
Little London. *Hants* 1E **24**
(nr. Basingstoke)
Little London. *Linc* 3D **76**
(nr. Long Sutton)
Little London. *Linc* 3B **76**
(nr. Spalding)
Little London. *Norf* 2E **79**
(nr. North Walsham)
Little London. *Norf* 1G **65**
(nr. Northwold)
Little London. *Norf* 2D **78**
(nr. Saxthorpe)
Little London. *Norf* 1F **65**
(nr. Southery)
Little London. *Powy* 2C **58**
Little Longstone. *Derbs* 3F **85**
Little Malvern. *Worc* 1C **48**
Little Maplestead. *Essx* 2B **54**
Little Marcle. *Here* 2B **48**
Little Marlow. *Buck* 3G **37**
Little Massingham. *Norf* 3G **77**
Little Melton. *Norf* 5D **78**
Littlemill. *Abers* 4H **151**
Littlemill. *E Ayr* 3D **116**
Littlemill. *High* 4D **158**
Little Mill. *Mon* 5G **47**
Little Milton. *Oxon* 5E **50**
Little Missenden. *Buck* 1A **38**
Littlemoor. *Derbs* 4A **86**
Littlemoor. *Dors* 4B **14**
Littlemore. *Oxon* 5D **50**
Little Mountain. *Flin* 4E **83**
Little Musgrave. *Cumb* 3A **104**
Little Ness. *Shrp* 4G **71**
Little Neston. *Ches W* 3E **83**
Little Newcastle. *Pemb* 2D **43**
Little Newsham. *Dur* 3E **105**
Little Oakley. *Essx* 3F **55**
Little Oakley. *Nptn* 2F **63**
Little Onn. *Staf* 4C **72**
Little Ormside. *Cumb* 3A **104**
Little Orton. *Cumb* 4E **113**
Little Orton. *Leics* 5H **73**
Little Ouse. *Norf* 2F **65**
Little Ouseburn. *N Yor* 3G **99**
Littleover. *Derb* 2H **73**
Little Packington. *Warw* 2G **61**
Little Paxton. *Cambs* 4A **64**
Little Petherick. *Corn* 1D **6**
Little Plumpton. *Lanc* 1B **90**
Little Plumstead. *Norf* 4F **79**
Little Ponton. *Linc* 2G **75**
Littleport. *Cambs* 2E **65**
Little Posbrook. *Hants* 2D **16**
Little Potheridge. *Devn* 1F **11**
Little Preston. *Nptn* 5C **62**
Little Raveley. *Cambs* 3B **64**
Little Reynoldston. *Swan* 4D **31**
Little Ribston. *N Yor* 4F **99**
Little Rissington. *Glos* 4G **49**
Little Rogart. *High* 3E **165**
Little Rollright. *Oxon* 2A **50**
Little Ryburgh. *Norf* 3B **78**
Little Ryle. *Nmbd* 3E **121**
Little Ryton. *Shrp* 5G **71**
Little Salkeld. *Cumb* 1G **103**
Little Sampford. *Essx* 2G **53**
Little Sandhurst. *Brac* 5G **37**
Little Saredon. *Staf* 5D **72**
Little Saxham. *Suff* 4G **65**
Little Scatwell. *High* 3F **157**
Little Shelford. *Cambs* 5D **64**
Little Shoddesden. *Hants* 2A **24**
Little Singleton. *Lanc* 1B **90**
Little Smeaton. *N Yor* 3F **93**
Little Snoring. *Norf* 2B **78**
Little Sodbury. *S Glo* 3C **34**
Little Somborne. *Hants* 3B **24**
Little Somerford. *Wilts* 3E **35**
Little Soudley. *Shrp* 3B **72**
Little Stainforth. *N Yor* 3H **97**
Little Stainton. *Darl* 3A **106**
Little Stanney. *Ches W* 3G **83**
Little Staughton. *Bed* 4A **64**
Little Steeping. *Linc* 4D **88**
Littlester. *Shet* 3G **173**
Little Stoke. *Staf* 2D **72**
Littlestone-on-Sea. *Kent* 3E **29**
Little Stonham. *Suff* 4D **66**
Little Stretton. *Leics* 5D **74**
Little Stretton. *Shrp* 1G **59**
Little Strickland. *Cumb* 3G **103**
Little Stukeley. *Cambs* 3B **64**
Little Sugnall. *Staf* 2C **72**
Little Sutton. *Ches W* 3F **83**
Little Sutton. *Linc* 3D **76**
Little Swinburne. *Nmbd* 2C **114**
Little Tew. *Oxon* 3B **50**
Little Tey. *Essx* 3B **54**
Little Thetford. *Cambs* 3E **65**
Little Thirkleby. *N Yor* 2G **99**
Little Thornage. *Norf* 2C **78**
Little Thornton. *Lanc* 5C **96**
Littlethorpe. *Leics* 1C **62**
Littlethorpe. *N Yor* 3F **99**
Little Thorpe. *W Yor* 2B **92**
Little Thurlow. *Suff* 5F **65**
Little Thurrock. *Thur* 3H **39**
Littleton. *Ches W* 4G **83**
Littleton. *Hants* 3C **24**
Littleton. *Som* 3H **21**
Littleton. *Surr* 1A **26**
(nr. Guildford)
Littleton. *Surr* 4B **38**
(nr. Staines)
Littleton Drew. *Wilts* 3D **34**
Littleton Pannell. *Wilts* 1F **23**
Littleton-upon-Severn. *S Glo* 3A **34**
Little Torboll. *High* 4E **165**
Little Torrington. *Devn* 1E **11**
Little Totham. *Essx* 4B **54**
Little Town. *Cumb* 3D **102**
Littletown. *Dur* 5G **115**
Littletown. *High* 5E **165**
Little Town. *Lanc* 1E **91**
Little Twycross. *Leics* 5H **73**
Little Urswick. *Cumb* 2B **96**
Little Wakering. *Essx* 2D **40**
Little Walden. *Essx* 1F **53**
Little Waldingfield. *Suff* 1C **54**
Little Walsingham. *Norf* 2B **78**
Little Waltham. *Essx* 4H **53**
Little Warley. *Essx* 1H **39**
Little Weighton. *E Yor* 1C **94**
Little Wenham. *Suff* 2D **54**
Little Wenlock. *Telf* 5A **72**
Little Whelnetham. *Suff* 4A **66**
Little Whittingham Green. *Suff* 3E **67**
Littlewick Green. *Wind* 4G **37**
Little Wilbraham. *Cambs* 5E **65**
Littlewindsor. *Dors* 2H **13**
Little Wisbeach. *Linc* 2A **76**
Little Witcombe. *Glos* 4E **49**
Little Witley. *Worc* 4B **60**
Little Wittenham. *Oxon* 2D **36**
Little Wolford. *Warw* 2A **50**
Littleworth. *Bed* 1A **52**
Littleworth. *Glos* 2G **49**
Littleworth. *Oxon* 2B **36**
Littleworth. *Staf* 4E **73**
(nr. Cannock)
Littleworth. *Staf* 3B **72**
(nr. Eccleshall)
Littleworth. *Staf* 3D **72**
(nr. Stafford)
Littleworth. *W Sus* 3C **26**
Littleworth. *Worc* 4D **61**
(nr. Redditch)
Littleworth. *Worc* 5C **60**
(nr. Worcester)
Little Wratting. *Suff* 1G **53**
Little Wymondley. *Herts* 3C **52**
Little Wyrley. *Staf* 5E **73**
Little Yeldham. *Essx* 2A **54**
Littley Green. *Essx* 4G **53**
Litton. *Derbs* 3F **85**
Litton. *N Yor* 2B **98**
Litton. *Som* 1A **22**
Litton Cheney. *Dors* 3A **14**
Liurbost. *W Isl* 5F **171**
Liverpool. *Mers* 1F **83**
Liverpool John Lennon Airport.
Mers 2G **83**
Liversedge. *W Yor* 2B **92**
Liverton. *Devn* 5B **12**
Liverton. *Red C* 3E **107**
Liverton Mines. *Red C* 3E **107**
Livingston. *W Lot* 3D **128**
Livingston Village. *W Lot* 3D **128**
Lixwm. *Flin* 3D **82**
Lizard. *Corn* 5E **5**
Llaingoch. *IOA* 2B **80**
Llaithddu. *Powy* 2C **58**
Llampha. *V Glam* 4C **32**
Llan. *Powy* 5A **70**
Llanaber. *Gwyn* 4F **69**
Llanaelhaearn. *Gwyn* 1C **68**
Llanaeron. *Cdgn* 4D **57**
Llanafan. *Cdgn* 3F **57**
Llanafan-fawr. *Powy* 5B **58**
Llanafan-fechan. *Powy* 5B **58**
Llanallgo. *IOA* 2D **81**
Llanandras. *Powy* 4F **59**
Llananno. *Powy* 3C **58**
Llanarmon. *Gwyn* 2D **68**
Llanarmon Dyffryn Ceiriog.
Wrex 2D **70**
Llanarmon-yn-Ial. *Den* 5D **82**
Llanarth. *Cdgn* 5D **56**
Llanarth. *Mon* 4G **47**
Llanarthne. *Carm* 3F **45**
Llanasa. *Flin* 2D **82**
Llanbabo. *IOA* 2C **80**
Llanbadarn Fawr. *Cdgn* 2F **57**
Llanbadarn Fynydd. *Powy* 3D **58**
Llanbadarn-y-garreg. *Powy* 1E **46**
Llanbadoc. *Mon* 5G **47**
Llanbadrig. *IOA* 1C **80**
Llanbeder. *Newp* 2G **33**
Llanbedr. *Gwyn* 3E **69**
Llanbedr. *Powy* 3F **47**
(nr. Crickhowell)
Llanbedr. *Powy* 1E **47**
(nr. Hay-on-Wye)
Llanbedr-Dyffryn-Clwyd. *Den* 5D **82**
Llanbedrgoch. *IOA* 2E **81**
Llanbedrog. *Gwyn* 2C **68**
Llanbedr Pont Steffan. *Cdgn* 1F **45**
Llanbedr-y-cennin. *Cnwy* 4G **81**
Llanberis. *Gwyn* 4E **81**
Llanbethery. *V Glam* 5D **32**
Llanbister. *Powy* 3D **58**
Llanblethian. *V Glam* 4C **32**
Llanboidy. *Carm* 2G **43**
Llanbradach. *Cphy* 2E **33**
Llanbrynmair. *Powy* 5A **70**
Llanbydderi. *V Glam* 5D **32**
Llancadle. *V Glam* 5D **32**
Llancarfan. *V Glam* 4D **32**
Llancatal. *V Glam* 5D **32**
Llancayo. *Mon* 5G **47**
Llancloudy. *Here* 3H **47**
Llancoch. *Powy* 3E **58**
Llancynfelyn. *Cdgn* 1F **57**
Llandaff. *Card* 4E **33**
Llandanwg. *Gwyn* 3E **69**
Llandarcy. *Neat* 3G **31**
Llandawke. *Carm* 3G **43**
Llanddaniel Fab. *IOA* 3D **81**
Llanddarog. *Carm* 4F **45**
Llanddeiniol. *Cdgn* 3E **57**
Llanddeiniolen. *Gwyn* 4E **81**
Llandderfel. *Gwyn* 2B **70**
Llanddeusant. *Carm* 3A **46**
Llanddeusant. *IOA* 2C **80**
Llanddew. *Powy* 2D **46**
Llanddewi. *Swan* 4D **30**
Llanddewi Brefi. *Cdgn* 5F **57**
Llanddewi'r Cwm. *Powy* 1D **46**
Llanddewi Rhydderch. *Mon* 4G **47**
Llanddewi Velfrey. *Pemb* 3F **43**
Llanddewi Ystradenni. *Powy* 4D **58**
Llanddoged. *Cnwy* 4H **81**
Llanddona. *IOA* 3E **81**
Llanddowror. *Carm* 3G **43**
Llanddulas. *Cnwy* 3B **82**
Llanddwywe. *Gwyn* 3E **69**
Llanddyfnan. *IOA* 3E **81**
Llandecwyn. *Gwyn* 2F **69**
Llandefaelog Fach. *Powy* 2D **46**
Llandefaelog-tre'r-graig. *Powy* 2E **47**
Llandefalle. *Powy* 2E **46**
Llandegfan. *IOA* 3E **81**
Llandegla. *Den* 5D **82**
Llandegley. *Powy* 4D **58**
Llandegveth. *Mon* 2G **33**
Llandeilo. *Carm* 3G **45**
Llandeilo Graban. *Powy* 1D **46**
Llandeilo'r Fan. *Powy* 2B **46**
Llandeloy. *Pemb* 2C **42**
Llandenny. *Mon* 5H **47**
Llandevaud. *Newp* 2H **33**
Llandevenny. *Mon* 3H **33**
Llandilo. *Pemb* 2F **43**
Llandinabo. *Here* 3A **48**
Llandinam. *Powy* 2C **58**
Llandissilio. *Pemb* 2F **43**
Llandogo. *Mon* 5A **48**
Llandough. *V Glam* 4C **32**
(nr. Cowbridge)
Llandough. *V Glam* 4E **33**
(nr. Penarth)
Llandovery. *Carm* 2A **46**
Llandow. *V Glam* 4C **32**
Llandre. *Cdgn* 2F **57**
Llandrillo. *Den* 2C **70**
Llandrillo-yn-Rhos. *Cnwy* 2H **81**
Llandrindod. *Powy* 4C **58**
Llandrindod Wells. *Powy* 4C **58**
Llandrinio. *Powy* 4E **71**
Llandudno. *Cnwy* 2G **81**
Llandudno Junction. *Cnwy* 3G **81**
Llandudoch. *Pemb* 1B **44**
Llandw. *V Glam* 4C **32**
Llandwrog. *Gwyn* 5D **80**
Llandybie. *Carm* 4G **45**
Llandyfaelog. *Carm* 4E **45**
Llandyfan. *Carm* 4G **45**
Llandyfriog. *Cdgn* 1D **44**
Llandyfrydog. *IOA* 2D **80**
Llandygai. *Gwyn* 3F **81**
Llandygwydd. *Cdgn* 1C **44**
Llandynan. *Den* 1D **70**
Llandyrnog. *Den* 4D **82**
Llandysilio. *Powy* 4E **71**
Llandyssil. *Powy* 1D **58**
Llandysul. *Cdgn* 1E **45**
Llanedeyrn. *Card* 3F **33**
Llaneglwys. *Powy* 2D **46**
Llanegryn. *Gwyn* 5F **69**
Llanegwad. *Carm* 3F **45**
Llaneilian. *IOA* 1D **80**
Llanelian-yn-Rhos. *Cnwy* 3A **82**
Llanelidan. *Den* 5D **82**
Llanelieu. *Powy* 2E **47**
Llanellen. *Mon* 4G **47**
Llanelli. *Carm* 3E **31**
Llanelltyd. *Gwyn* 4G **69**
Llanelly. *Mon* 4F **47**
Llanelly Hill. *Mon* 4F **47**
Llanelwedd. *Powy* 5C **58**
Llanelwy. *Den* 3C **82**
Llanenddwyn. *Gwyn* 3E **69**
Llanengan. *Gwyn* 3B **68**
Llanerch. *Powy* 1F **59**
Llanerchymedd. *IOA* 2D **80**
Llanerfyl. *Powy* 5C **70**
Llaneuddog. *IOA* 2D **80**
Llanfachraeth. *IOA* 2C **80**
Llanfachreth. *Gwyn* 3G **69**
Llanfaelog. *IOA* 3C **80**
Llanfaelrhys. *Gwyn* 3B **68**
Llanfaenor. *Mon* 4H **47**
Llanfaes. *IOA* 3F **81**
Llanfaes. *Powy* 3D **46**

Llanfaethlu. IOA ... 2C 80
Llanfaglan. Gwyn ... 4D 80
Llanfair. Gwyn ... 3E 69
Llanfair. Here ... 1F 47
Llanfair Caereinion. Powy ... 5D 70
Llanfair Clydogau. Cdgn ... 5F 57
Llanfair Dyffryn Clwyd. Den ... 5D 82
Llanfairfechan. Cnwy ... 3F 81
Llanfair-Nant-Gwyn. Pemb ... 1F 43
Llanfair Pwllgwyngyll. IOA ... 3E 81
Llanfair Talhaiarn. Cnwy ... 3B 82
Llanfair Waterdine. Shrp ... 3E 59
Llanfair-ym-Muallt. Powy ... 5C 58
Llanfairyneubwll. IOA ... 3C 80
Llanfairynghornwy. IOA ... 1C 80
Llanfallteg. Carm ... 3F 43
Llanfallteg West. Carm ... 3F 43
Llanfaredd. Powy ... 5C 58
Llanfarian. Cdgn ... 3E 57
Llanfechain. Powy ... 3D 70
Llanfechell. IOA ... 1C 80
Llanfendigaid. Gwyn ... 5E 69
Llanferres. Den ... 4D 82
Llan Ffestiniog. Gwyn ... 1G 69
Llanfflewyn. IOA ... 2C 80
Llanfihangel-ar-Arth. Carm ... 2E 45
Llanfihangel Glyn Myfyr. Cnwy ... 1B 70
Llanfihangel Nant Bran. Powy ... 2C 46
Llanfihangel-Nant-Melan. Powy ... 5D 58
Llanfihangel Rhydithon. Powy ... 4D 58
Llanfihangel Rogiet. Mon ... 3H 33
Llanfihangel Tal-y-llyn. Powy ... 3E 46
Llanfihangel-uwch-Gwili. Carm ... 3E 45
Llanfihangel-y-Creuddyn. Cdgn ... 3F 57
Llanfihangel-yng-Ngwynfa.
   Powy ... 4C 70
Llanfihangel yn Nhowyn. IOA ... 3C 80
Llanfihangel-y-pennant. Gwyn ... 1E 69
   (nr. Golan)
Llanfihangel-y-pennant. Gwyn ... 5F 69
   (nr. Tywyn)
Llanfihangel-y-traethau. Gwyn ... 2E 69
Llanfilo. Powy ... 2E 46
Llanfleiddan. V Glam ... 4C 32
Llanfoist. Mon ... 4F 47
Llanfor. Gwyn ... 2B 70
Llanfrechfa. Torf ... 2G 33
Llanfrothen. Gwyn ... 1F 69
Llanfrynach. Powy ... 3D 46
Llanfwrog. IOA ... 2C 80
Llanfwrog. Den ... 4D 70
Llanfyllin. Powy ... 3D 70
Llanfynydd. Carm ... 3F 45
Llanfynydd. Flin ... 5E 83
Llanfyrnach. Pemb ... 1G 43
Llangadfan. Powy ... 4C 70
Llangadog. Carm ... 3H 45
   (nr. Llandovery)
Llangadog. Carm ... 5E 45
   (nr. Llanelli)
Llangadwaladr. IOA ... 4C 80
Llangadwaladr. Powy ... 2D 70
Llangaffo. IOA ... 4D 80
Llangain. Carm ... 4D 45
Llangammarch Wells. Powy ... 1C 46
Llangan. V Glam ... 4C 32
Llangarron. Here ... 3A 48
Llangasty-Talyllyn. Powy ... 3E 47
Llangathen. Carm ... 3F 45
Llangattock. Powy ... 4F 47
Llangattock Lingoed. Mon ... 3G 47
Llangattock-Vibon-Avel. Mon ... 4H 47
Llangedwyn. Powy ... 3D 70
Llangefni. IOA ... 3D 80
Llangeinor. B'end ... 3C 32
Llangeitho. Cdgn ... 5F 57
Llangeler. Carm ... 2D 44
Llangelynin. Gwyn ... 5E 69
Llangendeirne. Carm ... 4E 45
Llangennech. Carm ... 5F 45
Llangennith. Swan ... 3D 30
Llangenny. Powy ... 4F 47
Llangernyw. Cnwy ... 4A 82
Llangian. Gwyn ... 3B 68
Llangiwg. Neat ... 5H 45

Llangloffan. Pemb ... 1D 42
Llanglydwen. Carm ... 2F 43
Llangoed. IOA ... 3F 81
Llangoedmor. Cdgn ... 1B 44
Llangollen. Den ... 1E 70
Llangolman. Pemb ... 2F 43
Llangorse. Powy ... 3E 47
Llangorwen. Cdgn ... 2F 57
Llangovan. Mon ... 5H 47
Llangower. Gwyn ... 2B 70
Llangranog. Cdgn ... 5C 56
Llangristiolus. IOA ... 3D 80
Llangrove. Here ... 4A 48
Llangua. Mon ... 3G 47
Llangunllo. Powy ... 3E 58
Llangunnor. Carm ... 3E 45
Llangurig. Powy ... 3B 58
Llangwm. Cnwy ... 1B 70
Llangwm. Mon ... 5H 47
Llangwm. Pemb ... 4D 43
Llangwm-isaf. Mon ... 5H 47
Llangwnnadl. Gwyn ... 2B 68
Llangwyfan. Den ... 4D 82
Llangwyfan-isaf. IOA ... 4C 80
Llangwyllog. IOA ... 3D 80
Llangwyryfon. Cdgn ... 3F 57
Llangybi. Cdgn ... 5F 57
Llangybi. Gwyn ... 1D 68
Llangybi. Mon ... 2G 33
Llangyfelach. Swan ... 3F 31
Llangynhafal. Den ... 4D 82
Llangynidr. Powy ... 4E 47
Llangynin. Carm ... 3G 43
Llangynog. Carm ... 3H 43
Llangynog. Powy ... 3C 70
Llangynwyd. B'end ... 3B 32
Llanhamlach. Powy ... 3D 46
Llanharan. Rhon ... 3D 32
Llanharry. Rhon ... 3D 32
Llanhennock. Mon ... 2G 33
Llanhilleth. Blae ... 5F 47
Llanidloes. Powy ... 2B 58
Llaniestyn. Gwyn ... 2B 68
Llanigon. Powy ... 1F 47
Llanilar. Cdgn ... 3F 57
Llanilid. Rhon ... 3C 32
Llanilltud Fawr. V Glam ... 5C 32
Llanishen. Card ... 3E 33
Llanishen. Mon ... 5H 47
Llanllawddog. Carm ... 3E 45
Llanllechid. Gwyn ... 4F 81
Llanllowell. Mon ... 2G 33
Llanllugan. Powy ... 5C 70
Llanllwch. Carm ... 4D 45
Llanllwchaiarn. Powy ... 1D 58
Llanllwni. Carm ... 2E 45
Llanllyfni. Gwyn ... 5D 80
Llanmadoc. Swan ... 3D 30
Llanmaes. V Glam ... 5C 32
Llanmartin. Newp ... 3G 33
Llanmihangel. V Glam ... 4C 32
Llan-mill. Pemb ... 3F 43
Llanmiloe. Carm ... 4G 43
Llanmorlais. Swan ... 3E 31
Llannefydd. Cnwy ... 3B 82
Llannon. Carm ... 5F 45
Llan-non. Cdgn ... 4E 57
Llannor. Gwyn ... 2C 68
Llanover. Mon ... 5G 47
Llanpumsaint. Carm ... 3E 45
Llanrhaeadr. Den ... 4C 82
Llanrhaeadr-ym-Mochnant.
   Powy ... 3D 70
Llanrhian. Pemb ... 1C 42
Llanrhidian. Swan ... 3D 31
Llanrhos. Cnwy ... 2G 81
Llanrhyddlad. IOA ... 2C 80
Llanrhystud. Cdgn ... 4E 57
Llanrothal. Here ... 4H 47
Llanrug. Gwyn ... 4E 81
Llanrumney. Card ... 3F 33
Llanrwst. Cnwy ... 4G 81
Llansadwrn. Carm ... 2G 45

Llansadwrn. IOA ... 3E 81
Llansaint. Carm ... 5D 45
Llansamlet. Swan ... 3F 31
Llansantffraid Glan Conwy.
   Cnwy ... 3H 81
Llansannan. Cnwy ... 4B 82
Llansannor. V Glam ... 4C 32
Llansantffraed. Cdgn ... 4E 57
Llansantffraed. Powy ... 3E 46
Llansantffraed Cwmdeuddwr.
   Powy ... 4B 58
Llansantffraed-in-Elwel. Powy ... 5C 58
Llansantffraid-ym-Mechain.
   Powy ... 3E 70
Llansawel. Carm ... 2G 45
Llansawel. Neat ... 3G 31
Llansilin. Powy ... 3E 70
Llansoy. Mon ... 5H 47
Llanspyddid. Powy ... 3D 46
Llanstadwell. Pemb ... 4D 42
Llansteffan. Carm ... 4D 44
Llanstephan. Powy ... 1E 46
Llantarnam. Torf ... 2G 33
Llanteg. Pemb ... 3F 43
Llanthony. Mon ... 3F 47
Llantilio Crossenny. Mon ... 4G 47
Llantilio Pertholey. Mon ... 4G 47
Llantood. Pemb ... 1B 44
Llantrisant. Mon ... 2G 33
Llantrisant. Rhon ... 3D 32
Llantrithyd. V Glam ... 4D 32
Llantwit Fardre. Rhon ... 3D 32
Llantwit Major. V Glam ... 5C 32
Llanuwchllyn. Gwyn ... 2A 70
Llanvaches. Newp ... 2H 33
Llanvair Discoed. Mon ... 2H 33
Llanvapley. Mon ... 4G 47
Llanvetherine. Mon ... 4G 47
Llanveynoe. Here ... 2G 47
Llanvihangel Crucorney. Mon ... 3G 47
Llanvihangel Gobion. Mon ... 5G 47
Llanvihangel Ystern-Llewern.
   Mon ... 4H 47
Llanwarne. Here ... 3A 48
Llanwddyn. Powy ... 4C 70
Llanwenarth. Mon ... 4F 47
Llanwenog. Cdgn ... 1E 45
Llanwern. Newp ... 3G 33
Llanwinio. Carm ... 2G 43
Llanwnda. Gwyn ... 5D 80
Llanwnda. Pemb ... 1D 42
Llanwnnen. Cdgn ... 1F 45
Llanwnog. Powy ... 1C 58
Llanwrda. Carm ... 2H 45
Llanwrin. Powy ... 5G 69
Llanwrthwl. Powy ... 4B 58
Llanwrtud. Powy ... 1B 46
Llanwrtyd. Powy ... 1B 46
Llanwrtyd Wells. Powy ... 1B 46
Llanyblodwel. Shrp ... 3E 71
Llanybri. Carm ... 3H 43
Llanybydder. Carm ... 1F 45
Llanycefn. Pemb ... 2E 43
Llanychaer. Pemb ... 1D 43
Llanycil. Gwyn ... 2B 70
Llanymawddwy. Gwyn ... 4B 70
Llanymddyfri. Carm ... 2A 46
Llanymynech. Shrp ... 3E 71
Llanynghenedl. IOA ... 2C 80
Llanynys. Den ... 4D 82
Llan-y-pwll. Wrex ... 5F 83
Llanyrafon. Torf ... 2G 33
Llanyre. Powy ... 4C 58
Llanystumdwy. Gwyn ... 2D 68
Llanywern. Powy ... 3E 46
Llawhaden. Pemb ... 3E 43
Llawndy. Flin ... 2D 82
Llawnt. Shrp ... 2E 71
Llawr Dref. Gwyn ... 3B 68
Llawryglyn. Powy ... 1B 58
Llay. Wrex ... 5F 83
Llechfaen. Powy ... 3D 46
Llechryd. Cphy ... 5E 47
Llechryd. Cdgn ... 1C 44

Llechrydau. Wrex ... 2E 71
Lledrod. Cdgn ... 3F 57
Llethrid. Swan ... 3E 31
Llidiad-Nenog. Carm ... 2F 45
Llidiart-y-Parc. Den ... 1D 70
Llithfaen. Gwyn ... 1C 68
Lloc. Flin ... 3D 82
Llong. Flin ... 4E 83
Llowes. Powy ... 1E 47
Lloyney. Powy ... 3E 59
Llundain-fach. Cdgn ... 5E 57
Llwydcoed. Rhon ... 5C 46
Llwyncelyn. Cdgn ... 5D 56
Llwyncelyn. Swan ... 5G 45
Llwyndafydd. Cdgn ... 5C 56
Llwynderw. Powy ... 5E 70
Llwyn-du. Mon ... 4F 47
Llwyngwril. Gwyn ... 5E 69
Llwynhendy. Carm ... 3E 31
Llwynmawr. Wrex ... 2E 71
Llwyn-on Village. Mer T ... 4D 46
Llwyn-teg. Carm ... 5F 45
Llwyn-y-brain. Carm ... 3F 43
Llwynygog. Powy ... 1A 58
Llwyn-y-groes. Cdgn ... 5E 57
Llwynypia. Rhon ... 2C 32
Llynclys. Shrp ... 3E 71
Llynfaes. IOA ... 3D 80
Llysfaen. Cnwy ... 3A 82
Llyswen. Powy ... 2E 47
Llysworney. V Glam ... 4C 32
Llys-y-fran. Pemb ... 2E 43
Llywel. Powy ... 2B 46
Llywernog. Cdgn ... 2G 57
Loan. Falk ... 2C 128
Loanend. Nmbd ... 4F 131
Loanhead. Midl ... 3G 129
Loaningfoot. Dum ... 4A 112
Loanreoch. High ... 1A 158
Loans. S Ayr ... 1C 116
Loansdean. Nmbd ... 1E 115
Lobb. Devn ... 3E 19
Lobhillcross. Devn ... 4E 11
Lochaber. Mor ... 4G 159
Loch a Charnain. W Isl ... 4D 170
Loch a Ghainmhich. W Isl ... 5E 171
Lochailort. High ... 5F 147
Lochaline. High ... 4A 140
Lochans. Dum ... 4F 109
Locharbriggs. Dum ... 1A 112
Lochardil. High ... 4A 158
Lochassynt Lodge. High ... 1F 163
Lochavich. Arg ... 2G 133
Lochawe. Arg ... 1A 134
Loch Baghasdail. W Isl ... 7C 170
Lochboisdale. W Isl ... 7C 170
Lochbuie. Arg ... 1D 132
Lochcarron. High ... 5A 156
Loch Choire Lodge. High ... 5G 167
Lochdochart House. Stir ... 1D 134
Lochdon. Arg ... 5B 140
Lochearnhead. Stir ... 1E 135
Lochee. D'dee ... 5C 144
Lochend. High ... 5A 157
   (nr. Inverness)
Lochend. High ... 2E 169
   (nr. Thurso)
Locherben. Dum ... 5B 118
Loch Euphort. W Isl ... 2D 170
Lochfoot. Dum ... 2F 111
Lochgair. Arg ... 4G 133
Lochgarthside. High ... 2H 149
Lochgelly. Fife ... 4D 136
Lochgilphead. Arg ... 1G 125
Lochgoilhead. Arg ... 3A 134
Loch Head. Dum ... 5A 110
Lochhill. Mor ... 2G 159
Lochindorb Lodge. High ... 5D 158
Lochinver. High ... 1E 163
Lochlane. Per ... 1H 135
Loch Lomond. Arg ... 3C 134
Loch Loyal Lodge. High ... 4G 167
Lochluichart. High ... 2F 157
Lochmaben. Dum ... 1B 112

Lochmaddy. W Isl ... 2E 170
Loch nam Madadh. W Isl ... 2E 170
Lochore. Fife ... 4D 136
Lochportain. W Isl ... 1E 170
Lochranza. N Ayr ... 4H 125
Loch Sgioport. W Isl ... 5D 170
Lochside. Abers ... 2G 145
Lochside. High ... 5A 168
   (nr. Achentoul)
Lochside. High ... 3C 158
   (nr. Nairn)
Lochslin. High ... 5F 165
Lochstack Lodge. High ... 4C 166
Lochton. Abers ... 4E 153
Lochty. Fife ... 3H 137
Lochuisge. High ... 3B 140
Lochussie. High ... 3G 157
Lochwinnoch. Ren ... 4E 127
Lochyside. High ... 1F 141
Lockengate. Corn ... 2E 7
Lockerbie. Dum ... 1C 112
Lockeridge. Wilts ... 5G 35
Lockerley. Hants ... 4A 24
Lockhills. Cumb ... 5G 113
Locking. N Som ... 1G 21
Lockington. E Yor ... 5D 101
Lockington. Leics ... 3B 74
Lockleywood. Shrp ... 3A 72
Locksgreen. IOW ... 3C 16
Locks Heath. Hants ... 2D 16
Lockton. N Yor ... 5F 107
Loddington. Leics ... 5E 75
Loddington. Nptn ... 3F 63
Loddiswell. Devn ... 4D 8
Loddon. Norf ... 1F 67
Lode. Cambs ... 4E 65
Loders. Dors ... 3H 13
Lodsworth. W Sus ... 3A 26
Lofthouse. N Yor ... 2D 98
Lofthouse. W Yor ... 2D 92
Lofthouse Gate. W Yor ... 2D 92
Loftus. Red C ... 3E 107
Logan. E Ayr ... 2E 117
Loganlea. W Lot ... 3C 128
Loggaston. Here ... 5F 59
Loggerheads. Staf ... 2B 72
Loggie. High ... 4F 163
Logie. Ang ... 2F 145
Logie. Fife ... 1G 137
Logie. Mor ... 3E 159
Logie Coldstone. Abers ... 3B 152
Logie Pert. Ang ... 2F 145
Logierait. Per ... 3G 143
Login. Carm ... 2F 43
Lolworth. Cambs ... 4C 64
Lonbain. High ... 3F 155
Londesborough. E Yor ... 5C 100
London. G Lon ... 2E 39
London Apprentice. Corn ... 3E 6
London Ashford (Lydd) Airport.
   Kent ... 3E 29
London City Airport. G Lon ... 2F 39
London Colney. Herts ... 5B 52
Londonderry. N Yor ... 2C 174
Londonderry. N Yor ... 1F 99
London Gatwick Airport.
   W Sus ... 1D 26
London Heathrow Airport.
   G Lon ... 3B 38
London Luton Airport. Lutn ... 3B 52
London Southend Airport. Essx ... 2C 40
London Stansted Airport. Essx ... 3F 53
Londonthorpe. Linc ... 2G 75
Londubh. High ... 5C 162
Lonemore. High ... 4D 166
   (nr. Dornoch)
Lonemore. High ... 1G 155
   (nr. Gairloch)
Long Ashton. N Som ... 4A 34
Long Bank. Worc ... 3B 60
Longbar. N Ayr ... 4E 127
Long Bennington. Linc ... 1F 75
Longbenton. Tyne ... 3F 115
Longborough. Glos ... 3G 49

Long Bredy—Lubcroy

Long Bredy. *Dors* 3A **14**
Longbridge. *Warw* 4G **61**
Longbridge. *W Mid* 3E **61**
Longbridge Deverill. *Wilts* 2D **22**
Long Buckby. *Nptn* 4D **62**
Long Buckby Wharf. *Nptn* 4D **62**
Longburgh. *Cumb* 4E **112**
Longburton. *Dors* 1B **14**
Long Clawson. *Leics* 3E **74**
Longcliffe. *Derbs* 5G **85**
Long Common. *Hants* 1D **16**
Long Compton. *Staf* 3C **72**
Long Compton. *Warw* 2A **50**
Longcot. *Oxon* 2A **36**
Long Crendon. *Buck* 5E **51**
Long Crichel. *Dors* 1E **15**
Longcroft. *Cumb* 4D **112**
Longcroft. *Falk* 2A **128**
Longcross. *Surr* 4A **38**
Longdale. *Cumb* 4H **103**
Longdales. *Cumb* 5G **113**
Longden. *Shrp* 5G **71**
Longden Common. *Shrp* 5G **71**
Long Ditton. *Surr* 4C **38**
Longdon. *Staf* 4E **73**
Longdon. *Worc* 2D **48**
Longdon Green. *Staf* 4E **73**
Longdon on Tern. *Telf* 4A **72**
Longdown. *Devn* 3B **12**
Longdowns. *Corn* 5B **6**
Long Drax. *N Yor* 2G **93**
Long Duckmanton. *Derbs* 3B **86**
Long Eaton. *Derbs* 2B **74**
Longfield. *Kent* 4H **39**
Longfield. *Shet* 10E **173**
Longfield Hill. *Kent* 4H **39**
Longford. *Derbs* 2G **73**
Longford. *Glos* 3D **48**
Longford. *G Lon* 3B **38**
Longford. *Shrp* 2A **72**
Longford. *Telf* 4B **72**
Longford. *W Mid* 2A **62**
Longforgan. *Per* 5C **144**
Longformacus. *Bord* 4C **130**
Longframlington. *Nmbd* 4F **121**
Long Gardens. *Essx* 2B **54**
Long Green. *Ches W* 3G **83**
Long Green. *Worc* 2D **48**
Longham. *Dors* 3F **15**
Longham. *Norf* 4B **78**
Long Hanborough. *Oxon* 4C **50**
Longhedge. *Wilts* 2D **22**
Longhill. *Abers* 3H **161**
Longhirst. *Nmbd* 1F **115**
Longhope. *Glos* 4B **48**
Longhope. *Orkn* 8C **172**
Longhorsley. *Nmbd* 5F **121**
Longhoughton. *Nmbd* 3G **121**
Long Itchington. *Warw* 4B **62**
Longlands. *Cumb* 1D **102**
Longlane. *Derbs* 2G **73**
Long Lane. *Telf* 4A **72**
Longlane. *W Ber* 4C **36**
Long Lawford. *Warw* 3B **62**
Long Lease. *N Yor* 4G **107**
Longley Green. *Worc* 5B **60**
Long Load. *Som* 4H **21**
Longmanhill. *Abers* 2E **161**
Long Marston. *Herts* 4G **51**
Long Marston. *N Yor* 4H **99**
Long Marston. *Warw* 1G **49**
Long Marton. *Cumb* 2H **103**
Long Meadow. *Cambs* 4E **65**
Long Meadowend. *Shrp* 2G **59**
Long Melford. *Suff* 1B **54**
Longmoor Camp. *Hants* 3F **25**
Longmorn. *Mor* 3G **159**
Longmoss. *Ches E* 3C **84**
Long Newnton. *Glos* 2E **35**
Longnewton. *Bord* 2H **119**
Long Newton. *Stoc T* 3A **106**
Longney. *Glos* 4C **48**
Longniddry. *E Lot* 2H **129**
Longnor. *Shrp* 5G **71**
Longnor. *Staf* 4E **85** (nr. Leek)
Longnor. *Staf* 4C **72** (nr. Stafford)
Longparish. *Hants* 2C **24**
Longpark. *Cumb* 3F **113**
Long Preston. *N Yor* 4H **97**
Longridge. *Lanc* 1E **90**
Longridge. *Staf* 4D **72**
Longridge. *W Lot* 3C **128**
Longriggend. *N Lan* 2B **128**
Long Riston. *E Yor* 5F **101**
Longrock. *Corn* 3C **4**
Longsdon. *Staf* 5D **84**
Longshaw. *G Man* 4D **90**
Longshaw. *Staf* 1E **73**
Longside. *Abers* 4H **161**
Longslow. *Shrp* 2A **72**
Longstanton. *Cambs* 4C **64**
Longstock. *Hants* 3B **24**
Longstowe. *Cambs* 5C **64**
Long Stratton. *Norf* 1D **66**
Long Street. *Mil* 1F **51**
Longstreet. *Wilts* 1G **23**
Long Sutton. *Hants* 2F **25**
Long Sutton. *Linc* 3D **76**
Long Sutton. *Som* 4H **21**
Longthorpe. *Pet* 1A **64**
Long Thurlow. *Suff* 4C **66**
Longthwaite. *Cumb* 2F **103**
Longton. *Lanc* 2C **90**
Longton. *Stoke* 1D **72**
Longtown. *Cumb* 3E **113**
Longtown. *Here* 3G **47**
Longville in the Dale. *Shrp* 1H **59**
Long Whatton. *Leics* 3B **74**
Longwick. *Buck* 5F **51**
Long Wittenham. *Oxon* 2D **36**
Longwitton. *Nmbd* 1D **115**
Longworth. *Oxon* 2B **36**
Longyester. *E Lot* 3B **130**
Lonmore. *High* 4B **154**
Looe. *Corn* 3G **7**
Loose. *Kent* 5B **40**
Loosegate. *Linc* 3C **76**
Loosley Row. *Buck* 5G **51**
Lopcombe Corner. *Wilts* 3A **24**
Lopen. *Som* 1H **13**
Loppington. *Shrp* 3G **71**
Lorbottle. *Nmbd* 4E **121**
Lordington. *W Sus* 2F **17**
Loscoe. *Derbs* 1B **74**
Loscombe. *Dors* 3A **14**
Losgaintir. *W Isl* 8C **171**
Lossiemouth. *Mor* 2G **159**
Lossit. *Arg* 4A **124**
Lostock Gralam. *Ches W* 3A **84**
Lostock Green. *Ches W* 3A **84**
Lostock Hall. *Lanc* 2D **90**
Lostock Junction. *G Man* 4E **91**
Lostwithiel. *Corn* 3F **7**
Lothbeg. *High* 2G **165**
Lothersdale. *N Yor* 5B **98**
Lothianbridge. *Midl* 3G **129**
Lothianburn. *Edin* 3F **129**
Lothmore. *High* 2G **165**
Lottisham. *Som* 3A **22**
Loudwater. *Buck* 1A **38**
Loughborough. *Leics* 4C **74**
Loughor. *Swan* 3E **31**
Loughton. *Essx* 1F **39**
Loughton. *Mil* 2G **51**
Loughton. *Shrp* 2A **60**
Lound. *Linc* 4H **75**
Lound. *Notts* 2D **86**
Lound. *Suff* 1H **67**
Lount. *Leics* 4A **74**
Louth. *Linc* 2C **88**
Love Clough. *Lanc* 2G **91**
Lovedean. *Hants* 1E **17**
Lover. *Wilts* 4H **23**
Loversall. *S Yor* 1C **86**
Loves Green. *Essx* 5G **53**
Loveston. *Pemb* 4E **43**
Lovington. *Som* 3A **22**
Low Ackworth. *W Yor* 3E **93**
Low Angerton. *Nmbd* 1D **115**
Low Ardwell. *Dum* 5F **109**
Low Ballochdowan. *S Ayr* 2F **109**
Lowbands. *Glos* 2C **48**
Low Barlings. *Linc* 3H **87**
Low Bell End. *N Yor* 5E **107**
Low Bentham. *N Yor* 3F **97**
Low Borrowbridge. *Cumb* 4H **103**
Low Bradfield. *S Yor* 1G **85**
Low Bradley. *N Yor* 5C **98**
Low Braithwaite. *Cumb* 5F **113**
Low Brunton. *Nmbd* 2C **114**
Low Burnham. *N Lin* 4A **94**
Lowca. *Cumb* 2A **102**
Low Catton. *E Yor* 4B **100**
Low Coniscliffe. *Darl* 3F **105**
Low Coylton. *S Ayr* 3D **116**
Low Crosby. *Cumb* 4F **113**
Low Dalby. *N Yor* 1C **100**
Lowdham. *Notts* 1D **74**
Low Dinsdale. *Darl* 3A **106**
Lowe. *Shrp* 2H **71**
Low Ellington. *N Yor* 1E **98**
Lower Amble. *Corn* 1D **6**
Lower Ansty. *Dors* 2C **14**
Lower Arboll. *High* 5F **165**
Lower Arncott. *Oxon* 4E **50**
Lower Ashton. *Devn* 4B **12**
Lower Assendon. *Oxon* 3F **37**
Lower Auchenreath. *Mor* 2A **160**
Lower Badcall. *High* 4B **166**
Lower Ballam. *Lanc* 1B **90**
Lower Basildon. *W Ber* 4E **36**
Lower Beeding. *W Sus* 3D **26**
Lower Benefield. *Nptn* 2G **63**
Lower Bentley. *Worc* 4D **61**
Lower Beobridge. *Shrp* 1B **60**
Lower Bockhampton. *Dors* 3C **14**
Lower Boddington. *Nptn* 5B **62**
Lower Bordean. *Hants* 4E **25**
Lower Brailes. *Warw* 2B **50**
Lower Breakish. *High* 1E **147**
Lower Broadheath. *Worc* 5C **60**
Lower Brynamman. *Neat* 4H **45**
Lower Bullingham. *Here* 2A **48**
Lower Bullington. *Hants* 2C **24**
Lower Burgate. *Hants* 1G **15**
Lower Cam. *Glos* 5C **48**
Lower Catesby. *Nptn* 5C **62**
Lower Chapel. *Powy* 2D **46**
Lower Cheriton. *Devn* 2E **12**
Lower Chicksgrove. *Wilts* 3E **23**
Lower Chute. *Wilts* 1B **24**
Lower Clopton. *Warw* 5F **61**
Lower Common. *Hants* 2E **25**
Lower Crossings. *Derbs* 2E **85**
Lower Cumberworth. *W Yor* 4C **92**
Lower Darwen. *Bkbn* 2E **91**
Lower Dean. *Bed* 4H **63**
Lower Dean. *Devn* 2D **8**
Lower Diabaig. *High* 2G **155**
Lower Dicker. *E Sus* 4G **27**
Lower Dounreay. *High* 2B **168**
Lower Down. *Shrp* 2F **59**
Lower Dunsforth. *N Yor* 3G **99**
Lower East Carleton. *Norf* 5D **78**
Lower Egleton. *Here* 1B **48**
Lower Ellastone. *Staf* 1F **73**
Lower End. *Nptn* 4F **63**
Lower Everleigh. *Wilts* 1G **23**
Lower Eype. *Dors* 3H **13**
Lower Failand. *N Som* 4A **34**
Lower Faintree. *Shrp* 2A **60**
Lower Farringdon. *Hants* 3F **25**
Lower Foxdale. *IOM* 4B **108**
Lower Frankton. *Shrp* 2F **71**
Lower Froyle. *Hants* 2F **25**
Lower Gabwell. *Devn* 2F **9**
Lower Gledfield. *High* 4C **164**
Lower Godney. *Som* 2H **21**
Lower Gravenhurst. *C Beds* 2B **52**
Lower Green. *Essx* 2E **53**
Lower Green. *Norf* 2B **78**
Lower Green. *W Ber* 5B **36**
Lower Halstow. *Kent* 4C **40**
Lower Hardres. *Kent* 5F **41**
Lower Hardwick. *Here* 5G **59**
Lower Hartshay. *Derbs* 5A **86**
Lower Hawthwaite. *Cumb* 1B **96**
Lower Hayton. *Shrp* 2H **59**
Lower Hergest. *Here* 5E **59**
Lower Heyford. *Oxon* 3C **50**
Lower Heysham. *Lanc* 3D **96**
Lower Higham. *Kent* 3B **40**
Lower Holbrook. *Suff* 2E **55**
Lower Holditch. *Dors* 2G **13**
Lower Hordley. *Shrp* 3F **71**
Lower Horncroft. *W Sus* 4B **26**
Lower Kilcott. *Glos* 3C **34**
Lower Killeyan. *Arg* 5A **124**
Lower Kingcombe. *Dors* 3A **14**
Lower Kingswood. *Surr* 5D **38**
Lower Kinnerton. *Ches W* 4F **83**
Lower Langford. *N Som* 5H **33**
Lower Largo. *Fife* 3G **137**
Lower Layham. *Suff* 1D **54**
Lower Ledwyche. *Shrp* 3H **59**
Lower Leigh. *Staf* 2E **73**
Lower Lemington. *Glos* 2H **49**
Lower Lenie. *High* 1H **149**
Lower Ley. *Glos* 4C **48**
Lower Llanfadog. *Powy* 4B **58**
Lower Lode. *Glos* 2D **49**
Lower Lovacott. *Devn* 4F **19**
Lower Loxhore. *Devn* 3G **19**
Lower Loxley. *Staf* 2E **73**
Lower Lydbrook. *Glos* 4A **48**
Lower Lye. *Here* 4G **59**
Lower Machen. *Newp* 3F **33**
Lower Maes-coed. *Here* 2G **47**
Lower Meend. *Glos* 5A **48**
Lower Midway. *Derbs* 3H **73**
Lower Milovaig. *High* 3A **154**
Lower Moor. *Worc* 1E **49**
Lower Morton. *S Glo* 2B **34**
Lower Mountain. *Flin* 5F **83**
Lower Nazeing. *Essx* 5D **53**
Lower Netchwood. *Shrp* 1A **60**
Lower Nyland. *Dors* 4C **22**
Lower Oakfield. *Fife* 4D **136**
Lower Oddington. *Glos* 3H **49**
Lower Ollach. *High* 5E **155**
Lower Penarth. *V Glam* 5E **33**
Lower Penn. *Staf* 1C **60**
Lower Pennington. *Hants* 3B **16**
Lower Peover. *Ches W* 3B **84**
Lower Pilsley. *Derbs* 4B **86**
Lower Pitkerrie. *High* 1C **158**
Lower Place. *G Man* 3H **91**
Lower Quinton. *Warw* 1G **49**
Lower Rainham. *Medw* 4C **40**
Lower Raydon. *Suff* 2D **54**
Lower Seagry. *Wilts* 3E **35**
Lower Shelton. *C Beds* 1H **51**
Lower Shiplake. *Oxon* 4F **37**
Lower Shuckburgh. *Warw* 4B **62**
Lower Sketty. *Swan* 3F **31**
Lower Slade. *Devn* 2F **19**
Lower Slaughter. *Glos* 3G **49**
Lower Soudley. *Glos* 4B **48**
Lower Stanton St Quintin. *Wilts* 3E **35**
Lower Stoke. *Medw* 3C **40**
Lower Stondon. *C Beds* 2B **52**
Lower Stonnall. *Staf* 5E **73**
Lower Stow Bedon. *Norf* 1B **66**
Lower Street. *Norf* 2E **79**
Lower Strensham. *Worc* 1E **49**
Lower Sundon. *C Beds* 3A **52**
Lower Swanwick. *Hants* 2C **16**
Lower Swell. *Glos* 3G **49**
Lower Tale. *Devn* 2D **12**
Lower Tean. *Staf* 2E **73**
Lower Thurlton. *Norf* 1G **67**
Lower Thurnham. *Lanc* 4D **96**
Lower Thurvaston. *Derbs* 2G **73**
Lowertown. *Corn* 4D **4**
Lower Town. *Here* 1B **48**
Lower Town. *IOS* 1B **4**
Lowertown. *Orkn* 8D **172**
Lower Town. *Pemb* 1D **42**
Lower Tysoe. *Warw* 1B **50**
Lower Upham. *Hants* 1D **16**
Lower Upnor. *Medw* 3B **40**
Lower Vexford. *Som* 3E **20**
Lower Walton. *Warr* 2A **84**
Lower Wear. *Devn* 4C **12**
Lower Weare. *Som* 1H **21**
Lower Welson. *Here* 5E **59**
Lower Whatcombe. *Dors* 2D **14**
Lower Whitley. *Ches W* 3A **84**
Lower Wield. *Hants* 2E **25**
Lower Withington. *Ches E* 4C **84**
Lower Woodend. *Buck* 3G **37**
Lower Woodford. *Wilts* 3G **23**
Lower Wraxall. *Dors* 2A **14**
Lower Wych. *Ches W* 1G **71**
Lower Wyche. *Worc* 1C **48**
Lowesby. *Leics* 5E **74**
Lowestoft. *Suff* 1H **67**
Loweswater. *Cumb* 2C **102**
Low Etherley. *Dur* 2E **105**
Lowfield Heath. *W Sus* 1D **26**
Lowford. *Hants* 1C **16**
Low Fulney. *Linc* 3B **76**
Low Gate. *Nmbd* 3C **114**
Lowgill. *Cumb* 5H **103**
Lowgill. *Lanc* 3F **97**
Low Grantley. *N Yor* 2E **99**
Low Green. *N Yor* 4E **98**
Low Habberley. *Worc* 3C **60**
Low Ham. *Som* 4H **21**
Low Hameringham. *Linc* 4C **88**
Low Hawsker. *N Yor* 4G **107**
Low Hesket. *Cumb* 5F **113**
Low Hesleyhurst. *Nmbd* 5E **121**
Lowick. *Cumb* 1B **96**
Lowick. *Nptn* 2G **63**
Lowick. *Nmbd* 1E **121**
Lowick Bridge. *Cumb* 1B **96**
Lowick Green. *Cumb* 1B **96**
Low Knipe. *Cumb* 2G **103**
Low Leighton. *Derbs* 2E **85**
Low Lorton. *Cumb* 2C **102**
Low Marishes. *N Yor* 2C **100**
Low Marnham. *Notts* 4F **87**
Low Mill. *N Yor* 5D **106**
Low Moor. *Lanc* 5G **97**
Low Moor. *W Yor* 2B **92**
Low Moorsley. *Tyne* 5G **115**
Low Newton-by-the-Sea. *Nmbd* 2G **121**
Lownie Moor. *Ang* 4D **145**
Lowood. *Bord* 1H **119**
Low Row. *Cumb* 3G **113** (nr. Brampton)
Low Row. *Cumb* 5C **112** (nr. Wigton)
Low Row. *N Yor* 5C **104**
Lowsonford. *Warw* 4F **61**
Low Street. *Norf* 5C **78**
Lowther. *Cumb* 2G **103**
Lowthorpe. *E Yor* 3E **101**
Lowton. *Devn* 2G **11**
Lowton. *G Man* 1A **84**
Lowton. *Som* 1E **13**
Lowton Common. *G Man* 1A **84**
Low Torry. *Fife* 1D **128**
Low Toynton. *Linc* 3B **88**
Low Valleyfield. *Fife* 1C **128**
Low Westwood. *Dur* 4E **115**
Low Whinnow. *Cumb* 4E **112**
Low Wood. *Cumb* 1C **96**
Low Worsall. *N Yor* 4A **106**
Low Wray. *Cumb* 4E **103**
Loxbeare. *Devn* 1C **12**
Loxhill. *Surr* 2B **26**
Loxhore. *Devn* 3G **19**
Loxley. *S Yor* 2H **85**
Loxley. *Warw* 5G **61**
Loxley Green. *Staf* 2E **73**
Loxton. *N Som* 1G **21**
Loxwood. *W Sus* 2B **26**
Lubcroy. *High* 3A **164**

Lubenham—Margaretting

Lubenham. *Leics* 2E 62
Lubinvullin. *High* 2F 167
Luccombe. *Som* 2C 20
Luccombe Village. *IOW* 4D 16
Lucker. *Nmbd* 1F 121
Luckett. *Corn* 5D 11
Luckington. *Wilts* 3D 34
Lucklawhill. *Fife* 1G 137
Luckwell Bridge. *Som* 3C 20
Lucton. *Here* 4G 59
Ludag. *W Isl* 7C 170
Ludborough. *Linc* 1B 88
Ludchurch. *Pemb* 3F 43
Luddenden. *W Yor* 2A 92
Luddenden Foot. *W Yor* 2A 92
Luddenham. *Kent* 4D 40
Ludderburn. *Cumb* 5F 103
Luddesdown. *Kent* 4A 40
Luddington. *N Lin* 3B 94
Luddington. *Warw* 5F 61
Luddington in the Brook. *Nptn* 2A 64
Ludford. *Linc* 2A 88
Ludford. *Shrp* 3H 59
Ludgershall. *Buck* 4E 51
Ludgershall. *Wilts* 1A 24
Ludgvan. *Corn* 3C 4
Ludham. *Norf* 4F 79
Ludlow. *Shrp* 3H 59
Ludstone. *Shrp* 1C 60
Ludwell. *Wilts* 4E 23
Ludworth. *Dur* 5G 115
Luffenhall. *Herts* 3C 52
Luffincott. *Devn* 3D 10
Lugar. *E Ayr* 2E 117
Luggate Burn. *E Lot* 2C 130
Lugg Green. *Here* 4G 59
Luggiebank. *N Lan* 2A 128
Lugton. *E Ayr* 4F 127
Lugwardine. *Here* 1A 48
Luib. *High* 1D 146
Luib. *Stir* 1D 135
Lulham. *Here* 1H 47
Lullington. *Derbs* 4G 73
Lullington. *E Sus* 5G 27
Lullington. *Som* 1C 22
Lulsgate Bottom. *N Som* 5A 34
Lulsley. *Worc* 5B 60
Lulworth Camp. *Dors* 4D 14
Lumb. *Lanc* 2G 91
Lumb. *W Yor* 2A 92
Lumby. *N Yor* 1E 93
Lumphanan. *Abers* 3C 152
Lumphinnans. *Fife* 4D 136
Lumsdaine. *Bord* 3E 131
Lumsden. *Abers* 1B 152
Lunan. *Ang* 3F 145
Lunanhead. *Ang* 3D 145
Luncarty. *Per* 1C 136
Lund. *E Yor* 5D 100
Lund. *N Yor* 1G 93
Lundie. *Ang* 5B 144
Lundin Links. *Fife* 3G 137
Lundy Green. *Norf* 1E 67
Lunna. *Shet* 5F 173
Lunning. *Shet* 5G 173
Lunnon. *Swan* 4E 31
Lunsford. *Kent* 5A 40
Lunsford's Cross. *E Sus* 4B 28
Lunt. *Mers* 4B 90
Luppitt. *Devn* 2E 13
Lupridge. *Devn* 3D 8
Lupset. *W Yor* 3D 92
Lupton. *Cumb* 1E 97
Lurgan. *Arm* 5F 175
Lurgashall. *W Sus* 3A 26
Lurley. *Devn* 1C 12
Lusby. *Linc* 4C 88
Luscombe. *Devn* 3D 9
Luson. *Devn* 4C 8
Luss. *Arg* 4C 134
Lussagiven. *Arg* 1E 125
Lusta. *High* 3B 154
Lustleigh. *Devn* 4A 12
Luston. *Here* 4G 59
Luthermuir. *Abers* 2F 145
Luthrie. *Fife* 2F 137
Lutley. *Staf* 2C 60
Luton. *Devn* 2D 12
(nr. Honiton)
Luton. *Devn* 5C 12
(nr. Teignmouth)
Luton. *Lutn* 3A 52
Luton (London) Airport. *Lutn* 3B 52
Lutterworth. *Leics* 2C 62
Lutton. *Devn* 3B 8
(nr. Ivybridge)
Lutton. *Devn* 2C 8
(nr. South Brent)
Lutton. *Linc* 3D 76
Lutton. *Nptn* 2A 64
Lutton Gowts. *Linc* 3D 76
Lutworthy. *Devn* 1A 12
Luxborough. *Som* 3C 20
Luxley. *Glos* 3B 48
Luxulyan. *Corn* 3E 7
Lybster. *High* 5E 169
Lydbury North. *Shrp* 2F 59
Lydcott. *Devn* 3G 19
Lydd. *Kent* 3E 29
Lydden. *Kent* 1G 29
(nr. Dover)
Lydden. *Kent* 4H 41
(nr. Margate)
Lyddington. *Rut* 1F 63
Lydd (London Ashford) Airport. *Kent* 3E 29
Lydd-on-Sea. *Kent* 3E 29
Lydeard St Lawrence. *Som* 3E 21
Lyde Green. *Hants* 1F 25
Lydford. *Devn* 4F 11
Lydford Fair Place. *Som* 3A 22
Lydgate. *G Man* 4H 91
Lydgate. *W Yor* 2H 91
Lydham. *Shrp* 1F 59
Lydiard Millicent. *Wilts* 3F 35
Lydiate. *Mers* 4B 90
Lydiate Ash. *Worc* 3D 61
Lydlinch. *Dors* 1C 14
Lydmarsh. *Som* 2G 13
Lydney. *Glos* 5B 48
Lydstep. *Pemb* 5E 43
Lye. *W Mid* 2D 60
Lye Green. *Buck* 5H 51
Lye Green. *E Sus* 2G 27
Lye Head. *Worc* 3B 60
Lye, The. *Shrp* 1A 60
Lyford. *Oxon* 2B 36
Lyham. *Nmbd* 1E 121
Lylestone. *N Ayr* 5E 127
Lymbridge Green. *Kent* 1F 29
Lyme Regis. *Dors* 3G 13
Lyminge. *Kent* 1F 29
Lymington. *Hants* 3B 16
Lyminster. *W Sus* 5B 26
Lymm. *Warr* 2A 84
Lymore. *Hants* 3A 16
Lympne. *Kent* 2F 29
Lympsham. *Som* 1G 21
Lympstone. *Devn* 4C 12
Lynaberack Lodge. *High* 4B 150
Lynbridge. *Devn* 2H 19
Lynch. *Som* 2C 20
Lynchat. *High* 3B 150
Lynch Green. *Norf* 5D 78
Lyndhurst. *Hants* 2B 16
Lyndon. *Rut* 5G 75
Lyne. *Bord* 5F 129
Lyne. *Surr* 4B 38
Lyneal. *Shrp* 2G 71
Lyne Down. *Here* 2B 48
Lyneham. *Oxon* 3A 50
Lyneham. *Wilts* 4F 35
Lyneholmeford. *Cumb* 2G 113
Lynemouth. *Nmbd* 5G 121
Lyne of Gorthleck. *High* 1H 149
Lyne of Skene. *Abers* 2E 153
Lynesack. *Dur* 2D 105
Lyness. *Orkn* 8C 172
Lyng. *Norf* 4C 78
Lyngate. *Norf* 2E 79
(nr. North Walsham)
Lyngate. *Norf* 3F 79
(nr. Worstead)
Lynmouth. *Devn* 2H 19
Lynn. *Staf* 5E 73
Lynn. *Telf* 4B 72
Lynsted. *Kent* 4D 40
Lynstone. *Corn* 2C 10
Lynton. *Devn* 2H 19
Lynwilg. *High* 2C 150
Lyon's Gate. *Dors* 2B 14
Lyonshall. *Here* 5F 59
Lytchett Matravers. *Dors* 3E 15
Lytchett Minster. *Dors* 3E 15
Lyth. *High* 2E 169
Lytham. *Lanc* 2B 90
Lytham St Anne's. *Lanc* 2B 90
Lythe. *N Yor* 3F 107
Lythes. *Orkn* 9D 172
Lythmore. *High* 2C 168

M

Mabe Burnthouse. *Corn* 5B 6
Mabie. *Dum* 2A 112
Mablethorpe. *Linc* 2E 89
Macbiehill. *Bord* 4E 129
Macclesfield. *Ches E* 3D 84
Macclesfield Forest. *Ches E* 3D 84
Macduff. *Abers* 2E 160
Machan. *S Lan* 4A 128
Macharioch. *Arg* 5B 122
Machen. *Cphy* 3F 33
Machrie. *N Ayr* 2C 122
Machrihanish. *Arg* 3A 122
Machroes. *Gwyn* 3C 68
Machynlleth. *Powy* 5G 69
Mackerye End. *Herts* 4B 52
Mackworth. *Derb* 2H 73
Macmerry. *E Lot* 2H 129
Madderty. *Per* 1B 136
Maddington. *Wilts* 2F 23
Maddiston. *Falk* 2C 128
Madehurst. *W Sus* 4A 26
Madeley. *Staf* 1B 72
Madeley. *Telf* 5A 72
Madeley Heath. *Staf* 1B 72
Madeley Heath. *Worc* 3D 60
Madford. *Devn* 1E 13
Madingley. *Cambs* 4C 64
Madley. *Here* 2H 47
Madresfield. *Worc* 1D 48
Madron. *Corn* 3B 4
Maenaddwyn. *IOA* 2D 80
Maenclochog. *Pemb* 2E 43
Maendy. *V Glam* 4D 32
Maenporth. *Corn* 4E 5
Maentwrog. *Gwyn* 1F 69
Maen-y-groes. *Cdgn* 5C 56
Maer. *Staf* 2B 72
Maerdy. *Carm* 3G 45
Maerdy. *Cnwy* 1C 70
Maerdy. *Rhon* 2C 32
Maesbrook. *Shrp* 3F 71
Maesbury. *Shrp* 3F 71
Maesbury Marsh. *Shrp* 3F 71
Maes-glas. *Flin* 3D 82
Maesgwyn-Isaf. *Powy* 4D 70
Maeshafn. *Den* 4E 82
Maes Llyn. *Cdgn* 1D 44
Maesmynis. *Powy* 1D 46
Maesteg. *B'end* 2B 32
Maestir. *Cdgn* 1F 45
Maesybont. *Carm* 4F 45
Maesycrugiau. *Carm* 1E 45
Maesycwmmer. *Cphy* 2E 33
Maesyrhandir. *Powy* 1C 58
Magdalen Laver. *Essx* 5F 53
Maggieknockater. *Mor* 4H 159
Maghaberry. *Lis* 4G 175
Magham Down. *E Sus* 4H 27
Maghera. *M Ulst* 2E 175
Magherafelt. *M Ulst* 3E 175
Magheralin. *Arm* 5G 175
Maghull. *Mers* 4B 90
Magna Park. *Leics* 2C 62
Magor. *Mon* 3H 33
Magpie Green. *Suff* 3C 66
Magwyr. *Mon* 3H 33
Maidenbower. *W Sus* 2D 27
Maiden Bradley. *Wilts* 3D 22
Maidencombe. *Torb* 2F 9
Maidenhayne. *Devn* 3F 13
Maidenhead. *Wind* 3G 37
Maiden Law. *Dur* 5E 115
Maiden Newton. *Dors* 3A 14
Maidens. *S Ayr* 4B 116
Maiden's Green. *Brac* 4G 37
Maidensgrove. *Oxon* 3F 37
Maidenwell. *Corn* 5B 10
Maidenwell. *Linc* 3C 88
Maiden Wells. *Pemb* 5D 42
Maidford. *Nptn* 5D 62
Maids Moreton. *Buck* 2F 51
Maidstone. *Kent* 5B 40
Maidwell. *Nptn* 3E 63
Mail. *Shet* 9F 173
Maindee. *Newp* 3G 33
Mainsforth. *Dur* 1A 106
Mains of Auchindachy. *Mor* 4B 160
Mains of Auchnagatt. *Abers* 4G 161
Mains of Drum. *Abers* 4F 153
Mains of Edingight. *Mor* 3C 160
Mainsriddle. *Dum* 4G 111
Mainstone. *Shrp* 2E 59
Maisemore. *Glos* 3D 48
Major's Green. *Worc* 3F 61
Makeney. *Derbs* 1A 74
Makerstoun. *Bord* 1A 120
Malacleit. *W Isl* 1C 170
Malaig. *High* 4E 147
Malaig Bheag. *High* 4E 147
Malborough. *Devn* 5D 8
Malcoff. *Derbs* 2E 85
Malcolmburn. *Mor* 3A 160
Malden Rushett. *G Lon* 4C 38
Maldon. *Essx* 5B 54
Malham. *N Yor* 3B 98
Maligar. *High* 2D 155
Malinslee. *Telf* 5A 72
Mallaig. *High* 4E 147
Malleny Mills. *Edin* 3E 129
Mallows Green. *Essx* 3E 53
Malltraeth. *IOA* 4D 80
Mallwyd. *Gwyn* 4A 70
Malmesbury. *Wilts* 3E 35
Malmsmead. *Devn* 2A 20
Malpas. *Ches W* 1G 71
Malpas. *Corn* 4C 6
Malpas. *Newp* 2G 33
Malswick. *Glos* 3C 48
Maltby. *S Yor* 1C 86
Maltby. *Stoc T* 3B 106
Maltby le Marsh. *Linc* 2D 88
Malt Lane. *Arg* 3H 133
Maltman's Hill. *Kent* 1D 28
Malton. *N Yor* 2B 100
Malvern Link. *Worc* 1C 48
Malvern Wells. *Worc* 1C 48
Mamble. *Worc* 3A 60
Mamhilad. *Mon* 5G 47
Manaccan. *Corn* 4E 5
Manafon. *Powy* 5D 70
Manais. *W Isl* 9D 171
Manaton. *Devn* 4A 12
Manby. *Linc* 2C 88
Mancetter. *Warw* 1H 61
Manchester. *G Man* 1C 84
Manchester Airport. *G Man* 2C 84
Mancot. *Flin* 4F 83
Manea. *Cambs* 2D 65
Maney. *W Mid* 1F 61
Manfield. *N Yor* 3F 105
Mangotsfield. *S Glo* 4B 34
Mangurstadh. *W Isl* 4C 171
Mankinholes. *W Yor* 2H 91
Manley. *Ches W* 3H 83
Manmoel. *Cphy* 5E 47
Mannal. *Arg* 4A 138
Mannerston. *Falk* 2D 128
Manningford Bohune. *Wilts* 1G 23
Manningford Bruce. *Wilts* 1G 23
Manningham. *W Yor* 1B 92
Mannings Heath. *W Sus* 3D 26
Mannington. *Dors* 2F 15
Manningtree. *Essx* 2E 54
Mannofield. *Aber* 3G 153
Manorbier. *Pemb* 5E 43
Manorbier Newton. *Pemb* 5E 43
Manordeilo. *Carm* 3G 45
Manorowen. *Pemb* 1D 42
Manor Park. *G Lon* 2F 39
Mansell Gamage. *Here* 1G 47
Mansell Lacy. *Here* 1H 47
Mansergh. *Cumb* 1F 97
Mansewood. *Glas* 3G 127
Mansfield. *E Ayr* 3F 117
Mansfield. *Notts* 4C 86
Mansfield Woodhouse. *Notts* 4C 86
Mansriggs. *Cumb* 1B 96
Manston. *Dors* 1D 14
Manston. *Kent* 4H 41
Manston. *W Yor* 1D 92
Manswood. *Dors* 2E 15
Manthorpe. *Linc* 4H 75
(nr. Bourne)
Manthorpe. *Linc* 2G 75
(nr. Grantham)
Manton. *N Lin* 4C 94
Manton. *Notts* 3C 86
Manton. *Rut* 5F 75
Manton. *Wilts* 5G 35
Manuden. *Essx* 3E 53
Maperton. *Som* 4B 22
Maplebeck. *Notts* 4E 86
Maple Cross. *Herts* 1B 38
Mapledurham. *Oxon* 4E 37
Mapledurwell. *Hants* 1E 25
Maplehurst. *W Sus* 3C 26
Maplescombe. *Kent* 4G 39
Mapleton. *Derbs* 1F 73
Mapperley. *Derbs* 1B 74
Mapperley. *Notts* 1C 74
Mapperley Park. *Nott* 1C 74
Mapperton. *Dors* 3A 14
(nr. Beaminster)
Mapperton. *Dors* 3E 15
(nr. Poole)
Mappleborough Green. *Warw* 4E 61
Mappleton. *E Yor* 5G 101
Mapplewell. *S Yor* 4D 92
Mappowder. *Dors* 2C 14
Maraig. *W Isl* 7E 171
Marazion. *Corn* 3C 4
Marbhig. *W Isl* 6G 171
Marbury. *Ches E* 1H 71
March. *Cambs* 1D 64
Marcham. *Oxon* 2C 36
Marchamley. *Shrp* 3H 71
Marchington. *Staf* 2F 73
Marchington Woodlands. *Staf* 3F 73
Marchwiel. *Wrex* 1F 71
Marchwood. *Hants* 1B 16
Marcross. *V Glam* 5C 32
Marden. *Here* 1A 48
Marden. *Kent* 1B 28
Marden. *Wilts* 1F 23
Marden Beech. *Kent* 1B 28
Marden Thorn. *Kent* 1B 28
Mardu. *Shrp* 2E 59
Mardy. *Mon* 4G 47
Marefield. *Leics* 5E 75
Mareham le Fen. *Linc* 4B 88
Mareham on the Hill. *Linc* 4B 88
Marehay. *Derbs* 1B 74
Marehill. *W Sus* 4B 26
Maresfield. *E Sus* 3F 27
Marfleet. *Hull* 2E 95
Marford. *Wrex* 5F 83
Margam. *Neat* 3A 32
Margaret Marsh. *Dors* 1D 14
Margaret Roding. *Essx* 4F 53
Margaretting. *Essx* 5G 53

Mere Green—Milton of Balgonie

Mere Green. *Worc* 4D **60**
Mere Heath. *Ches W* 3A **84**
Mereside. *Bkpl* 1B **90**
Meretown. *Staf* 3B **72**
Mereworth. *Kent* 5A **40**
Meriden. *W Mid* 2G **61**
Merkadale. *High* 5C **154**
Merkland. *S Ayr* 5B **116**
Merkland Lodge. *High* 1A **164**
Merley. *Pool* 3F **15**
Merlin's Bridge. *Pemb* 3D **42**
Merridge. *Som* 3F **21**
Merrington. *Shrp* 3G **71**
Merrion. *Pemb* 5D **42**
Merriott. *Som* 1H **13**
Merrivale. *Devn* 5F **11**
Merrow. *Surr* 5B **38**
Merrybent. *Darl* 3F **105**
Merry Lees. *Leics* 5B **74**
Merrymeet. *Corn* 2G **7**
Mersham. *Kent* 2E **29**
Merstham. *Surr* 5D **39**
Merston. *W Sus* 2G **17**
Merstone. *IOW* 4D **16**
Merther. *Corn* 4C **6**
Merthyr. *Carm* 3D **44**
Merthyr Cynog. *Powy* 2C **46**
Merthyr Dyfan. *V Glam* 4E **32**
Merthyr Mawr. *B'end* 4B **32**
Merthyr Tudful. *Mer T* 5D **46**
Merthyr Tydfil. *Mer T* 5D **46**
Merthyr Vale. *Mer T* 5D **46**
Merton. *Devn* 1F **11**
Merton. *G Lon* 4D **38**
Merton. *Norf* 1B **66**
Merton. *Oxon* 4D **50**
Meshaw. *Devn* 1A **12**
Messing. *Essx* 4B **54**
Messingham. *N Lin* 4B **94**
Metcombe. *Devn* 3D **12**
Metfield. *Suff* 2E **67**
Metherell. *Corn* 2A **8**
Metheringham. *Linc* 4H **87**
Methil. *Fife* 4F **137**
Methilhill. *Fife* 4F **137**
Methley. *W Yor* 2D **93**
Methley Junction. *W Yor* 2D **93**
Methlick. *Abers* 5F **161**
Methven. *Per* 1C **136**
Methwold. *Norf* 1G **65**
Methwold Hythe. *Norf* 1G **65**
Mettingham. *Suff* 2F **67**
Metton. *Norf* 2D **78**
Mevagissey. *Corn* 4E **6**
Mexborough. *S Yor* 4E **93**
Mey. *High* 1E **169**
Meysey Hampton. *Glos* 2G **35**
Miabhag. *W Isl* 8D **171**
Miabhaig. *W Isl* 7C **171** (nr. Cliasmol)
Miabhaig. *W Isl* 4C **171** (nr. Timsgearraidh)
Mial. *High* 1G **155**
Michaelchurch. *Here* 3A **48**
Michaelchurch Escley. *Here* 2G **47**
Michaelchurch-on-Arrow. *Powy* 5E **59**
Michaelston-le-Pit. *V Glam* 4E **33**
Michaelston-y-Fedw. *Newp* 3F **33**
Michaelstow. *Corn* 5A **10**
Michelcombe. *Devn* 2C **8**
Micheldever. *Hants* 3D **24**
Micheldever Station. *Hants* 2D **24**
Michelmersh. *Hants* 4B **24**
Mickfield. *Suff* 4D **66**
Micklebring. *S Yor* 1C **86**
Mickleby. *N Yor* 3F **107**
Micklefield. *W Yor* 1E **93**
Micklefield Green. *Herts* 1B **38**
Mickleham. *Surr* 5C **38**
Mickleover. *Derb* 2H **73**
Micklethwaite. *Cumb* 4D **112**
Micklethwaite. *W Yor* 5D **98**
Mickleton. *Dur* 2C **104**
Mickleton. *Glos* 1G **49**
Mickletown. *W Yor* 2D **93**
Mickle Trafford. *Ches W* 4G **83**
Mickley. *N Yor* 2E **99**
Mickley Green. *Suff* 5H **65**
Mickley Square. *Nmbd* 3D **115**
Mid Ardlaw. *Abers* 2G **161**
Midbea. *Orkn* 3D **172**
Mid Beltie. *Abers* 3D **152**
Mid Calder. *W Lot* 3D **129**
Mid Clyth. *High* 5E **169**
Middle Assendon. *Oxon* 3F **37**
Middle Aston. *Oxon* 3C **50**
Middle Barton. *Oxon* 3C **50**
Middlebie. *Dum* 2D **112**
Middle Chinnock. *Som* 1H **13**
Middle Claydon. *Buck* 3F **51**
Middlecliffe. *S Yor* 4E **93**
Middlecott. *Devn* 4H **11**
Middle Drums. *Ang* 3E **145**
Middle Duntisbourne. *Glos* 5E **49**
Middle Essie. *Abers* 3H **161**
Middleforth Green. *Lanc* 2D **90**
Middleham. *N Yor* 1D **98**
Middle Handley. *Derbs* 3B **86**
Middle Harling. *Norf* 2B **66**
Middlehope. *Shrp* 2G **59**
Middle Littleton. *Worc* 1F **49**
Middle Maes-coed. *Here* 2G **47**
Middlemarsh. *Dors* 2B **14**
Middle Marwood. *Devn* 3F **19**
Middle Mayfield. *Staf* 1F **73**
Middlemoor. *Devn* 5E **11**
Middlemuir. *Abers* 4F **161** (nr. New Deer)
Middlemuir. *Abers* 3G **161** (nr. Strichen)
Middle Rainton. *Tyne* 5G **115**
Middle Rasen. *Linc* 2H **87**
Middlesbrough. *Midd* 3B **106**
Middlesceugh. *Cumb* 5E **113**
Middleshaw. *Cumb* 1E **97**
Middlesmoor. *N Yor* 2C **98**
Middles, The. *Dur* 4F **115**
Middlestone. *Dur* 1F **105**
Middlestone Moor. *Dur* 1F **105**
Middle Stoughton. *Som* 2H **21**
Middlestown. *W Yor* 3C **92**
Middle Street. *Glos* 5C **48**
Middle Taphouse. *Corn* 2F **7**
Middleton. *Ang* 4E **145**
Middleton. *Arg* 4A **138**
Middleton. *Cumb* 1F **97**
Middleton. *Derbs* 4F **85** (nr. Bakewell)
Middleton. *Derbs* 5G **85** (nr. Wirksworth)
Middleton. *Essx* 2B **54**
Middleton. *G Man* 4G **91**
Middleton. *Hants* 2C **24**
Middleton. *Hart* 1C **106**
Middleton. *Here* 4H **59**
Middleton. *IOW* 4B **16**
Middleton. *Lanc* 4D **96**
Middleton. *Midl* 4G **129**
Middleton. *Norf* 4F **77**
Middleton. *Nptn* 2F **63**
Middleton. *Nmbd* 1F **121** (nr. Belford)
Middleton. *Nmbd* 1D **114** (nr. Morpeth)
Middleton. *N Yor* 5D **98** (nr. Ilkley)
Middleton. *N Yor* 1B **100** (nr. Pickering)
Middleton. *Per* 3D **136**
Middleton. *Shrp* 3H **59** (nr. Ludlow)
Middleton. *Shrp* 3F **71** (nr. Oswestry)
Middleton. *Suff* 4G **67**
Middleton. *Swan* 4D **30**
Middleton. *Warw* 1F **61**
Middleton. *W Yor* 2C **92**
Middleton Cheney. *Nptn* 1D **50**
Middleton Green. *Staf* 2D **73**
Middleton-in-Teesdale. *Dur* 2C **104**
Middleton One Row. *Darl* 3A **106**
Middleton-on-Leven. *N Yor* 4B **106**
Middleton-on-Sea. *W Sus* 5A **26**
Middleton on the Hill. *Here* 4H **59**
Middleton-on-the-Wolds. *E Yor* 5D **100**
Middleton Priors. *Shrp* 1A **60**
Middleton Quernhow. *N Yor* 2F **99**
Middleton St George. *Darl* 3A **106**
Middleton Scriven. *Shrp* 2A **60**
Middleton Stoney. *Oxon* 3D **50**
Middleton Tyas. *N Yor* 4F **105**
Middletown. *Cumb* 4A **102**
Middle Town. *IOS* 1B **4**
Middletown. *Powy* 4F **71**
Middle Tysoe. *Warw* 1B **50**
Middle Wallop. *Hants* 3A **24**
Middlewich. *Ches E* 4B **84**
Middle Winterslow. *Wilts* 3H **23**
Middlewood. *Corn* 5C **10**
Middlewood. *S Yor* 1H **85**
Middle Woodford. *Wilts* 3G **23**
Middlewood Green. *Suff* 4C **66**
Middleyard. *Glos* 5D **48**
Middlezoy. *Som* 3G **21**
Middridge. *Dur* 2F **105**
Midelney. *Som* 4H **21**
Midfield. *High* 2F **167**
Midford. *Bath* 5C **34**
Mid Garrary. *Dum* 2C **110**
Midge Hall. *Lanc* 2D **90**
Midgeholme. *Cumb* 4H **113**
Midgham. *W Ber* 5D **36**
Midgley. *W Yor* 2A **92** (nr. Halifax)
Midgley. *W Yor* 3C **92** (nr. Horbury)
Mid Ho. *Shet* 2G **173**
Midhopestones. *S Yor* 1G **85**
Midhurst. *W Sus* 4G **25**
Mid Kirkton. *N Ayr* 4C **126**
Mid Lambrook. *Som* 1H **13**
Midland. *Orkn* 7C **172**
Mid Lavant. *W Sus* 2G **17**
Midlem. *Bord* 2H **119**
Midney. *Som* 4A **22**
Midsomer Norton. *Bath* 1B **22**
Midton. *Inv* 2D **126**
Midtown. *High* 5C **162** (nr. Poolewe)
Midtown. *High* 2F **167** (nr. Tongue)
Midville. *Linc* 5C **88**
Mid Walls. *Shet* 7C **173**
Mid Yell. *Shet* 2G **173**
Migdale. *High* 4D **164**
Migvie. *Abers* 3B **152**
Milborne Port. *Som* 1B **14**
Milborne St Andrew. *Dors* 3D **14**
Milborne Wick. *Som* 4B **22**
Milbourne. *Nmbd* 2E **115**
Milbourne. *Wilts* 3E **35**
Milburn. *Cumb* 2H **103**
Milbury Heath. *S Glo* 2B **34**
Milby. *N Yor* 3G **99**
Milcombe. *Oxon* 2C **50**
Milden. *Suff* 1C **54**
Mildenhall. *Suff* 3G **65**
Mildenhall. *Wilts* 5H **35**
Milebrook. *Powy* 3F **59**
Milebush. *Kent* 1B **28**
Mile End. *Cambs* 2F **65**
Mile End. *Essx* 3C **54**
Mileham. *Norf* 4B **78**
Mile Oak. *Brig* 5D **26**
Miles Green. *Staf* 5C **84**
Miles Hope. *Here* 4H **59**
Milesmark. *Fife* 1D **128**
Mile Town. *Kent* 3D **40**
Milfield. *Nmbd* 1D **120**
Milford. *Derbs* 1A **74**
Milford. *Devn* 4C **18**
Milford. *Powy* 1C **58**
Milford. *Staf* 3D **72**
Milford. *Surr* 1A **26**
Milford Haven. *Pemb* 4D **42**
Milford on Sea. *Hants* 3A **16**
Milkwall. *Glos* 5A **48**
Milkwell. *Wilts* 4E **23**
Milland. *W Sus* 4G **25**
Millbank. *High* 2D **168**
Mill Bank. *W Yor* 2A **92**
Millbeck. *Cumb* 2D **102**
Millbounds. *Orkn* 4E **172**
Millbreck. *Abers* 4H **161**
Millbridge. *Surr* 2G **25**
Millbrook. *C Beds* 2A **52**
Millbrook. *Corn* 3A **8**
Millbrook. *G Man* 1D **85**
Millbrook. *Sotn* 1B **16**
Mill Common. *Suff* 2G **67**
Mill Corner. *E Sus* 3C **28**
Milldale. *Staf* 5F **85**
Millden Lodge. *Ang* 1E **145**
Milldens. *Ang* 3E **145**
Millearn. *Per* 2B **136**
Mill End. *Buck* 3F **37**
Mill End. *Cambs* 5F **65**
Millend. *Glos* 2C **34** (nr. Dursley)
Mill End. *Glos* 4G **49** (nr. Northleach)
Mill End. *Herts* 2D **52**
Millerhill. *Midl* 3G **129**
Miller's Dale. *Derbs* 3F **85**
Millers Green. *Derbs* 5G **85**
Millerston. *N Lan* 3H **127**
Millfield. *Abers* 4B **152**
Millfield. *Pet* 5A **76**
Millgate. *Lanc* 3G **91**
Mill Green. *Essx* 5G **53**
Mill Green. *Norf* 2D **66**
Mill Green. *Shrp* 3A **72**
Mill Green. *Staf* 3E **73**
Mill Green. *Suff* 1C **54**
Millhalf. *Here* 1F **47**
Millhall. *E Ren* 4G **127**
Millhayes. *Devn* 2F **13** (nr. Honiton)
Millhayes. *Devn* 1E **13** (nr. Wellington)
Millhead. *Lanc* 2D **97**
Millheugh. *S Lan* 4A **128**
Mill Hill. *Bkbn* 2E **91**
Mill Hill. *G Lon* 1D **38**
Millholme. *Cumb* 5G **103**
Millhouse. *Arg* 2A **126**
Millhouse. *Cumb* 1E **103**
Millhousebridge. *Dum* 1C **112**
Millhouses. *S Yor* 2H **85**
Millikenpark. *Ren* 3F **127**
Millington. *E Yor* 4C **100**
Millington Green. *Derbs* 1G **73**
Millisle. *N Dwn* 4J **175**
Mill Knowe. *Arg* 3B **122**
Mill Lane. *Hants* 1F **25**
Millmeece. *Staf* 2C **72**
Mill of Craigievar. *Abers* 2C **152**
Mill of Fintray. *Abers* 2F **153**
Mill of Haldane. *W Dun* 1F **127**
Millom. *Cumb* 1A **96**
Millow. *C Beds* 1C **52**
Millpool. *Corn* 5B **10**
Millport. *N Ayr* 4C **126**
Mill Side. *Cumb* 1D **96**
Mill Street. *Norf* 4C **78** (nr. Lyng)
Mill Street. *Norf* 4C **78** (nr. Swanton Morley)
Millthorpe. *Derbs* 3H **85**
Millthorpe. *Linc* 2A **76**
Millthrop. *Cumb* 5H **103**
Milltimber. *Aber* 3F **153**
Milltown. *Abers* 3G **151** (nr. Corgarff)
Milltown. *Abers* 2B **152** (nr. Lumsden)
Milltown. *Corn* 3F **7**
Milltown. *Derbs* 4A **86**
Milltown. *Devn* 3F **19**
Milltown. *Dum* 2E **113**
Milltown of Aberdalgie. *Per* 1C **136**
Milltown of Auchindoun. *Mor* 4A **160**
Milltown of Campfield. *Abers* 3D **152**
Milltown of Edinvillie. *Mor* 4G **159**
Milltown of Rothiemay. *Mor* 4C **160**
Milltown of Towie. *Abers* 2B **152**
Milnacraig. *Ang* 3B **144**
Milnathort. *Per* 3D **136**
Milngavie. *E Dun* 2G **127**
Milnholm. *Stir* 1A **128**
Milnrow. *G Man* 3H **91**
Milnthorpe. *Cumb* 1D **97**
Milnthorpe. *W Yor* 3D **92**
Milson. *Shrp* 3A **60**
Milstead. *Kent* 5D **40**
Milston. *Wilts* 2G **23**
Milthorpe. *Nptn* 1D **50**
Milton. *Ang* 4C **144**
Milton. *Cambs* 4D **65**
Milton. *Cumb* 3G **113** (nr. Brampton)
Milton. *Cumb* 1E **97** (nr. Crooklands)
Milton. *Derbs* 3H **73**
Milton. *Dum* 2F **111** (nr. Crocketford)
Milton. *Dum* 4H **109** (nr. Glenluce)
Milton. *Glas* 3G **127**
Milton. *High* 3F **157** (nr. Achnasheen)
Milton. *High* 4G **155** (nr. Applecross)
Milton. *High* 5G **157** (nr. Drumnadrochit)
Milton. *High* 1B **158** (nr. Invergordon)
Milton. *High* 4H **157** (nr. Inverness)
Milton. *High* 3F **169** (nr. Wick)
Milton. *Mor* 2C **160** (nr. Cullen)
Milton. *Mor* 2F **151** (nr. Tomintoul)
Milton. *N Som* 5G **33**
Milton. *Notts* 3E **86**
Milton. *Oxon* 2C **50** (nr. Bloxham)
Milton. *Oxon* 2C **36** (nr. Didcot)
Milton. *Pemb* 4E **43**
Milton. *Port* 3E **17**
Milton. *Som* 4H **21**
Milton. *S Ayr* 2D **116**
Milton. *Stir* 3E **135** (nr. Aberfoyle)
Milton. *Stir* 4D **134** (nr. Drymen)
Milton. *Stoke* 5D **84**
Milton. *W Dun* 2F **127**
Milton Abbas. *Dors* 2D **14**
Milton Abbot. *Devn* 5E **11**
Milton Auchlossan. *Abers* 3C **152**
Milton Bridge. *Midl* 3F **129**
Milton Bryan. *C Beds* 2H **51**
Milton Clevedon. *Som* 3B **22**
Milton Coldwells. *Abers* 5G **161**
Milton Combe. *Devn* 2A **8**
Milton Common. *Oxon* 5E **51**
Milton Damerel. *Devn* 1D **11**
Miltonduff. *Mor* 2F **159**
Milton End. *Glos* 5G **49**
Milton Ernest. *Bed* 5H **63**
Milton Green. *Ches W* 5G **83**
Milton Hill. *Devn* 5C **12**
Milton Hill. *Oxon* 2C **36**
Milton Keynes. *Mil* 2G **51**
Milton Keynes Village. *Mil* 2G **51**
Milton Lilbourne. *Wilts* 5G **35**
Milton Malsor. *Nptn* 5E **63**
Milton Morenish. *Per* 5D **142**
Milton of Auchinhove. *Abers* 3C **152**
Milton of Balgonie. *Fife* 3F **137**

Milton of Barras—Mount Pleasant

Milton of Barras. *Abers* 1H **145**
Milton of Campsie. *E Dun* 2H **127**
Milton of Cultoquhey. *Per* 1A **136**
Milton of Cushnie. *Abers* 2C **152**
Milton of Finavon. *Ang* 3D **145**
Milton of Gollanfield. *High* 3B **158**
Milton of Lesmore. *Abers* 1B **152**
Milton of Leys. *High* 4A **158**
Milton of Tullich. *Abers* 4A **152**
Milton on Stour. *Dors* 4C **22**
Milton Regis. *Kent* 4C **40**
Milton Street. *E Sus* 5G **27**
Milton-under-Wychwood. *Oxon* 4A **50**
Milverton. *Som* 4E **20**
Milverton. *Warw* 4H **61**
Milwich. *Staf* 2D **72**
Mimbridge. *Surr* 4A **38**
Minard. *Arg* 4G **133**
Minchington. *Dors* 1E **15**
Minchinhampton. *Glos* 5D **48**
Mindrum. *Nmbd* 1C **120**
Minehead. *Som* 2C **20**
Minera. *Wrex* 5E **83**
Minety. *Wilts* 2F **35**
Minffordd. *Gwyn* 2E **69**
Mingarrypark. *High* 2A **140**
Mingary. *High* 2G **139**
Mingearraidh. *W Isl* 6C **170**
Miningsby. *Linc* 4C **88**
Minions. *Corn* 5C **10**
Minishant. *S Ayr* 3C **116**
Minllyn. *Gwyn* 4A **70**
Minnigaff. *Dum* 3B **110**
Minorca. *IOM* 3D **108**
Minskip. *N Yor* 3F **99**
Minstead. *Hants* 1A **16**
Minsted. *W Sus* 4G **25**
Minster. *Kent* 4H **41** (nr. Ramsgate)
Minster. *Kent* 3D **40** (nr. Sheerness)
Minsteracres. *Nmbd* 4D **114**
Minsterley. *Shrp* 5F **71**
Minster Lovell. *Oxon* 4B **50**
Minsterworth. *Glos* 4C **48**
Minterne Magna. *Dors* 2B **14**
Minterne Parva. *Dors* 2B **14**
Minting. *Linc* 3A **88**
Mintlaw. *Abers* 4H **161**
Minto. *Bord* 2H **119**
Minton. *Shrp* 1G **59**
Minwear. *Pemb* 3E **43**
Minworth. *W Mid* 1F **61**
Miodar. *Arg* 4B **138**
Mirbister. *Orkn* 5C **172**
Mirehouse. *Cumb* 3A **102**
Mireland. *High* 2F **169**
Mirfield. *W Yor* 3C **92**
Miserden. *Glos* 5E **49**
Miskin. *Rhon* 3D **32**
Misson. *Notts* 1D **86**
Misterton. *Leics* 2C **62**
Misterton. *Notts* 1E **87**
Misterton. *Som* 2H **13**
Mistley. *Essx* 2E **54**
Mistley Heath. *Essx* 2E **55**
Mitcham. *G Lon* 4D **39**
Mitcheldean. *Glos* 4B **48**
Mitchell. *Corn* 3C **6**
Mitchel Troy. *Mon* 4H **47**
Mitcheltroy Common. *Mon* 5H **47**
Mitford. *Nmbd* 1E **115**
Mithian. *Corn* 3B **6**
Mitton. *Staf* 4C **72**
Mixbury. *Oxon* 2E **50**
Mixenden. *W Yor* 2A **92**
Mixon. *Staf* 5E **85**
Moaness. *Orkn* 7B **172**
Moarfield. *Shet* 1G **173**
Moat. *Cumb* 2F **113**
Moats Tye. *Suff* 5C **66**
Mobberley. *Ches E* 3B **84**
Mobberley. *Staf* 1E **73**
Moccas. *Here* 1G **47**
Mochdre. *Cnwy* 3H **81**
Mochdre. *Powy* 2C **58**
Mochrum. *Dum* 5A **110**
Mockbeggar. *Hants* 2G **15**
Mockerkin. *Cumb* 2B **102**
Modbury. *Devn* 3C **8**
Moddershall. *Staf* 2D **72**
Modsarie. *High* 2G **167**
Moelfre. *Cnwy* 3B **82**
Moelfre. *IOA* 2E **81**
Moelfre. *Powy* 3D **70**
Moffat. *Dum* 4C **118**
Moggerhanger. *C Beds* 1B **52**
Mogworthy. *Devn* 1B **12**
Moira. *Leics* 4H **73**
Moira. *Lis* 4G **175**
Molash. *Kent* 5E **41**
Mol-chlach. *High* 2C **146**
Mold. *Flin* 4E **83**
Molehill Green. *Essx* 3F **53**
Molescroft. *E Yor* 5E **101**
Molesden. *Nmbd* 1E **115**
Molesworth. *Cambs* 3H **63**
Moll. *High* 1D **146**
Molland. *Devn* 4B **20**
Mollington. *Ches W* 3F **83**
Mollington. *Oxon* 1C **50**
Mollinsburn. *N Lan* 2A **128**
Monachty. *Cdgn* 4E **57**
Monachyle. *Stir* 2D **135**
Monar Lodge. *High* 4E **156**
Monaughty. *Powy* 4E **59**
Monewden. *Suff* 5E **67**
Moneydie. *Per* 1C **136**
Moneymore. *M Ulst* 3E **175**
Moneyrow Green. *Wind* 4G **37**
Moniaive. *Dum* 5G **117**
Monifieth. *Ang* 5E **145**
Monikie. *Ang* 5E **145**
Monimail. *Fife* 2E **137**
Monington. *Pemb* 1B **44**
Monk Bretton. *S Yor* 4D **92**
Monken Hadley. *G Lon* 1D **38**
Monk Fryston. *N Yor* 2F **93**
Monk Hesleden. *Dur* 1B **106**
Monkhide. *Here* 1B **48**
Monkhill. *Cumb* 4E **113**
Monkhopton. *Shrp* 1A **60**
Monkland. *Here* 5G **59**
Monkleigh. *Devn* 4E **19**
Monknash. *V Glam* 4C **32**
Monkokehampton. *Devn* 2F **11**
Monkseaton. *Tyne* 2G **115**
Monks Eleigh. *Suff* 1C **54**
Monk's Gate. *W Sus* 3D **26**
Monk's Heath. *Ches E* 3C **84**
Monk Sherborne. *Hants* 1E **24**
Monkshill. *Abers* 4E **161**
Monksilver. *Som* 3D **20**
Monks Kirby. *Warw* 2B **62**
Monk Soham. *Suff* 4E **66**
Monk Soham Green. *Suff* 4E **66**
Monkspath. *W Mid* 3F **61**
Monks Risborough. *Buck* 5G **51**
Monksthorpe. *Linc* 4D **88**
Monk Street. *Essx* 3G **53**
Monkswood. *Mon* 5G **47**
Monkton. *Devn* 2E **13**
Monkton. *Kent* 4G **41**
Monkton. *Pemb* 4D **42**
Monkton. *S Ayr* 2C **116**
Monkton Combe. *Bath* 5C **34**
Monkton Deverill. *Wilts* 3D **22**
Monkton Farleigh. *Wilts* 5D **34**
Monkton Heathfield. *Som* 4F **21**
Monktonhill. *S Ayr* 2C **116**
Monkton Up Wimborne. *Dors* 1F **15**
Monkton Wyld. *Dors* 3G **13**
Monkwearmouth. *Tyne* 4G **115**
Monkwood. *Dors* 3H **13**
Monkwood. *Hants* 3E **25**
Monmarsh. *Here* 1A **48**
Monmouth. *Mon* 4A **48**
Monnington on Wye. *Here* 1G **47**
Monreith. *Dum* 5A **110**
Montacute. *Som* 1H **13**
Montford. *Arg* 3C **126**
Montford. *Shrp* 4G **71**
Montford Bridge. *Shrp* 4G **71**
Montgarrie. *Abers* 2C **152**
Montgarswood. *E Ayr* 2E **117**
Montgomery. *Powy* 1E **58**
Montgreenan. *N Ayr* 5E **127**
Montrave. *Fife* 3F **137**
Montrose. *Ang* 3G **145**
Monxton. *Hants* 2B **24**
Monyash. *Derbs* 4F **85**
Monymusk. *Abers* 2D **152**
Monzie. *Per* 1A **136**
Moodiesburn. *N Lan* 2H **127**
Moon's Green. *Kent* 3C **28**
Moonzie. *Fife* 2F **137**
Moor. *Som* 1H **13**
Moor Allerton. *W Yor* 1C **92**
Moorbath. *Dors* 3H **13**
Moorbrae. *Shet* 3F **173**
Moorby. *Linc* 4B **88**
Moorcot. *Here* 5F **59**
Moor Crichel. *Dors* 2E **15**
Moor Cross. *Devn* 3C **8**
Moordown. *Bour* 3F **15**
Moore. *Hal* 2H **83**
Moorend. *Dum* 2D **112**
Moor End. *E Yor* 1B **94**
Moorend. *Glos* 5C **48** (nr. Dursley)
Moorend. *Glos* 4D **48** (nr. Gloucester)
Moorends. *S Yor* 3G **93**
Moorgate. *S Yor* 1B **86**
Moorgreen. *Hants* 1C **16**
Moorgreen. *Notts* 1B **74**
Moor Green. *Wilts* 5D **34**
Moorhaigh. *Notts* 4C **86**
Moorhall. *Derbs* 3H **85**
Moorhampton. *Here* 1G **47**
Moorhouse. *Cumb* 4E **113** (nr. Carlisle)
Moorhouse. *Cumb* 4D **112** (nr. Wigton)
Moorhouse. *Notts* 4E **87**
Moorhouse. *Surr* 5F **39**
Moorhouses. *Linc* 5B **88**
Moorland. *Som* 3G **21**
Moorlinch. *Som* 3H **21**
Moor Monkton. *N Yor* 4H **99**
Moor of Granary. *Mor* 3E **159**
Moor Row. *Cumb* 3B **102** (nr. Whitehaven)
Moor Row. *Cumb* 5D **112** (nr. Wigton)
Moorsholm. *Red C* 3D **107**
Moorside. *Dors* 1C **14**
Moorside. *G Man* 4H **91**
Moor, The. *Kent* 3B **28**
Moortown. *Devn* 3D **10**
Moortown. *Hants* 2G **15**
Moortown. *IOW* 4C **16**
Moortown. *Linc* 1H **87**
Moortown. *Telf* 4A **72**
Moortown. *W Yor* 1D **92**
Morangie. *High* 5E **165**
Morar. *High* 4E **147**
Morborne. *Cambs* 1A **64**
Morchard Bishop. *Devn* 2A **12**
Morcombelake. *Dors* 3H **13**
Morcott. *Rut* 5G **75**
Morda. *Shrp* 3E **71**
Morden. *G Lon* 4D **38**
Mordiford. *Here* 2A **48**
Mordon. *Dur* 2A **106**
More. *Shrp* 1F **59**
Morebath. *Devn* 4C **20**
Morebattle. *Bord* 2B **120**
Morecambe. *Lanc* 3D **96**
Morefield. *High* 4F **163**
Moreleigh. *Devn* 3D **8**
Morenish. *Per* 5C **142**
Moresby Parks. *Cumb* 3A **102**
Morestead. *Hants* 4D **24**
Moreton. *Dors* 4D **14**
Moreton. *Essx* 5F **53**
Moreton. *Here* 4H **59**
Moreton. *Mers* 1E **83**
Moreton. *Oxon* 5E **51**
Moreton. *Staf* 4B **72**
Moreton Corbet. *Shrp* 3H **71**
Moretonhampstead. *Devn* 4A **12**
Moreton-in-Marsh. *Glos* 2H **49**
Moreton Jeffries. *Here* 1B **48**
Moreton Morrell. *Warw* 5H **61**
Moreton on Lugg. *Here* 1A **48**
Moreton Pinkney. *Nptn* 1D **50**
Moreton Say. *Shrp* 2A **72**
Moreton Valence. *Glos* 5C **48**
Morfa. *Cdgn* 5C **56**
Morfa Bach. *Carm* 4D **44**
Morfa Bychan. *Gwyn* 2E **69**
Morfa Glas. *Neat* 5B **46**
Morfa Nefyn. *Gwyn* 1B **68**
Morganstown. *Card* 3E **33**
Morgan's Vale. *Wilts* 4G **23**
Morham. *E Lot* 2B **130**
Moriah. *Cdgn* 3F **57**
Morland. *Cumb* 2G **103**
Morley. *Ches E* 2C **84**
Morley. *Derbs* 1A **74**
Morley. *Dur* 2E **105**
Morley. *W Yor* 2C **92**
Morley St Botolph. *Norf* 1C **66**
Morningside. *Edin* 2F **129**
Morningside. *N Lan* 4B **128**
Morningthorpe. *Norf* 1E **66**
Morpeth. *Nmbd* 1F **115**
Morrey. *Staf* 4F **73**
Morridge Side. *Staf* 5E **85**
Morridge Top. *Staf* 4E **85**
Morrington. *Dum* 1F **111**
Morris Green. *Essx* 2H **53**
Morriston. *Swan* 3F **31**
Morston. *Norf* 1C **78**
Mortehoe. *Devn* 2E **19**
Morthen. *S Yor* 2B **86**
Mortimer. *W Ber* 5E **37**
Mortimer's Cross. *Here* 4G **59**
Mortimer West End. *Hants* 5E **37**
Mortomley. *S Yor* 1H **85**
Morton. *Cumb* 1F **103** (nr. Calthwaite)
Morton. *Cumb* 4E **113** (nr. Carlisle)
Morton. *Derbs* 4B **86**
Morton. *Linc* 3H **75** (nr. Bourne)
Morton. *Linc* 1F **87** (nr. Gainsborough)
Morton. *Linc* 4F **87** (nr. Lincoln)
Morton. *Norf* 4D **78**
Morton. *Notts* 5E **87**
Morton. *Shrp* 3E **71**
Morton. *S Glo* 2B **34**
Morton Bagot. *Warw* 4F **61**
Morton Mill. *Shrp* 3H **71**
Morton-on-Swale. *N Yor* 5A **106**
Morton Tinmouth. *Dur* 2E **105**
Morvah. *Corn* 3B **4**
Morval. *Corn* 3G **7**
Morvich. *High* 3E **165** (nr. Golspie)
Morvich. *High* 1B **148** (nr. Shiel Bridge)
Morvil. *Pemb* 1E **43**
Morville. *Shrp* 1A **60**
Morwenstow. *Corn* 1C **10**
Morwick. *Nmbd* 4G **121**
Mosborough. *S Yor* 2B **86**
Moscow. *E Ayr* 5F **127**
Mose. *Shrp* 1B **60**
Mosedale. *Cumb* 1E **103**
Moseley. *W Mid* 2E **61** (nr. Birmingham)
Moseley. *W Mid* 5D **72** (nr. Wolverhampton)
Moseley. *Worc* 5C **60**
Moss. *Arg* 4A **138**
Moss. *High* 2A **140**
Moss. *S Yor* 3F **93**
Moss. *Wrex* 5F **83**
Mossatt. *Abers* 2B **152**
Moss Bank. *Mers* 1H **83**
Mossbank. *Shet* 4F **173**
Mossblown. *S Ayr* 2D **116**
Mossbrow. *G Man* 2B **84**
Mossburnford. *Bord* 3A **120**
Mossdale. *Dum* 2D **110**
Mossedge. *Cumb* 3F **113**
Mossend. *N Lan* 3A **128**
Mossgate. *Staf* 2D **72**
Moss Lane. *Ches E* 3D **84**
Mossley. *Ches E* 4C **84**
Mossley. *G Man* 4H **91**
Mossley Hill. *Mers* 2F **83**
Moss of Barmuckity. *Mor* 2G **159**
Mosspark. *Glas* 3G **127**
Mosspaul. *Bord* 5G **119**
Moss Side. *Cumb* 4C **112**
Moss Side. *G Man* 1C **84**
Moss-side. *High* 3C **158**
Moss Side. *Lanc* 1B **90** (nr. Blackpool)
Moss Side. *Lanc* 2D **90** (nr. Preston)
Moss Side. *Mers* 4B **90**
Moss-side of Cairness. *Abers* 2H **161**
Mosstodloch. *Mor* 2H **159**
Mosswood. *Nmbd* 4D **114**
Mossy Lea. *Lanc* 3D **90**
Mosterton. *Dors* 2H **13**
Moston. *Shrp* 3H **71**
Moston Green. *Ches E* 4B **84**
Mostyn. *Flin* 2D **82**
Mostyn Quay. *Flin* 2D **82**
Motcombe. *Dors* 4D **22**
Mothecombe. *Devn* 4C **8**
Motherby. *Cumb* 2F **103**
Motherwell. *N Lan* 4A **128**
Mottingham. *G Lon* 3F **39**
Mottisfont. *Hants* 4B **24**
Mottistone. *IOW* 4C **16**
Mottram in Longdendale. *G Man* 1D **85**
Mottram St Andrew. *Ches E* 3C **84**
Mott's Mill. *E Sus* 2G **27**
Mouldsworth. *Ches W* 3H **83**
Moulin. *Per* 3G **143**
Moulsecoomb. *Brig* 5E **27**
Moulsford. *Oxon* 3D **36**
Moulsoe. *Mil* 1H **51**
Moulton. *Ches W* 4A **84**
Moulton. *Linc* 3C **76**
Moulton. *Nptn* 4E **63**
Moulton. *N Yor* 4F **105**
Moulton. *Suff* 4F **65**
Moulton. *V Glam* 4D **32**
Moulton Chapel. *Linc* 4B **76**
Moulton Eaugate. *Linc* 4C **76**
Moulton St Mary. *Norf* 5F **79**
Moulton Seas End. *Linc* 3C **76**
Mount. *Corn* 2F **7** (nr. Bodmin)
Mount. *Corn* 3B **6** (nr. Newquay)
Mountain Ash. *Rhon* 2D **32**
Mountain Cross. *Bord* 5E **129**
Mountain Street. *Kent* 5E **41**
Mountain Water. *Pemb* 2D **42**
Mount Ambrose. *Corn* 4B **6**
Mountbenger. *Bord* 2F **119**
Mountblow. *W Dun* 2F **127**
Mount Bures. *Essx* 2C **54**
Mountfield. *E Sus* 3B **28**
Mountgerald. *High* 2H **157**
Mount Hawke. *Corn* 4B **6**
Mount High. *High* 2A **158**
Mountjoy. *Corn* 2C **6**
Mount Lothian. *Midl* 4F **129**
Mountnessing. *Essx* 1H **39**
Mounton. *Mon* 2A **34**
Mount Pleasant. *Buck* 2E **51**
Mount Pleasant. *Ches E* 5C **84**

Mount Pleasant—Newbiggin

Mount Pleasant. *Derbs* 1H 73
(nr. Derby)
Mount Pleasant. *Derbs* 4G 73
(nr. Swadlincote)
Mount Pleasant. *E Sus* 4F 27
Mount Pleasant. *Hants* 3A 16
Mount Pleasant. *Norf* 1B 66
Mount Skippett. *Oxon* 4B 50
Mountsorrel. *Leics* 4C 74
Mount Stuart. *Arg* 4C 126
Mousehole. *Corn* 4B 4
Mouswald. *Dum* 2B 112
Mow Cop. *Ches E* 5C 84
Mowden. *Darl* 3F 105
Mowhaugh. *Bord* 2C 120
Mowmacre Hill. *Leic* 5C 74
Mowsley. *Leics* 2D 62
Moy. *High* 5B 158
Moy. *M Ulst* 5E 175
Moygashel. *M Ulst* 4E 175
Moylgrove. *Pemb* 1B 44
Moy Lodge. *High* 5G 149
Muasdale. *Arg* 5E 125
Muchalls. *Abers* 4G 153
Much Birch. *Here* 2A 48
Much Cowarne. *Here* 1B 48
Much Dewchurch. *Here* 2H 47
Muchelney. *Som* 4H 21
Muchelney Ham. *Som* 4H 21
Much Hadham. *Herts* 4E 53
Much Hoole. *Lanc* 2C 90
Muchlarnick. *Corn* 3G 7
Much Marcle. *Here* 2B 48
Muchrachd. *High* 5E 157
Much Wenlock. *Shrp* 5A 72
Mucking. *Thur* 2A 40
Muckle Breck. *Shet* 5G 173
Muckleford. *Dors* 3B 14
Mucklestone. *Staf* 2B 72
Muckleton. *Norf* 2H 77
Muckleton. *Shrp* 3H 71
Muckley. *Shrp* 1A 60
Muckley Corner. *Staf* 5E 73
Muckton. *Linc* 2C 88
Mudale. *High* 5F 167
Muddiford. *Devn* 3F 19
Mudeford. *Dors* 3G 15
Mudford. *Som* 1A 14
Mudgley. *Som* 2H 21
Mugdock. *Stir* 2G 127
Mugeary. *High* 5D 154
Mugginton. *Derbs* 1G 73
Muggintonlane End. *Derbs* 1G 73
Muggleswick. *Dur* 4D 114
Mugswell. *Surr* 5D 38
Muie. *High* 3D 164
Muirden. *Abers* 3E 160
Muirdrum. *Ang* 5E 145
Muiredge. *Per* 1E 137
Muirend. *Glas* 3G 127
Muirhead. *Ang* 5C 144
Muirhead. *Fife* 3E 137
Muirhead. *N Lan* 3H 127
Muirhouses. *Falk* 1D 128
Muirkirk. *E Ayr* 2F 117
Muir of Alford. *Abers* 2C 152
Muir of Fairburn. *High* 3G 157
Muir of Fowlis. *Abers* 2C 152
Muir of Miltonduff. *Mor* 3F 159
Muir of Ord. *High* 3H 157
Muir of Tarradale. *High* 3H 157
Muirshearlich. *High* 5D 148
Muirtack. *Abers* 5G 161
Muirton. *High* 2B 158
Muirton. *Per* 1D 136
Muirton of Ardblair. *Per* 4A 144
Muirtown. *Per* 2B 136
Muiryfold. *Abers* 3E 161
Muker. *N Yor* 5C 104
Mulbarton. *Norf* 5D 78
Mulben. *Mor* 3A 160
Mulindry. *Arg* 4B 124
Mulla. *Shet* 5F 173
Mullach Charlabhaigh. *W Isl* 3E 171
Mullacott. *Devn* 2F 19
Mullion. *Corn* 5D 5
Mullion Cove. *Corn* 5D 4
Mumbles. *Swan* 4F 31
Mumby. *Linc* 3E 89
Munderfield Row. *Here* 5A 60
Munderfield Stocks. *Here* 5A 60
Mundesley. *Norf* 2F 79
Mundford. *Norf* 1H 65
Mundham. *Norf* 1F 67
Mundon. *Essx* 5B 54
Munerigie. *High* 3E 149
Muness. *Shet* 1H 173
Mungasdale. *High* 4D 162
Mungrisdale. *Cumb* 1E 103
Munlochy. *High* 3A 158
Munsley. *Here* 1B 48
Munslow. *Shrp* 2H 59
Murchington. *Devn* 4G 11
Murcot. *Worc* 1F 49
Murcott. *Oxon* 4D 50
Murdishaw. *Hal* 2H 83
Murieston. *W Lot* 3D 128
Murkle. *High* 2D 168
Murlaggan. *High* 4C 148
Murra. *Orkn* 7B 172
Murrayfield. *Edin* 2F 129
Murray, The. *S Lan* 4H 127
Murrell Green. *Hants* 1F 25
Murroes. *Ang* 5D 144
Murrow. *Cambs* 5C 76
Mursley. *Buck* 3G 51
Murthly. *Per* 5H 143
Murton. *Cumb* 2A 104
Murton. *Dur* 5G 115
Murton. *Nmbd* 5F 131
Murton. *Swan* 4E 31
Murton. *York* 4A 100
Musbury. *Devn* 3F 13
Muscoates. *N Yor* 1A 100
Muscott. *Nptn* 4D 62
Musselburgh. *E Lot* 2G 129
Muston. *Leics* 2F 75
Muston. *N Yor* 2E 101
Mustow Green. *Worc* 3C 60
Muswell Hill. *G Lon* 2D 39
Mutehill. *Dum* 5D 111
Mutford. *Suff* 2G 67
Muthill. *Per* 2A 136
Mutterton. *Devn* 2D 12
Muxton. *Telf* 4B 72
Mwmbwls. *Swan* 4F 31
Mybster. *High* 3D 168
Myddfai. *Carm* 2A 46
Myddle. *Shrp* 3G 71
Mydroilyn. *Cdgn* 5D 56
Myerscough. *Lanc* 1C 90
Mylor Bridge. *Corn* 5C 6
Mylor Churchtown. *Corn* 5C 6
Mynachlog-ddu. *Pemb* 1F 43
Mynydd-bach. *Mon* 2H 33
Mynydd Isa. *Flin* 4E 83
Mynyddislwyn. *Cphy* 2E 33
Mynydd Llandegai. *Gwyn* 4F 81
Mynydd Mechell. *IOA* 1C 80
Mynydd-y-briw. *Powy* 3D 70
Mynyddygarreg. *Carm* 5E 45
Mynytho. *Gwyn* 2C 68
Myrebird. *Abers* 4E 153
Myrelandhorn. *High* 3E 169
Mytchett. *Surr* 1G 25
Mythe, The. *Glos* 2D 49
Mytholmroyd. *W Yor* 2A 92
Myton-on-Swale. *N Yor* 3G 99
Mytton. *Shrp* 4G 71

N

Naast. *High* 5C 162
Na Buirgh. *W Isl* 8C 171
Naburn. *York* 5H 99
Nab Wood. *W Yor* 1B 92
Nackington. *Kent* 5F 41
Nacton. *Suff* 1F 55
Nafferton. *E Yor* 4E 101
Na Gearrannan. *W Isl* 3D 171
Nailbridge. *Glos* 4B 48
Nailsbourne. *Som* 4F 21
Nailsea. *N Som* 4H 33
Nailstone. *Leics* 5B 74
Nailsworth. *Glos* 2D 34
Nairn. *High* 3C 158
Nalderswood. *Surr* 1D 26
Nancegollan. *Corn* 3D 4
Nancledra. *Corn* 3B 4
Nangreaves. *G Man* 3G 91
Nanhyfer. *Pemb* 1E 43
Nannerch. *Flin* 4D 82
Nanpantan. *Leics* 4C 74
Nanpean. *Corn* 3D 6
Nanstallon. *Corn* 2E 7
Nant-ddu. *Powy* 4D 46
Nanternis. *Cdgn* 5C 56
Nantgaredig. *Carm* 3E 45
Nantgarw. *Rhon* 3E 33
Nant Glas. *Powy* 4B 58
Nantglyn. *Den* 4C 82
Nantgwyn. *Powy* 3B 58
Nantlle. *Gwyn* 5E 81
Nantmawr. *Shrp* 3E 71
Nantmel. *Powy* 4C 58
Nantmor. *Gwyn* 1F 69
Nant Peris. *Gwyn* 5F 81
Nantwich. *Ches E* 5A 84
Nant-y-bai. *Carm* 1A 46
Nant-y-bwch. *Blae* 4E 47
Nant-y-Derry. *Mon* 5G 47
Nant-y-dugoed. *Powy* 4B 70
Nant-y-felin. *Cnwy* 3F 81
Nantyffyllon. *B'end* 2B 32
Nantyglo. *Blae* 4E 47
Nant-y-meichiaid. *Powy* 4D 70
Nant-y-moel. *B'end* 2C 32
Nant-y-Pandy. *Cnwy* 3F 81
Naphill. *Buck* 2G 37
Nappa. *N Yor* 4A 98
Napton on the Hill. *Warw* 4B 62
Narberth. *Pemb* 3F 43
Narberth Bridge. *Pemb* 3F 43
Narborough. *Leics* 1C 62
Narborough. *Norf* 4G 77
Narkurs. *Corn* 3H 7
Narth, The. *Mon* 5A 48
Narthwaite. *Cumb* 5A 104
Nasareth. *Gwyn* 5D 80
Naseby. *Nptn* 3D 62
Nash. *Buck* 2F 51
Nash. *Here* 4F 59
Nash. *Kent* 5G 41
Nash. *Newp* 3G 33
Nash. *Shrp* 3A 60
Nash Lee. *Buck* 5G 51
Nassington. *Nptn* 1H 63
Nasty. *Herts* 3D 52
Natcott. *Devn* 4C 18
Nateby. *Cumb* 4A 104
Nateby. *Lanc* 5D 96
Nately Scures. *Hants* 1F 25
Natland. *Cumb* 1E 97
Naughton. *Suff* 1D 54
Naunton. *Glos* 3G 49
Naunton. *Worc* 2D 49
Naunton Beauchamp. *Worc* 5D 60
Navenby. *Linc* 5G 87
Navestock. *Essx* 1G 39
Navestock Side. *Essx* 1G 39
Navidale. *High* 2H 165
Nawton. *N Yor* 1A 100
Nayland. *Suff* 2C 54
Nazeing. *Essx* 5E 53
Neacroft. *Hants* 3G 15
Nealhouse. *Cumb* 4E 113
Neal's Green. *Warw* 2H 61
Neap House. *N Lin* 3B 94
Near Sawrey. *Cumb* 5E 103
Neasden. *G Lon* 2D 38
Neasham. *Darl* 3A 106
Neath. *Neat* 2A 32
Neath Abbey. *Neat* 3G 31
Neatishead. *Norf* 3F 79
Neaton. *Norf* 5B 78
Nebo. *Cdgn* 4E 57
Nebo. *Cnwy* 5H 81
Nebo. *Gwyn* 5D 81
Nebo. *IOA* 1D 80
Necton. *Norf* 5A 78
Nedd. *High* 5B 166
Nedderton. *Nmbd* 1F 115
Nedging. *Suff* 1D 54
Nedging Tye. *Suff* 1D 54
Needham. *Norf* 2E 67
Needham Market. *Suff* 5C 66
Needham Street. *Suff* 4G 65
Needingworth. *Cambs* 3C 64
Needwood. *Staf* 3F 73
Neen Savage. *Shrp* 3A 60
Neen Sollars. *Shrp* 3A 60
Neenton. *Shrp* 2A 60
Nefyn. *Gwyn* 1C 68
Neilston. *E Ren* 4F 127
Neithrop. *Oxon* 1C 50
Nelly Andrews Green. *Powy* 5E 71
Nelson. *Cphy* 2E 32
Nelson. *Lanc* 1G 91
Nelson Village. *Nmbd* 2F 115
Nemphlar. *S Lan* 5B 128
Nempnett Thrubwell. *Bath* 5A 34
Nene Terrace. *Linc* 5B 76
Nenthall. *Cumb* 5A 114
Nenthead. *Cumb* 5A 114
Nenthorn. *Bord* 1A 120
Nercwys. *Flin* 4E 83
Neribus. *Arg* 4A 124
Nerston. *S Lan* 4H 127
Nesbit. *Nmbd* 1D 121
Nesfield. *N Yor* 5C 98
Ness. *Ches W* 3F 83
Nesscliffe. *Shrp* 4F 71
Ness of Tenston. *Orkn* 6B 172
Neston. *Ches W* 3E 83
Neston. *Wilts* 5D 34
Nethanfoot. *S Lan* 5B 128
Nether Alderley. *Ches E* 3C 84
Netheravon. *Wilts* 2G 23
Nether Blainslie. *Bord* 5B 130
Netherbrae. *Abers* 3E 161
Netherbrough. *Orkn* 6C 172
Nether Broughton. *Leics* 3D 74
Netherburn. *S Lan* 5B 128
Nether Burrow. *Lanc* 2F 97
Netherbury. *Dors* 3H 13
Netherby. *Cumb* 2E 113
Nether Careston. *Ang* 3E 145
Nether Cerne. *Dors* 3B 14
Nether Compton. *Dors* 1A 14
Nethercote. *Glos* 3G 49
Nethercote. *Warw* 4C 62
Nethercott. *Devn* 3E 19
Nethercott. *Oxon* 3C 50
Nether Dallachy. *Mor* 2A 160
Nether Durdie. *Per* 1E 136
Nether End. *Derbs* 3G 85
Netherend. *Glos* 5A 48
Nether Exe. *Devn* 2C 12
Netherfield. *E Sus* 4B 28
Netherfield. *Notts* 1D 74
Nethergate. *Norf* 3C 78
Netherhampton. *Wilts* 4G 23
Nether Handley. *Derbs* 3B 86
Nether Haugh. *S Yor* 1B 86
Nether Heage. *Derbs* 5A 86
Nether Heyford. *Nptn* 5D 62
Netherhouses. *Cumb* 1B 96
Nether Howcleugh. *S Lan* 3C 118
Nether Kellet. *Lanc* 3E 97
Nether Kinmundy. *Abers* 4H 161
Netherland Green. *Staf* 2F 73
Nether Langwith. *Notts* 3C 86
Netherlaw. *Dum* 5E 111
Netherley. *Abers* 4F 153
Nethermill. *Dum* 1B 112
Nethermills. *Mor* 3C 160
Nether Moor. *Derbs* 4A 86
Nether Padley. *Derbs* 3G 85
Netherplace. *E Ren* 4G 127
Nether Poppleton. *York* 4H 99
Netherseal. *Derbs* 4G 73
Nether Silton. *N Yor* 5B 106
Nether Stowey. *Som* 3E 21
Nether Street. *Essx* 4F 53
Netherstreet. *Wilts* 5E 35
Netherthird. *E Ayr* 3E 117
Netherthong. *W Yor* 4B 92
Netherton. *Ang* 3E 145
Netherton. *Cumb* 1B 102
Netherton. *Devn* 5B 12
Netherton. *Hants* 1B 24
Netherton. *Here* 3A 48
Netherton. *Mers* 1F 83
Netherton. *N Lan* 4A 128
Netherton. *Nmbd* 4D 121
Netherton. *Per* 3A 144
Netherton. *Shrp* 2B 60
Netherton. *Stir* 2G 127
Netherton. *W Mid* 2D 60
Netherton. *W Yor* 3C 92
(nr. Horbury)
Netherton. *W Yor* 3B 92
(nr. Huddersfield)
Netherton. *Worc* 1E 49
Nethertown. *Cumb* 4A 102
Nethertown. *High* 1F 169
Nethertown. *Staf* 4F 73
Nether Urquhart. *Fife* 3D 136
Nether Wallop. *Hants* 3B 24
Nether Wasdale. *Cumb* 4C 102
Nether Welton. *Cumb* 5E 113
Nether Westcote. *Glos* 3H 49
Nether Whitacre. *Warw* 1G 61
Nether Winchendon. *Buck* 4F 51
Netherwitton. *Nmbd* 5F 121
Nether Worton. *Oxon* 2C 50
Nethy Bridge. *High* 1E 151
Netley. *Hants* 2C 16
Netley. *Shrp* 5G 71
Netley Marsh. *Hants* 1B 16
Nettlebed. *Oxon* 3F 37
Nettlebridge. *Som* 2B 22
Nettlecombe. *Dors* 3A 14
Nettlecombe. *IOW* 5D 16
Nettleden. *Herts* 4A 52
Nettleham. *Linc* 3H 87
Nettlestead. *Kent* 5A 40
Nettlestead Green. *Kent* 5A 40
Nettlestone. *IOW* 3E 16
Nettlesworth. *Dur* 5F 115
Nettleton. *Linc* 4E 94
Nettleton. *Wilts* 4D 34
Netton. *Devn* 4B 8
Netton. *Wilts* 3G 23
Neuadd. *Powy* 5C 70
Neuk, The. *Abers* 4E 153
Nevendon. *Essx* 1B 40
Nevern. *Pemb* 1E 43
New Abbey. *Dum* 3A 112
New Aberdour. *Abers* 2F 161
New Addington. *G Lon* 4E 39
Newall. *W Yor* 5E 98
New Alresford. *Hants* 3D 24
New Alyth. *Per* 4B 144
Newark. *Orkn* 3G 172
Newark. *Pet* 5B 76
Newark-on-Trent. *Notts* 5E 87
New Arley. *Warw* 2G 61
Newarthill. *N Lan* 4A 128
New Ash Green. *Kent* 4H 39
New Balderton. *Notts* 5F 87
New Barn. *Kent* 4H 39
New Barnetby. *N Lin* 3D 94
Newbattle. *Midl* 3G 129
New Bewick. *Nmbd* 2E 121
Newbie. *Dum* 3C 112
Newbiggin. *Cumb* 2H 103
(nr. Appleby)
Newbiggin. *Cumb* 3B 96
(nr. Barrow-in-Furness)
Newbiggin. *Cumb* 5G 113
(nr. Cumrew)
Newbiggin. *Cumb* 2F 103
(nr. Penrith)

Newton upon Derwent—North Water Bridge

Newton upon Derwent. *E Yor* 5B **100**
Newton Valence. *Hants* 3F **25**
Newton-with-Scales. *Lanc* 1C **90**
Newtown. *Abers* 2E **160**
Newtown. *Cambs* 4H **63**
Newtown. *Corn* 5C **10**
Newtown. *Cumb* 5B **112**
(nr. Aspatria)
Newtown. *Cumb* 3G **113**
(nr. Brampton)
Newtown. *Cumb* 2G **103**
(nr. Penrith)
Newtown. *Derbs* 2D **85**
Newtown. *Devn* 4A **20**
Newtown. *Dors* 2H **13**
(nr. Beaminster)
New Town. *Dors* 1E **15**
(nr. Sixpenny Handley)
New Town. *E Lot* 2H **129**
Newtown. *Falk* 1C **128**
Newtown. *Glos* 5B **48**
(nr. Lydney)
Newtown. *Glos* 2E **49**
(nr. Tewkesbury)
Newtown. *Hants* 1D **16**
(nr. Bishop's Waltham)
Newtown. *Hants* 3G **25**
(nr. Liphook)
Newtown. *Hants* 1A **16**
(nr. Lyndhurst)
Newtown. *Hants* 5C **36**
(nr. Newbury)
Newtown. *Hants* 4B **24**
(nr. Romsey)
Newtown. *Hants* 2C **16**
(nr. Warsash)
Newtown. *Hants* 1E **16**
(nr. Wickham)
Newtown. *Here* 2A **48**
(nr. Little Dewchurch)
Newtown. *Here* 1B **48**
(nr. Stretton Grandison)
Newtown. *High* 3F **149**
Newtown. *IOM* 4C **108**
Newtown. *IOW* 3C **16**
Newtown. *Lanc* 3D **90**
New Town. *Lutn* 3A **52**
Newtown. *Nmbd* 4E **121**
(nr. Rothbury)
Newtown. *Nmbd* 2E **121**
(nr. Wooler)
Newtown. *Pool* 3F **15**
Newtown. *Powy* 1D **58**
Newtown. *Rhon* 2D **32**
Newtown. *Shet* 3F **173**
Newtown. *Shrp* 2G **71**
Newtown. *Som* 1F **13**
Newtown. *Staf* 4D **84**
(nr. Biddulph)
Newtown. *Staf* 5D **73**
(nr. Cannock)
Newtown. *Staf* 4E **85**
(nr. Longnor)
New Town. *W Yor* 2E **93**
Newtown. *Wilts* 4E **23**
Newtownabbey. *Ant* 3H **175**
Newtownards. *N Dwn* 4H **175**
Newtown-in-St Martin. *Corn* 4E **5**
Newtown Linford. *Leics* 5C **74**
Newtown St Boswells. *Bord* 1H **119**
Newtownstewart. *Derr* 3C **174**
New Tredegar. *Cphy* 5E **47**
Newtyle. *Ang* 4B **144**
New Village. *E Yor* 1D **94**
New Village. *S Yor* 4F **93**
New Walsoken. *Cambs* 5D **76**
New Waltham. *NE Lin* 4F **95**
New Winton. *E Lot* 2H **129**
New World. *Cambs* 1C **64**
New Yatt. *Oxon* 4B **50**
Newyears Green. *G Lon* 2B **38**
New York. *Linc* 5B **88**
New York. *Tyne* 2G **115**
Nextend. *Here* 5F **59**
Neyland. *Pemb* 4D **42**
Nib Heath. *Shrp* 4G **71**
Nicholashayne. *Devn* 1E **12**
Nicholaston. *Swan* 4E **31**
Nidd. *N Yor* 3F **99**
Niddrie. *Edin* 2G **129**
Niddry. *Edin* 2D **129**
Nigg. *Aber* 3G **153**
Nigg. *High* 1C **158**
Nigg Ferry. *High* 2B **158**
Nightcott. *Som* 4B **20**
Nimmer. *Som* 1G **13**
Nine Ashes. *Essx* 5F **53**
Ninebanks. *Nmbd* 4A **114**
Nine Elms. *Swin* 3G **35**
Ninemile Bar. *Dum* 2F **111**
Nine Mile Burn. *Midl* 4E **129**
Ninfield. *E Sus* 4B **28**
Ningwood. *IOW* 4C **16**
Nisbet. *Bord* 2A **120**
Nisbet Hill. *Bord* 4D **130**
Niton. *IOW* 5D **16**
Nitshill. *Glas* 3G **127**
Niwbwrch. *IOA* 4D **80**
Noak Hill. *G Lon* 1G **39**
Nobold. *Shrp* 4G **71**
Nobottle. *Nptn* 4D **62**
Nocton. *Linc* 4H **87**
Nogdam End. *Norf* 5F **79**
Noke. *Oxon* 4D **50**
Nolton. *Pemb* 3C **42**
Nolton Haven. *Pemb* 3C **42**
No Man's Heath. *Ches W* 1H **71**
No Man's Heath. *Warw* 5G **73**
Nomansland. *Devn* 1B **12**
Nomansland. *Wilts* 1A **16**
Noneley. *Shrp* 3G **71**
Noness. *Shet* 9F **173**
Nonikiln. *High* 1A **158**
Nonington. *Kent* 5G **41**
Nook. *Cumb* 2F **113**
(nr. Longtown)
Nook. *Cumb* 1E **97**
(nr. Milnthorpe)
Noranside. *Ang* 2D **144**
Norbreck. *Bkpl* 5C **96**
Norbridge. *Here* 1C **48**
Norbury. *Ches E* 1H **71**
Norbury. *Derbs* 1F **73**
Norbury. *Shrp* 1F **59**
Norbury. *Staf* 3B **72**
Norby. *N Yor* 1G **99**
Norby. *Shet* 6C **173**
Norcross. *Lanc* 5C **96**
Nordelph. *Norf* 5E **77**
Norden. *G Man* 3G **91**
Nordley. *Shrp* 1A **60**
Norfolk Broads. *Norf* 5G **79**
Norham. *Nmbd* 5F **131**
Norland Town. *W Yor* 2A **92**
Norley. *Ches W* 3H **83**
Norleywood. *Hants* 3B **16**
Normanby. *N Lin* 3B **94**
Normanby. *N Yor* 1B **100**
Normanby. *Red C* 3C **106**
Normanby-by-Spital. *Linc* 2H **87**
Normanby le Wold. *Linc* 1A **88**
Norman Cross. *Cambs* 1A **64**
Normandy. *Surr* 5A **38**
Norman's Bay. *E Sus* 5A **28**
Norman's Green. *Devn* 2D **12**
Normanton. *Derb* 2H **73**
Normanton. *Leics* 1F **75**
Normanton. *Linc* 1G **75**
Normanton. *Notts* 5E **86**
Normanton. *W Yor* 2D **93**
Normanton le Heath. *Leics* 4A **74**
Normanton on Soar. *Notts* 3C **74**
Normanton-on-the-Wolds. *Notts* 2D **74**
Normanton on Trent. *Notts* 4E **87**
Normoss. *Lanc* 1B **90**
Norrington Common. *Wilts* 5D **35**
Norris Green. *Mers* 1F **83**
Norris Hill. *Leics* 4H **73**
Norristhorpe. *W Yor* 2C **92**
Northacre. *Norf* 1B **66**
Northall. *Buck* 3H **51**
Northallerton. *N Yor* 5A **106**
Northam. *Devn* 4E **19**
Northam. *Sotn* 1C **16**
Northampton. *Nptn* 4E **63**
North Anston. *S Yor* 2C **86**
North Ascot. *Brac* 4A **38**
North Aston. *Oxon* 3C **50**
Northaw. *Herts* 5C **52**
Northay. *Som* 1F **13**
North Baddesley. *Hants* 4B **24**
North Balfern. *Dum* 4B **110**
North Ballachulish. *High* 2E **141**
North Barrow. *Som* 4B **22**
North Barsham. *Norf* 2B **78**
Northbeck. *Linc* 1H **75**
North Benfleet. *Essx* 2B **40**
North Bersted. *W Sus* 5A **26**
North Berwick. *E Lot* 1B **130**
North Bitchburn. *Dur* 1E **105**
North Blyth. *Nmbd* 1G **115**
North Boarhunt. *Hants* 1E **16**
North Bockhampton. *Dors* 3G **15**
Northborough. *Pet* 5A **76**
Northbourne. *Kent* 5H **41**
Northbourne. *Oxon* 3D **36**
North Bovey. *Devn* 4H **11**
North Bowood. *Dors* 3H **13**
North Bradley. *Wilts* 1D **22**
North Brentor. *Devn* 4E **11**
North Brewham. *Som* 3C **22**
Northbrook. *Oxon* 3C **50**
North Brook End. *Cambs* 1C **52**
North Broomhill. *Nmbd* 4G **121**
North Buckland. *Devn* 2E **19**
North Burlingham. *Norf* 4F **79**
North Cadbury. *Som* 4B **22**
North Carlton. *Linc* 3G **87**
North Cave. *E Yor* 1B **94**
North Cerney. *Glos* 5F **49**
North Chailey. *E Sus* 3E **27**
Northchapel. *W Sus* 3A **26**
North Charford. *Hants* 1G **15**
North Charlton. *Nmbd* 2F **121**
North Cheriton. *Som* 4B **22**
North Chideock. *Dors* 3H **13**
Northchurch. *Herts* 5H **51**
North Cliffe. *E Yor* 1B **94**
North Clifton. *Notts* 3F **87**
North Close. *Dur* 1F **105**
North Cockerington. *Linc* 1C **88**
North Coker. *Som* 1A **14**
North Collafirth. *Shet* 3E **173**
North Common. *E Sus* 3E **27**
North Commonty. *Abers* 4F **161**
North Coombe. *Devn* 1B **12**
North Cornelly. *B'end* 3B **32**
North Cotes. *Linc* 4G **95**
Northcott. *Devn* 3D **10**
(nr. Boyton)
Northcott. *Devn* 1D **12**
(nr. Culmstock)
Northcourt. *Oxon* 2D **36**
North Cove. *Suff* 2G **67**
North Cowton. *N Yor* 4F **105**
North Craigo. *Ang* 2F **145**
North Crawley. *Mil* 1H **51**
North Cray. *G Lon* 3F **39**
North Creake. *Norf* 2A **78**
North Curry. *Som* 4G **21**
North Dalton. *E Yor* 4D **100**
North Deighton. *N Yor* 4F **99**
North Dronley. *Ang* 5C **144**
North Duffield. *N Yor* 1G **93**
Northdyke. *Orkn* 5B **172**
Northedge. *Derbs* 4A **86**
North Elkington. *Linc* 1B **88**
North Elmham. *Norf* 3B **78**
North Elmsall. *W Yor* 3E **93**
Northend. *Buck* 2F **37**
North End. *E Yor* 1F **95**
North End. *Essx* 4G **53**
(nr. Great Dunmow)
North End. *Essx* 2A **54**
(nr. Great Yeldham)
North End. *Hants* 5C **36**
North End. *Leics* 4C **74**
North End. *Linc* 1B **76**
North End. *Norf* 1B **66**
North End. *N Som* 5H **33**
North End. *Port* 2E **17**
Northend. *Warw* 5A **62**
North End. *W Sus* 5C **26**
North End. *Wilts* 2F **35**
North Erradale. *High* 5B **162**
North Evington. *Leic* 5D **74**
North Fambridge. *Essx* 1C **40**
North Fearns. *High* 5E **155**
North Featherstone. *W Yor* 2E **93**
North Feorline. *N Ayr* 3D **122**
North Ferriby. *E Yor* 2C **94**
Northfield. *Aber* 3F **153**
Northfield. *E Yor* 2D **94**
Northfield. *Som* 3F **21**
Northfield. *W Mid* 3E **61**
Northfleet. *Kent* 3H **39**
North Frodingham. *E Yor* 4F **101**
Northgate. *Linc* 3A **76**
North Gluss. *Shet* 4E **173**
North Gorley. *Hants* 1G **15**
North Green. *Norf* 2E **66**
North Green. *Suff* 4F **67**
(nr. Framlingham)
North Green. *Suff* 3F **67**
(nr. Halesworth)
North Green. *Suff* 4F **67**
(nr. Saxmundham)
North Greetwell. *Linc* 3H **87**
North Grimston. *N Yor* 3C **100**
North Halling. *Medw* 4B **40**
North Hayling. *Hants* 2F **17**
North Hazelrigg. *Nmbd* 1E **121**
North Heasley. *Devn* 3H **19**
North Heath. *W Sus* 3B **26**
North Hill. *Corn* 5C **10**
North Holmwood. *Surr* 1C **26**
North Huish. *Devn* 3D **8**
North Hykeham. *Linc* 4G **87**
Northiam. *E Sus* 3C **28**
Northill. *C Beds* 1B **52**
Northington. *Hants* 3D **24**
North Kelsey. *Linc* 4D **94**
North Kelsey Moor. *Linc* 4D **94**
North Kessock. *High* 4A **158**
North Killingholme. *N Lin* 3E **95**
North Kilvington. *N Yor* 1G **99**
North Kilworth. *Leics* 2D **62**
North Kyme. *Linc* 5A **88**
North Lancing. *W Sus* 5C **26**
Northlands. *Linc* 5C **88**
Northleach. *Glos* 4G **49**
North Lee. *Buck* 5G **51**
North Lees. *N Yor* 2E **99**
Northleigh. *Devn* 3G **19**
(nr. Barnstaple)
Northleigh. *Devn* 3E **13**
(nr. Honiton)
North Leigh. *Kent* 1F **29**
North Leigh. *Oxon* 4B **50**
North Leverton. *Notts* 2E **87**
Northlew. *Devn* 3F **11**
North Littleton. *Worc* 1F **49**
North Lopham. *Norf* 2C **66**
North Luffenham. *Rut* 5G **75**
North Marden. *W Sus* 1G **17**
North Marston. *Buck* 3F **51**
North Middleton. *Midl* 4G **129**
North Middleton. *Nmbd* 2E **121**
North Molton. *Devn* 4H **19**
North Moor. *N Yor* 1D **100**
Northmoor. *Oxon* 5C **50**
Northmoor Green. *Som* 3G **21**
North Moreton. *Oxon* 3D **36**
Northmuir. *Ang* 3C **144**
North Mundham. *W Sus* 2G **17**
North Murie. *Per* 1E **137**
North Muskham. *Notts* 5E **87**
North Ness. *Orkn* 8C **172**
North Newbald. *E Yor* 1C **94**
North Newington. *Oxon* 2C **50**
North Newnton. *Wilts* 1G **23**
North Newton. *Som* 3F **21**
Northney. *Hants* 2F **17**
North Nibley. *Glos* 2C **34**
North Oakley. *Hants* 1D **24**
North Ockendon. *G Lon* 2G **39**
Northolt. *G Lon* 2C **38**
Northop. *Flin* 4E **83**
Northop Hall. *Flin* 4E **83**
North Ormesby. *Midd* 3C **106**
North Ormsby. *Linc* 1B **88**
Northorpe. *Linc* 4H **75**
(nr. Bourne)
Northorpe. *Linc* 2B **76**
(nr. Donington)
Northorpe. *Linc* 1F **87**
(nr. Gainsborough)
North Otterington. *N Yor* 1F **99**
Northover. *Som* 3H **21**
(nr. Glastonbury)
Northover. *Som* 4A **22**
(nr. Yeovil)
North Owersby. *Linc* 1H **87**
Northowram. *W Yor* 2B **92**
North Perrott. *Som* 2H **13**
North Petherton. *Som* 3F **21**
North Petherwin. *Corn* 4C **10**
North Pickenham. *Norf* 5A **78**
North Piddle. *Worc* 5D **60**
North Poorton. *Dors* 3A **14**
North Port. *Arg* 1H **133**
Northport. *Dors* 4E **15**
North Queensferry. *Fife* 1E **129**
North Radworthy. *Devn* 3A **20**
North Rauceby. *Linc* 1H **75**
Northrepps. *Norf* 2E **79**
North Rigton. *N Yor* 5E **99**
North Rode. *Ches E* 4C **84**
North Roe. *Shet* 3E **173**
North Ronaldsay Airport. *Orkn* 2G **172**
North Row. *Cumb* 1D **102**
North Runcton. *Norf* 4F **77**
North Sannox. *N Ayr* 5B **126**
North Scale. *Cumb* 2A **96**
North Scarle. *Linc* 4F **87**
North Seaton. *Nmbd* 1F **115**
North Seaton Colliery. *Nmbd* 1F **115**
North Sheen. *G Lon* 3C **38**
North Shian. *Arg* 4D **140**
North Shields. *Tyne* 3G **115**
North Shoebury. *S'end* 2D **40**
North Shore. *Bkpl* 1B **90**
North Side. *Cumb* 2B **102**
North Skelton. *Red C* 3D **106**
North Somercotes. *Linc* 1D **88**
North Stainley. *N Yor* 2E **99**
North Stainmore. *Cumb* 3B **104**
North Stifford. *Thur* 2H **39**
North Stoke. *Bath* 5C **34**
North Stoke. *Oxon* 3E **36**
North Stoke. *W Sus* 4B **26**
Northstowe. *Cambs* 4D **64**
North Street. *Hants* 3E **25**
North Street. *Kent* 5E **40**
North Street. *Medw* 3C **40**
North Street. *W Ber* 4E **37**
North Sunderland. *Nmbd* 1G **121**
North Tamerton. *Corn* 3D **10**
North Tawton. *Devn* 2G **11**
North Thoresby. *Linc* 1B **88**
North Tidworth. *Wilts* 2H **23**
North Town. *Devn* 2F **11**
Northtown. *Orkn* 8D **172**
North Town. *Shet* 10E **173**
North Tuddenham. *Norf* 4C **78**
North Walbottle. *Tyne* 3E **115**
Northwall. *Orkn* 3G **172**
North Walney. *Cumb* 3A **96**
North Walsham. *Norf* 2E **79**
North Waltham. *Hants* 2D **24**
North Warnborough. *Hants* 1F **25**
North Water Bridge. *Ang* 2F **145**

Pont-y-pant—Pwllheli

Pont-y-pant. *Cnwy* 5G **81**
Pontypool. *Torf* 2F **33**
Pontypridd. *Rhon* 3D **32**
Pontypwl. *Torf* 2F **33**
Pontywaun. *Cphy* 2F **33**
Pooksgreen. *Hants* 1B **16**
Pool. *Corn* 4A **6**
Pool. *W Yor* 5E **99**
Poole. *N Yor* 2E **93**
Poole. *Pool* 3F **15**
Poole. *Som* 4E **21**
Poole Keynes. *Glos* 2E **35**
Poolend. *Staf* 5D **84**
Poolewe. *High* 5C **162**
Pooley Bridge. *Cumb* 2F **103**
Poolfold. *Staf* 5C **84**
Pool Head. *Here* 5H **59**
Pool Hey. *Lanc* 3B **90**
Poolhill. *Glos* 3C **48**
Poolmill. *Here* 3A **48**
Pool o' Muckhart. *Clac* 3C **136**
Pool Quay. *Powy* 4E **71**
Poolsbrook. *Derbs* 3B **86**
Pool Street. *Essx* 2A **54**
Pootings. *Kent* 1F **27**
Pope Hill. *Pemb* 3D **42**
Pope's Hill. *Glos* 4B **48**
Popeswood. *Brac* 5G **37**
Popham. *Hants* 2D **24**
Poplar. *G Lon* 2E **39**
Popley. *Hants* 1E **25**
Porchfield. *IOW* 3C **16**
Porin. *High* 3F **157**
Poringland. *Norf* 5E **79**
Porkellis. *Corn* 5A **6**
Porlock. *Som* 2B **20**
Porlock Weir. *Som* 2B **20**
Portachoillan. *Arg* 4F **125**
Port Adhair Bheinn na Faoghla. *W Isl* 3C **170**
Port Adhair Thirlodh. *Arg* 4B **138**
Portadown. *Arm* 5F **175**
Portaferry. *N Dwn* 5J **175**
Port Ann. *Arg* 1H **125**
Port Appin. *Arg* 4D **140**
Port Asgaig. *Arg* 3C **124**
Port Askaig. *Arg* 3C **124**
Portavadie. *Arg* 3H **125**
Portavogie. *N Dwn* 4J **175**
Portballintrae. *Caus* 1F **175**
Port Bannatyne. *Arg* 3B **126**
Portbury. *N Som* 4A **34**
Port Carlisle. *Cumb* 3D **112**
Port Charlotte. *Arg* 4A **124**
Portchester. *Hants* 2E **16**
Port Clarence. *Stoc T* 2B **106**
Port Driseach. *Arg* 2A **126**
Port Dundas. *Glas* 3G **127**
Port Ellen. *Arg* 5B **124**
Port Elphinstone. *Abers* 1E **153**
Portencalzie. *Dum* 2F **109**
Portencross. *N Ayr* 5C **126**
Port Erin. *IOM* 5A **108**
Port Erroll. *Abers* 5H **161**
Porter's Fen Corner. *Norf* 5E **77**
Portesham. *Dors* 4B **14**
Portessie. *Mor* 2B **160**
Port e Vullen. *IOM* 2D **108**
Port-Eynon. *Swan* 4D **30**
Portfield. *Som* 4H **21**
Portfield Gate. *Pemb* 3D **42**
Portgate. *Devn* 4E **11**
Port Gaverne. *Corn* 4A **10**
Port Glasgow. *Inv* 2E **127**
Portglenone. *ME Ant* 2F **175**
Portgordon. *Mor* 2A **160**
Portgower. *High* 2H **165**
Porth. *Corn* 2C **6**
Porth. *Rhon* 2D **32**
Porthaethwy. *IOA* 3E **81**
Porthallow. *Corn* 3G **7**
(nr. Looe)
Porthallow. *Corn* 4E **5**
(nr. St Keverne)
Porthcawl. *B'end* 4B **32**
Porthceri. *V Glam* 5D **32**
Porthcothan. *Corn* 1C **6**
Porthcurno. *Corn* 4A **4**
Port Henderson. *High* 1G **155**
Porthgain. *Pemb* 1C **42**
Porthgwarra. *Corn* 4A **4**
Porthill. *Shrp* 4G **71**
Porthkerry. *V Glam* 5D **32**
Porthleven. *Corn* 4D **4**
Porthllechog. *IOA* 1D **80**
Porthmadog. *Gwyn* 2E **69**
Porthmeor. *Corn* 3B **4**
Porth Navas. *Corn* 4E **5**
Portholland. *Corn* 4D **6**
Porthoustock. *Corn* 4F **5**
Porthtowan. *Corn* 4A **6**
Porth Tywyn. *Carm* 5E **45**
Porth-y-felin. *IOA* 2B **80**
Porthyrhyd. *Carm* 4F **45**
(nr. Carmarthen)
Porthyrhyd. *Carm* 2H **45**
(nr. Llandovery)
Porth-y-waen. *Shrp* 3E **71**
Portincaple. *Arg* 4B **134**
Portington. *E Yor* 1A **94**
Portinnisherrich. *Arg* 2G **133**
Portinscale. *Cumb* 2D **102**
Port Isaac. *Corn* 1D **6**
Portishead. *N Som* 4H **33**
Portknockie. *Mor* 2B **160**
Port Lamont. *Arg* 2B **126**
Portlethen. *Abers* 4G **153**
Portlethen Village. *Abers* 4G **153**
Portling. *Dum* 4F **111**
Port Lion. *Pemb* 4D **43**
Portloe. *Corn* 5D **6**
Port Logan. *Dum* 5F **109**
Portmahomack. *High* 5G **165**
Port Mead. *Swan* 3F **31**
Portmeirion. *Gwyn* 2E **69**
Portmellon. *Corn* 4E **6**
Port Mholair. *W Isl* 4H **171**
Port Mor. *High* 1F **139**
Portmore. *Hants* 3B **16**
Port Mulgrave. *N Yor* 3E **107**
Portnacroish. *Arg* 4D **140**
Portnahaven. *Arg* 4A **124**
Portnalong. *High* 5C **154**
Portnaluchaig. *High* 5E **147**
Portnancon. *High* 2E **167**
Port Nan Giuran. *W Isl* 4H **171**
Port nan Long. *W Isl* 1D **170**
Port Nis. *W Isl* 1H **171**
Portobello. *Edin* 2G **129**
Portobello. *W Yor* 3D **92**
Port of Menteith. *Stir* 3E **135**
Porton. *Wilts* 3G **23**
Portormin. *High* 5D **168**
Portpatrick. *Dum* 4F **109**
Port Quin. *Corn* 1D **6**
Port Ramsay. *Arg* 4C **140**
Portreath. *Corn* 4A **6**
Portree. *High* 4D **155**
Port Righ. *High* 4D **155**
Portrush. *Caus* 1E **175**
Port St Mary. *IOM* 5B **108**
Portscatho. *Corn* 5C **6**
Portsea. *Port* 2E **17**
Portskerra. *High* 2A **168**
Portskewett. *Mon* 3A **34**
Portslade-by-Sea. *Brig* 5D **26**
Portsmouth. *Port* 2E **17**
Portsmouth. *W Yor* 2H **91**
Port Soderick. *IOM* 4C **108**
Port Solent. *Port* 2E **17**
Portsonachan. *Arg* 1H **133**
Portsoy. *Abers* 2C **160**
Portstewart. *Caus* 1E **175**
Port Sunlight. *Mers* 2F **83**
Portswood. *Sotn* 1C **16**
Port Talbot. *Neat* 3A **32**
Porttannachy. *Mor* 2A **160**
Port Tennant. *Swan* 3F **31**
Portuairk. *High* 2F **139**
Portway. *Here* 1H **47**
Portway. *Worc* 3E **61**
Port Wemyss. *Arg* 4A **124**
Port William. *Dum* 5A **110**
Portwrinkle. *Corn* 3H **7**
Poslingford. *Suff* 1A **54**
Postbridge. *Devn* 5G **11**
Postcombe. *Oxon* 2F **37**
Post Green. *Dors* 3E **15**
Postling. *Kent* 2F **29**
Postlip. *Glos* 3F **49**
Post-Mawr. *Cdgn* 5D **56**
Postwick. *Norf* 5E **79**
Potarch. *Abers* 4D **152**
Potsgrove. *C Beds* 3H **51**
Potten End. *Herts* 5A **52**
Potter Brompton. *N Yor* 2D **101**
Pottergate Street. *Norf* 1D **66**
Potterhanworth. *Linc* 4H **87**
Potterhanworth Booths. *Linc* 4H **87**
Potter Heigham. *Norf* 4G **79**
Potter Hill. *Leics* 3E **75**
Potteries, The. *Stoke* 1C **72**
Potterne. *Wilts* 1E **23**
Potterne Wick. *Wilts* 1F **23**
Potternewton. *W Yor* 1D **92**
Potters Bar. *Herts* 5C **52**
Potters Brook. *Lanc* 4D **97**
Potter's Cross. *Staf* 2C **60**
Potters Crouch. *Herts* 5B **52**
Potter Somersal. *Derbs* 2F **73**
Potterspury. *Nptn* 1F **51**
Potter Street. *Essx* 5E **53**
Potterton. *Abers* 2G **153**
Potthorpe. *Norf* 3B **78**
Pottle Street. *Wilts* 2D **22**
Potto. *N Yor* 4B **106**
Potton. *C Beds* 1C **52**
Pott Row. *Norf* 3G **77**
Pott Shrigley. *Ches E* 3D **84**
Poughill. *Corn* 2C **10**
Poughill. *Devn* 2B **12**
Poulner. *Hants* 2G **15**
Poulshot. *Wilts* 1E **23**
Poulton. *Glos* 5G **49**
Poulton-le-Fylde. *Lanc* 1B **90**
Pound Bank. *Worc* 3B **60**
Poundbury. *Dors* 3B **14**
Poundfield. *E Sus* 2G **27**
Poundgate. *E Sus* 3F **27**
Pound Green. *E Sus* 3G **27**
Pound Green. *Suff* 5G **65**
Pound Hill. *W Sus* 2D **27**
Poundland. *S Ayr* 1G **109**
Poundon. *Buck* 3E **51**
Poundsgate. *Devn* 5H **11**
Poundstock. *Corn* 3C **10**
Pound Street. *Hants* 5C **36**
Pounsley. *E Sus* 3G **27**
Powburn. *Nmbd* 3E **121**
Powderham. *Devn* 4C **12**
Powerstock. *Dors* 3A **14**
Powfoot. *Dum* 3C **112**
Powick. *Worc* 5C **60**
Powmill. *Per* 4C **136**
Poxwell. *Dors* 4C **14**
Poyle. *Slo* 3B **38**
Poynings. *W Sus* 4D **26**
Poyntington. *Dors* 4B **22**
Poynton. *Ches E* 2D **84**
Poynton. *Telf* 4H **71**
Poynton Green. *Telf* 4H **71**
Poystreet Green. *Suff* 5B **66**
Praa Sands. *Corn* 4C **4**
Pratt's Bottom. *G Lon* 4F **39**
Praze-an-Beeble. *Corn* 3D **4**
Prees. *Shrp* 2H **71**
Preesall. *Lanc* 5C **96**
Preesall Park. *Lanc* 5C **96**
Prees Green. *Shrp* 2H **71**
Prees Higher Heath. *Shrp* 2H **71**
Prendergast. *Pemb* 3D **42**
Prendwick. *Nmbd* 3E **121**
Pren-gwyn. *Cdgn* 1E **45**
Prenteg. *Gwyn* 1E **69**
Prenton. *Mers* 2F **83**
Prescot. *Mers* 1G **83**
Prescott. *Devn* 1D **12**
Prescott. *Shrp* 3G **71**
Preshute. *Wilts* 5G **35**
Pressen. *Nmbd* 1C **120**
Prestatyn. *Den* 2C **82**
Prestbury. *Ches E* 3D **84**
Prestbury. *Glos* 3E **49**
Presteigne. *Powy* 4F **59**
Presthope. *Shrp* 1H **59**
Prestleigh. *Som* 2B **22**
Preston. *Brig* 5E **27**
Preston. *Devn* 5B **12**
Preston. *Dors* 4C **14**
Preston. *E Lot* 2B **130**
(nr. East Linton)
Preston. *E Lot* 2G **129**
(nr. Prestonpans)
Preston. *E Yor* 1E **95**
Preston. *Glos* 5F **49**
Preston. *Herts* 3B **52**
Preston. *Kent* 4G **41**
(nr. Canterbury)
Preston. *Kent* 4E **41**
(nr. Faversham)
Preston. *Lanc* 2D **90**
Preston. *Nmbd* 2F **121**
Preston. *Rut* 5F **75**
Preston. *Bord* 4D **130**
Preston. *Shrp* 4H **71**
Preston. *Suff* 5B **66**
Preston. *Wilts* 4A **36**
(nr. Aldbourne)
Preston. *Wilts* 4F **35**
(nr. Lyneham)
Preston Bagot. *Warw* 4F **61**
Preston Bissett. *Buck* 3E **51**
Preston Bowyer. *Som* 4E **21**
Preston Brockhurst. *Shrp* 3H **71**
Preston Brook. *Hal* 2H **83**
Preston Candover. *Hants* 2E **24**
Preston Capes. *Nptn* 5C **62**
Preston Cross. *Glos* 2B **48**
Preston Gubbals. *Shrp* 4G **71**
Preston-le-Skerne. *Dur* 2A **106**
Preston Marsh. *Here* 1A **48**
Prestonmill. *Dum* 4A **112**
Preston on Stour. *Warw* 1H **49**
Preston on the Hill. *Hal* 2H **83**
Preston on Wye. *Here* 1G **47**
Prestonpans. *E Lot* 2G **129**
Preston Plucknett. *Som* 1A **14**
Preston-under-Scar. *N Yor* 5D **104**
Preston upon the Weald Moors. *Telf* 4A **72**
Preston Wynne. *Here* 1A **48**
Prestwich. *G Man* 4G **91**
Prestwick. *Nmbd* 2E **115**
Prestwick. *S Ayr* 2C **116**
Prestwold. *Leics* 3C **74**
Prestwood. *Buck* 5G **51**
Prestwood. *Staf* 1F **73**
Price Town. *B'end* 2C **32**
Prickwillow. *Cambs* 2E **65**
Priddy. *Som* 1A **22**
Priestcliffe. *Derbs* 3F **85**
Priesthill. *Glas* 3G **127**
Priest Hutton. *Lanc* 2E **97**
Priestland. *E Ayr* 1E **117**
Priest Weston. *Shrp* 1E **59**
Priestwood. *Brac* 4G **37**
Priestwood. *Kent* 4A **40**
Primethorpe. *Leics* 1C **62**
Primrose Green. *Norf* 4C **78**
Primrose Hill. *Derbs* 5B **86**
Primrose Hill. *Glos* 5B **48**
Primrose Hill. *Lanc* 4B **90**
Primrose Valley. *N Yor* 2F **101**
Primsidemill. *Bord* 2C **120**
Princes Gate. *Pemb* 3F **43**
Princes Risborough. *Buck* 5G **51**
Princethorpe. *Warw* 3B **62**
Princetown. *Devn* 5F **11**
Prinsted. *W Sus* 2F **17**
Prion. *Den* 4C **82**
Prior Muir. *Fife* 2H **137**
Prior's Frome. *Here* 2A **48**
Priors Halton. *Shrp* 3G **59**
Priors Hardwick. *Warw* 5B **62**
Priorslee. *Telf* 4B **72**
Priors Marston. *Warw* 5B **62**
Prior's Norton. *Glos* 3D **48**
Priory, The. *W Ber* 5B **36**
Priory Wood. *Here* 1F **47**
Priston. *Bath* 5B **34**
Pristow Green. *Norf* 2D **66**
Prittlewell. *S'end* 2C **40**
Privett. *Hants* 4E **25**
Prixford. *Devn* 3F **19**
Probus. *Corn* 4C **6**
Prospect. *Cumb* 5C **112**
Prospect Village. *Staf* 4E **73**
Provanmill. *Glas* 3H **127**
Prudhoe. *Nmbd* 3D **115**
Publow. *Bath* 5B **34**
Puckeridge. *Herts* 3D **53**
Puckington. *Som* 1G **13**
Pucklechurch. *S Glo* 4B **34**
Puckrup. *Glos* 2D **49**
Puddinglake. *Ches W* 4B **84**
Puddington. *Ches W* 3F **83**
Puddington. *Devn* 1B **12**
Puddlebrook. *Glos* 4B **48**
Puddledock. *Norf* 1C **66**
Puddletown. *Dors* 3C **14**
Pudleston. *Here* 5H **59**
Pudsey. *W Yor* 1C **92**
Pulborough. *W Sus* 4B **26**
Puleston. *Telf* 3B **72**
Pulford. *Ches W* 5F **83**
Pulham. *Dors* 2C **14**
Pulham Market. *Norf* 2D **66**
Pulham St Mary. *Norf* 2E **66**
Pulley. *Shrp* 5G **71**
Pulloxhill. *C Beds* 2A **52**
Pulpit Hill. *Arg* 1F **133**
Pulverbatch. *Shrp* 5G **71**
Pumpherston. *W Lot* 3D **128**
Pumsaint. *Carm* 1G **45**
Puncheston. *Pemb* 2E **43**
Puncknowle. *Dors* 4A **14**
Punnett's Town. *E Sus* 3H **27**
Purbrook. *Hants* 2E **17**
Purfleet. *Thur* 3G **39**
Puriton. *Som* 2G **21**
Purleigh. *Essx* 5B **54**
Purley. *G Lon* 4E **39**
Purley on Thames. *W Ber* 4E **37**
Purlogue. *Shrp* 3E **59**
Purl's Bridge. *Cambs* 2D **65**
Purse Caundle. *Dors* 1B **14**
Purslow. *Shrp* 2F **59**
Purston Jaglin. *W Yor* 3E **93**
Purtington. *Som* 2G **13**
Purton. *Glos* 5B **48**
(nr. Lydney)
Purton. *Glos* 5B **48**
(nr. Sharpness)
Purton. *Wilts* 3F **35**
Purton Stoke. *Wilts* 2F **35**
Pury End. *Nptn* 1F **51**
Pusey. *Oxon* 2B **36**
Putley. *Here* 2B **48**
Putney. *G Lon* 3D **38**
Putsborough. *Devn* 2E **19**
Puttenham. *Herts* 4G **51**
Puttenham. *Surr* 1A **26**
Puttock End. *Essx* 1B **54**
Puttock's End. *Essx* 4F **53**
Puxey. *Dors* 1C **14**
Puxton. *N Som* 5H **33**
Pwll. *Carm* 5E **45**
Pwll. *Powy* 5D **70**
Pwllcrochan. *Pemb* 4D **42**
Pwll-glas. *Den* 5D **82**
Pwllgloyw. *Powy* 2D **46**
Pwllheli. *Gwyn* 2C **68**

Rexon—Rose Green

Rexon. *Devn* 4E **11**
Reybridge. *Wilts* 5E **35**
Reydon. *Suff* 3H **67**
Reymerston. *Norf* 5C **78**
Reynalton. *Pemb* 4E **43**
Reynoldston. *Swan* 4D **31**
Rezare. *Corn* 5D **10**
Rhadyr. *Mon* 5G **47**
Rhaeadr Gwy. *Powy* 4B **58**
Rhandirmwyn. *Carm* 1A **46**
Rhayader. *Powy* 4B **58**
Rheindown. *High* 4H **157**
Rhemore. *High* 3G **139**
Rhenetra. *High* 3D **154**
Rhewl. *Den* 1D **70**
(nr. Llangollen)
Rhewl. *Den* 4D **82**
(nr. Ruthin)
Rhewl. *Shrp* 2F **71**
Rhewl-Mostyn. *Flin* 2D **82**
Rhian. *High* 2C **164**
Rhian Breck. *High* 3C **164**
Rhicarn. *High* 1E **163**
Rhiconich. *High* 3C **166**
Rhicullen. *High* 1A **158**
Rhidorroch. *High* 4F **163**
Rhifail. *High* 4H **167**
Rhigos. *Rhon* 5C **46**
Rhilochan. *High* 3E **165**
Rhiroy. *High* 5F **163**
Rhitongue. *High* 3G **167**
Rhiw. *Gwyn* 3B **68**
Rhiwabon. *Wrex* 1F **71**
Rhiwbina. *Card* 3E **33**
Rhiwbryfdir. *Gwyn* 1F **69**
Rhiwderin. *Newp* 3F **33**
Rhiwlas. *Gwyn* 2B **70**
(nr. Bala)
Rhiwlas. *Gwyn* 4E **81**
(nr. Bangor)
Rhiwlas. *Powy* 2D **70**
Rhodes. *G Man* 4G **91**
Rhodesia. *Notts* 2C **86**
Rhodes Minnis. *Kent* 1F **29**
Rhodiad-y-Brenin. *Pemb* 2B **42**
Rhondda. *Rhon* 2C **32**
Rhonehouse. *Dum* 4E **111**
Rhoose. *V Glam* 5D **32**
Rhos. *Carm* 2D **45**
Rhos. *Neat* 5H **45**
Rhosaman. *Carm* 4H **45**
Rhoscefnhir. *IOA* 3E **81**
Rhoscolyn. *IOA* 3B **80**
Rhos Common. *Powy* 4E **71**
Rhoscrowther. *Pemb* 4D **42**
Rhos-ddu. *Gwyn* 2B **68**
Rhosdylluan. *Gwyn* 3A **70**
Rhosesmor. *Flin* 4E **82**
Rhos-fawr. *Gwyn* 2C **68**
Rhosgadfan. *Gwyn* 5E **81**
Rhosgoch. *IOA* 2D **80**
Rhosgoch. *Powy* 1E **47**
Rhos Haminiog. *Cdgn* 4E **57**
Rhos-hill. *Pemb* 1B **44**
Rhoshirwaun. *Gwyn* 3A **68**
Rhoslan. *Gwyn* 1D **69**
Rhoslefain. *Gwyn* 5E **69**
Rhosllanerchrugog. *Wrex* 1E **71**
Rhôs Lligwy. *IOA* 2D **81**
Rhosmaen. *Carm* 3G **45**
Rhosmeirch. *IOA* 3D **80**
Rhosneigr. *IOA* 3C **80**
Rhos-on-Sea. *Cnwy* 2H **81**
Rhossili. *Swan* 4D **30**
Rhosson. *Pemb* 2B **42**
Rhos, The. *Pemb* 3E **43**
Rhostrenwfa. *IOA* 3D **80**
Rhostryfan. *Gwyn* 5D **81**
Rhostyllen. *Wrex* 1F **71**
Rhoswiel. *Shrp* 2E **71**
Rhosybol. *IOA* 2D **80**
Rhos-y-brithdir. *Powy* 3D **70**
Rhos-y-garth. *Cdgn* 3F **57**
Rhos-y-gwaliau. *Gwyn* 2B **70**
Rhos-y-llan. *Gwyn* 2B **68**
Rhos-y-meirch. *Powy* 4E **59**
Rhu. *Arg* 1D **126**
Rhuallt. *Den* 3C **82**
Rhubha Stoer. *High* 1E **163**
Rhubodach. *Arg* 2B **126**
Rhuddall Heath. *Ches W* 4H **83**
Rhuddlan. *Cdgn* 1E **45**
Rhuddlan. *Den* 3C **82**
Rhue. *High* 4E **163**
Rhulen. *Powy* 1E **47**
Rhunahaorine. *Arg* 5F **125**
Rhuthun. *Den* 5D **82**
Rhuvoult. *High* 3C **166**
Rhyd. *Gwyn* 1F **69**
Rhydaman. *Carm* 4G **45**
Rhydargaeau. *Carm* 3E **45**
Rhydcymerau. *Carm* 2F **45**
Rhydd. *Worc* 1D **48**
Rhyd-Ddu. *Gwyn* 5E **81**
Rhydding. *Neat* 3G **31**
Rhydfudr. *Cdgn* 4E **57**
Rhydlanfair. *Cnwy* 5H **81**
Rhydlewis. *Cdgn* 1D **44**
Rhydlios. *Gwyn* 2A **68**
Rhydlydan. *Cnwy* 5A **82**
Rhyd-meirionydd. *Cdgn* 2F **57**
Rhydowen. *Cdgn* 1E **45**
Rhyd-Rosser. *Cdgn* 4E **57**
Rhydspence. *Powy* 1F **47**
Rhydtalog. *Flin* 5E **83**
Rhyd-uchaf. *Gwyn* 2B **70**
Rhydwyn. *IOA* 2C **80**
Rhyd-y-clafdy. *Gwyn* 2C **68**
Rhydycroesau. *Shrp* 2E **71**
Rhydyfelin. *Cdgn* 3E **57**
Rhydyfelin. *Rhon* 3E **32**
Rhyd-y-foel. *Cnwy* 3B **82**
Rhyd-y-fro. *Neat* 5H **45**
Rhydymain. *Gwyn* 3H **69**
Rhyd-y-meudwy. *Den* 5D **82**
Rhydymwyn. *Flin* 4E **82**
Rhyd-yr-onen. *Gwyn* 5F **69**
Rhyd-y-sarn. *Gwyn* 1F **69**
Rhyl. *Den* 2C **82**
Rhymney. *Cphy* 5E **46**
Rhymni. *Cphy* 5E **46**
Rhynd. *Per* 1D **136**
Rhynie. *Abers* 1B **152**
Ribbesford. *Worc* 3B **60**
Ribbleton. *Lanc* 1D **90**
Ribby. *Lanc* 1C **90**
Ribchester. *Lanc* 1E **91**
Riber. *Derbs* 5H **85**
Ribigill. *High* 3F **167**
Riby. *Linc* 4E **95**
Riccall. *N Yor* 1G **93**
Riccarton. *E Ayr* 1D **116**
Richards Castle. *Here* 4G **59**
Richborough Port. *Kent* 4H **41**
Richhill. *Arm* 5F **175**
Richings Park. *Buck* 3B **38**
Richmond. *G Lon* 3C **38**
Richmond. *N Yor* 4E **105**
Rickarton. *Abers* 5F **153**
Rickerby. *Cumb* 4F **113**
Rickerscote. *Staf* 3D **72**
Rickford. *N Som* 1H **21**
Rickham. *Devn* 5D **8**
Rickinghall. *Suff* 3C **66**
Rickleton. *Tyne* 4F **115**
Rickling. *Essx* 2E **53**
Rickling Green. *Essx* 3F **53**
Rickmansworth. *Herts* 1B **38**
Riddings. *Derbs* 5B **86**
Riddlecombe. *Devn* 1G **11**
Riddlesden. *W Yor* 5C **98**
Ridge. *Dors* 4E **15**
Ridge. *Herts* 5C **52**
Ridge. *Wilts* 3E **23**
Ridgebourne. *Powy* 4C **58**
Ridge Lane. *Warw* 1G **61**
Ridgeway. *Derbs* 5A **86**
(nr. Alfreton)
Ridgeway. *Derbs* 2B **86**
(nr. Sheffield)
Ridgeway. *Stoke* 5C **84**
Ridgeway Cross. *Here* 1C **48**
Ridgeway Moor. *Derbs* 2B **86**
Ridgewell. *Essx* 1H **53**
Ridgewood. *E Sus* 3F **27**
Ridgmont. *C Beds* 2H **51**
Ridgwardine. *Shrp* 2A **72**
Riding Mill. *Nmbd* 3D **114**
Ridley. *Kent* 4H **39**
Ridley. *Nmbd* 3A **114**
Ridlington. *Norf* 2F **79**
Ridlington. *Rut* 5F **75**
Ridsdale. *Nmbd* 1C **114**
Riemore Lodge. *Per* 4H **143**
Rievaulx. *N Yor* 1H **99**
Rift House. *Hart* 1B **106**
Rigg. *Dum* 3D **112**
Riggend. *N Lan* 2A **128**
Rigsby. *Linc* 3D **88**
Rigside. *S Lan* 1A **118**
Riley Green. *Lanc* 2E **90**
Rileyhill. *Staf* 4F **73**
Rilla Mill. *Corn* 5C **10**
Rillington. *N Yor* 2C **100**
Rimington. *Lanc* 5H **97**
Rimpton. *Som* 4B **22**
Rimsdale. *High* 4H **167**
Rimswell. *E Yor* 2G **95**
Ringasta. *Shet* 10E **173**
Ringford. *Dum* 4D **111**
Ringing Hill. *Leics* 4B **74**
Ringinglow. *S Yor* 2G **85**
Ringland. *Norf* 4D **78**
Ringlestone. *Kent* 5C **40**
Ringmer. *E Sus* 4F **27**
Ringmore. *Devn* 4C **8**
(nr. Kingsbridge)
Ringmore. *Devn* 5C **12**
(nr. Teignmouth)
Ring o' Bells. *Lanc* 3C **90**
Ring's End. *Cambs* 5C **76**
Ringsfield. *Suff* 2G **67**
Ringsfield Corner. *Suff* 2G **67**
Ringshall. *Buck* 4H **51**
Ringshall. *Suff* 5C **66**
Ringshall Stocks. *Suff* 5C **66**
Ringstead. *Norf* 1G **77**
Ringstead. *Nptn* 3G **63**
Ringwood. *Hants* 2G **15**
Ringwould. *Kent* 1H **29**
Rinmore. *Abers* 2B **152**
Rinnigill. *Orkn* 8C **172**
Rinsey. *Corn* 4C **4**
Riof. *W Isl* 4D **171**
Ripe. *E Sus* 4G **27**
Ripley. *Derbs* 5B **86**
Ripley. *Hants* 3G **15**
Ripley. *N Yor* 3E **99**
Ripley. *Surr* 5B **38**
Riplingham. *E Yor* 1C **94**
Riplington. *Hants* 4E **25**
Ripon. *N Yor* 2F **99**
Rippingale. *Linc* 3H **75**
Ripple. *Kent* 1H **29**
Ripple. *Worc* 2D **48**
Ripponden. *W Yor* 3A **92**
Rireavach. *High* 4E **163**
Risabus. *Arg* 5B **124**
Risbury. *Here* 5H **59**
Risby. *E Yor* 1D **94**
Risby. *N Lin* 3C **94**
Risby. *Suff* 4G **65**
Risca. *Cphy* 2F **33**
Rise. *E Yor* 5F **101**
Riseden. *E Sus* 2H **27**
Riseden. *Kent* 2B **28**
Rise End. *Derbs* 5G **85**
Risegate. *Linc* 3B **76**
Riseholme. *Linc* 3G **87**
Riseley. *Bed* 4H **63**
Riseley. *Wok* 5F **37**
Rishangles. *Suff* 4D **66**
Rishton. *Lanc* 1F **91**
Rishworth. *W Yor* 3A **92**
Risley. *Derbs* 2B **74**
Risley. *Warr* 1A **84**
Risplith. *N Yor* 3E **99**
Rispond. *High* 2E **167**
Rivar. *Wilts* 5B **36**
Rivenhall. *Essx* 4B **54**
Rivenhall End. *Essx* 4B **54**
River. *Kent* 1G **29**
River. *W Sus* 3A **26**
River Bank. *Cambs* 4E **65**
Riverhead. *Kent* 5G **39**
Rivington. *Lanc* 3E **91**
Roach Bridge. *Lanc* 2D **90**
Roachill. *Devn* 4B **20**
Roade. *Nptn* 5E **63**
Road Green. *Norf* 1E **67**
Roadhead. *Cumb* 2G **113**
Roadmeetings. *S Lan* 5B **128**
Roadside. *High* 2D **168**
Roadside of Catterline.
Abers 1H **145**
Roadside of Kinneff. *Abers* 1H **145**
Roadwater. *Som* 3D **20**
Road Weedon. *Nptn* 5D **62**
Roag. *High* 4B **154**
Roa Island. *Cumb* 3B **96**
Roath. *Card* 4E **33**
Roberton. *Bord* 3G **119**
Roberton. *S Lan* 2B **118**
Robertsbridge. *E Sus* 3B **28**
Robertstown. *Mor* 4G **159**
Robertstown. *Rhon* 5C **46**
Roberttown. *W Yor* 2B **92**
Robeston Back. *Pemb* 3E **43**
Robeston Wathen. *Pemb* 3E **43**
Robeston West. *Pemb* 4C **42**
Robin Hood. *Lanc* 3D **90**
Robin Hood. *W Yor* 2D **92**
Robin Hood Airport Doncaster Sheffield.
S Yor 1D **86**
Robinhood End. *Essx* 2H **53**
Robin Hood's Bay. *N Yor* 4G **107**
Roborough. *Devn* 1F **11**
(nr. Great Torrington)
Roborough. *Devn* 2B **8**
(nr. Plymouth)
Rob Roy's House. *Arg* 2A **134**
Roby Mill. *Lanc* 4D **90**
Rocester. *Staf* 2F **73**
Roch. *Pemb* 2C **42**
Rochdale. *G Man* 3G **91**
Roche. *Corn* 2D **6**
Rochester. *Medw* 4B **40**
Rochester. *Nmbd* 5C **120**
Rochford. *Essx* 1C **40**
Rock. *Corn* 1D **6**
Rock. *Nmbd* 2G **121**
Rock. *W Sus* 4C **26**
Rock. *Worc* 3B **60**
Rockbeare. *Devn* 3D **12**
Rockbourne. *Hants* 1G **15**
Rockcliffe. *Cumb* 3E **113**
Rockcliffe. *Dum* 4F **111**
Rockcliffe Cross. *Cumb* 3E **113**
Rock Ferry. *Mers* 2F **83**
Rockfield. *High* 5G **165**
Rockfield. *Mon* 4H **47**
Rockford. *Hants* 2G **15**
Rockgreen. *Shrp* 3H **59**
Rockhampton. *S Glo* 2B **34**
Rockhead. *Corn* 4A **10**
Rockingham. *Nptn* 1F **63**
Rockland All Saints. *Norf* 1B **66**
Rockland St Mary. *Norf* 5F **79**
Rockland St Peter. *Norf* 1B **66**
Rockley. *Wilts* 4G **35**
Rockwell End. *Buck* 3F **37**
Rockwell Green. *Som* 1E **13**
Rodborough. *Glos* 5D **48**
Rodbourne. *Wilts* 3E **35**
Rodd. *Here* 4F **59**
Roddam. *Nmbd* 2E **121**
Rodden. *Dors* 4B **14**
Roddenloft. *E Ayr* 2D **117**
Roddymoor. *Dur* 1E **105**
Rode. *Som* 1D **22**
Rodeheath. *Ches E* 4C **84**
(nr. Congleton)
Rode Heath. *Ches E* 5C **84**
(nr. Kidsgrove)
Rodel. *W Isl* 9C **171**
Roden. *Telf* 4H **71**
Rodhuish. *Som* 3D **20**
Rodington. *Telf* 4H **71**
Rodington Heath. *Telf* 4H **71**
Rodley. *Glos* 4C **48**
Rodmarton. *Glos* 2E **35**
Rodmell. *E Sus* 5F **27**
Rodmersham. *Kent* 4D **40**
Rodmersham Green. *Kent* 4D **40**
Rodney Stoke. *Som* 2H **21**
Rodsley. *Derbs* 1G **73**
Rodway. *Som* 3F **21**
Rodway. *Telf* 4A **72**
Rodwell. *Dors* 5B **14**
Roecliffe. *N Yor* 3F **99**
Roe Green. *Herts* 2D **52**
Roehampton. *G Lon* 3D **38**
Roesound. *Shet* 5E **173**
Roffey. *W Sus* 2C **26**
Rogart. *High* 3E **165**
Rogate. *W Sus* 4G **25**
Roger Ground. *Cumb* 5E **103**
Rogerstone. *Newp* 3F **33**
Rogiet. *Mon* 3H **33**
Rogue's Alley. *Cambs* 5C **76**
Roke. *Oxon* 2E **37**
Rokemarsh. *Oxon* 2E **36**
Roker. *Tyne* 4H **115**
Rollesby. *Norf* 4G **79**
Rolleston. *Leics* 5E **75**
Rolleston. *Notts* 5E **87**
Rolleston on Dove. *Staf* 3G **73**
Rolston. *E Yor* 5G **101**
Rolvenden. *Kent* 2C **28**
Rolvenden Layne. *Kent* 2C **28**
Romaldkirk. *Dur* 2C **104**
Roman Bank. *Shrp* 1H **59**
Romanby. *N Yor* 5A **106**
Roman Camp. *W Lot* 2D **129**
Romannobridge. *Bord* 5E **129**
Romansleigh. *Devn* 4H **19**
Romers Common. *Worc* 4H **59**
Romesdal. *High* 3D **154**
Romford. *Dors* 2F **15**
Romford. *G Lon* 2G **39**
Romiley. *G Man* 1D **84**
Romsey. *Hants* 4B **24**
Romsley. *Shrp* 2B **60**
Romsley. *Worc* 3D **60**
Ronague. *IOM* 4B **108**
Ronaldsvoe. *Orkn* 8D **172**
Rookby. *Cumb* 3B **104**
Rookhope. *Dur* 5C **114**
Rooking. *Cumb* 3F **103**
Rookley. *IOW* 4D **16**
Rooks Bridge. *Som* 1G **21**
Rooksey Green. *Suff* 5B **66**
Rook's Nest. *Som* 3D **20**
Rookwood. *W Sus* 3F **17**
Roos. *E Yor* 1F **95**
Roosebeck. *Cumb* 3B **96**
Roosecote. *Cumb* 3B **96**
Rootfield. *High* 3H **157**
Rootham's Green. *Bed* 5A **64**
Rootpark. *S Lan* 4C **128**
Ropley. *Hants* 3E **25**
Ropley Dean. *Hants* 3E **25**
Ropsley. *Linc* 2G **75**
Rora. *Abers* 3H **161**
Rorandle. *Abers* 2D **152**
Rorrington. *Shrp* 5F **71**
Rose. *Corn* 3B **6**
Roseacre. *Lanc* 1C **90**
Rose Ash. *Devn* 4A **20**
Rosebank. *S Lan* 5B **128**
Rosebush. *Pemb* 2E **43**
Rosedale Abbey. *N Yor* 5E **107**
Roseden. *Nmbd* 2E **121**
Rose Green. *Essx* 3B **54**
Rose Green. *Suff* 1C **54**

S

St Helens—Scalpay House

St Helens. *IOW* 4E 17
St Helens. *Mers* 1H 83
St Hilary. *Corn* 3C 4
St Hilary. *V Glam* 4D 32
Saint Hill. *Devn* 2D 12
Saint Hill. *W Sus* 2E 27
St Illtyd. *Blae* 5F 47
St Ippolyts. *Herts* 3B 52
St Ishmael. *Carm* 5D 44
St Ishmael's. *Pemb* 4C 42
St Issey. *Corn* 1D 6
St Ive. *Corn* 2H 7
St Ives. *Cambs* 3C 64
St Ives. *Corn* 2C 4
St Ives. *Dors* 2G 15
St James' End. *Nptn* 4E 63
St James South Elmham. *Suff* 2F 67
St Jidgey. *Corn* 2D 6
St John. *Corn* 3A 8
St John's. *IOM* 3B 108
St Johns. *Worc* 5C 60
St John's Chapel. *Devn* 4F 19
St John's Chapel. *Dur* 1B 104
St John's Fen End. *Norf* 4E 77
St John's Town of Dalry. *Dum* 1D 110
St Judes. *IOM* 2C 108
St Just. *Corn* 3A 4
St Just in Roseland. *Corn* 5C 6
St Katherines. *Abers* 5E 161
St Keverne. *Corn* 4E 5
St Kew. *Corn* 5A 10
St Kew Highway. *Corn* 5A 10
St Keyne. *Corn* 2G 7
St Lawrence. *Corn* 2E 7
St Lawrence. *Essx* 5C 54
St Lawrence. *IOW* 5D 16
St Leonards. *Buck* 5H 51
St Leonards. *Dors* 2G 15
St Leonards. *E Sus* 5B 28
St Levan. *Corn* 4A 4
St Lythans. *V Glam* 4E 32
St Mabyn. *Corn* 5A 10
St Madoes. *Per* 1D 136
St Margarets. *Here* 2G 47
St Margaret's. *Herts* 4A 52
(nr. Hemel Hempstead)
St Margarets. *Herts* 4D 53
(nr. Hoddesdon)
St Margaret's. *Wilts* 5H 35
St Margaret's at Cliffe. *Kent* 1H 29
St Margaret's Hope. *Orkn* 8D 172
St Margaret South Elmham. *Suff* 2F 67
St Mark's. *IOM* 4B 108
St Martin. *Corn* 4E 5
(nr. Helston)
St Martin. *Corn* 3G 7
(nr. Looe)
St Martins. *Per* 5A 144
St Martin's. *Shrp* 2F 71
St Mary Bourne. *Hants* 1C 24
St Marychurch. *Torb* 2F 9
St Mary Church. *V Glam* 4D 32
St Mary Cray. *G Lon* 4F 39
St Mary Hill. *V Glam* 4C 32
St Mary Hoo. *Medw* 3C 40
St Mary in the Marsh. *Kent* 3E 29
St Mary's. *Orkn* 7D 172
St Mary's Bay. *Kent* 3E 29
St Maughan's Green. *Mon* 4H 47
St Mawes. *Corn* 5C 6
St Mawgan. *Corn* 2C 6
St Mellion. *Corn* 2H 7
St Mellons. *Card* 3F 33
St Merryn. *Corn* 1C 6
St Mewan. *Corn* 3D 6
St Michael Caerhays. *Corn* 4D 6
St Michael Penkevil. *Corn* 4C 6
St Michaels. *Kent* 2C 28
St Michaels. *Torb* 3E 9
St Michaels. *Worc* 4H 59
St Michael's on Wyre. *Lanc* 5D 96
St Michael South Elmham. *Suff* 2F 67
St Minver. *Corn* 1D 6
St Monans. *Fife* 3H 137
St Neot. *Corn* 2F 7
St Neots. *Cambs* 4A 64
St Newlyn East. *Corn* 3C 6
St Nicholas. *Pemb* 1C 42
St Nicholas. *V Glam* 4D 32
St Nicholas at Wade. *Kent* 4G 41
St Nicholas South Elmham. *Suff* 2F 67
St Ninians. *Stir* 4G 135
St Olaves. *Norf* 1G 67
St Osyth. *Essx* 4E 54
St Osyth Heath. *Essx* 4E 55
St Owen's Cross. *Here* 3A 48
St Paul's Cray. *G Lon* 4F 39
St Paul's Walden. *Herts* 3B 52
St Peter's. *Kent* 4H 41
St Peter The Great. *Worc* 5C 60
St Petrox. *Pemb* 5D 42
St Pinnock. *Corn* 2G 7
St Quivox. *S Ayr* 2C 116
St Ruan. *Corn* 5E 5
St Stephen. *Corn* 3D 6
St Stephens. *Corn* 4D 10
(nr. Launceston)
St Stephens. *Corn* 3A 8
(nr. Saltash)
St Teath. *Corn* 4A 10
St Thomas. *Devn* 3C 12
St Thomas. *Swan* 3F 31
St Tudy. *Corn* 5A 10
St Twynnells. *Pemb* 5D 42
St Veep. *Corn* 3F 7
St Vigeans. *Ang* 4F 145
St Wenn. *Corn* 2D 6
St Weonards. *Here* 3H 47
St Winnolls. *Corn* 3H 7
St Winnow. *Corn* 3F 7
Salcombe. *Devn* 5D 8
Salcombe Regis. *Devn* 4E 13
Salcott. *Essx* 4C 54
Sale. *G Man* 1B 84
Saleby. *Linc* 3D 88
Sale Green. *Worc* 5D 60
Salehurst. *E Sus* 3B 28
Salem. *Carm* 3G 45
Salem. *Cdgn* 2F 57
Salen. *Arg* 4G 139
Salen. *High* 2A 140
Salesbury. *Lanc* 1E 91
Saleway. *Worc* 5D 60
Salford. *C Beds* 2H 51
Salford. *G Man* 1C 84
Salford. *Oxon* 3A 50
Salford Priors. *Warw* 5E 61
Salfords. *Surr* 1D 27
Salhouse. *Norf* 4F 79
Saligo. *Arg* 3A 124
Saline. *Fife* 4C 136
Salisbury. *Wilts* 3G 23
Salkeld Dykes. *Cumb* 1G 103
Sallachan. *High* 2D 141
Sallachy. *High* 3C 164
(nr. Lairg)
Sallachy. *High* 5B 156
(nr. Stromeferry)
Salle. *Norf* 3D 78
Salmonby. *Linc* 3C 88
Salmond's Muir. *Ang* 5E 145
Salperton. *Glos* 3F 49
Salph End. *Bed* 5H 63
Salsburgh. *N Lan* 3B 128
Salt. *Staf* 3D 72
Salta. *Cumb* 5B 112
Saltaire. *W Yor* 1B 92
Saltash. *Corn* 3A 8
Saltburn. *High* 2B 158
Saltburn-by-the-Sea. *Red C* 2D 106
Saltby. *Leics* 3F 75
Saltcoats. *Cumb* 5B 102
Saltcoats. *N Ayr* 5D 126
Saltdean. *Brig* 5E 27
Salt End. *E Yor* 2E 95
Salter. *Lanc* 3F 97
Salterforth. *Lanc* 5A 98
Salters Lode. *Norf* 5E 77
Salterswall. *Ches W* 4A 84
Salterton. *Wilts* 3G 23
Saltfleet. *Linc* 1D 88
Saltfleetby All Saints. *Linc* 1D 88
Saltfleetby St Clements. *Linc* 1D 88
Saltfleetby St Peter. *Linc* 2D 88
Saltford. *Bath* 5B 34
Salthouse. *Norf* 1C 78
Saltmarshe. *E Yor* 2A 94
Saltmead. *Card* 4E 33
Saltness. *Orkn* 9B 172
Saltness. *Shet* 7D 173
Saltney. *Flin* 4F 83
Salton. *N Yor* 2B 100
Saltrens. *Devn* 4E 19
Saltwick. *Nmbd* 2E 115
Saltwood. *Kent* 2F 29
Salum. *Arg* 4B 138
Salwarpe. *Worc* 4C 60
Salwayash. *Dors* 3H 13
Samalaman. *High* 1A 140
Sambourne. *Warw* 4E 61
Sambourne. *Wilts* 2D 22
Sambrook. *Telf* 3B 72
Samhia. *W Isl* 2C 170
Samlesbury. *Lanc* 1D 90
Samlesbury Bottoms. *Lanc* 2E 90
Sampford Arundel. *Som* 1E 12
Sampford Brett. *Som* 2D 20
Sampford Courtenay. *Devn* 2G 11
Sampford Peverell. *Devn* 1D 12
Sampford Spiney. *Devn* 5F 11
Samsonslane. *Orkn* 5F 172
Samuelston. *E Lot* 2A 130
Sanaigmore. *Arg* 2A 124
Sancreed. *Corn* 4B 4
Sancton. *E Yor* 1C 94
Sand. *High* 4D 162
Sand. *Shet* 7E 173
Sand. *Som* 2H 21
Sandaig. *Arg* 4A 138
Sandaig. *High* 3F 147
Sandale. *Cumb* 5D 112
Sandal Magna. *W Yor* 3D 92
Sandavore. *High* 5C 146
Sanday Airport. *Orkn* 3F 172
Sandbach. *Ches E* 4B 84
Sandbank. *Arg* 1C 126
Sandbanks. *Pool* 4F 15
Sandend. *Abers* 2C 160
Sanderstead. *G Lon* 4E 39
Sandfields. *Neat* 3G 31
Sandford. *Cumb* 3A 104
Sandford. *Devn* 2B 12
Sandford. *Dors* 4E 15
Sandford. *Hants* 2G 15
Sandford. *IOW* 4D 16
Sandford. *N Som* 1H 21
Sandford. *Shrp* 3F 71
(nr. Oswestry)
Sandford. *Shrp* 2H 71
(nr. Whitchurch)
Sandford. *S Lan* 5A 128
Sandfordhill. *Abers* 4H 161
Sandford-on-Thames. *Oxon* 5D 50
Sandford Orcas. *Dors* 4B 22
Sandford St Martin. *Oxon* 3C 50
Sandgate. *Kent* 2F 29
Sandgreen. *Dum* 4C 110
Sandhaven. *Abers* 2G 161
Sandhead. *Dum* 4F 109
Sandhill. *Cambs* 2E 65
Sandhills. *Dors* 1B 14
Sandhills. *Oxon* 5D 50
Sandhills. *Surr* 2A 26
Sandhoe. *Nmbd* 3C 114
Sand Hole. *E Yor* 1B 94
Sandholme. *E Yor* 1B 94
Sandholme. *Linc* 2C 76
Sandhurst. *Brac* 5G 37
Sandhurst. *Glos* 3D 48
Sandhurst. *Kent* 3B 28
Sandhurst Cross. *Kent* 3B 28
Sandhutton. *N Yor* 1F 99
(nr. Thirsk)
Sand Hutton. *N Yor* 4A 100
(nr. York)
Sandiacre. *Derbs* 2B 74
Sandilands. *Linc* 2E 89
Sandiway. *Ches W* 3A 84
Sandleheath. *Hants* 1G 15
Sandling. *Kent* 5B 40
Sandlow Green. *Ches E* 4B 84
Sandness. *Shet* 6C 173
Sandon. *Essx* 5H 53
Sandon. *Herts* 2D 52
Sandon. *Staf* 3D 72
Sandonbank. *Staf* 3D 72
Sandown. *IOW* 4D 16
Sandplace. *Corn* 3G 7
Sandridge. *Herts* 4B 52
Sandringham. *Norf* 3F 77
Sandsend. *N Yor* 3F 107
Sandside. *Cumb* 2C 96
Sandsound. *Shet* 7E 173
Sands, The. *Surr* 2G 25
Sandtoft. *N Lin* 4H 93
Sandvoe. *Shet* 2E 173
Sandway. *Kent* 5C 40
Sandwich. *Kent* 5H 41
Sandwick. *Cumb* 3F 103
Sandwick. *Orkn* 6B 172
(on Mainland)
Sandwick. *Orkn* 9D 172
(on South Ronaldsay)
Sandwick. *Shet* 9F 173
(on Mainland)
Sandwick. *Shet* 5G 173
(on Whalsay)
Sandwith. *Cumb* 3A 102
Sandy. *Carm* 5E 45
Sandy. *C Beds* 1B 52
Sandy Bank. *Linc* 5B 88
Sandycroft. *Flin* 4F 83
Sandy Cross. *Here* 5A 60
Sandygate. *Devn* 5B 12
Sandygate. *IOM* 2C 108
Sandy Haven. *Pemb* 4C 42
Sandyhills. *Dum* 4F 111
Sandylands. *Lanc* 3D 96
Sandylane. *Swan* 4E 31
Sandy Lane. *Wilts* 5E 35
Sandystones. *Bord* 2H 119
Sandyway. *Here* 3H 47
Sangobeg. *High* 2E 167
Sangomore. *High* 2E 166
Sankyn's Green. *Worc* 4B 60
Sanna. *High* 2F 139
Sanndabhaig. *W Isl* 4G 171
(on Isle of Lewis)
Sanndabhaig. *W Isl* 4D 170
(on South Uist)
Sannox. *N Ayr* 5B 126
Sanquhar. *Dum* 3G 117
Santon. *Cumb* 4B 102
Santon Bridge. *Cumb* 4C 102
Santon Downham. *Suff* 2H 65
Sapcote. *Leics* 1B 62
Sapey Common. *Here* 4B 60
Sapiston. *Suff* 3B 66
Sapley. *Cambs* 3B 64
Sapperton. *Derbs* 2F 73
Sapperton. *Glos* 5E 49
Sapperton. *Linc* 2H 75
Saracen's Head. *Linc* 3C 76
Sarclet. *High* 4F 169
Sardis. *Carm* 5F 45
Sardis. *Pemb* 4D 42
(nr. Milford Haven)
Sardis. *Pemb* 4F 43
(nr. Tenby)
Sarisbury. *Hants* 2D 16
Sarn. *B'end* 3C 32
Sarn. *Powy* 1E 58
Sarnau. *Carm* 3E 45
Sarnau. *Cdgn* 5C 56
Sarnau. *Gwyn* 2B 70
Sarnau. *Powy* 2D 46
(nr. Brecon)
Sarnau. *Powy* 4E 71
(nr. Welshpool)
Sarn Bach. *Gwyn* 3C 68
Sarnesfield. *Here* 5F 59
Sarn Meyllteyrn. *Gwyn* 2B 68
Saron. *Carm* 4G 45
(nr. Ammanford)
Saron. *Carm* 2D 45
(nr. Newcastle Emlyn)
Saron. *Gwyn* 4E 81
(nr. Bethel)
Saron. *Gwyn* 5D 80
(nr. Bontnewydd)
Sarratt. *Herts* 1B 38
Sarre. *Kent* 4G 41
Sarsden. *Oxon* 3A 50
Satley. *Dur* 5E 115
Satron. *N Yor* 5C 104
Satterleigh. *Devn* 4G 19
Satterthwaite. *Cumb* 5E 103
Satwell. *Oxon* 3F 37
Sauchen. *Abers* 2D 152
Saucher. *Per* 5A 144
Saughall. *Ches W* 3F 83
Saughtree. *Bord* 5H 119
Saul. *Glos* 5C 48
Saundby. *Notts* 2E 87
Saundersfoot. *Pemb* 4F 43
Saunderton. *Buck* 5F 51
Saunderton Lee. *Buck* 2G 37
Saunton. *Devn* 3E 19
Sausthorpe. *Linc* 4C 88
Saval. *High* 3C 164
Saverley Green. *Staf* 2D 72
Sawbridge. *Warw* 4C 62
Sawbridgeworth. *Herts* 4E 53
Sawdon. *N Yor* 1D 100
Sawley. *Derbs* 2B 74
Sawley. *Lanc* 5G 97
Sawley. *N Yor* 3E 99
Sawston. *Cambs* 1E 53
Sawtry. *Cambs* 2A 64
Saxby. *Leics* 3F 75
Saxby. *Linc* 2H 87
Saxby All Saints. *N Lin* 3C 94
Saxelby. *Leics* 3D 74
Saxelbye. *Leics* 3D 74
Saxham Street. *Suff* 4C 66
Saxilby. *Linc* 3F 87
Saxlingham. *Norf* 2C 78
Saxlingham Green. *Norf* 1E 67
Saxlingham Nethergate. *Norf* 1E 67
Saxlingham Thorpe. *Norf* 1E 66
Saxmundham. *Suff* 4F 67
Saxondale. *Notts* 1D 74
Saxon Street. *Cambs* 5F 65
Saxtead. *Suff* 4E 67
Saxtead Green. *Suff* 4E 67
Saxthorpe. *Norf* 2D 78
Saxton. *N Yor* 1E 93
Sayers Common. *W Sus* 4D 26
Scackleton. *N Yor* 2A 100
Scadabhagh. *W Isl* 8D 171
Scaftworth. *Notts* 1D 86
Scagglethorpe. *N Yor* 2C 100
Scaitcliffe. *Lanc* 2F 91
Scaladal. *W Isl* 6D 171
Scalasaig. *Arg* 4A 132
Scalby. *E Yor* 2B 94
Scalby. *N Yor* 5H 107
Scalby Mills. *N Yor* 5H 107
Scaldwell. *Nptn* 3E 63
Scaleby. *Cumb* 3F 113
Scaleby Hill. *Cumb* 3F 113
Scale Houses. *Cumb* 5G 113
Scales. *Cumb* 2B 96
(nr. Barrow-in-Furness)
Scales. *Cumb* 2E 103
(nr. Keswick)
Scalford. *Leics* 3E 75
Scaling. *Red C* 3E 107
Scaling Dam. *Red C* 3E 107
Scalloway. *Shet* 8F 173
Scalpaigh. *W Isl* 8E 171
Scalpay House. *High* 1E 147

Skirpenbeck—Southrepps

Skirpenbeck. *E Yor* 4B **100**
Skirwith. *Cumb* 1H **103**
Skirwith. *N Yor* 2G **97**
Skirza. *High* 2F **169**
Skitby. *Cumb* 3F **113**
Skitham. *Lanc* 5D **96**
Skittle Green. *Buck* 5F **51**
Skroo. *Shet* 1B **172**
Skulamus. *High* 1E **147**
Skullomie. *High* 2G **167**
Skyborry Green. *Shrp* 3E **59**
Skye Green. *Essx* 3B **54**
Skye of Curr. *High* 1D **151**
Slack. *W Yor* 2H **91**
Slackhall. *Derbs* 2E **85**
Slack Head. *Cumb* 2D **97**
Slackhead. *Mor* 2B **160**
Slackholme End. *Linc* 3E **89**
Slacks of Cairnbanno. *Abers* 4F **161**
Slack, The. *Dur* 2E **105**
Slad. *Glos* 5D **48**
Slade. *Swan* 4D **31**
Slade End. *Oxon* 2D **36**
Slade Field. *Cambs* 2C **64**
Slade Green. *G Lon* 3G **39**
Slade Heath. *Staf* 5D **72**
Slade Hooton. *S Yor* 2C **86**
Sladesbridge. *Corn* 5A **10**
Slade, The. *W Ber* 5D **36**
Slaggyford. *Nmbd* 4H **113**
Slaidburn. *Lanc* 4G **97**
Slaid Hill. *W Yor* 5F **99**
Slaithwaite. *W Yor* 3A **92**
Slaley. *Derbs* 5G **85**
Slaley. *Nmbd* 4C **114**
Slamannan. *Falk* 2B **128**
Slapton. *Buck* 3H **51**
Slapton. *Devn* 4E **9**
Slapton. *Nptn* 1E **51**
Slattocks. *G Man* 4G **91**
Slaugham. *W Sus* 3D **26**
Slaughterbridge. *Corn* 4B **10**
Slaughterford. *Wilts* 4D **34**
Slawston. *Leics* 1E **63**
Sleaford. *Hants* 3G **25**
Sleaford. *Linc* 1H **75**
Sleagill. *Cumb* 3G **103**
Sleap. *Shrp* 3G **71**
Sledmere. *E Yor* 3D **100**
Sleightholme. *Dur* 3C **104**
Sleights. *N Yor* 4F **107**
Slepe. *Dors* 3E **15**
Slickly. *High* 2E **169**
Sliddery. *N Ayr* 3D **122**
Sligachan. *High* 1C **146**
Slimbridge. *Glos* 5C **48**
Slindon. *Staf* 2C **72**
Slindon. *W Sus* 5A **26**
Slinfold. *W Sus* 2C **26**
Slingsby. *N Yor* 2A **100**
Slip End. *C Beds* 4A **52**
Slipton. *Nptn* 3G **63**
Slitting Mill. *Staf* 4E **73**
Slochd. *High* 1C **150**
Slockavullin. *Arg* 4F **133**
Sloley. *Norf* 3E **79**
Sloncombe. *Devn* 4H **11**
Sloothby. *Linc* 3D **89**
Slough. *Slo* 3A **38**
Slough Green. *Som* 4F **21**
Slough Green. *W Sus* 3D **27**
Sluggan. *High* 1C **150**
Slyne. *Lanc* 3D **97**
Smailholm. *Bord* 1A **120**
Smallbridge. *G Man* 3H **91**
Smallbrook. *Devn* 3B **12**
Smallburgh. *Norf* 3F **79**
Smallburn. *E Ayr* 2F **117**
Smalldale. *Derbs* 3E **85**
Small Dole. *W Sus* 4D **26**
Smalley. *Derbs* 1B **74**
Smallfield. *Surr* 1E **27**
Small Heath. *W Mid* 2E **61**
Smallholm. *Dum* 2C **112**
Small Hythe. *Kent* 2C **28**
Smallrice. *Staf* 2D **72**
Smallridge. *Devn* 2G **13**
Smallwood Hey. *Lanc* 5C **96**
Smallworth. *Norf* 2C **66**
Smannell. *Hants* 2B **24**
Smardale. *Cumb* 4A **104**
Smarden. *Kent* 1C **28**
Smarden Bell. *Kent* 1C **28**
Smart's Hill. *Kent* 1G **27**
Smeatharpe. *Devn* 1F **13**
Smeeth. *Kent* 2E **29**
Smeeth, The. *Norf* 4E **77**
Smeeton Westerby. *Leics* 1D **62**
Smeircleit. *W Isl* 7C **170**
Smerral. *High* 5D **168**
Smestow. *Staf* 1C **60**
Smethwick. *W Mid* 2E **61**
Smirisary. *High* 1A **140**
Smisby. *Derbs* 4H **73**
Smitham Hill. *Bath* 1A **22**
Smith End Green. *Worc* 5B **60**
Smithfield. *Cumb* 3F **113**
Smith Green. *Lanc* 4D **97**
Smithies, The. *Shrp* 1A **60**
Smithincott. *Devn* 1D **12**
Smith's Green. *Essx* 3F **53**
Smithstown. *High* 1G **155**
Smithton. *High* 4B **158**
Smithwood Green. *Suff* 5B **66**
Smithy Bridge. *G Man* 3H **91**
Smithy Green. *Ches E* 3B **84**
Smithy Lane Ends. *Lanc* 3C **90**
Smockington. *Leics* 2B **62**
Smoogro. *Orkn* 7C **172**
Smyth's Green. *Essx* 4C **54**
Snaigow House. *Per* 4H **143**
Snailbeach. *Shrp* 5F **71**
Snailwell. *Cambs* 4F **65**
Snainton. *N Yor* 1D **100**
Snaith. *E Yor* 2G **93**
Snape. *N Yor* 1E **99**
Snape. *Suff* 5F **67**
Snape Green. *Lanc* 3B **90**
Snapper. *Devn* 3F **19**
Snarestone. *Leics* 5H **73**
Snarford. *Linc* 2H **87**
Snargate. *Kent* 3D **28**
Snave. *Kent* 3E **28**
Sneachill. *Worc* 5D **60**
Snead. *Powy* 1F **59**
Snead Common. *Worc* 4B **60**
Sneaton. *N Yor* 4F **107**
Sneatonthorpe. *N Yor* 4G **107**
Snelland. *Linc* 2H **87**
Snelston. *Derbs* 1F **73**
Snetterton. *Norf* 1B **66**
Snettisham. *Norf* 2F **77**
Snibston. *Leics* 4B **74**
Sniseabhal. *W Isl* 5C **170**
Snitter. *Nmbd* 4E **121**
Snitterby. *Linc* 1G **87**
Snitterfield. *Warw* 5G **61**
Snitton. *Shrp* 3H **59**
Snodhill. *Here* 1G **47**
Snodland. *Kent* 4B **40**
Snods Edge. *Nmbd* 4D **114**
Snowdonia. *Gwyn* 2G **69**
Snowshill. *Glos* 2F **49**
Snow Street. *Norf* 2C **66**
Snydale. *W Yor* 2E **93**
Soake. *Hants* 1E **17**
Soar. *Carm* 3G **45**
Soar. *Gwyn* 2F **69**
Soar. *IOA* 3C **80**
Soar. *Powy* 2C **46**
Soberton. *Hants* 1E **16**
Soberton Heath. *Hants* 1E **16**
Sockbridge. *Cumb* 2G **103**
Sockburn. *Darl* 4A **106**
Sodom. *Den* 3C **82**
Sodom. *Shet* 5G **173**
Soham. *Cambs* 3E **65**
Soham Cotes. *Cambs* 3E **65**
Solas. *W Isl* 1D **170**
Soldon Cross. *Devn* 1D **10**
Soldridge. *Hants* 3E **25**
Solent Breezes. *Hants* 2D **16**
Sole Street. *Kent* 4A **40**
(nr. Meopham)
Sole Street. *Kent* 1E **29**
(nr. Waltham)
Solihull. *W Mid* 2F **61**
Sollers Dilwyn. *Here* 5G **59**
Sollers Hope. *Here* 2B **48**
Sollom. *Lanc* 3C **90**
Solva. *Pemb* 2B **42**
Somerby. *Leics* 4E **75**
Somerby. *Linc* 4D **94**
Somercotes. *Derbs* 5B **86**
Somerford. *Dors* 3G **15**
Somerford. *Staf* 5C **72**
Somerford Keynes. *Glos* 2F **35**
Somerley. *W Sus* 3G **17**
Somerleyton. *Suff* 1G **67**
Somersal Herbert. *Derbs* 2F **73**
Somersby. *Linc* 3C **88**
Somersham. *Cambs* 3C **64**
Somersham. *Suff* 1D **54**
Somerton. *Oxon* 3C **50**
Somerton. *Som* 4H **21**
Somerton. *Suff* 5H **65**
Sompting. *W Sus* 5C **26**
Sonning. *Wok* 4F **37**
Sonning Common. *Oxon* 3F **37**
Sonning Eye. *Oxon* 4F **37**
Sookholme. *Notts* 4C **86**
Sopley. *Hants* 3G **15**
Sopworth. *Wilts* 3D **34**
Sorbie. *Dum* 5B **110**
Sordale. *High* 2D **168**
Sorisdale. *Arg* 2D **138**
Sorn. *E Ayr* 2E **117**
Sornhill. *E Ayr* 1E **117**
Sortat. *High* 2E **169**
Sotby. *Linc* 3B **88**
Sots Hole. *Linc* 4A **88**
Sotterley. *Suff* 2G **67**
Soudley. *Shrp* 1G **59**
(nr. Church Stretton)
Soudley. *Shrp* 3B **72**
(nr. Market Drayton)
Soughton. *Flin* 4E **83**
Soulbury. *Buck* 3G **51**
Soulby. *Cumb* 3A **104**
(nr. Appleby)
Soulby. *Cumb* 2F **103**
(nr. Penrith)
Souldern. *Oxon* 2D **50**
Souldrop. *Bed* 4G **63**
Sound. *Ches E* 1A **72**
Sound. *Shet* 7F **173**
(nr. Lerwick)
Sound. *Shet* 6E **173**
(nr. Tresta)
Soundwell. *S Glo* 4B **34**
Sourhope. *Bord* 2C **120**
Sourin. *Orkn* 4D **172**
Sour Nook. *Cumb* 5E **113**
Sourton. *Devn* 3F **11**
Soutergate. *Cumb* 1B **96**
South Acre. *Norf* 4H **77**
Southall. *G Lon* 3C **38**
South Allington. *Devn* 5D **9**
South Alloa. *Falk* 4A **136**
Southam. *Glos* 3E **49**
Southam. *Warw* 4B **62**
South Ambersham. *W Sus* 3A **26**
Southampton. *Sotn* 1C **16**
Southampton Airport. *Hants* 1C **16**
Southannan. *N Ayr* 4D **126**
South Anston. *S Yor* 2C **86**
South Ascot. *Wind* 4A **38**
South Baddesley. *Hants* 3B **16**
South Balfern. *Dum* 4B **110**
South Ballachulish. *High* 3E **141**
South Bank. *Red C* 2C **106**
South Barrow. *Som* 4B **22**
South Benfleet. *Essx* 2B **40**
South Bents. *Tyne* 3H **115**
South Bersted. *W Sus* 5A **26**
Southborough. *Kent* 1G **27**
Southbourne. *Bour* 3G **15**
Southbourne. *W Sus* 2F **17**
South Bowood. *Dors* 3H **13**
South Brent. *Devn* 3C **8**
South Brewham. *Som* 3C **22**
South Broomage. *Falk* 1B **128**
South Broomhill. *Nmbd* 5G **121**
Southburgh. *Norf* 5B **78**
South Burlingham. *Norf* 5F **79**
Southburn. *E Yor* 4D **101**
South Cadbury. *Som* 4B **22**
South Carlton. *Linc* 3G **87**
South Cave. *E Yor* 1C **94**
South Cerney. *Glos* 2F **35**
South Chard. *Som* 2G **13**
South Charlton. *Nmbd* 2F **121**
South Cheriton. *Som* 4B **22**
South Church. *Dur* 2F **105**
Southchurch. *S'end* 2D **40**
South Cleatlam. *Dur* 3E **105**
South Cliffe. *E Yor* 1B **94**
South Clifton. *Notts* 3F **87**
South Clunes. *High* 4H **157**
South Cockerington. *Linc* 2C **88**
South Common. *Devn* 2G **13**
South Common. *E Sus* 4E **27**
South Cornelly. *B'end* 3B **32**
Southcott. *Devn* 1E **11**
(nr. Great Torrington)
Southcott. *Devn* 3F **11**
(nr. Okehampton)
Southcott. *Wilts* 1G **23**
Southcourt. *Buck* 4G **51**
South Cove. *Suff* 2G **67**
South Creagan. *Arg* 4D **141**
South Creake. *Norf* 2A **78**
South Crosland. *W Yor* 3B **92**
South Croxton. *Leics* 4D **74**
South Dalton. *E Yor* 5D **100**
South Darenth. *Kent* 4G **39**
Southdean. *Bord* 4A **120**
Southdown. *Bath* 5C **34**
South Downs. *W Sus* 5D **26**
South Duffield. *N Yor* 1G **93**
Southease. *E Sus* 5F **27**
South Elkington. *Linc* 2B **88**
South Elmsall. *W Yor* 3E **93**
Southend. *Arg* 5A **122**
South End. *Cumb* 3B **96**
Southend. *Glos* 2C **34**
South End. *N Lin* 2E **94**
South End. *W Ber* 4D **36**
Southend (London) Airport.
Essx 2C **40**
Southend-on-Sea. *S'end* 2C **40**
Southerfield. *Cumb* 5C **112**
Southerhouse. *Shet* 8E **173**
Southerly. *Devn* 4F **11**
Southernden. *Kent* 1C **28**
Southerndown. *V Glam* 4B **32**
Southerness. *Dum* 4A **112**
South Erradale. *High* 1G **155**
Southerton. *Devn* 3D **12**
Southery. *Norf* 1F **65**
Southey Green. *Essx* 2A **54**
South Fambridge. *Essx* 1C **40**
South Fawley. *W Ber* 3B **36**
South Feorline. *N Ayr* 3D **122**
South Ferriby. *N Lin* 2C **94**
South Field. *E Yor* 2D **94**
Southfleet. *Kent* 3H **39**
South Garvan. *High* 1D **141**
Southgate. *Cdgn* 2E **57**
Southgate. *G Lon* 1E **39**
Southgate. *Norf* 3D **78**
(nr. Aylsham)
Southgate. *Norf* 2A **78**
(nr. Fakenham)
Southgate. *Swan* 4E **31**
South Gluss. *Shet* 4E **173**
South Godstone. *Surr* 1E **27**
South Gorley. *Hants* 1G **15**
South Green. *Essx* 1A **40**
(nr. Billericay)
South Green. *Essx* 4D **54**
(nr. Colchester)
South Green. *Kent* 4C **40**
South Hanningfield. *Essx* 1B **40**
South Harting. *W Sus* 1F **17**
South Hayling. *Hants* 3F **17**
South Hazelrigg. *Nmbd* 1E **121**
South Heath. *Buck* 5H **51**
South Heath. *Essx* 4E **54**
South Heighton. *E Sus* 5F **27**
South Hetton. *Dur* 5G **115**
South Hiendley. *W Yor* 3D **93**
South Hill. *Corn* 5D **10**
South Hill. *Som* 4H **21**
South Hinksey. *Oxon* 5D **50**
South Hole. *Devn* 4C **18**
South Holme. *N Yor* 2B **100**
South Holmwood. *Surr* 1C **26**
South Hornchurch. *G Lon* 2G **39**
South Huish. *Devn* 4C **8**
South Hykeham. *Linc* 4G **87**
South Hylton. *Tyne* 4G **115**
Southill. *C Beds* 1B **52**
Southington. *Hants* 2D **24**
South Kelsey. *Linc* 1H **87**
South Kessock. *High* 4A **158**
South Killingholme. *N Lin* 3E **95**
South Kilvington. *N Yor* 1G **99**
South Kilworth. *Leics* 2D **62**
South Kirkby. *W Yor* 3E **93**
South Kirkton. *Abers* 3E **153**
South Knighton. *Devn* 5B **12**
South Kyme. *Linc* 1A **76**
South Lancing. *W Sus* 5C **26**
South Ledaig. *Arg* 5D **140**
Southleigh. *Devn* 3F **13**
South Leigh. *Oxon* 5B **50**
South Leverton. *Notts* 2E **87**
South Littleton. *Worc* 1F **49**
South Lopham. *Norf* 2C **66**
South Luffenham. *Rut* 5G **75**
South Malling. *E Sus* 4F **27**
South Marston. *Swin* 3G **35**
South Middleton. *Nmbd* 2D **121**
South Milford. *N Yor* 1E **93**
South Milton. *Devn* 4D **8**
South Mimms. *Herts* 5C **52**
Southminster. *Essx* 1D **40**
South Molton. *Devn* 4H **19**
South Moor. *Dur* 4E **115**
Southmoor. *Oxon* 2B **36**
South Moreton. *Oxon* 3D **36**
South Mundham. *W Sus* 2G **17**
South Muskham. *Notts* 5E **87**
South Newbald. *E Yor* 1C **94**
South Newington. *Oxon* 2C **50**
South Newsham. *Nmbd* 2G **115**
South Newton. *N Ayr* 4H **125**
South Newton. *Wilts* 3F **23**
South Normanton. *Derbs* 5B **86**
South Norwood. *G Lon* 4E **39**
South Nutfield. *Surr* 1E **27**
South Ockendon. *Thur* 2G **39**
Southoe. *Cambs* 4A **64**
Southolt. *Suff* 4D **66**
South Ormsby. *Linc* 3C **88**
Southorpe. *Pet* 5H **75**
South Otterington. *N Yor* 1F **99**
South Owersby. *Linc* 1H **87**
Southowram. *W Yor* 2B **92**
South Oxhey. *Herts* 1C **38**
South Perrott. *Dors* 2H **13**
South Petherton. *Som* 1H **13**
South Petherwin. *Corn* 4D **10**
South Pickenham. *Norf* 5A **78**
South Pool. *Devn* 4D **9**
South Poorton. *Dors* 3A **14**
South Port. *Arg* 1H **133**
Southport. *Mers* 3B **90**
Southpunds. *Shet* 10F **173**
South Queensferry. *Edin* 2E **129**
South Radworthy. *Devn* 3A **20**
South Rauceby. *Linc* 1H **75**
South Raynham. *Norf* 3A **78**
Southrepps. *Norf* 2E **79**

South Reston—Staxton

South Reston. *Linc* 2D **88**
Southrey. *Linc* 4A **88**
Southrop. *Glos* 5G **49**
Southrope. *Hants* 2E **25**
South Runcton. *Norf* 5F **77**
South Scarle. *Notts* 4F **87**
Southsea. *Port* 3E **17**
South Shields. *Tyne* 3G **115**
South Shore. *Bkpl* 1B **90**
Southside. *Orkn* 5E **172**
South Somercotes. *Linc* 1D **88**
South Stainley. *N Yor* 3F **99**
South Stainmore. *Cumb* 3B **104**
South Stifford. *Thur* 3G **39**
South Stoke. *Bath* 5C **34**
South Stoke. *Oxon* 3D **36**
South Stoke. *W Sus* 5B **26**
South Street. *E Sus* 4E **27**
South Street. *Kent* 5E **41** (nr. Faversham)
South Street. *Kent* 4F **41** (nr. Whitstable)
South Tawton. *Devn* 3G **11**
South Thoresby. *Linc* 3D **88**
South Tidworth. *Wilts* 2H **23**
South Town. *Devn* 4C **12**
South Town. *Hants* 3E **25**
Southtown. *Norf* 5H **79**
Southtown. *Orkn* 8D **172**
South View. *Shet* 7E **173**
Southwaite. *Cumb* 5F **113**
South Walsham. *Norf* 4F **79**
South Warnborough. *Hants* 2F **25**
Southwater. *W Sus* 3C **26**
Southwater Street. *W Sus* 3C **26**
Southway. *Som* 2A **22**
South Weald. *Essx* 1G **39**
South Weirs. *Hants* 2A **16**
Southwell. *Dors* 5B **14**
Southwell. *Notts* 5E **86**
South Weston. *Oxon* 2F **37**
South Wheatley. *Corn* 3C **10**
South Wheatley. *Notts* 2E **87**
Southwick. *Hants* 2E **17**
Southwick. *Nptn* 1H **63**
Southwick. *Tyne* 4G **115**
Southwick. *W Sus* 5D **26**
Southwick. *Wilts* 1D **22**
South Widcombe. *Bath* 1A **22**
South Wigston. *Leics* 1C **62**
South Willingham. *Linc* 2A **88**
South Wingfield. *Derbs* 5A **86**
South Witham. *Linc* 4G **75**
Southwold. *Suff* 3H **67**
South Wonston. *Hants* 3C **24**
Southwood. *Norf* 5F **79**
Southwood. *Som* 3A **22**
South Woodham Ferrers. *Essx* 1C **40**
South Wootton. *Norf* 3F **77**
South Wraxall. *Wilts* 5D **34**
South Zeal. *Devn* 3G **11**
Soval Lodge. *W Isl* 5F **171**
Sowerby. *N Yor* 1G **99**
Sowerby. *W Yor* 2A **92**
Sowerby Bridge. *W Yor* 2A **92**
Sowerby Row. *Cumb* 5E **113**
Sower Carr. *Lanc* 5C **96**
Sowley Green. *Suff* 5G **65**
Sowood. *W Yor* 3A **92**
Sowton. *Devn* 3C **12**
Soyal. *High* 4C **164**
Soyland Town. *W Yor* 2A **92**
Spacey Houses. *N Yor* 4F **99**
Spa Common. *Norf* 2E **79**
Spalding. *Linc* 3B **76**
Spaldington. *E Yor* 1A **94**
Spaldwick. *Cambs* 3A **64**
Spalford. *Notts* 4F **87**
Spanby. *Linc* 2H **75**
Sparham. *Norf* 4C **78**
Sparhamhill. *Norf* 4C **78**
Spark Bridge. *Cumb* 1C **96**
Sparket. *Cumb* 2F **103**
Sparkford. *Som* 4B **22**
Sparkwell. *Devn* 3B **8**
Sparrow Green. *Norf* 4B **78**
Sparrowpit. *Derbs* 2E **85**
Sparrow's Green. *E Sus* 2H **27**
Sparsholt. *Hants* 3C **24**
Sparsholt. *Oxon* 3B **36**
Spartylea. *Nmbd* 5B **114**
Spath. *Staf* 2E **73**
Spaunton. *N Yor* 1B **100**
Spaxton. *Som* 3F **21**
Spean Bridge. *High* 5E **149**
Spear Hill. *W Sus* 4C **26**
Speen. *Buck* 2G **37**
Speen. *W Ber* 5C **36**
Speeton. *N Yor* 2F **101**
Speke. *Mers* 2G **83**
Speldhurst. *Kent* 1G **27**
Spellbrook. *Herts* 4E **53**
Spelsbury. *Oxon* 3B **50**
Spencers Wood. *Wok* 5F **37**
Spennithorne. *N Yor* 1D **98**
Spennymoor. *Dur* 1F **105**
Spernall. *Warw* 4E **61**
Spetchley. *Worc* 5C **60**
Spetisbury. *Dors* 2E **15**
Spexhall. *Suff* 2F **67**
Speybank. *High* 3C **150**
Spey Bay. *Mor* 2A **160**
Speybridge. *High* 1E **151**
Speyview. *Mor* 4G **159**
Spilsby. *Linc* 4C **88**
Spindlestone. *Nmbd* 1F **121**
Spinkhill. *Derbs* 3B **86**
Spinney Hills. *Leic* 5D **74**
Spinningdale. *High* 5D **164**
Spital. *Mers* 2F **83**
Spitalhill. *Derbs* 1F **73**
Spital in the Street. *Linc* 1G **87**
Spithurst. *E Sus* 4F **27**
Spittal. *Dum* 4A **110**
Spittal. *E Lot* 2A **130**
Spittal. *High* 3D **168**
Spittal. *Nmbd* 4G **131**
Spittal. *Pemb* 2D **43**
Spittalfield. *Per* 4A **144**
Spittal of Glenmuick. *Abers* 5H **151**
Spittal of Glenshee. *Per* 1A **144**
Spittal-on-Rule. *Bord* 3H **119**
Spixworth. *Norf* 4E **79**
Splatt. *Corn* 4C **10**
Spofforth. *N Yor* 4F **99**
Spondon. *Derb* 2B **74**
Spon End. *W Mid* 3H **61**
Spooner Row. *Norf* 1C **66**
Sporle. *Norf* 4H **77**
Spott. *E Lot* 2C **130**
Spratton. *Nptn* 3E **62**
Spreakley. *Surr* 2G **25**
Spreyton. *Devn* 3H **11**
Spridlington. *Linc* 2H **87**
Springburn. *Glas* 3H **127**
Springfield. *Dum* 3E **113**
Springfield. *Fife* 2F **137**
Springfield. *High* 2A **158**
Springfield. *W Mid* 2E **61**
Springhill. *Staf* 5D **73**
Spring Hill. *W Mid* 1C **60**
Springholm. *Dum* 3F **111**
Springside. *N Ayr* 1C **116**
Springthorpe. *Linc* 2F **87**
Spring Vale. *IOW* 3E **16**
Spring Valley. *IOM* 4C **108**
Springwell. *Tyne* 4F **115**
Sproatley. *E Yor* 1E **95**
Sproston Green. *Ches W* 4B **84**
Sprotbrough. *S Yor* 4F **93**
Sproughton. *Suff* 1E **54**
Sprouston. *Bord* 1B **120**
Sprowston. *Norf* 4E **79**
Sproxton. *Leics* 3F **75**
Sproxton. *N Yor* 1A **100**
Sprunston. *Cumb* 5F **113**
Spurstow. *Ches E* 5H **83**
Squires Gate. *Lanc* 1B **90**
Sraid Ruadh. *Arg* 4A **138**
Srannda. *W Isl* 9C **171**
Sron an t-Sithein. *High* 2C **140**
Sronphadruig Lodge. *Per* 1E **142**
Sruth Mor. *W Isl* 2E **170**
Stableford. *Shrp* 1B **60**
Stackhouse. *N Yor* 3H **97**
Stackpole. *Pemb* 5D **43**
Stackpole Elidor. *Pemb* 5D **43**
Stacksford. *Norf* 1C **66**
Stacksteads. *Lanc* 2G **91**
Staddiscombe. *Plym* 3B **8**
Staddlethorpe. *E Yor* 2B **94**
Staddon. *Devn* 2D **10**
Staden. *Derbs* 3E **85**
Stadhampton. *Oxon* 2E **36**
Stadhlaigearraidh. *W Isl* 5C **170**
Stafainn. *High* 2D **155**
Staffield. *Cumb* 5G **113**
Staffin. *High* 2D **155**
Stafford. *Staf* 3D **72**
Stafford Park. *Telf* 5B **72**
Stagden Cross. *Essx* 4G **53**
Stagsden. *Bed* 1H **51**
Stag's Head. *Devn* 4G **19**
Stainburn. *Cumb* 2B **102**
Stainburn. *N Yor* 5E **99**
Stainby. *Linc* 3G **75**
Staincliffe. *W Yor* 2C **92**
Staincross. *S Yor* 3D **92**
Staindrop. *Dur* 2E **105**
Staines-upon-Thames. *Surr* 3B **38**
Stainfield. *Linc* 3H **75** (nr. Bourne)
Stainfield. *Linc* 3A **88** (nr. Lincoln)
Stainforth. *N Yor* 3H **97**
Stainforth. *S Yor* 3G **93**
Staining. *Lanc* 1B **90**
Stainland. *W Yor* 3A **92**
Stainsacre. *N Yor* 4G **107**
Stainton. *Cumb* 4E **113** (nr. Carlisle)
Stainton. *Cumb* 1E **97** (nr. Kendal)
Stainton. *Cumb* 2F **103** (nr. Penrith)
Stainton. *Dur* 3D **104**
Stainton. *Midd* 3B **106**
Stainton. *N Yor* 5E **105**
Stainton. *S Yor* 1C **86**
Stainton by Langworth. *Linc* 3H **87**
Staintondale. *N Yor* 5G **107**
Stainton le Vale. *Linc* 1A **88**
Stainton with Adgarley. *Cumb* 2B **96**
Stair. *Cumb* 2D **102**
Stair. *E Ayr* 2D **116**
Stairhaven. *Dum* 4H **109**
Staithes. *N Yor* 3E **107**
Stakeford. *Nmbd* 1F **115**
Stake Pool. *Lanc* 5D **96**
Stakes. *Hants* 2E **17**
Stalbridge. *Dors* 1C **14**
Stalbridge Weston. *Dors* 1C **14**
Stalham. *Norf* 3F **79**
Stalham Green. *Norf* 3F **79**
Stalisfield Green. *Kent* 5D **40**
Stallen. *Dors* 1B **14**
Stallingborough. *NE Lin* 3F **95**
Stalling Busk. *N Yor* 1B **98**
Stallington. *Staf* 2D **72**
Stalmine. *Lanc* 5C **96**
Stalybridge. *G Man* 1D **84**
Stambourne. *Essx* 2H **53**
Stamford. *Linc* 5H **75**
Stamford. *Nmbd* 3G **121**
Stamford Bridge. *Ches W* 4G **83**
Stamford Bridge. *E Yor* 4B **100**
Stamfordham. *Nmbd* 2D **115**
Stamperland. *E Ren* 4G **127**
Stanah. *Lanc* 5C **96**
Stanborough. *Herts* 4C **52**
Stanbridge. *C Beds* 3H **51**
Stanbridge. *Dors* 2F **15**
Stanbury. *W Yor* 1A **92**
Stand. *N Lan* 3A **128**
Standburn. *Falk* 2C **128**
Standeford. *Staf* 5D **72**
Standen. *Kent* 1C **28**
Standen Street. *Kent* 2C **28**
Standerwick. *Som* 1D **22**
Standford. *Hants* 3G **25**
Standford Bridge. *Telf* 3B **72**
Standingstone. *Cumb* 5D **112**
Standish. *Glos* 5D **48**
Standish. *G Man* 3D **90**
Standish Lower Ground. *G Man* 4D **90**
Standlake. *Oxon* 5B **50**
Standon. *Hants* 4C **24**
Standon. *Herts* 3D **53**
Standon. *Staf* 2C **72**
Standon Green End. *Herts* 4D **52**
Stane. *N Lan* 4B **128**
Stanecastle. *N Ayr* 1C **116**
Stanfield. *Norf* 3B **78**
Stanford. *C Beds* 1B **52**
Stanford. *Kent* 2F **29**
Stanford Bishop. *Here* 5A **60**
Stanford Bridge. *Worc* 4B **60**
Stanford Dingley. *W Ber* 4D **36**
Stanford in the Vale. *Oxon* 2B **36**
Stanford-le-Hope. *Thur* 2A **40**
Stanford on Avon. *Nptn* 3C **62**
Stanford on Soar. *Notts* 3C **74**
Stanford on Teme. *Worc* 4B **60**
Stanford Rivers. *Essx* 5F **53**
Stanfree. *Derbs* 3B **86**
Stanghow. *Red C* 3D **107**
Stanground. *Pet* 1B **64**
Stanhoe. *Norf* 2H **77**
Stanhope. *Dur* 1C **104**
Stanhope. *Bord* 2D **118**
Stanion. *Nptn* 2G **63**
Stanley. *Derbs* 1B **74**
Stanley. *Dur* 4E **115**
Stanley. *Per* 5A **144**
Stanley. *Shrp* 2B **60**
Stanley. *Staf* 5D **84**
Stanley. *W Yor* 2D **92**
Stanley Common. *Derbs* 1B **74**
Stanley Crook. *Dur* 1E **105**
Stanley Hill. *Here* 1B **48**
Stanlow. *Ches W* 3G **83**
Stanmer. *Brig* 5E **27**
Stanmore. *G Lon* 1C **38**
Stanmore. *Hants* 4C **24**
Stanmore. *W Ber* 4C **36**
Stannersburn. *Nmbd* 1A **114**
Stanningfield. *Suff* 5A **66**
Stannington. *Nmbd* 2F **115**
Stannington. *S Yor* 2H **85**
Stansbatch. *Here* 4F **59**
Stansfield. *Suff* 5G **65**
Stanshope. *Staf* 5F **85**
Stanstead. *Suff* 1B **54**
Stanstead Abbotts. *Herts* 4D **53**
Stansted. *Kent* 4H **39**
Stansted (London) Airport. *Essx* 3F **53**
Stansted Mountfitchet. *Essx* 3F **53**
Stanthorne. *Ches W* 4A **84**
Stanton. *Derbs* 4G **73**
Stanton. *Glos* 2F **49**
Stanton. *Nmbd* 5F **121**
Stanton. *Staf* 1F **73**
Stanton. *Suff* 3B **66**
Stanton by Bridge. *Derbs* 3A **74**
Stanton by Dale. *Derbs* 2B **74**
Stanton Chare. *Suff* 3B **66**
Stanton Drew. *Bath* 5A **34**
Stanton Fitzwarren. *Swin* 2G **35**
Stanton Harcourt. *Oxon* 5C **50**
Stanton Hill. *Notts* 4B **86**
Stanton in Peak. *Derbs* 4G **85**
Stanton Lacy. *Shrp* 3G **59**
Stanton Long. *Shrp* 1H **59**
Stanton-on-the-Wolds. *Notts* 2D **74**
Stanton Prior. *Bath* 5B **34**
Stanton St Bernard. *Wilts* 5F **35**
Stanton St John. *Oxon* 5D **50**
Stanton St Quintin. *Wilts* 4E **35**
Stanton Street. *Suff* 4B **66**
Stanton under Bardon. *Leics* 4B **74**
Stanton upon Hine Heath. *Shrp* 3H **71**
Stanton Wick. *Bath* 5B **34**
Stanwardine in the Fields. *Shrp* 3G **71**
Stanwardine in the Wood. *Shrp* 3G **71**
Stanway. *Essx* 3C **54**
Stanway. *Glos* 2F **49**
Stanwell. *Surr* 3B **38**
Stanwell Green. *Suff* 3D **66**
Stanwell Moor. *Surr* 3B **38**
Stanwick. *Nptn* 3G **63**
Stanydale. *Shet* 6D **173**
Staoinebrig. *W Isl* 5C **170**
Stape. *N Yor* 5E **107**
Stapehill. *Dors* 2F **15**
Stapeley. *Ches E* 1A **72**
Stapenhill. *Staf* 3G **73**
Staple. *Kent* 5G **41**
Staple Cross. *Devn* 4D **20**
Staplecross. *E Sus* 3B **28**
Staplefield. *W Sus* 3D **27**
Staple Fitzpaine. *Som* 1F **13**
Stapleford. *Cambs* 5D **64**
Stapleford. *Herts* 4D **52**
Stapleford. *Leics* 4F **75**
Stapleford. *Linc* 5F **87**
Stapleford. *Notts* 2B **74**
Stapleford. *Wilts* 3F **23**
Stapleford Abbotts. *Essx* 1G **39**
Stapleford Tawney. *Essx* 1G **39**
Staplegrove. *Som* 4F **21**
Staplehay. *Som* 4F **21**
Staple Hill. *S Glo* 4B **34**
Staplehurst. *Kent* 1B **28**
Staplers. *IOW* 4D **16**
Stapleton. *Bris* 4B **34**
Stapleton. *Cumb* 2G **113**
Stapleton. *Here* 4F **59**
Stapleton. *Leics* 1B **62**
Stapleton. *N Yor* 3F **105**
Stapleton. *Shrp* 5G **71**
Stapleton. *Som* 4H **21**
Stapley. *Som* 1E **13**
Staploe. *Bed* 4A **64**
Staplow. *Here* 1B **48**
Star. *Fife* 3F **137**
Star. *Pemb* 1G **43**
Starbeck. *N Yor* 4F **99**
Starbotton. *N Yor* 2B **98**
Starcross. *Devn* 4C **12**
Stareton. *Warw* 3H **61**
Starkholmes. *Derbs* 5H **85**
Starling. *G Man* 3F **91**
Starling's Green. *Essx* 2E **53**
Starston. *Norf* 2E **67**
Start. *Devn* 4E **9**
Startforth. *Dur* 3D **104**
Start Hill. *Essx* 3F **53**
Startley. *Wilts* 3E **35**
Stathe. *Som* 4G **21**
Stathern. *Leics* 2E **75**
Station Town. *Dur* 1B **106**
Staughton Green. *Cambs* 4A **64**
Staughton Highway. *Cambs* 4A **64**
Staunton. *Glos* 3C **48** (nr. Cheltenham)
Staunton. *Glos* 4A **48** (nr. Monmouth)
Staunton in the Vale. *Notts* 1F **75**
Staunton on Arrow. *Here* 4F **59**
Staunton on Wye. *Here* 1G **47**
Staveley. *Cumb* 5F **103**
Staveley. *Derbs* 3B **86**
Staveley. *N Yor* 3F **99**
Staveley-in-Cartmel. *Cumb* 1C **96**
Staverton. *Devn* 2D **9**
Staverton. *Glos* 3D **49**
Staverton. *Nptn* 4C **62**
Staverton. *Wilts* 5D **34**
Stawell. *Som* 3G **21**
Stawley. *Som* 4D **20**
Staxigoe. *High* 3F **169**
Staxton. *N Yor* 2E **101**

Thornley—Tongwynlais

Thornley. *Dur* 1A **106**
(nr. Durham)
Thornley. *Dur* 1E **105**
(nr. Tow Law)
Thornley Gate. *Nmbd* 4B **114**
Thornliebank. *E Ren* 3G **127**
Thornroan. *Abers* 5F **161**
Thorns. *Suff* 5G **65**
Thornsett. *Derbs* 2E **85**
Thornthwaite. *Cumb* 2D **102**
Thornthwaite. *N Yor* 4D **98**
Thornton. *Ang* 4C **144**
Thornton. *Buck* 2F **51**
Thornton. *E Yor* 5B **100**
Thornton. *Fife* 4E **137**
Thornton. *Lanc* 5C **96**
Thornton. *Leics* 5B **74**
Thornton. *Linc* 4B **88**
Thornton. *Mers* 4B **90**
Thornton. *Midd* 3B **106**
Thornton. *Nmbd* 5F **131**
Thornton. *Pemb* 4D **42**
Thornton. *W Yor* 1A **92**
Thornton Curtis. *N Lin* 3D **94**
Thorntonhall. *S Lan* 4G **127**
Thornton Heath. *G Lon* 4E **39**
Thornton Hough. *Mers* 2F **83**
Thornton in Craven. *N Yor* 5B **98**
Thornton in Lonsdale. *N Yor* 2F **97**
Thornton-le-Beans. *N Yor* 5A **106**
Thornton-le-Clay. *N Yor* 3A **100**
Thornton-le-Dale. *N Yor* 1C **100**
Thornton le Moor. *Linc* 1H **87**
Thornton-le-Moor. *N Yor* 1F **99**
Thornton-le-Moors. *Ches W* 3G **83**
Thornton-le-Street. *N Yor* 1G **99**
Thorntonloch. *E Lot* 2D **130**
Thornton Rust. *N Yor* 1B **98**
Thornton Steward. *N Yor* 1D **98**
Thornton Watlass. *N Yor* 1E **99**
Thornwood Common. *Essx* 5E **53**
Thornythwaite. *Cumb* 2E **103**
Thoroton. *Notts* 1E **75**
Thorp Arch. *W Yor* 5G **99**
Thorpe. *Derbs* 5F **85**
Thorpe. *E Yor* 5D **101**
Thorpe. *Linc* 2D **89**
Thorpe. *Norf* 1G **67**
Thorpe. *N Yor* 3C **98**
Thorpe. *Notts* 1E **75**
Thorpe. *Surr* 4B **38**
Thorpe Abbotts. *Norf* 3D **66**
Thorpe Acre. *Leics* 3C **74**
Thorpe Arnold. *Leics* 3E **75**
Thorpe Audlin. *W Yor* 3E **93**
Thorpe Bassett. *N Yor* 2C **100**
Thorpe Bay. *S'end* 2D **40**
Thorpe by Water. *Rut* 1F **63**
Thorpe Common. *S Yor* 1A **86**
Thorpe Common. *Suff* 2F **55**
Thorpe Constantine. *Staf* 5G **73**
Thorpe End. *Norf* 4E **79**
Thorpe Fendike. *Linc* 4D **88**
Thorpe Green. *Essx* 3E **55**
Thorpe Green. *Suff* 5B **66**
Thorpe Hall. *N Yor* 2H **99**
Thorpe Hamlet. *Norf* 5E **79**
Thorpe Hesley. *S Yor* 1A **86**
Thorpe in Balne. *S Yor* 3F **93**
Thorpe in the Fallows. *Linc* 2G **87**
Thorpe Langton. *Leics* 1E **63**
Thorpe Larches. *Dur* 2A **106**
Thorpe Latimer. *Linc* 1A **76**
Thorpe-le-Soken. *Essx* 3E **55**
Thorpe le Street. *E Yor* 5C **100**
Thorpe Malsor. *Nptn* 3F **63**
Thorpe Mandeville. *Nptn* 1D **50**
Thorpe Market. *Norf* 2E **79**
Thorpe Marriott. *Norf* 4D **78**
Thorpe Morieux. *Suff* 5B **66**
Thorpeness. *Suff* 5G **67**
Thorpe on the Hill. *Linc* 4G **87**
Thorpe on the Hill. *W Yor* 2D **92**
Thorpe St Andrew. *Norf* 5E **79**
Thorpe St Peter. *Linc* 4D **89**
Thorpe Salvin. *S Yor* 2C **86**
Thorpe Satchville. *Leics* 4E **75**
Thorpe Thewles. *Stoc T* 2A **106**
Thorpe Tilney. *Linc* 5A **88**
Thorpe Underwood. *N Yor* 4G **99**
Thorpe Waterville. *Nptn* 2H **63**
Thorpe Willoughby. *N Yor* 1F **93**
Thorpland. *Norf* 5F **77**
Thorrington. *Essx* 3D **54**
Thorverton. *Devn* 2C **12**
Thrandeston. *Suff* 3D **66**
Thrapston. *Nptn* 3G **63**
Thrashbush. *N Lan* 3A **128**
Threapland. *Cumb* 1C **102**
Threapland. *N Yor* 3B **98**
Threapwood. *Ches W* 1G **71**
Threapwood. *Staf* 1E **73**
Three Ashes. *Here* 3A **48**
Three Bridges. *Linc* 2D **88**
Three Bridges. *W Sus* 2D **27**
Three Burrows. *Corn* 4B **6**
Three Chimneys. *Kent* 2C **28**
Three Cocks. *Powy* 2E **47**
Three Crosses. *Swan* 3E **31**
Three Cups Corner. *E Sus* 3H **27**
Threehammer Common. *Norf* 3F **79**
Three Holes. *Norf* 5E **77**
Threekingham. *Linc* 2H **75**
Three Leg Cross. *E Sus* 2A **28**
Three Legged Cross. *Dors* 2F **15**
Three Mile Cross. *Wok* 5F **37**
Threemilestone. *Corn* 4B **6**
Three Oaks. *E Sus* 4C **28**
Threlkeld. *Cumb* 2E **102**
Threshfield. *N Yor* 3B **98**
Thrigby. *Norf* 4G **79**
Thringarth. *Dur* 2C **104**
Thringstone. *Leics* 4B **74**
Thrintoft. *N Yor* 5A **106**
Thriplow. *Cambs* 1E **53**
Throckenholt. *Linc* 5C **76**
Throcking. *Herts* 2D **52**
Throckley. *Tyne* 3E **115**
Throckmorton. *Worc* 1E **49**
Throop. *Bour* 3G **15**
Throphill. *Nmbd* 1E **115**
Thropton. *Nmbd* 4E **121**
Throsk. *Stir* 4A **136**
Througham. *Glos* 5E **49**
Throughgate. *Dum* 1F **111**
Throwleigh. *Devn* 3G **11**
Throwley. *Kent* 5D **40**
Throwley Forstal. *Kent* 5D **40**
Throxenby. *N Yor* 1E **101**
Thrumpton. *Notts* 2C **74**
Thrumster. *High* 4F **169**
Thrunton. *Nmbd* 3E **121**
Thrupp. *Glos* 5D **48**
Thrupp. *Oxon* 4C **50**
Thrushelton. *Devn* 4E **11**
Thrushgill. *Lanc* 3F **97**
Thrussington. *Leics* 4D **74**
Thruxton. *Hants* 2A **24**
Thruxton. *Here* 2H **47**
Thrybergh. *S Yor* 1B **86**
Thulston. *Derbs* 2B **74**
Thundergay. *N Ayr* 5G **125**
Thundersley. *Essx* 2B **40**
Thundridge. *Herts* 4D **52**
Thurcaston. *Leics* 4C **74**
Thurcroft. *S Yor* 2B **86**
Thurdon. *Corn* 1C **10**
Thurgarton. *Norf* 2D **78**
Thurgarton. *Notts* 1D **74**
Thurgoland. *S Yor* 4C **92**
Thurlaston. *Leics* 1C **62**
Thurlaston. *Warw* 3B **62**
Thurlbear. *Som* 4F **21**
Thurlby. *Linc* 3D **89**
(nr. Alford)
Thurlby. *Linc* 4A **76**
(nr. Baston)
Thurlby. *Linc* 4G **87**
(nr. Lincoln)
Thurleigh. *Bed* 5H **63**
Thurlestone. *Devn* 4C **8**
Thurloxton. *Som* 3F **21**
Thurlstone. *S Yor* 4C **92**
Thurlton. *Norf* 1G **67**
Thurmaston. *Leics* 5D **74**
Thurnby. *Leics* 5D **74**
Thurne. *Norf* 4G **79**
Thurnham. *Kent* 5C **40**
Thurning. *Norf* 3C **78**
Thurning. *Nptn* 2H **63**
Thurnscoe. *S Yor* 4E **93**
Thursby. *Cumb* 4E **113**
Thursford. *Norf* 2B **78**
Thursford Green. *Norf* 2B **78**
Thursley. *Surr* 2A **26**
Thurso. *High* 2D **168**
Thurso East. *High* 2D **168**
Thurstaston. *Mers* 2E **83**
Thurston. *Suff* 4B **66**
Thurston End. *Suff* 5G **65**
Thurstonfield. *Cumb* 4E **112**
Thurstonland. *W Yor* 3B **92**
Thurton. *Norf* 5F **79**
Thurvaston. *Derbs* 2F **73**
(nr. Ashbourne)
Thurvaston. *Derbs* 2G **73**
(nr. Derby)
Thuxton. *Norf* 5C **78**
Thwaite. *Dur* 3D **104**
Thwaite. *N Yor* 5B **104**
Thwaite. *Suff* 4D **66**
Thwaite Head. *Cumb* 5E **103**
Thwaites. *W Yor* 5C **98**
Thwaite St Mary. *Norf* 1F **67**
Thwing. *E Yor* 2E **101**
Tibbermore. *Per* 1C **136**
Tibberton. *Glos* 3C **48**
Tibberton. *Telf* 3A **72**
Tibberton. *Worc* 5D **60**
Tibenham. *Norf* 2D **66**
Tibshelf. *Derbs* 4B **86**
Tibthorpe. *E Yor* 4D **100**
Ticehurst. *E Sus* 2A **28**
Tichborne. *Hants* 3D **24**
Tickencote. *Rut* 5G **75**
Tickenham. *N Som* 4H **33**
Tickhill. *S Yor* 1C **86**
Ticklerton. *Shrp* 1G **59**
Ticknall. *Derbs* 3A **74**
Tickton. *E Yor* 5E **101**
Tidbury Green. *W Mid* 3F **61**
Tidcombe. *Wilts* 1A **24**
Tiddington. *Oxon* 5E **51**
Tiddington. *Warw* 5G **61**
Tiddleywink. *Wilts* 4D **34**
Tidebrook. *E Sus* 3H **27**
Tideford. *Corn* 3H **7**
Tideford Cross. *Corn* 2H **7**
Tidenham. *Glos* 2A **34**
Tideswell. *Derbs* 3F **85**
Tidmarsh. *W Ber* 4E **37**
Tidmington. *Warw* 2A **50**
Tidpit. *Hants* 1F **15**
Tidworth. *Wilts* 2H **23**
Tidworth Camp. *Wilts* 2H **23**
Tiers Cross. *Pemb* 3D **42**
Tiffield. *Nptn* 5D **62**
Tifty. *Abers* 4E **161**
Tigerton. *Ang* 2E **145**
Tighnabruaich. *Arg* 2A **126**
Tigley. *Devn* 2D **8**
Tilbrook. *Cambs* 4H **63**
Tilbury. *Thur* 3H **39**
Tilbury Green. *Essx* 1H **53**
Tilbury Juxta Clare. *Essx* 1A **54**
Tile Hill. *W Mid* 3G **61**
Tilehurst. *Read* 4E **37**
Tilford. *Surr* 2G **25**
Tilgate Forest Row. *W Sus* 2D **26**
Tillathrowie. *Abers* 5B **160**
Tillers Green. *Glos* 2B **48**
Tillery. *Abers* 1G **153**
Tilley. *Shrp* 3H **71**
Tillicoultry. *Clac* 4B **136**
Tillingham. *Essx* 5C **54**
Tillington. *Here* 1H **47**
Tillington. *W Sus* 3A **26**
Tillington Common. *Here* 1H **47**
Tillybirloch. *Abers* 3D **152**
Tillyfourie. *Abers* 2D **152**
Tilmanstone. *Kent* 5H **41**
Tilney All Saints. *Norf* 4E **77**
Tilney Fen End. *Norf* 4E **77**
Tilney High End. *Norf* 4E **77**
Tilney St Lawrence. *Norf* 4E **77**
Tilshead. *Wilts* 2F **23**
Tilstock. *Shrp* 2H **71**
Tilston. *Ches W* 5G **83**
Tilstone Fearnall. *Ches W* 4H **83**
Tilsworth. *C Beds* 3H **51**
Tilton on the Hill. *Leics* 5E **75**
Tiltups End. *Glos* 2D **34**
Timberland. *Linc* 5A **88**
Timbersbrook. *Ches E* 4C **84**
Timberscombe. *Som* 2C **20**
Timble. *N Yor* 4D **98**
Timperley. *G Man* 2B **84**
Timsbury. *Bath* 1B **22**
Timsbury. *Hants* 4B **24**
Timsgearraidh. *W Isl* 4C **171**
Timworth Green. *Suff* 4A **66**
Tincleton. *Dors* 3C **14**
Tindale. *Cumb* 4H **113**
Tindale Crescent. *Dur* 2F **105**
Tingewick. *Buck* 2E **51**
Tingrith. *C Beds* 2A **52**
Tingwall. *Orkn* 5D **172**
Tinhay. *Devn* 4D **11**
Tinshill. *W Yor* 1C **92**
Tinsley. *S Yor* 1B **86**
Tinsley Green. *W Sus* 2D **27**
Tintagel. *Corn* 4A **10**
Tintern. *Mon* 5A **48**
Tintinhull. *Som* 1H **13**
Tintwistle. *Derbs* 1E **85**
Tinwald. *Dum* 1B **112**
Tinwell. *Rut* 5H **75**
Tippacott. *Devn* 2A **20**
Tipperty. *Abers* 1G **153**
Tipps End. *Cambs* 1E **65**
Tiptoe. *Hants* 3A **16**
Tipton. *W Mid* 1D **60**
Tipton St John. *Devn* 3D **12**
Tiptree. *Essx* 4B **54**
Tiptree Heath. *Essx* 4B **54**
Tirabad. *Powy* 1B **46**
Tircoed. *Swan* 5G **45**
Tiree Airport. *Arg* 4B **138**
Tirinie. *Per* 2F **143**
Tirley. *Glos* 3D **48**
Tirnewydd. *Flin* 3D **82**
Tiroran. *Arg* 1B **132**
Tirphil. *Cphy* 5E **47**
Tirril. *Cumb* 2G **103**
Tirryside. *High* 2C **164**
Tir-y-dail. *Carm* 4G **45**
Tisbury. *Wilts* 4E **23**
Tisman's Common. *W Sus* 2B **26**
Tissington. *Derbs* 5F **85**
Titchberry. *Devn* 4C **18**
Titchfield. *Hants* 2D **16**
Titchmarsh. *Nptn* 3H **63**
Titchwell. *Norf* 1G **77**
Tithby. *Notts* 2D **74**
Titley. *Here* 5F **59**
Titlington. *Nmbd* 3E **121**
Titsey. *Surr* 5F **39**
Titson. *Corn* 2C **10**
Tittensor. *Staf* 2C **72**
Tittleshall. *Norf* 3A **78**
Titton. *Worc* 4C **60**
Tiverton. *Ches W* 4H **83**
Tiverton. *Devn* 1C **12**
Tivetshall St Margaret. *Norf* 2D **66**
Tivetshall St Mary. *Norf* 2D **66**
Tivington. *Som* 2C **20**
Tixall. *Staf* 3D **73**
Tixover. *Rut* 5G **75**
Toab. *Orkn* 7E **172**
Toab. *Shet* 10E **173**
Toadmoor. *Derbs* 5A **86**
Tobermory. *Arg* 3G **139**
Toberonochy. *Arg* 3E **133**
Tobha-Beag. *W Isl* 1E **170**
(on North Uist)
Tobha Beag. *W Isl* 5C **170**
(on South Uist)
Tobha Mor. *W Isl* 5C **170**
Tobhtarol. *W Isl* 4D **171**
Tobson. *W Isl* 4D **171**
Tocabhaig. *High* 2E **147**
Tocher. *Abers* 5D **160**
Tockenham. *Wilts* 4F **35**
Tockenham Wick. *Wilts* 3F **35**
Tockholes. *Bkbn* 2E **91**
Tockington. *S Glo* 3B **34**
Tockwith. *N Yor* 4G **99**
Todber. *Dors* 4D **22**
Todding. *Here* 3G **59**
Toddington. *C Beds* 3A **52**
Toddington. *Glos* 2F **49**
Todenham. *Glos* 2H **49**
Todhills. *Cumb* 3E **113**
Todmorden. *W Yor* 2H **91**
Todwick. *S Yor* 2B **86**
Toft. *Cambs* 5C **64**
Toft. *Linc* 4H **75**
Toft Hill. *Dur* 2E **105**
Toft Monks. *Norf* 1G **67**
Toft next Newton. *Linc* 2H **87**
Toftrees. *Norf* 3A **78**
Tofts. *High* 2F **169**
Toftwood. *Norf* 4B **78**
Togston. *Nmbd* 4G **121**
Tokavaig. *High* 2E **147**
Tokers Green. *Oxon* 4F **37**
Tolastadh a Chaolais. *W Isl* 4D **171**
Tolladine. *Worc* 5C **60**
Tolland. *Som* 3E **20**
Tollard Farnham. *Dors* 1E **15**
Tollard Royal. *Wilts* 1E **15**
Toll Bar. *S Yor* 4F **93**
Toller Fratrum. *Dors* 3A **14**
Toller Porcorum. *Dors* 3A **14**
Tollerton. *N Yor* 3H **99**
Tollerton. *Notts* 2D **74**
Toller Whelme. *Dors* 2A **14**
Tollesbury. *Essx* 4C **54**
Tolleshunt D'Arcy. *Essx* 4C **54**
Tolleshunt Knights. *Essx* 4C **54**
Tolleshunt Major. *Essx* 4C **54**
Tollie. *High* 3H **157**
Tollie Farm. *High* 1A **156**
Tolm. *W Isl* 4G **171**
Tolpuddle. *Dors* 3C **14**
Tolstadh bho Thuath. *W Isl* 3H **171**
Tolworth. *G Lon* 4C **38**
Tomachlaggan. *Mor* 1F **151**
Tomaknock. *Per* 1A **136**
Tomatin. *High* 1C **150**
Tombuidhe. *Arg* 3H **133**
Tomdoun. *High* 3D **148**
Tomich. *High* 1F **149**
(nr. Cannich)
Tomich. *High* 1B **158**
(nr. Invergordon)
Tomich. *High* 3D **164**
(nr. Lairg)
Tomintoul. *Mor* 2F **151**
Tomnavoulin. *Mor* 1G **151**
Tomsléibhe. *Arg* 5A **140**
Ton. *Mon* 2G **33**
Tonbridge. *Kent* 1G **27**
Tondu. *B'end* 3B **32**
Tonedale. *Som* 4E **21**
Tonfanau. *Gwyn* 5E **69**
Tong. *Shrp* 5B **72**
Tonge. *Leics* 3B **74**
Tong Forge. *Shrp* 5B **72**
Tongham. *Surr* 2G **25**
Tongland. *Dum* 4D **111**
Tong Norton. *Shrp* 5B **72**
Tongue. *High* 3F **167**
Tongue End. *Linc* 4A **76**
Tongwynlais. *Card* 3E **33**

Trondavoe—Upper Green

Trondavoe. *Shet* 4E 173
Troon. *Corn* 5A 6
Troon. *S Ayr* 1C 116
Troqueer. *Dum* 2A 112
Troston. *Suff* 3A 66
Trottiscliffe. *Kent* 4H 39
Trotton. *W Sus* 4G 25
Troutbeck. *Cumb* 4F 103
(nr. Ambleside)
Troutbeck. *Cumb* 2E 103
(nr. Penrith)
Troutbeck Bridge. *Cumb* 4F 103
Troway. *Derbs* 3A 86
Trowbridge. *Wilts* 1D 22
Trowell. *Notts* 2B 74
Trowle Common. *Wilts* 1D 22
Trowley Bottom. *Herts* 4A 52
Trowse Newton. *Norf* 5E 79
Trudoxhill. *Som* 2C 22
Trull. *Som* 4F 21
Trumaisgearraidh. *W Isl* 1D 170
Trumpan. *High* 2B 154
Trumpet. *Here* 2B 48
Trumpington. *Cambs* 5D 64
Trumps Green. *Surr* 4A 38
Trunch. *Norf* 2E 79
Trunnah. *Lanc* 5C 96
Truro. *Corn* 4C 6
Trusham. *Devn* 4B 12
Trusley. *Derbs* 2G 73
Trusthorpe. *Linc* 2E 89
Tryfil. *IOA* 2D 80
Trysull. *Staf* 1C 60
Tubney. *Oxon* 2C 36
Tuckenhay. *Devn* 3E 9
Tuckhill. *Shrp* 2B 60
Tuckingmill. *Corn* 4A 6
Tuckton. *Bour* 3G 15
Tuddenham. *Suff* 3G 65
Tuddenham St Martin. *Suff* 1E 55
Tudeley. *Kent* 1H 27
Tudhoe. *Dur* 1F 105
Tudhoe Grange. *Dur* 1F 105
Tudorville. *Here* 3A 48
Tudweiliog. *Gwyn* 2B 68
Tuesley. *Surr* 1A 26
Tufton. *Hants* 2C 24
Tufton. *Pemb* 2E 43
Tugby. *Leics* 5E 75
Tugford. *Shrp* 2H 59
Tughall. *Nmbd* 2G 121
Tulchan. *Per* 1B 136
Tullibardine. *Per* 2B 136
Tullibody. *Clac* 4A 136
Tullich. *Arg* 2H 133
Tullich. *High* 4B 156
(nr. Lochcarron)
Tullich. *High* 1C 158
(nr. Tain)
Tullich. *Mor* 4H 159
Tullich Muir. *High* 1B 158
Tulliemet. *Per* 3G 143
Tulloch. *Abers* 5F 161
Tulloch. *High* 4D 164
(nr. Bonar Bridge)
Tulloch. *High* 5F 149
(nr. Fort William)
Tulloch. *High* 2D 151
(nr. Grantown-on-Spey)
Tulloch. *Per* 1C 136
Tullochgorm. *Arg* 4G 133
Tullybeagles Lodge. *Per* 5H 143
Tullymurdoch. *Per* 3B 144
Tullynessle. *Abers* 2C 152
Tumble. *Carm* 4F 45
Tumbler's Green. *Essx* 3B 54
Tumby. *Linc* 4B 88
Tumby Woodside. *Linc* 5B 88
Tummel Bridge. *Per* 3E 143
Tunbridge Wells, Royal. *Kent* 2G 27
Tunga. *W Isl* 4G 171
Tungate. *Norf* 3E 79
Tunley. *Bath* 1B 22
Tunstall. *E Yor* 1G 95
Tunstall. *Kent* 4C 40
Tunstall. *Lanc* 2F 97
Tunstall. *Norf* 5G 79
Tunstall. *N Yor* 5F 105
Tunstall. *Staf* 3B 72
Tunstall. *Stoke* 5C 84
Tunstall. *Suff* 5F 67
Tunstall. *Tyne* 4G 115
Tunstead. *Derbs* 3F 85
Tunstead. *Norf* 3E 79
Tunstead Milton. *Derbs* 2E 85
Tunworth. *Hants* 2E 25
Tupsley. *Here* 1A 48
Tupton. *Derbs* 4A 86
Turfholm. *S Lan* 1H 117
Turfmoor. *Devn* 2F 13
Turgis Green. *Hants* 1E 25
Turkdean. *Glos* 4G 49
Turkey Island. *Hants* 1D 16
Tur Langton. *Leics* 1E 62
Turleigh. *Wilts* 5D 34
Turlin Moor. *Pool* 3E 15
Turnastone. *Here* 2G 47
Turnberry. *S Ayr* 4B 116
Turnchapel. *Plym* 3A 8
Turnditch. *Derbs* 1G 73
Turners Hill. *W Sus* 2E 27
Turners Puddle. *Dors* 3D 14
Turnford. *Herts* 5D 52
Turnhouse. *Edin* 2E 129
Turnworth. *Dors* 2D 14
Turriff. *Abers* 4E 161
Tursdale. *Dur* 1A 106
Turton Bottoms. *Bkbn* 3F 91
Turtory. *Mor* 4C 160
Turves Green. *W Mid* 3E 61
Turvey. *Bed* 5G 63
Turville. *Buck* 2F 37
Turville Heath. *Buck* 2F 37
Turweston. *Buck* 2E 50
Tushielaw. *Bord* 3F 119
Tutbury. *Staf* 3G 73
Tutnall. *Worc* 3D 61
Tutshill. *Glos* 2A 34
Tuttington. *Norf* 3E 79
Tutts Clump. *W Ber* 4D 36
Tutwell. *Corn* 5D 11
Tuxford. *Notts* 3E 87
Twatt. *Orkn* 5B 172
Twatt. *Shet* 6E 173
Twechar. *E Dun* 2H 127
Tweedale. *Telf* 5B 72
Tweedmouth. *Nmbd* 4F 131
Tweedsmuir. *Bord* 2C 118
Twelveheads. *Corn* 4B 6
Twemlow Green. *Ches E* 4B 84
Twenty. *Linc* 3A 76
Twerton. *Bath* 5C 34
Twickenham. *G Lon* 3C 38
Twigworth. *Glos* 3D 48
Twineham. *W Sus* 4D 26
Twinhoe. *Bath* 1C 22
Twinstead. *Essx* 2B 54
Twinstead Green. *Essx* 2B 54
Twiss Green. *Warr* 1A 84
Twiston. *Lanc* 5H 97
Twitchen. *Devn* 3A 20
Twitchen. *Shrp* 3F 59
Two Bridges. *Devn* 5G 11
Two Bridges. *Glos* 5B 48
Two Dales. *Derbs* 4G 85
Two Gates. *Staf* 5G 73
Two Mile Oak. *Devn* 2E 9
Twycross. *Leics* 5H 73
Twyford. *Buck* 3E 51
Twyford. *Derbs* 3H 73
Twyford. *Dors* 1D 14
Twyford. *Hants* 4C 24
Twyford. *Leics* 4E 75
Twyford. *Norf* 3C 78
Twyford. *Wok* 4F 37
Twyford Common. *Here* 2A 48
Twyncarno. *Cphy* 5E 46
Twynholm. *Dum* 4D 110
Twyning. *Glos* 2D 49
Twyning Green. *Glos* 2E 49
Twynllanan. *Carm* 3A 46
Twyn-y-Sheriff. *Mon* 5H 47
Twywell. *Nptn* 3G 63
Tyberton. *Here* 2G 47
Tyburn. *W Mid* 1F 61
Tyby. *Norf* 3C 78
Tycroes. *Carm* 4G 45
Tycrwyn. *Powy* 4D 70
Tyddewi. *Pemb* 2B 42
Tydd Gote. *Linc* 4D 76
Tydd St Giles. *Cambs* 4D 76
Tydd St Mary. *Linc* 4D 76
Tye. *Hants* 2F 17
Tye Green. *Essx* 3F 53
(nr. Bishop's Stortford)
Tye Green. *Essx* 3A 54
(nr. Braintree)
Tye Green. *Essx* 2F 53
(nr. Saffron Walden)
Tyersal. *W Yor* 1B 92
Ty Issa. *Powy* 2D 70
Tyldesley. *G Man* 4E 91
Tyler Hill. *Kent* 4F 41
Tylers Green. *Buck* 2G 37
Tyler's Green. *Essx* 5F 53
Tylorstown. *Rhon* 2D 32
Tylwch. *Powy* 2B 58
Ty-nant. *Cnwy* 1B 70
Tyndrum. *Stir* 5H 141
Tyneham. *Dors* 4D 15
Tynehead. *Midl* 4G 129
Tynemouth. *Tyne* 3G 115
Tyneside. *Tyne* 3F 115
Tyne Tunnel. *Tyne* 3G 115
Tynewydd. *Rhon* 2C 32
Tyninghame. *E Lot* 2C 130
Tynron. *Dum* 5H 117
Ty'n-y-bryn. *Rhon* 3D 32
Tyn-y-celyn. *Wrex* 2D 70
Tyn-y-cwm. *Swan* 5G 45
Tyn-y-ffridd. *Powy* 2D 70
Tynygongl. *IOA* 2E 81
Tynygraig. *Cdgn* 4F 57
Ty'n-y-groes. *Cnwy* 3G 81
Ty'n-yr-eithin. *Cdgn* 4F 57
Tyn-y-rhyd. *Powy* 4C 70
Tyn-y-wern. *Powy* 3C 70
Tyrie. *Abers* 2G 161
Tyringham. *Mil* 1G 51
Tythecott. *Devn* 1E 11
Tythegston. *B'end* 4B 32
Tytherington. *Ches E* 3D 84
Tytherington. *Som* 2C 22
Tytherington. *S Glo* 3B 34
Tytherington. *Wilts* 2E 23
Tytherleigh. *Devn* 2G 13
Tywardreath. *Corn* 3E 7
Tywardreath Highway. *Corn* 3E 7
Tywyn. *Cnwy* 3G 81
Tywyn. *Gwyn* 5E 69

U

Uachdar. *W Isl* 3D 170
Uags. *High* 5G 155
Ubbeston Green. *Suff* 3F 67
Ubley. *Bath* 1A 22
Uckerby. *N Yor* 4F 105
Uckfield. *E Sus* 3F 27
Uckinghall. *Worc* 2D 48
Uckington. *Glos* 3E 49
Uckington. *Shrp* 5H 71
Uddingston. *S Lan* 3H 127
Uddington. *S Lan* 1A 118
Udimore. *E Sus* 4C 28
Udny Green. *Abers* 1F 153
Udny Station. *Abers* 1G 153
Udston. *S Lan* 4H 127
Udstonhead. *S Lan* 5A 128
Uffcott. *Wilts* 4G 35
Uffculme. *Devn* 1D 12
Uffington. *Linc* 5H 75
Uffington. *Oxon* 3B 36
Uffington. *Shrp* 4H 71
Ufford. *Pet* 5H 75
Ufford. *Suff* 5E 67
Ufton. *Warw* 4A 62
Ufton Nervet. *W Ber* 5E 37
Ugadale. *Arg* 3B 122
Ugborough. *Devn* 3C 8
Ugford. *Wilts* 3F 23
Uggeshall. *Suff* 2G 67
Ugglebarnby. *N Yor* 4F 107
Ugley. *Essx* 3F 53
Ugley Green. *Essx* 3F 53
Ugthorpe. *N Yor* 3E 107
Uidh. *W Isl* 9B 170
Uig. *Arg* 3C 138
Uig. *High* 2C 154
(nr. Balgown)
Uig. *High* 3A 154
(nr. Dunvegan)
Uigshader. *High* 4D 154
Uisken. *Arg* 2A 132
Ulbster. *High* 4F 169
Ulcat Row. *Cumb* 2F 103
Ulceby. *Linc* 3D 88
Ulceby. *N Lin* 3E 94
Ulceby Skitter. *N Lin* 3E 94
Ulcombe. *Kent* 1C 28
Uldale. *Cumb* 1D 102
Uley. *Glos* 2C 34
Ulgham. *Nmbd* 5G 121
Ullapool. *High* 4F 163
Ullenhall. *Warw* 4F 61
Ulleskelf. *N Yor* 1F 93
Ullesthorpe. *Leics* 2C 62
Ulley. *S Yor* 2B 86
Ullingswick. *Here* 5H 59
Ullinish. *High* 5C 154
Ullock. *Cumb* 2B 102
Ulpha. *Cumb* 5C 102
Ulrome. *E Yor* 4F 101
Ulsta. *Shet* 3F 173
Ulting. *Essx* 5B 54
Ulva House. *Arg* 5F 139
Ulverston. *Cumb* 2B 96
Ulwell. *Dors* 4F 15
Umberleigh. *Devn* 4G 19
Unapool. *High* 5C 166
Underbarrow. *Cumb* 5F 103
Undercliffe. *W Yor* 1B 92
Underdale. *Shrp* 4H 71
Underhoull. *Shet* 1G 173
Underriver. *Kent* 5G 39
Under Tofts. *S Yor* 2H 85
Underton. *Shrp* 1A 60
Underwood. *Newp* 3G 33
Underwood. *Notts* 5B 86
Underwood. *Plym* 3B 8
Undley. *Suff* 2F 65
Undy. *Mon* 3H 33
Union Mills. *IOM* 4C 108
Union Street. *E Sus* 2B 28
Unstone. *Derbs* 3A 86
Unstone Green. *Derbs* 3A 86
Unthank. *Cumb* 5E 113
(nr. Carlisle)
Unthank. *Cumb* 5H 113
(nr. Gamblesby)
Unthank. *Cumb* 1F 103
(nr. Penrith)
Unthank End. *Cumb* 1F 103
Upavon. *Wilts* 1G 23
Up Cerne. *Dors* 2B 14
Upchurch. *Kent* 4C 40
Upcott. *Devn* 2F 11
Upcott. *Here* 5F 59
Upend. *Cambs* 5F 65
Up Exe. *Devn* 2C 12
Upgate. *Norf* 4D 78
Upgate Street. *Norf* 1C 66
Uphall. *Dors* 2A 14
Uphall. *W Lot* 2D 128
Uphall Station. *W Lot* 2D 128
Upham. *Devn* 2B 12
Upham. *Hants* 4D 24
Uphampton. *Here* 4F 59
Uphampton. *Worc* 4C 60
Up Hatherley. *Glos* 3E 49
Uphill. *N Som* 1G 21
Up Holland. *Lanc* 4D 90
Uplawmoor. *E Ren* 4F 127
Upleadon. *Glos* 3C 48
Upleatham. *Red C* 3D 106
Uplees. *Kent* 4D 40
Uploders. *Dors* 3A 14
Uplowman. *Devn* 1D 12
Uplyme. *Devn* 3G 13
Up Marden. *W Sus* 1F 17
Upminster. *G Lon* 2G 39
Up Nately. *Hants* 1E 25
Upottery. *Devn* 2F 13
Uppat. *High* 3F 165
Upper Affcot. *Shrp* 2G 59
Upper Arley. *Worc* 2B 60
Upper Armley. *W Yor* 1C 92
Upper Arncott. *Oxon* 4E 50
Upper Astrop. *Nptn* 2D 50
Upper Badcall. *High* 4B 166
Upper Bangor. *Gwyn* 3E 81
Upper Basildon. *W Ber* 4D 36
Upper Batley. *W Yor* 2C 92
Upper Beeding. *W Sus* 4C 26
Upper Benefield. *Nptn* 2G 63
Upper Bentley. *Worc* 4D 61
Upper Bighouse. *High* 3A 168
Upper Boddam. *Abers* 5D 160
Upper Boddington. *Nptn* 5B 62
Upper Bogside. *Mor* 3G 159
Upper Booth. *Derbs* 2F 85
Upper Borth. *Cdgn* 2F 57
Upper Boyndlie. *Abers* 2G 161
Upper Brailes. *Warw* 1B 50
Upper Breinton. *Here* 1H 47
Upper Broadheath. *Worc* 5C 60
Upper Broughton. *Notts* 3D 74
Upper Brynamman. *Carm* 4H 45
Upper Bucklebury. *W Ber* 5D 36
Upper Bullington. *Hants* 2C 24
Upper Burgate. *Hants* 1G 15
Upper Caldecote. *C Beds* 1B 52
Upper Canterton. *Hants* 1A 16
Upper Catesby. *Nptn* 5C 62
Upper Chapel. *Powy* 1D 46
Upper Cheddon. *Som* 4F 21
Upper Chicksgrove. *Wilts* 4E 23
Upper Church Village. *Rhon* 3D 32
Upper Chute. *Wilts* 1A 24
Upper Clatford. *Hants* 2B 24
Upper Coberley. *Glos* 4E 49
Upper Coedcae. *Torf* 5F 47
Upper Common. *Hants* 2E 25
Upper Cound. *Shrp* 5H 71
Upper Cudworth. *S Yor* 4D 93
Upper Cumberworth. *W Yor* 4C 92
Upper Cuttlehill. *Abers* 4B 160
Upper Cwmbran. *Torf* 2F 33
Upper Dallachy. *Mor* 2A 160
Upper Dean. *Bed* 4H 63
Upper Denby. *W Yor* 4C 92
Upper Derraid. *High* 5E 159
Upper Diabaig. *High* 2H 155
Upper Dicker. *E Sus* 5G 27
Upper Dinchope. *Shrp* 2G 59
Upper Dochcarty. *High* 2H 157
Upper Dounreay. *High* 2B 168
Upper Dovercourt. *Essx* 2F 55
Upper Dunsforth. *N Yor* 3G 99
Upper Dunsley. *Herts* 4H 51
Upper Eastern Green. *W Mid* 2G 61
Upper Elkstone. *Staf* 5E 85
Upper Ellastone. *Staf* 1F 73
Upper End. *Derbs* 3E 85
Upper Enham. *Hants* 2B 24
Upper Farmcote. *Shrp* 1B 60
Upper Farringdon. *Hants* 3F 25
Upper Framilode. *Glos* 4C 48
Upper Froyle. *Hants* 2F 25
Upper Gills. *High* 1F 169
Upper Glenfintaig. *High* 5E 149
Upper Godney. *Som* 2H 21
Upper Gravenhurst. *C Beds* 2B 52
Upper Green. *Essx* 2E 53

Upper Green—Walnut Grove

Upper Green. *W Ber* 5B **36**
Upper Green. *W Yor* 2C **92**
Upper Grove Common. *Here* 3A **48**
Upper Hackney. *Derbs* 4G **85**
Upper Hale. *Surr* 2G **25**
Upper Halliford. *Surr* 4B **38**
Upper Halling. *Medw* 4A **40**
Upper Hambleton. *Rut* 5G **75**
Upper Hardres Court. *Kent* 5F **41**
Upper Hardwick. *Here* 5G **59**
Upper Hartfield. *E Sus* 2F **27**
Upper Haugh. *S Yor* 1B **86**
Upper Hayton. *Shrp* 2H **59**
Upper Heath. *Shrp* 2H **59**
Upper Hellesdon. *Norf* 4E **78**
Upper Helmsley. *N Yor* 4A **100**
Upper Hengoed. *Shrp* 2E **71**
Upper Hergest. *Here* 5E **59**
Upper Heyford. *Nptn* 5D **62**
Upper Heyford. *Oxon* 3C **50**
Upper Hill. *Here* 5G **59**
Upper Hindhope. *Bord* 4B **120**
Upper Hopton. *W Yor* 3B **92**
Upper Howsell. *Worc* 1C **48**
Upper Hulme. *Staf* 4E **85**
Upper Inglesham. *Swin* 2H **35**
Upper Kilcott. *Glos* 3C **34**
Upper Killay. *Swan* 3E **31**
Upper Kirkton. *Abers* 5E **161**
Upper Kirkton. *N Ayr* 4C **126**
Upper Knockando. *Mor* 4F **159**
Upper Knockchoilum. *High* 2G **149**
Upper Lambourn. *W Ber* 3B **36**
Upper Langford. *N Som* 1H **21**
Upper Langwith. *Derbs* 4C **86**
Upper Largo. *Fife* 3G **137**
Upper Latheron. *High* 5D **169**
Upper Layham. *Suff* 1D **54**
Upper Leigh. *Staf* 2E **73**
Upper Lenie. *High* 1H **149**
Upper Lochton. *Abers* 4D **152**
Upper Longdon. *Staf* 4E **73**
Upper Longwood. *Shrp* 5A **72**
Upper Lybster. *High* 5E **169**
Upper Lydbrook. *Glos* 4B **48**
Upper Lye. *Here* 4F **59**
Upper Maes-coed. *Here* 2G **47**
Upper Midway. *Derbs* 3G **73**
Uppermill. *G Man* 4H **91**
Upper Millichope. *Shrp* 2H **59**
Upper Milovaig. *High* 4A **154**
Upper Minety. *Wilts* 2F **35**
Upper Mitton. *Worc* 3C **60**
Upper Nash. *Pemb* 4E **43**
Upper Neepaback. *Shet* 3G **173**
Upper Netchwood. *Shrp* 1A **60**
Upper Nobut. *Staf* 2E **73**
Upper North Dean. *Buck* 2G **37**
Upper Norwood. *W Sus* 4A **26**
Upper Nyland. *Dors* 4C **22**
Upper Oddington. *Glos* 3H **49**
Upper Ollach. *High* 5E **155**
Upper Outwoods. *Staf* 3G **73**
Upper Padley. *Derbs* 3G **85**
Upper Pennington. *Hants* 3B **16**
Upper Poppleton. *York* 4H **99**
Upper Quinton. *Warw* 1G **49**
Upper Rissington. *Glos* 4H **49**
Upper Rochford. *Worc* 4A **60**
Upper Rusko. *Dum* 3C **110**
Upper Sandaig. *High* 2F **147**
Upper Sanday. *Orkn* 7E **172**
Upper Sapey. *Here* 4A **60**
Upper Seagry. *Wilts* 3E **35**
Upper Shelton. *C Beds* 1H **51**
Upper Sheringham. *Norf* 1D **78**
Upper Skelmorlie. *N Ayr* 3C **126**
Upper Slaughter. *Glos* 3G **49**
Upper Sonachan. *Arg* 1H **133**
Upper Soudley. *Glos* 4B **48**
Upper Staploe. *Bed* 5A **64**
Upper Stoke. *Norf* 5E **79**
Upper Stondon. *C Beds* 2B **52**
Upper Stowe. *Nptn* 5D **62**
Upper Street. *Hants* 1G **15**
Upper Street. *Norf* 4F **79** (nr. Horning)
Upper Street. *Norf* 4F **79** (nr. Hoveton)
Upper Street. *Suff* 2E **55**
Upper Strensham. *Worc* 2E **49**
Upper Studley. *Wilts* 1D **22**
Upper Sundon. *C Beds* 3A **52**
Upper Swell. *Glos* 3G **49**
Upper Tankersley. *S Yor* 1H **85**
Upper Tean. *Staf* 2E **73**
Upperthong. *W Yor* 4B **92**
Upperthorpe. *N Lin* 4A **94**
Upper Thurnham. *Lanc* 4D **96**
Upper Tillyrie. *Per* 3D **136**
Upperton. *W Sus* 3A **26**
Upper Tooting. *G Lon* 3D **39**
Uppertown. *Derbs* 4H **85** (nr. Ashover)
Upper Town. *Derbs* 5G **85** (nr. Bonsall)
Upper Town. *Derbs* 5G **85** (nr. Hognaston)
Upper Town. *Here* 1A **48**
Uppertown. *High* 1F **169**
Upper Town. *N Som* 5A **34**
Uppertown. *Nmbd* 2B **114**
Uppertown. *Orkn* 8D **172**
Upper Tysoe. *Warw* 1B **50**
Upper Upham. *Wilts* 4H **35**
Upper Upnor. *Medw* 3B **40**
Upper Urquhart. *Fife* 3D **136**
Upper Wardington. *Oxon* 1C **50**
Upper Weald. *Mil* 2F **51**
Upper Weedon. *Nptn* 5D **62**
Upper Wellingham. *E Sus* 4F **27**
Upper Whiston. *S Yor* 2B **86**
Upper Wield. *Hants* 3E **25**
Upper Winchendon. *Buck* 4F **51**
Upperwood. *Derbs* 5G **85**
Upper Woodford. *Wilts* 3G **23**
Upper Wootton. *Hants* 1D **24**
Upper Wraxall. *Wilts* 4D **34**
Upper Wyche. *Here* 1C **48**
Uppincott. *Devn* 2B **12**
Uppingham. *Rut* 1F **63**
Uppington. *Shrp* 5A **72**
Upsall. *N Yor* 1G **99**
Upsettlington. *Bord* 5E **131**
Upshire. *Essx* 5E **53**
Up Somborne. *Hants* 3B **24**
Upstreet. *Kent* 4G **41**
Up Sydling. *Dors* 2B **14**
Upthorpe. *Suff* 3B **66**
Upton. *Buck* 4F **51**
Upton. *Cambs* 3A **64**
Upton. *Ches W* 4G **83**
Upton. *Corn* 2C **10** (nr. Bude)
Upton. *Corn* 5C **10** (nr. Liskeard)
Upton. *Cumb* 1E **102**
Upton. *Devn* 2D **12** (nr. Honiton)
Upton. *Devn* 4D **8** (nr. Kingsbridge)
Upton. *Dors* 3E **15** (nr. Poole)
Upton. *Dors* 4C **14** (nr. Weymouth)
Upton. *E Yor* 4F **101**
Upton. *Hants* 1B **24** (nr. Andover)
Upton. *Hants* 1B **16** (nr. Southampton)
Upton. *IOW* 3D **16**
Upton. *Leics* 1A **62**
Upton. *Linc* 2F **87**
Upton. *Mers* 2E **83**
Upton. *Norf* 4F **79**
Upton. *Nptn* 4E **62**
Upton. *Notts* 3E **87** (nr. Retford)
Upton. *Notts* 5E **87** (nr. Southwell)
Upton. *Oxon* 3D **36**
Upton. *Pemb* 4E **43**
Upton. *Pet* 5A **76**
Upton. *Slo* 3A **38**
Upton. *Som* 4H **21** (nr. Somerton)
Upton. *Som* 4C **20** (nr. Wiveliscombe)
Upton. *Warw* 5F **61**
Upton. *W Yor* 3E **93**
Upton. *Wilts* 3D **22**
Upton Bishop. *Here* 3B **48**
Upton Cheyney. *S Glo* 5B **34**
Upton Cressett. *Shrp* 1A **60**
Upton Crews. *Here* 3B **48**
Upton Cross. *Corn* 5C **10**
Upton End. *C Beds* 2B **52**
Upton Grey. *Hants* 2E **25**
Upton Heath. *Ches W* 4G **83**
Upton Hellions. *Devn* 2B **12**
Upton Lovell. *Wilts* 2E **23**
Upton Magna. *Shrp* 4H **71**
Upton Noble. *Som* 3C **22**
Upton Pyne. *Devn* 3C **12**
Upton St Leonards. *Glos* 4D **48**
Upton Scudamore. *Wilts* 2D **22**
Upton Snodsbury. *Worc* 5D **60**
Upton upon Severn. *Worc* 1D **48**
Upton Warren. *Worc* 4D **60**
Upwaltham. *W Sus* 4A **26**
Upware. *Cambs* 3E **65**
Upwell. *Norf* 5E **77**
Upwey. *Dors* 4B **14**
Upwick Green. *Herts* 3E **53**
Upwood. *Cambs* 2B **64**
Urafirth. *Shet* 4E **173**
Uragaig. *Arg* 4A **132**
Urchany. *High* 4C **158**
Urchfont. *Wilts* 1F **23**
Urdimarsh. *Here* 1A **48**
Ure. *Shet* 4D **173**
Ure Bank. *N Yor* 2F **99**
Urgha. *W Isl* 8D **171**
Urlay Nook. *Stoc T* 3B **106**
Urmston. *G Man* 1B **84**
Urquhart. *Mor* 2G **159**
Urra. *N Yor* 4C **106**
Urray. *High* 3H **157**
Usan. *Ang* 3G **145**
Ushaw Moor. *Dur* 5F **115**
Usk. *Mon* 5G **47**
Usselby. *Linc* 1H **87**
Usworth. *Tyne* 4G **115**
Utkinton. *Ches W* 4H **83**
Uton. *Devn* 3B **12**
Utterby. *Linc* 1C **88**
Uttoxeter. *Staf* 2E **73**
Uwchmynydd. *Gwyn* 3A **68**
Uxbridge. *G Lon* 2B **38**
Uyeasound. *Shet* 1G **173**
Uzmaston. *Pemb* 3D **42**

V

Valley. *IOA* 3B **80**
Valley End. *Surr* 4A **38**
Valley Truckle. *Corn* 4B **10**
Valsgarth. *Shet* 1H **173**
Valtos. *High* 2E **155**
Van. *Powy* 2B **58**
Vange. *Essx* 2B **40**
Varteg. *Torf* 5F **47**
Vatsetter. *Shet* 3G **173**
Vatten. *High* 4B **154**
Vaul. *Arg* 4B **138**
Vauld, The. *Here* 1A **48**
Vaynol. *Gwyn* 3E **81**
Vaynor. *Mer T* 4D **46**
Veensgarth. *Shet* 7F **173**
Velindre. *Powy* 2E **47**
Vellow. *Som* 3D **20**
Velly. *Devn* 4C **18**
Veness. *Orkn* 5E **172**
Venhay. *Devn* 1A **12**
Venn. *Devn* 4D **8**
Venngreen. *Devn* 1D **11**
Vennington. *Shrp* 5F **71**
Venn Ottery. *Devn* 3D **12**
Venn's Green. *Here* 1A **48**
Venny Tedburn. *Devn* 3B **12**
Venterdon. *Corn* 5D **10**
Ventnor. *IOW* 5D **16**
Vernham Dean. *Hants* 1B **24**
Vernham Street. *Hants* 1B **24**
Vernolds Common. *Shrp* 2G **59**
Verwood. *Dors* 2F **15**
Veryan. *Corn* 5D **6**
Veryan Green. *Corn* 5D **6**
Vicarage. *Devn* 4F **13**
Vickerstown. *Cumb* 3A **96**
Victoria. *Corn* 2D **6**
Vidlin. *Shet* 5F **173**
Viewpark. *N Lan* 3A **128**
Vigo. *W Mid* 5E **73**
Vigo Village. *Kent* 4H **39**
Vinehall Street. *E Sus* 3B **28**
Vine's Cross. *E Sus* 4G **27**
Viney Hill. *Glos* 5B **48**
Virginia Water. *Surr* 4A **38**
Virginstow. *Devn* 3D **11**
Vobster. *Som* 2C **22**
Voe. *Shet* 5F **173** (nr. Hillside)
Voe. *Shet* 3E **173** (nr. Swinister)
Vole. *Som* 2G **21**
Vowchurch. *Here* 2G **47**
Voxter. *Shet* 4E **173**
Voy. *Orkn* 6B **172**
Vulcan Village. *Mers* 1H **83**

W

Waberthwaite. *Cumb* 5C **102**
Wackerfield. *Dur* 2E **105**
Wacton. *Norf* 1D **66**
Wadbister. *Shet* 7F **173**
Wadborough. *Worc* 1E **49**
Wadbrook. *Devn* 2G **13**
Waddesdon. *Buck* 4F **51**
Waddeton. *Devn* 3E **9**
Waddicar. *Mers* 1F **83**
Waddingham. *Linc* 1G **87**
Waddington. *Lanc* 5G **97**
Waddington. *Linc* 4G **87**
Waddon. *Devn* 5B **12**
Wadebridge. *Corn* 1D **6**
Wadeford. *Som* 1G **13**
Wadenhoe. *Nptn* 2H **63**
Wadesmill. *Herts* 4D **52**
Wadhurst. *E Sus* 2H **27**
Wadshelf. *Derbs* 3H **85**
Wadsley. *S Yor* 1H **85**
Wadsley Bridge. *S Yor* 1H **85**
Wadswick. *Wilts* 5D **34**
Wadwick. *Hants* 1C **24**
Wadworth. *S Yor* 1C **86**
Waen. *Den* 4D **82** (nr. Llandymog)
Waen. *Den* 4B **82** (nr. Nantglyn)
Waen. *Powy* 1B **58**
Waen Fach. *Powy* 4E **70**
Waen Goleugoed. *Den* 3C **82**
Wag. *High* 1H **165**
Wainfleet All Saints. *Linc* 5D **89**
Wainfleet Bank. *Linc* 5D **88**
Wainfleet St Mary. *Linc* 5D **89**
Wainhouse Corner. *Corn* 3B **10**
Wainscott. *Medw* 3B **40**
Wainstalls. *W Yor* 2A **92**
Waitby. *Cumb* 4A **104**
Waithe. *Linc* 4F **95**
Wakefield. *W Yor* 2D **92**
Wakerley. *Nptn* 1G **63**
Wakes Colne. *Essx* 3B **54**
Walberswick. *Suff* 3G **67**
Walberton. *W Sus* 5A **26**
Walbottle. *Tyne* 3E **115**
Walby. *Cumb* 3F **113**
Walcombe. *Som* 2A **22**
Walcot. *Linc* 2H **75**
Walcot. *N Lin* 2B **94**
Walcot. *Swin* 3G **35**
Walcot. *Telf* 4H **71**
Walcot. *Warw* 5F **61**
Walcote. *Leics* 2C **62**
Walcot Green. *Norf* 2D **66**
Walcott. *Linc* 5A **88**
Walcott. *Norf* 2F **79**
Walden. *N Yor* 1C **98**
Walden Head. *N Yor* 1B **98**
Walden Stubbs. *N Yor* 3F **93**
Walderslade. *Medw* 4B **40**
Walderton. *W Sus* 1F **17**
Walditch. *Dors* 3H **13**
Waldley. *Derbs* 2F **73**
Waldridge. *Dur* 4F **115**
Waldringfield. *Suff* 1F **55**
Waldron. *E Sus* 4G **27**
Wales. *S Yor* 2B **86**
Walesby. *Linc* 1A **88**
Walesby. *Notts* 3D **86**
Walford. *Here* 3F **59** (nr. Leintwardine)
Walford. *Here* 3A **48** (nr. Ross-on-Wye)
Walford. *Shrp* 3G **71**
Walford. *Staf* 2C **72**
Walford Heath. *Shrp* 4G **71**
Walgherton. *Ches E* 1A **72**
Walgrave. *Nptn* 3F **63**
Walhampton. *Hants* 3B **16**
Walkden. *G Man* 4F **91**
Walker. *Tyne* 3F **115**
Walkerburn. *Bord* 1F **119**
Walker Fold. *Lanc* 5F **97**
Walkeringham. *Notts* 1E **87**
Walkerith. *Linc* 1E **87**
Walkern. *Herts* 3C **52**
Walker's Green. *Here* 1A **48**
Walkerton. *Fife* 3E **137**
Walkerville. *N Yor* 5F **105**
Walkford. *Dors* 3H **15**
Walkhampton. *Devn* 2B **8**
Walkington. *E Yor* 1C **94**
Walkley. *S Yor* 2H **85**
Walk Mill. *Lanc* 1G **91**
Wall. *Corn* 3D **4**
Wall. *Nmbd* 3C **114**
Wall. *Staf* 5F **73**
Wallaceton. *Dum* 1F **111**
Wallacetown. *Shet* 6E **173**
Wallacetown. *S Ayr* 2C **116** (nr. Ayr)
Wallacetown. *S Ayr* 4B **116** (nr. Dailly)
Wallands Park. *E Sus* 4F **27**
Wallasey. *Mers* 1E **83**
Wallaston Green. *Pemb* 4D **42**
Wallbrook. *W Mid* 1D **60**
Wallcrouch. *E Sus* 2A **28**
Wall End. *Cumb* 1B **96**
Wallend. *Medw* 3C **40**
Wall Heath. *W Mid* 2C **60**
Wallingford. *Oxon* 3E **36**
Wallington. *G Lon* 4D **39**
Wallington. *Hants* 2D **16**
Wallington. *Herts* 2C **52**
Wallis. *Pemb* 2E **43**
Wallisdown. *Pool* 3F **15**
Walliswood. *Surr* 2C **26**
Wall Nook. *Dur* 5F **115**
Walls. *Shet* 7D **173**
Wallsend. *Tyne* 3G **115**
Wallsworth. *Glos* 3D **48**
Wall under Heywood. *Shrp* 1H **59**
Wallyford. *E Lot* 2G **129**
Walmer. *Kent* 5H **41**
Walmer Bridge. *Lanc* 2C **90**
Walmersley. *G Man* 3G **91**
Walmley. *W Mid* 1F **61**
Walnut Grove. *Per* 1D **136**

Walpole. Suff ... 3F 67
Walpole Cross Keys. Norf ... 4E 77
Walpole Gate. Norf ... 4E 77
Walpole Highway. Norf ... 4E 77
Walpole Marsh. Norf ... 4D 77
Walpole St Andrew. Norf ... 4E 77
Walpole St Peter. Norf ... 4E 77
Walsall. *W Mid* ... 1E 61
Walsall Wood. W Mid ... 5E 73
Walsden. W Yor ... 2H 91
Walsgrave on Sowe. W Mid ... 2A 62
Walsham le Willows. Suff ... 3C 66
Walshaw. G Man ... 3F 91
Walshford. N Yor ... 4G 99
Walsoken. Cambs ... 4D 76
Walston. S Lan ... 5D 128
Walsworth. Herts ... 2B 52
Walter's Ash. Buck ... 2G 37
Walterston. V Glam ... 4D 32
Walterstone. Here ... 3G 47
Waltham. Kent ... 1F 29
Waltham. NE Lin ... 4F 95
Waltham Abbey. *Essx* ... 5D 53
Waltham Chase. Hants ... 1D 16
Waltham Cross. Herts ... 5D 52
Waltham on the Wolds. Leics ... 3F 75
Waltham St Lawrence. Wind ... 4G 37
Waltham's Cross. Essx ... 2G 53
Walthamstow. *G Lon* ... 2E 39
Walton. Cumb ... 3G 113
Walton. Derbs ... 4A 86
Walton. Leics ... 2C 62
Walton. Mers ... 1F 83
Walton. Mil ... 2G 51
Walton. Pet ... 5A 76
Walton. Powy ... 5E 59
Walton. Som ... 3H 21
Walton. Staf ... 3C 72
(nr. Eccleshall)
Walton. Staf ... 2C 72
(nr. Stone)
Walton. Suff ... 2F 55
Walton. Telf ... 4H 71
Walton. Warw ... 5G 61
Walton. W Yor ... 3D 92
(nr. Wakefield)
Walton. W Yor ... 5G 99
(nr. Wetherby)
Walton Cardiff. Glos ... 2E 49
Walton East. Pemb ... 2E 43
Walton Elm. Dors ... 1C 14
Walton Highway. Norf ... 4D 77
Walton-in-Gordano. N Som ... 4H 33
Walton-le-Dale. Lanc ... 2D 90
Walton-on-Thames. *Surr* ... 4C 38
Walton-on-the-Hill. Staf ... 3D 72
Walton on the Hill. Surr ... 5D 38
Walton-on-the-Naze. *Essx* ... 3F 55
Walton on the Wolds. Leics ... 4C 74
Walton-on-Trent. Derbs ... 4G 73
Walton West. Pemb ... 3C 42
Walwick. Nmbd ... 2C 114
Walworth. Darl ... 3F 105
Walworth Gate. Darl ... 2F 105
Walwyn's Castle. Pemb ... 3C 42
Wambrook. Som ... 2F 13
Wampool. Cumb ... 4D 112
Wanborough. Surr ... 1A 26
Wanborough. Swin ... 3H 35
Wandel. S Lan ... 2B 118
Wandsworth. *G Lon* ... 3D 38
Wangford. Suff ... 2G 65
(nr. Lakenheath)
Wangford. Suff ... 2H 67
(nr. Southwold)
Wanlip. Leics ... 4C 74
Wanlockhead. Dum ... 3A 118
Wannock. E Sus ... 5G 27
Wansford. E Yor ... 4E 101
Wansford. Pet ... 1H 63
Wanshurst Green. Kent ... 1B 28
Wanstead. *G Lon* ... 2F 39
Wanstrow. Som ... 2C 22
Wanswell. Glos ... 5B 48
Wantage. Oxon ... 3C 36

Wapley. S Glo ... 4C 34
Wappenbury. Warw ... 4A 62
Wappenham. Nptn ... 1E 51
Warbleton. E Sus ... 4H 27
Warblington. Hants ... 2F 17
Warborough. Oxon ... 2D 36
Warboys. Cambs ... 2C 64
Warbreck. Bkpl ... 1B 90
Warburton. G Man ... 2B 84
Warcop. Cumb ... 3A 104
Warden. Kent ... 3E 40
Warden. Nmbd ... 3C 114
Ward End. W Mid ... 2F 61
Ward Green. Suff ... 4C 66
Ward Green Cross. Lanc ... 1E 91
Wardhedges. C Beds ... 2A 52
Wardhouse. Abers ... 5C 160
Wardington. Oxon ... 1C 50
Wardle. Ches E ... 5A 84
Wardle. G Man ... 3H 91
Wardley. Rut ... 5F 75
Wardley. W Sus ... 4G 25
Wardlow. Derbs ... 3F 85
Wardsend. Ches E ... 2D 84
Wardy Hill. Cambs ... 2D 64
Ware. *Herts* ... 4D 52
Ware. Kent ... 4G 41
Wareham. Dors ... 4E 15
Warehorne. Kent ... 2D 28
Warenford. Nmbd ... 2F 121
Waren Mill. Nmbd ... 1F 121
Warenton. Nmbd ... 1F 121
Wareside. Herts ... 4D 53
Waresley. Cambs ... 5B 64
Waresley. Worc ... 4C 60
Warfield. Brac ... 4G 37
Warfleet. Devn ... 3E 9
Wargate. Linc ... 2B 76
Wargrave. Wok ... 4F 37
Warham. Norf ... 1B 78
Waringstown. Arm ... 5G 175
Wark. Nmbd ... 1C 120
(nr. Coldstream)
Wark. Nmbd ... 2B 114
(nr. Hexham)
Warkleigh. Devn ... 4G 19
Warkton. Nptn ... 3F 63
Warkworth. Nptn ... 1C 50
Warkworth. Nmbd ... 4G 121
Warlaby. N Yor ... 5A 106
Warland. W Yor ... 2H 91
Warleggan. Corn ... 2F 7
Warlingham. *Surr* ... 5E 39
Warmanbie. Dum ... 3C 112
Warmfield. W Yor ... 2D 93
Warmingham. Ches E ... 4B 84
Warminghurst. W Sus ... 4C 26
Warmington. Nptn ... 1H 63
Warmington. Warw ... 1C 50
Warminster. *Wilts* ... 2D 23
Warmley. S Glo ... 4B 34
Warmsworth. S Yor ... 4F 93
Warmwell. Dors ... 4C 14
Warndon. Worc ... 5C 60
Warners End. Herts ... 5A 52
Warnford. Hants ... 4E 24
Warnham. W Sus ... 2C 26
Warningcamp. W Sus ... 5B 26
Warninglid. W Sus ... 3D 26
Warren. Ches E ... 3C 84
Warren. Pemb ... 5D 42
Warrenby. Red C ... 2C 106
Warren Corner. Hants ... 2G 25
(nr. Aldershot)
Warren Corner. Hants ... 4G 25
(nr. Petersfield)
Warrenpoint. New M ... 6G 175
Warren Row. Wind ... 3G 37
Warren Street. Kent ... 5D 40
Warrington. Mil ... 5F 63
Warrington. *Warr* ... 2A 84
Warsash. Hants ... 2C 16
Warse. High ... 1F 169
Warslow. Staf ... 5E 85

Warsop. *Notts* ... 4C 86
Warsop Vale. Notts ... 4C 86
Warter. E Yor ... 4C 100
Warthermarske. N Yor ... 2E 98
Warthill. N Yor ... 4A 100
Wartling. E Sus ... 5A 28
Wartnaby. Leics ... 3E 74
Warton. Lanc ... 2C 90
(nr. Carnforth)
Warton. Lanc ... 2C 90
(nr. Freckleton)
Warton. Nmbd ... 4E 121
Warton. Warw ... 5G 73
Warwick. *Warw* ... 4G 61
Warwick Bridge. Cumb ... 4F 113
Warwick-on-Eden. Cumb ... 4F 113
Warwick Wold. Surr ... 5E 39
Wasbister. Orkn ... 4C 172
Wasdale Head. Cumb ... 4C 102
Wash. Derbs ... 2E 85
Washaway. Corn ... 2E 7
Washbourne. Devn ... 3D 9
Washbrook. Suff ... 1E 54
Wash Common. W Ber ... 5C 36
Washerwall. Staf ... 1D 72
Washfield. Devn ... 1C 12
Washford. N Yor ... 4D 104
Washford. Som ... 2D 20
Washford Pyne. Devn ... 1B 12
Washingborough. Linc ... 3H 87
Washington. *Tyne* ... 4G 115
Washington. W Sus ... 4C 26
Washington Village. Tyne ... 4G 115
Waskerley. Dur ... 5D 114
Wasperton. Warw ... 5G 61
Wasp Green. Surr ... 1E 27
Wasps Nest. Linc ... 4H 87
Wass. N Yor ... 2H 99
Watchet. Som ... 2D 20
Watchfield. Oxon ... 2H 35
Watchgate. Cumb ... 5G 103
Watchhill. Cumb ... 5C 112
Watcombe. Torb ... 2F 9
Watendlath. Cumb ... 3D 102
Water. Devn ... 4A 12
Water. Lanc ... 2G 91
Waterbeach. Cambs ... 4D 65
Waterbeach. W Sus ... 2G 17
Waterbeck. Dum ... 2D 112
Waterditch. Hants ... 3G 15
Water End. C Beds ... 2A 52
Water End. E Yor ... 1A 94
Water End. Essx ... 1F 53
Water End. Herts ... 5C 52
(nr. Hatfield)
Water End. Herts ... 4A 52
(nr. Hemel Hempstead)
Waterfall. Staf ... 5E 85
Waterfoot. E Ren ... 4G 127
Waterfoot. Lanc ... 2G 91
Waterford. Herts ... 4D 52
Water Fryston. W Yor ... 2E 93
Waterhead. Cumb ... 4E 103
Waterhead. E Ayr ... 3E 117
Waterhead. S Ayr ... 5C 116
Waterheads. Bord ... 4F 129
Waterhouses. Dur ... 5E 115
Waterhouses. Staf ... 5E 85
Wateringbury. Kent ... 5A 40
Waterlane. Glos ... 5E 49
Waterlip. Som ... 2B 22
Waterloo. Cphy ... 3E 33
Waterloo. Corn ... 5B 10
Waterloo. Here ... 1G 47
Waterloo. High ... 1E 147
Waterloo. Mers ... 1F 83
Waterloo. N Lan ... 4B 128
Waterloo. Pemb ... 4D 42
Waterloo. Per ... 5H 143
Waterloo. Pool ... 3F 15
Waterloo. Shrp ... 2G 71
Waterlooville. *Hants* ... 2E 17
Watermead. Buck ... 4G 51
Watermillock. Cumb ... 2F 103

Water Newton. Cambs ... 1A 64
Water Orton. Warw ... 1F 61
Waterperry. Oxon ... 5E 51
Waterrow. Som ... 4D 20
Watersfield. W Sus ... 4B 26
Waterside. Buck ... 5H 51
Waterside. Cambs ... 3F 65
Waterside. Cumb ... 5D 112
Waterside. E Ayr ... 4D 116
(nr. Ayr)
Waterside. E Ayr ... 5F 127
(nr. Kilmarnock)
Waterside. E Dun ... 2H 127
Waterstein. High ... 4A 154
Waterstock. Oxon ... 5E 51
Waterston. Pemb ... 4D 42
Water Stratford. Buck ... 2E 51
Waters Upton. Telf ... 4A 72
Water Yeat. Cumb ... 1B 96
Watford. *Herts* ... 1C 38
Watford. Nptn ... 4D 62
Wath. Cumb ... 4H 103
Wath. N Yor ... 3D 98
(nr. Pateley Bridge)
Wath. N Yor ... 2F 99
(nr. Ripon)
Wath Brow. Cumb ... 3B 102
Wath upon Dearne. *S Yor* ... 4E 93
Watlington. Norf ... 4F 77
Watlington. Oxon ... 2E 37
Watten. High ... 3E 169
Wattisfield. Suff ... 3C 66
Wattisham. Suff ... 5C 66
Wattlesborough Heath. Shrp ... 4F 71
Watton. Dors ... 3H 13
Watton. E Yor ... 4E 101
Watton. Norf ... 5B 78
Watton at Stone. Herts ... 4C 52
Wattston. N Lan ... 2A 128
Wattstown. Rhon ... 2D 32
Wattsville. Cphy ... 2F 33
Wauldby. E Yor ... 2C 94
Waulkmill. Abers ... 4D 152
Waun. Powy ... 4E 71
Waunarlwydd. Swan ... 3F 31
Waun Fawr. Cdgn ... 2F 57
Waunfawr. Gwyn ... 5E 81
Waungilwen. Carm ... 1H 43
Waunlwyd. Blae ... 5E 47
Waun-y-Clyn. Carm ... 5E 45
Wavendon. Mil ... 2H 51
Waverbridge. Cumb ... 5D 112
Waverley. Surr ... 2G 25
Waverton. Ches W ... 4G 83
Waverton. Cumb ... 5D 112
Wavertree. Mers ... 2F 83
Wawne. E Yor ... 1D 94
Waxham. Norf ... 3G 79
Waxholme. E Yor ... 2G 95
Wayford. Som ... 2H 13
Way Head. Cambs ... 2D 65
Waytown. Dors ... 3H 13
Way Village. Devn ... 1B 12
Wdig. Pemb ... 1D 42
Wealdstone. G Lon ... 2C 38
Weardley. W Yor ... 5E 99
Weare. Som ... 1H 21
Weare Giffard. Devn ... 4E 19
Wearhead. Dur ... 1B 104
Wearne. Som ... 4H 21
Weasdale. Cumb ... 4H 103
Weasenham All Saints. Norf ... 3H 77
Weasenham St Peter. Norf ... 3A 78
Weaverham. Ches W ... 3A 84
Weaverthorpe. N Yor ... 2D 100
Webheath. Worc ... 4E 61
Webton. Here ... 2H 47
Wedderlairs. Abers ... 5F 161
Weddington. Warw ... 1A 62
Wedhampton. Wilts ... 1F 23
Wedmore. Som ... 2H 21
Wednesbury. W Mid ... 1D 61
Wednesfield. W Mid ... 5D 72
Weecar. Notts ... 4F 87
Weedon. Buck ... 4G 51

Weedon Bec. Nptn ... 5D 62
Weedon Lois. Nptn ... 1E 50
Weeford. Staf ... 5F 73
Week. Devn ... 4F 19
(nr. Barnstaple)
Week. Devn ... 2G 11
(nr. Okehampton)
Week. Devn ... 1H 11
(nr. South Molton)
Week. Devn ... 2D 9
(nr. Totnes)
Week. Som ... 3C 20
Weeke. Devn ... 2A 12
Weeke. Hants ... 3C 24
Week Green. Corn ... 3C 10
Weekley. Nptn ... 2F 63
Week St Mary. Corn ... 3C 10
Weel. E Yor ... 1D 94
Weeley. Essx ... 3E 55
Weeley Heath. Essx ... 3E 55
Weem. Per ... 4F 143
Weeping Cross. Staf ... 3D 72
Weethly. Warw ... 5E 61
Weeting. Norf ... 2G 65
Weeton. E Yor ... 2G 95
Weeton. Lanc ... 1B 90
Weeton. N Yor ... 5E 99
Weetwood Hall. Nmbd ... 2E 121
Weir. Lanc ... 2G 91
Welborne. Norf ... 4C 78
Welbourn. Linc ... 5G 87
Welburn. N Yor ... 1A 100
(nr. Kirkbymoorside)
Welburn. N Yor ... 3B 100
(nr. Malton)
Welbury. N Yor ... 4A 106
Welby. Linc ... 2G 75
Welches Dam. Cambs ... 2D 64
Welcombe. Devn ... 1C 10
Weld Bank. Lanc ... 3D 90
Weldon. Nptn ... 2G 63
Weldon. Nmbd ... 5F 121
Welford. Nptn ... 2D 62
Welford. W Ber ... 4C 36
Welford-on-Avon. Warw ... 5F 61
Welham. Leics ... 1E 63
Welham. Notts ... 2E 87
Welham Green. Herts ... 5C 52
Well. Hants ... 2F 25
Well. Linc ... 3D 88
Well. N Yor ... 1E 99
Welland. Worc ... 1C 48
Wellbank. Ang ... 5D 144
Well Bottom. Dors ... 1E 15
Welldale. Dum ... 3C 112
Wellesbourne. Warw ... 5G 61
Well Hill. Kent ... 4F 39
Wellhouse. W Ber ... 4D 36
Welling. G Lon ... 3F 39
Wellingborough. *Nptn* ... 4F 63
Wellingham. Norf ... 3A 78
Wellingore. Linc ... 5G 87
Wellington. Cumb ... 4B 102
Wellington. Here ... 1H 47
Wellington. *Som* ... 4E 21
Wellington. Telf ... 4A 72
Wellington Heath. Here ... 1C 48
Wellow. Bath ... 1C 22
Wellow. IOW ... 4B 16
Wellow. Notts ... 4D 86
Wellpond Green. Herts ... 3E 53
Wells. *Som* ... 2A 22
Wellsborough. Leics ... 5A 74
Wells Green. Ches E ... 5A 84
Wells-next-the-Sea. Norf ... 1B 78
Wellswood. Torb ... 2F 9
Wellwood. Fife ... 1D 129
Welney. Norf ... 1E 65
Welsford. Devn ... 4C 18
Welshampton. Shrp ... 2G 71
Welsh End. Shrp ... 2H 71
Welsh Frankton. Shrp ... 2F 71
Welsh Hook. Pemb ... 2D 42
Welsh Newton. Herts ... 4H 47
Welsh Newton Common. Here ... 4A 48